JAPAN'S PAST
AND PRESENT

JAPAN'S PAST
AND PRESENT

EDITED BY
KURT ALMQVIST & YUKIKO DUKE BERGMAN

BOKFÖRLAGET STOLPE   AXEL AND MARGARET AX:SON JOHNSONS FOUNDATION FOR PUBLIC BENEFIT

CONTENTS

Kurt Almqvist
Preface 9

THE IDEA OF UNIQUENESS

Kosaku Yoshino
Cultural Nationalism In Japan 15

John Lie
My Country Great or Not 37

Dick Stegewerns
From Chinese World Order to Japan's Modern Mindset 57

Roger Goodman
Education and the Construction of Japanese National Identity 77

Anne E. Imamura
Finding One's Place 93

Pia Moberg
Japanese Work Identity in International Encounters 109

Inken Prohl
Religions in Japan 123

Jaqueline Berndt
Manga as Japanese 139

JAPANESE ARCHITECTURE: TRADITION AND MODERNITY

Elisabet Yanagisawa Avén
From Concrete to Abstract 153

Kristina Fridh
En – Interacting Spaces in japanese architecture 173

Blaine Brownell
Evoking Ihyou 193

JAPAN'S CHRISTIAN CENTURY AND THE KAKURE KIRISHITAN

M. Antoni J. Ucerler, S.J.
Early Jesuit Encounters with 'Warring States' Japan 215

Stephen Turnbull
The Christian Threat to Japan 233

Christal Whelan
Japan's Hidden Christians in Light of Martin Scorsese's *Silence* 247

Mark Williams
The Power of *Silence* 263

THE MAKING OF SAMURAI IN TOKUGAWA JAPAN

Stephen Turnbull
The Trials of the Tokugawa and the Passing of the Samurai 281

Anne Walthall
Samurai Women in Early Modern Japan 297

Thomas D. Conlan
The Rise of Warriors During the Warring States Period 317

Karl Friday
Martial Ways, Whys and Whens 333

Natasha Bennett
Armour for an Age of Peace 351

Constantine N. Vaporis
Performance, Display, and the Spectacular 369

Michael Wert
The Invention of the Samurai in Early Modern Japan 389

Oleg Benesch
Constructing the Samurai, Constructing the Nation 405

JAPAN'S PAST AND PRESENT

James L. Huffman
The Faces of Meiji 423

Naoki Sakai
From an Outward-Looking Society to an Inward-Looking One 441

Peter Nosco
Seeking Knowledge throughout the World 457

Margaret Mehl
Chinese Learning [Kangaku] Between Classical And National Scholarship 473

John Breen
Shinto in Meiji Japan: Reflections on Ise 489

James E. Ketelaar
The Buddha Is Dead, Long Live the Buddha 509

M. Antoni J. Ucerler, S.J.
The Last Persecution of Christianity in Meiji Japan 529

Lars Vargö
The Dramatic Changes of the Twentieth Century 547

Contributors 561

Image rights 563

PREFACE

Japan is today one of the world's largest economies. But it is facing enormous challenges on social, cultural, financial and political levels. These challenges are highlighted and analysed in this book through themes and topics from Japanese history, including identity, architecture, religion, manga, Christianity, the samurais and many other subjects.

Some 150 years ago, in 1868, Sweden became the first nation in the world, to sign a treaty with Japan's newly-installed Meiji government. Japan was taking giant leaps towards modernity. Only a decade was needed for the country to become an industrialised democracy comparable to many countries in the West.

How did the dramatic changes since the Meiji Restoration affect the Japanese self-image and national spirit? And to what degree do the old Japanese traditions live on?

In 1868 the Tokugawa shogun, lost his power and the emperor was restored to the supreme position. The emperor took the name Meiji –"enlightened rule"– as his sovereignty name, and this occurrence became known as the Meiji Restoration. With the Meiji epoch ending in 1912, Japan had a centralised, bureaucratic government, a constitution and elected parliament. How was Japan's modernisation possible?

In Japan, *nihonjinron* – "the study of the Japanese", became popular after the Second World War in an attempt to explain the uniqueness of Japanese culture and character. Some of the essays in this volume deals with these issues and explore aspects of the Japanese quest for a national identity.

The essays stem from a three-year Ax:son Johnson Foundation project to promote understanding of Japanese society and commemorate 150-years of Swedish-Japanese relations. The seminars occured between 2016 and 2018, and were also televised on the Foundation's TV channel, Axess TV. The first one on the 8th of September 2016 at the Engelsberg

Ironworks in Västmanland, bore the title Japanese Self-images: The Idea of Uniqueness; the second took place in Stockholm, on the 3rd of November 2016 and addressed Japanese Architecture – Tradition and Modernity, followed by Japan's Christian Century and the Kakure Kirishitan which took place on the 2nd of March 2017, and The Making of the Samurai in Tokugawa Japan, which took place at Engelsberg Ironworks on the 17th of May 2017. On March 5th, 2018 the last seminar, Japan Past and Present: Society, Thought and Religion in Meiji Japan, took place at the Ricci institute at the University of San Francisco, USA.

The Foundation would like to convey its sincere gratitude to the project leader Yukiko Duke Bergman, and in particular also to M. Antoni J. Ucerler, S.J., director at the Ricci Institute for Chinese-Western Cultural History at the University of San Francisco, who has been helpful with both ideas and names of people knowledgeable about Japan and Japanese history. We would also like to thank all the participants in the seminars for their contributions in the form of lectures as well for the essays in this volume.

Ösmo, Sweden, January, 2020
Kurt Almqvist, President, Axel and Margaret Ax:son Johnson
Foundation for Public Benefit

THE IDEA OF UNIQUENESS

"The End of Negotiations": 1904 French political cartoon about the Russo-Japanese War.

CULTURAL NATIONALISM IN JAPAN

Kosaku Yoshino

Cultural nationalism aims to regenerate a national community by creating, preserving or strengthening cultural identity when it is felt to be lacking, inadequate or threatened. It is concerned with the distinctiveness of a nation as a cultural and historical community. This essay addresses the case of contemporary Japan. Cultural nationalism works differently for different groups and different individuals, and diverse processes are at work in forming the phenomenon. The essay, therefore, does not aim to furnish an overview of contemporary Japanese cultural nationalism. Rather, a focus will be set on one of its processes, that is, the "intellectualisation of culture", to borrow the phrase used by sociologists Gerard Delanty and Patrick O'Mahony.[1]

The intellectualisation of culture consists of two phases. Or, rather, it is generally performed by two types of intellectuals: "productive" intellectuals, who produce or formulate ideas of a nation's cultural identity, and "reproductive" intellectuals who reproduce and disseminate such ideas by relating them to their own social, economic and political or other interests and activities. Most scholars of cultural nationalism are only interested in the first aspect and neglect the second. I argue that it is both necessary and important to enquire sociologically into the manner in which ideas of national distinctiveness get disseminated among wider sections of the population.

This essay first takes a brief look at the historical patterns of the intellectualisation of culture or, to be more specific, national cultural distinctiveness. Secondly, it focuses on discourses on Japanese distinctiveness that developed after 1945. Such discourses are generally referred to as *nihonjinron*. The essay looks into changes and continuities between the "old" *nihonjinron* of the 1970s and 1980s and the "new" *nihonjinron* of the 2010s.

In the modern history of Japan, the intellectualisation of culture or of national cultural distinctiveness has appeared periodically. The "outward looking" and "inward looking" periods have alternated. By this it is meant that the actively open attitude to the outside world has been followed by the actively conscious marking of the symbolic boundary of "our Japanese realm" – a source of Japanese identity – in which intellectuals have engaged.

Japanese distinctiveness is a theme that has periodically concerned intellectuals in modern Japan. Following the first two decades of Westernisation in the Meiji period (which began in 1868), the next two decades witnessed intellectuals showing a strong interest in exploring indigenous and distinctively Japanese ideas. This led to the *kokusui hozon* [preservation of the national essence] movement. By the turn of the century, emphasis on Japanese distinctiveness took on a more active tone, reflecting the mood of the victorious nation after the SinoJapanese War (1894–95). The nationalist ideology, called *nihonshugi* [Japanism], not merely rejected foreign religions and values and advocated the worship of imperial ancestors, but also urged the people to enhance national solidarity and to honour the military. The period following Japan's victory in the RussoJapanese War (1904–05) was characterised by a desire to rationalise the nation's greatness rather than by a mere search for its uniqueness. Notions such as *bushidō* [the way of samurai] and *kokutai* [unity of the Japanese people centred on the imperial family] were emphasised. The ways in which Japanese intellectuals interpreted the nation's uniqueness thus varied from one historical period to another. Such shifts are reflected in changes in the editorial content of the leading nationalist journal *Nihonjin* [The Japanese]. Prior to the SinoJapanese War, this journal represented the views of the "preservation of the national essence". Before and during the RussoJapanese War, it reflected the views of Japanism. In 1907, the journal changed its name to *Nihon oyobi Nihonjin* [Japan and the Japanese] and adopted a new editorial policy which stressed spiritual superiority, but assumed a more tolerant attitude towards foreign ideas and institutions, reflecting the relatively peaceful and prosperous mood of the nation. The late 1930s and early 1940s saw another boom in national character literature, this time called *nihongaku* [study of Japan], reasserting Japanese uniqueness and greatness.[2]

Following Japan's defeat in 1945, a massive wave of Americanisation and modernisation swept over the country. Towards the end of the 1960s, Japanese intellectuals began to engage in discourses on the distinctiveness of Japanese society and culture, generally referred to as *nihonjinron*:

Man influenced by the West.

Next pages: Japanese schoolchildren.

a significant source of contemporary cultural nationalism. From the 1990s onwards we saw the pervasive influences of globalisation as well as multiculturalisation. Subsequently, today's Japan is experiencing another wave of cultural nationalism, in which the new *nihonjinron* are playing an important part.

★

Since the *nihonjinron* of the 1970s and 1980s set the tone for subsequent discourses on "Japaneseness" in contemporary Japan, it is in order to provide a summary of their contents as well as their roles in society. What, for the sake of our discussion, may be called the old *nihonjinron* emerged mainly as a response to modernisation-cum-Americanisation during the 1950s and 60s. Modernisation was a unilinear development perspective, which was the hallmark of the postwar understanding of world history. The US clearly was the model that Japan should follow.

During this period, a huge number of intellectuals of diverse occupations participated in discourses on Japanese distinctiveness. For the present purpose, it will suffice to summarise briefly the four main themes prominent in the *nihonjinron*. First, Japanese society is characterised by group-orientation, interpersonalism [*kanjinshugi*], vertical stratification (intra-company solidarity) and dependence (other-directedness), in contrast to Western society which is represented as individualistic, horizontal (class-based solidarity) and valuing independence (self-autonomy). Second, Japanese patterns of interpersonal communication are characterised by a lack of emphasis on logical and linguistic presentation in contrast to Western patterns, which are supposed to encourage logical and linguistic confrontation. In other words, essential communication among the Japanese is supposed to be performed empathetically without the use of explicit spoken words and logical presentation. Third, Japanese society is characterised as being homogeneous and *tan'itsu minzoku* [uni-racial] in contrast to the heterogeneous and multiracial society of the West. Fourth, the *nihonjinron* closely associates the cultural and racial distinctiveness of the Japanese, thereby promoting the perception that the Japanese mode of thinking and behaving is so unique so that one has to be born Japanese to understand it, as well as the notion that Japanese culture is the exclusive property of the Japanese "race".[3]

Now, how did intellectuals' discourses on national distinctiveness spread among wider sections of the population, thereby fostering a climate of cultural nationalism? Here, we must pay attention to the role of reproducers who convert abstract ideas into a form that can be consumed by ordinary people. The sociologist Edward Shils referred to "reproductive intellectuals" who engage in the interpretation and transmission of intellectual works as opposed to "productive intellectuals" who produce intellectual works. Reproductive intellectuals played an important role in reproducing academics' theories of Japaneseness in a form that could be consumed by ordinary people to suit their practical concerns. S.N. Eisenstadt similarly pointed out that reproductive intellectuals – "secondary intellectuals" in his own words – "serve as channels of institutionalisation, and even as possible creators of new types of symbols of cultural orientations, of traditions, and of collective and cultural identity" through their activities in teaching, communications, entertainment and so on.[4] Pierre Bourdieu draws special attention to what he calls "new intellectuals", who stand between "classic" intellectuals and the masses, increasingly playing an important role as transmitters and intermediaries for the popularisation of intellectuals' ideas in contemporary society. Following Bourdieu, Mike Featherstone takes special note of the expanding group of "cultural intermediaries", who are engaged in providing symbolic goods and services such as marketing and advertising, along with public relations personnel, television producers and presenters, social workers and counsellors.[5]

In my earlier work, I analysed the role of the business sector during this period, scrutinising how they acted as typical cultural intermediaries, reproducing the *nihonjinron* in their efforts to educate the internationally-minded Japanese.[6] Among the many intercultural communication guidebooks produced for English learners, the following serves as a good example. It is an excerpt from a book called *Talking About Japan* by the Nippon Steel Corp. It is designed for businessmen or, for that matter, any learners of practical English who wish to explain Japanese things in English. Here, cultural differences between Japan and the West are presented in the form of dialogue between Mr Suzuki, a Japanese businessman, and Mr Jones, an American. In this excerpt, Japanese groupism is contrasted with American individualism. The US is represented as the significant other to highlight the uniqueness of Japanese culture.

Mr Jones: ... I don't think I could ever learn to make the subtle distinctions you need in Japanese.
Mr Suzuki: It's so tied in with the whole culture. It's difficult to master for someone who grew up in another country. Also, most Japanese tend to avoid doing anything that sets them off from others. They worry about what others think and change their behavior accordingly.
Mr J: That's probably one of the reasons why people talk about Japanese groupism.
Mr S: It's a factor. It's also why Japanese are poor at asserting themselves. We tend to speak and act only after considering the other person's feelings and point of view.
Mr J: You can't say that for most Westerners. In America, we try to teach our children to be independent, take individual responsibility ... We also try to train them to think logically, and learn how to express their thoughts and opinions.
Mr S: Yes, I know ... Foreigners often criticize us Japanese for not giving clear-cut yes or no answers. This is probably connected to our being basically a homogeneous society and our traditional tendency to try to avoid conflicts ...[7]

In the increasingly popular field of intercultural communication, conscious recognition of Japanese peculiarities was widely assumed as a necessary step towards understanding. In general, ethnicity is understood as "the process by which '*their*' difference is used to enhance the sense of '*us*' for the purposes of organisation or identification."[8] In the old *nihonjinron*, it was not *their* differences but *our* differences that were actively used for the enhancement of our national identity. In intellectualising culture, elites in Japan constructed identity through emphasis of the difference of Japan's particularistic culture from the "central" and "universal" civilisations of the West in general and the US in particular. This type of thinking may be referred to as ethnoperipherism (as opposed to ethnocentrism). There is a tendency to equate nationalism with ethnocentrism, but here the equation does not hold true.

Present-day Japanese society is experiencing a phase of cultural nationalism in which the new *nihonjinron* are playing an integral part in a way that differs from the old *nihonjinron*. Some of its features will be discussed here.

1. *Representation of Japan in the age of multiculturalisation*

First, whereas the old *nihonjinron* were a response to modernisation and Americanisation, the new *nihonjinron* developed as a response to globalisation and multiculturalisation. Unlike the earlier process, which was predicated upon the obvious presence of a centre (or centres) of the world, globalisation is a complex process by which both centre and periphery are "de-territorialised". Numerous societies across the globe have undergone what may be called multiculturalisation, and Japan is no longer an exception.

The notion of Japan as a *tan'itsu minzoku* [uni-racial/ethnic nation] – the third proposition of the old *nihonjinron* – attracted strong criticism as part of the increasingly dominant trend towards the demythologisation of a homogeneous Japan. A critique of the myth was also stimulated by the increasing number of foreign residents in Japan, as well as the development of scholarly interests in multiculturalism. In addition, the notion that Japanese culture is the exclusive property of the Japanese "race" – the fourth proposition of the old *nihonjinron* – has become challenged by the increasing presence of foreign-looking non-Japanese who have acquired Japaneseness linguistically, culturally and socially – as well as the mixed-ethnicity Japanese often with "not very Japanese" names. These cases of "very Japanese" foreigners and "not very Japanese" Japanese have generated a lack of fit between cultural and racial boundaries of difference, thereby causing an inconsistency in and inefficacy of the symbolic boundary system that defines Japanese identity. The traditional assumptions behind Japanese identity have been challenged by the increasing occurrence of such boundary dissonance in the wake of multiculturalisation.

This leads to the second feature of the new *nihonjinron*. In general, national identity is the antiimage of foreignness. Previously, Japanese identity was affirmed by formulating the image of the West in general, and the US in particular, as the other. Following nearly two decades of globalisation and multiculturalisation, significant others for the Japanese have diversified to cover a wider range of countries, including Asian countries.

Thirdly, whereas the old *nihonjinron* emphasised the allegedly *intrinsic* differences of the Japanese from others without explicitly attaching any positive values to such differences, the new *nihonjinron* are more evaluative

Next pages: American film poster in Tokyo, 1961.

and express Japanese identity in a more positive way. This has to do with a rise in national pride, dating from the 2000s. Most previous surveys, including the World Values Surveys, show Japanese national pride as lower than that of most other countries. Recent surveys reveal a change. Among a number of reasons for the change, two major ones are mentioned here.

2. Market-driven patriotism and removal of postwar constraints

Following Japan's defeat in 1945, the democratisation of space Japanese society took place, eliminating nationalistic institutions and ideas under the supervision of the occupation forces. Criticisms of feudalistic social legacies as well as state-initiated nationalism came from among Japanese thinkers themselves. Two opposing sentiments existed side by side throughout the postwar period until fairly recently. On the one hand, particular caution was exercised to prevent a revival of those symbols and practices reminiscent of prewar and wartime ultra-nationalism, symbolised by the display of the Hinomaru flag and singing of the Kimigayo anthem at school ceremonies. On the other hand, there was an attempt by state actors to restore a sense of national pride and patriotism. The development of nationalism from 1945 onward may best be seen in terms of the occupation-imposed and self-imposed restraints on it, and reactions against these.

Interestingly, throughout the postwar period until recently, there were significant numbers of Japanese people whose opposition to nationalism was reinforced precisely because of nationalistic rituals such as the display of the national flag, the singing of the national anthem in schools, visits by cabinet ministers to the Yasukuni Shrine and so on. Precisely because state-initiated nationalism used obviously nationalistic symbols, it failed to elicit voluntary and active support from large sections of the population.

It was around 2002, the year when Japan and South Korea jointly hosted the FIFA World Cup, that these postwar constraints on expressions of national pride were largely removed. In photos taken at the time, young people were seen waving the national flag, as well as wrapping themselves in it, and chanting "Nippon, Nippon". This should not immediately be interpreted as a growing sense of nationalism, but rather as

"Cool Japan": Japanese talk show.

football spectators promoting a sense of togetherness among themselves. What is important is that this sporting event was instrumental in eliminating negative images associated with the national flag and anthem.

To fly the Hinomaru proudly was the very thing that the ministry of education had been trying to make happen for fifty years since the 1950s. The World Cup did it overnight, more or less. Given that this was an extremely interesting and important development, I had a student research project team at the University of Tokyo look into this issue. Their original findings merit reporting here.

The research team consisted of seven students, all ardent football fans. In June 2003, they first went to soccer bars where fans gathered to watch games on a television screen. As they observed and interviewed the crowd, one question formed: why were people cheering in exactly the same manner as they were at the stadium during the World Cup?

It so happened that one of the students worked part-time at a company that transmitted soccer results to mobile phone users. The student found out that the firm's president was a cheerleader, and not only that, was the key agent orchestrating football events. He turned out to be the very person who, at the request of a major advertising company, invented the particular cheering style for the stadium. He composed a song, along with the way of singing it, the manner of waving hands, the flag, and so on. Upon hearing this amazing story, the students met people from the advertising agency who confirmed it. This particular way of cheering was invented to create a sense of solidarity among spectators supporting the Japanese team. The person in question was also asked by the advertising agency to orchestrate cheering at a public event at a stadium where people watched a football game on a large TV screen – the first such event ever to have been attempted in Japan. He was so successful that whoever came to the stadium felt a sense of togetherness. Other students conducted fieldwork at television stations and among sponsors to hear their side of the story.[9]

The invention of this way of cheering – a "cheering culture" – around the time of the 2002 World Cup was a major contributing factor to removing both negative values attached to national symbols and previous constraints on patriotic expression. It is worthy of praise that the students successfully identified the process whereby this extremely skilful orchestration of collective cheering was invented. But this does not suggest that this alone explains a rise in demonstrative patriotism.

Needless to say, a plurality of actors and their roles should be taken into consideration.

3. *The 2011 earthquake and tsunami*

One such consideration is related to the 2011 earthquake, tsunami and ensuing nuclear catastrophe. The devastated nation was eventually able to boost its sense of confidence and solidarity. It is not possible to furnish a comprehensive discussion of the complex ways in which the catastrophe worked to promote patriotism. Suffice to mention here only that an outpouring of praise for the Japanese national character from around the world helped to console and encourage not just victims of the disasters, but the Japanese public in general.

Much of this praise was quoted and reported in the Japanese media. Here are some examples:

> "'I think they are coping as well as could be expected or even better, if you imagine us being in that situation,' he said. 'That strength and resilience are rooted in a culture that has historically relied on social organisation.'" (*ABC News*, March 15, 2011, quoting an American resident in Japan)

> "Everywhere, Japan's stoic resilience and its tightly woven community fabric are on display. Outside the hotel front door is a line of locals waiting patiently, as perhaps only Japanese people can." (John Garnaut, *Sydney Morning Herald*, March 15, 2011)

> "I find something noble and courageous in Japan's resilience and perseverance, and it will be on display in the coming days. This will also be a time when the tight knit of Japan's social fabric, its toughness and resilience, shine through. And my hunch is that the Japanese will, by and large, work together – something of a contrast to the polarization and bickering and dog-eat-dog model of politics now on display from Wisconsin to Washington. So maybe we can learn just a little bit from Japan. In short, our hearts go out to Japan, and we extend our deepest sympathy for the tragic quake. But also, our deepest admiration." (Nicholas Kristof, *The New York Times*, March 11, 2011)

Anti-American demonstrations in Tokyo, 1960.

It is important to note here that these statements nearly always assume the usual dichotomy of socially cohesive Japan as opposed to the individualistic West.

It may be said that this international praise became a catalyst in changing the tone of discourses on Japanese national distinctiveness. This leads to our next discussion about the new type of actors involved in reproducing and disseminating the *nihonjinron* as well as the changed tone of such discourses in today's Japan.

4. *The nihonjinron as a form of infotainment*

In the last decade or so, the types of reproducers of *nihonjinron* have grown and expanded considerably. Particularly worthy of attention here are the Japanese television "infotainment" programmes which reproduce *nihonjinron* to a wide audience. Such programmes are broadcast every day between seven and nine pm – peak-viewing time, and each one of the main TV channels has at least one such programme.

You wa nani shini Nippon e? [Why Did You Come to Japan?], which TV Tokyo launched in 2013, is probably the first programme of this genre in which non-Japanese visitors are interviewed and narrate how "awesome" Japan is for the enjoyment of viewers. In this weekly show, a camera crew visits airports to ask overseas visitors why they came to Japan. The travellers usually have interesting stories to tell, and the crew sometimes follow them. For example, an Australian visits one city after another, eating and praising local varieties of Japanese hamburgers; a Japanophile Frenchman auditions to be a fashion model. In these episodes, visitors interact with all types of ordinary Japanese people, and are pleasantly surprised at how "awesome" they and their culture are. One episode features an American retiree, who has visited Japan fifty times, acting as a voluntary tourist guide. He says:

> I don't do this for money … 'cos they don't know what they're missing. Japan is extraordinary. Japan is not just *Shikansen* and geisha. It's not just Mount Fuji. Five thousand people can get on and off the subway without a problem and no litter. You're amazing people.[10]

This show was so popular that it triggered a number of similar programmes, including *Nepu to Imoto no sekaibanzuke* [Nepu and Imoto's World Ranking], launched in 2014. In one episode called National Character Derby, a method similar to *Candid Camera* space is employed. A young girl pretends to be lost and alone in the street. Concealed cameras film the reactions of passers-by and count the number of people who offer help. The show creates the same situation in several other countries (Brazil, France, Germany and Nigeria) and comes up with what they call a world ranking of considerate and kind society. Japan ranks first.[11]

NHK, a public broadcaster, also launched a programme, *Cool Japan* in 2006. Their website has the following to say:

> The keywords, 'Cool Japan', are flying all around the world. From fashion, anime, games, and food, various cultures that the Japanese take for granted are being accepted as cool and trendy by foreigners.
> 'COOL JAPAN Discovering what makes Japan cool', uses the sense of foreigners to the fullest, to dig up and examine the appeal and secrets of these cool cultural aspects.[12]

Every week, about twenty foreign residents are invited to the NHK studio to compare Japan and their own countries regarding given topics, eventually narrating how 'awesome' Japan is. Subjects include: Japanese coffee shops; Japanised foreign dishes; department stores; vending machines; packaging; strange manners; wives; senior citizens; bento; *washoku* [cuisine]; *izakaya* [informal restaurants, literally, "sake shop"]; and various districts of Tokyo.

It is important to point out that, although such programmes discuss a variety of institutions and practices, their ultimate concern is to stress the cultural ethos or, to be more exact, the characteristic mode of behaving and thinking of the Japanese that underlie objectified institutions and practices. This holistic approach to national distinctiveness is characteristic of Japanese thinking elites' discourses on Japanese distinctiveness [*nihonjinron*].[13]

In another example – a programme called *Sekai ga odoroita Nippon! Sugo-i desune!! Shisatsudan* [Japan that Surprised the World! Awesome!! Inspectors], launched in 2014 – foreigners in the same occupation are invited to Japan to compare how apparently similar work is done here and in their own countries. Jobs covered include underground railway staff, hospital workers, fire-fighters, supermarket employees, and so on. In one episode, nursery school teachers from France and Finland are invited to observe a Japanese school. Here are their observations about queueing:

> *French teacher*: Japanese children can queue in such an orderly manner. French children are not capable of this.
> *Finnish teacher*: In Finland, too, such an orderly queue is impossible.
> *Japanese teacher*: In Japan children acquire the skill of living in a group.
> *French*: In France we are brought up respecting the principle of individualism from babyhood. That is why it is so difficult to teach group discipline in a nursery school.
> *Japanese*: Human beings cannot live alone. We all live around people. We learn this from a very young age. That is why each one of us tries not to stand out from others but finds joy in doing the same thing together.[14]

This show normally zeroes in on what non-Japanese visitors love about Japan. In this episode, however, the French and Finnish teachers are rather critical of the Japanese institution. This is offset by a chorus of praise for Japanese nursery schools by a group of foreign residents in Japan from six countries (India, Uzbekistan, Germany, New Zealand, Sweden, Senegal).

It is interesting that the old *nihonjinron* themes discussed earlier – to be more specific, the first and second propositions, group orientation and empathetic communications – should be reproduced over and over again in the mass and digital media.

★

It has become a truism to say that globalisation often results in an emphasis of differences and particularism. Global capitalism thrives on diversified micro-markets where various types of cultural intermediaries commodify particularistic differences in terms of nation, ethnicity, race, gender and class. National differences comprise one of the most prominent particularisms in the age of global modernity. In the increasingly globalised world, cultural nationalism unfolds in the context of supply of and demand for differences between national cultures. The preceding discussion drew attention to the activities of cultural intermediaries in Japanese television media, who commodify and reproduce discourses on cultural differences.

Furthermore, we should note another, new type of cultural intermediary who not only watches these programmes but reproduces their contents by uploading them to video-sharing websites such as YouTube and Dailymotion. These clips are not simply passively consumed, but are commented upon by another group of viewers who participate in discussions. Digital technology is making us re-examine concepts that previously required no detailed analysis in media studies, such as interactivity among anonymous internet users, as it symbolises the nature of online spaces where such users copy, reproduce and post comments. The *nihonjinron* have expanded beyond the realm of mass media to become a popular narrative among intermediaries for digitalised cultural nationalism. Careful research into this new, important subject will be necessary for a further update of understanding of cultural nationalism in Japan.

1. Delanty, Gerard and O'Mahony, Patrick, *Nationalism and Social Theory: Modernity and the Recalcitrance of the Nation,* (London: Sage, 2002).
2. See Yoshino, Kosaku, *Cultural Nationalism in Contemporary Japan: A Sociological Enquiry,* (London and New York: Routledge, 1992); Brown, Delmer M., *Nationalism in Japan: An Introductory Historical Analysis,* (New York: Russell & Russell, 1955).
3. See Yoshino, *ibid.*
4. Shils, Edward, "Intellectuals, Tradition, and the Traditions of Intellectuals: Some Preliminary Considerations", and Eisenstadt, S.N., "Intellectuals and Tradition", in *Daedalus,* Spring 1972.
5. Bourdieu, Pierre, *Distinction* (London: Routledge, 1984), p.370; Featherstone, Mike, *Consumer Culture and Postmodernism,* (London: Sage, 1991), pp.43, 90–94.
6. See Yoshino, *Cultural Nationalism in Contemporary Japan*; Yoshino, *Consuming Ethnicity and Nationalism: Asian Experiences* (London: Curzon Press/Honolulu: The University of Hawai'i Press, 1999).
7. Nippon Steel Human Resources Development Co. Ltd., *Talking About Japan/Nihon o kataru* (Tokyo: ALC, 1987), p.405.
8. Wallman, Sandra, "Introduction: The Scope for Ethnicity", in S. Wallman (ed.) *Ethnicity at Work* (London: Macmillan, 1979), p.3.
9. See Yoshino, "Wakamono no ukeika/hoshuka to nashonarizumu: shakaichosa o toshite daigakusei to tomo ni kangaeru" [Youth and Nationalism in Contemporary Japan: Enquiring into the Issue with University Students], *The Annual Review of Sociology*, Kanto Sociological Association, no. 20, 2007.
10. TV Tokyo, May 23, 2016, uploaded to Dailymotion, http://www.dailymotion.com/video/x4c5vvn, accessed September 23, 2016.
11. NTV, April 13, 2012, uploaded to YouTube, https://www.youtube.com/watch?v= l33n0sWg7D8, accessed September 23, 2016.
12. NHK, http://www6.nhk.or.jp/cooljapan/en/about/, accessed October 1, 2016
13. https://www.youtube.com/watch?v=0AwPCNQuMnA, accessed November 24, 2016.
14. TV Asahi, 21 May 2016, uploaded to YouTube, https://www.youtube.com/watch?v=fUIFYQGWL3I, accessed November 24, 2016.

The organisation expert Marie Kondo appears at a media event to introduce her new line of storage boxes in New York.

MY COUNTRY GREAT OR NOT

John Lie

Since the property bubble burst in the early 1990s, the prevailing understanding of Japaneseness shifted from "Japan as number one" to the "Japanese disease". Several decades of rapid economic growth since the end of World War II led to Japan becoming an economic power house, but after 1990 the vision of grandeur faded. The most common categorisation of the last quarter century in Japan is as the "lost decades" (now threatening to become three decades). In the early 21st century, public discussion often revolves around turning Japanese society and the economy around: to "cure" what is commonly called the Japanese disease. Simultaneously, there is a persistent, popular belief in Japan as the most desirable country in which to live. These and other conceptualisations of contemporary Japanese society share a strong belief in the integrity and uniqueness of Japan. In short, few question the robust boundary of Japanese society and Japaneseness.

In the early 21st century, many topics concern thinking people around the world: Grexit and Brexit, the rise of China and the radicalisation of Islam, transnational epidemics and natural disasters, financial globalisation and counter-globalisation movements, and so on and on. Very few non-Japanese people would, however, be thinking about Japan, except possibly as a delightful land of sushi and anime. Almost no one would have foreseen this state of affairs a few decades ago. After all, the 1980s were rife with shrill debates on the rise of Japan and its impending status as "number one". Given the tenor of the discussion at the time, one could have been excused for thinking that the 21st century would be the "Japanese Century". The decline or disappearance of Japan from the global stage is strange given its continuing significance as an economic power and a cultural presence.

My contrarian view is that Japan stands to be more significant in the 2020s than in the 1980s. While the rise of Japan in the post-World War II decades was but one permutation of rapid industrialisation – something

Next pages: Members of a media tour group with employees from Tokyo Electric Power Co. at the Fukushima nuclear power plant.

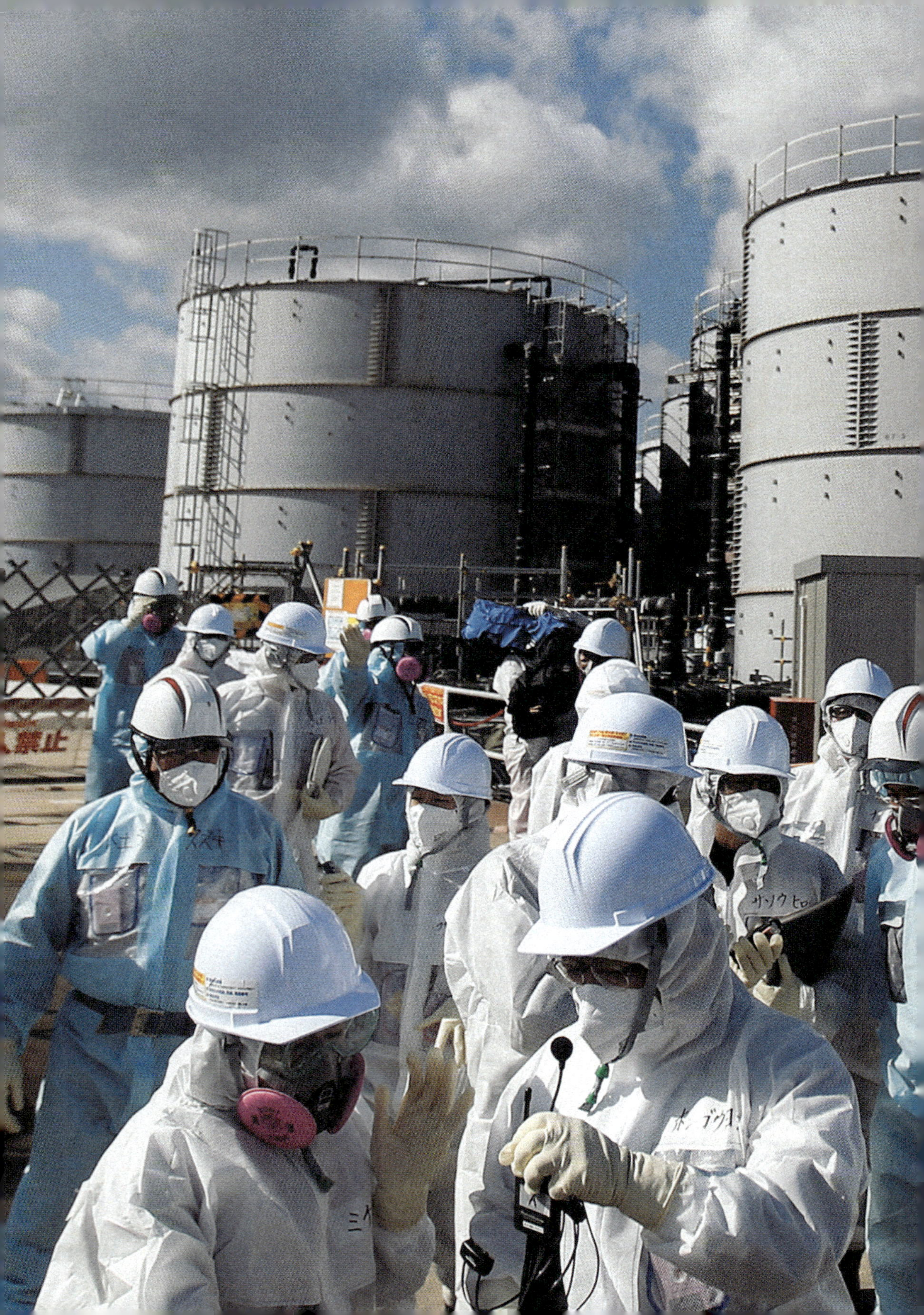
入禁止

地下水バイパ
一時貯留タン
G-1-1

that China is currently undergoing – and a story that is very much a reprise, even if idiosyncratic variations exist across different national experiences, of the Eurocentric past – Japan as what I call "The Stationary Society" places it at the forefront of the challenges facing the world today, especially among advanced industrial societies, ranging from environment and energy to an ageing society and a post-growth-oriented economy.

How Japan will deal with the leading-edge problems of the 21st century will depend in part on how it thinks of itself. Regarding itself as a unique country, will it succumb to reactionary impulses and revive nationalism and militarism? Or will it find a suitable modus vivendi in a world of environmental constraints and economic stasis? The point of this essay, then, is to explore the changing and competing understanding of Japanese people and culture: a topic of interest not only in and of itself but also one with some lessons for other post-industrial societies.

★

The 1868 Meiji Restoration – the demise of samurai rule and the restoration of imperial sovereignty – marks the conventional divide between traditional and modern Japan. The self-reflectively modernising Meiji regime achieved many things, but perhaps the most consequential was the construction of the modern nation and peoplehood. Hitherto separated by status distinctions and regional differences, the post-Meiji transformation created a more or less culturally unified nation. Beyond economic, social, and cultural changes – important as they are in making possible the infrastructural integration of modern Japan, from transportation and communication to universal schooling and national mass media – lies the almost constant state of warfare. Most crucially, what some Japanese historians call the Fifteen Years' War, which reached its crescendo with the Pacific War, forged a nation with a shared sense of purpose. There's nothing like having a common enemy to strengthen social solidarity, and all the hardships and suffering – creating in turn a mirage of equality – merely cemented it. Symptomatic is that the end of the war brought a call for the hundred million Japanese to repent together [*ichioku sōzange*], bearing collectively and thereby diffusely war responsibility and war guilt, including imperial subjects such as Koreans and Taiwanese. In so doing, all Japanese became victims of World War II, from Emperor Hirohito to an impoverished *Zainichi* [Korean] seamstress or coal miner, who had in varying degrees helped to bring it about. Be that as it may, perhaps the most significant legacy of modernising and militarised Japan was a sense of collective identity qua Japanese.

Numerous circumstances, contexts, and contingencies led to over four decades of rapid economic growth after 1945: from the generally favourable economic climate under the Pax Americana (ironically the two major drivers were the demand generated by the Korean and Vietnamese wars) to the general global economic expansion and prosperity. One important factor was the sense of social solidarity forged during the war years: not only a sense of privileging collective goals, but also the institutionalisation of cooperation and the valourisation of harmony. People learned to work together, disguising and devaluing individual and instrumental goals, in the context of modern organisations that emphasised precision and punctuality, division of labour and separation of execution from conception. Undergirding these ideals and practices was the fact that modern Japan had become relatively integrated and homogeneous with the spread of a common language and common identity. Linguistic unification facilitated a common cultural identity that sought to delineate Japanese people as collective-minded and other-oriented, as well as patient and diligent, punctual and loyal.

Largely unplanned, the solidarity of Japaneseness underwent several major transformations after 1945. First, it excised former Japanese subjects, such as Koreans and Chinese who were part of the erstwhile empire. In the post-World War II period, there have been very few reflections on the multi-ethnic constitution of Japan, prewar or postwar, because the modern nation building was successful in creating a relatively integrated population, and the postwar period had jettisoned and excluded non-ethnic-Japanese populations. Furthermore, unlike other industrial countries such as France or Germany, Japan did not rely on foreign migrant workers, exploiting instead its large domestic rural population. On the two occasions when low-paid foreign workers might have become significant, external factors – the 1973 oil crisis and the aforementioned bursting of the property speculation bubble – dampened demand. Non-ethnic Japanese groups, such as ethnic Koreans [*Zainichi*] or Okinawans, sought to pass as ordinary Japanese, and precisely when they became more vocal the Japanese government sought to ameliorate their conditions, whether because of the desire to follow international norms or to quell domestic

Share prices tumble on the Tokyo Stock Exchange, 13 October, 1997.

dissent. In any case, the very definition of Japaneseness remained mono-ethnic and homogeneous.

Secondly, the tragedy of war and the collapse of the empire ushered in a series of new predicates of Japaneseness. Rather than glorifying martial virtues, such as bravery and conquest, much more modest and mundane ideals were disseminated: the stress on quotidian happiness or the desire for security. Combined with the prewar ideals of solidarity and harmony, the predominant postwar Japanese view of itself was as a small island country, largely oblivious to the travails and tribulations of the larger world. In part this was made plausible because the major source of comparison in postwar Japan was with the United States, an altogether unusual country. Being Japanese or non-Japanese emerged as one of the cardinal distinctions in life, with the former state inevitably believed to be in isolation and homogeneous to boot. The relative seclusion of Japanese people was paradoxically made possible by having perhaps the largest homogeneous market in the world. This is puzzling in part because the engine of postwar Japanese economic growth was almost universally believed to be export-led, and Japanese people have been, and are, eager to consume foreign goods. Yet the salient reality was the belief in the relative isolation and integrity of Japan, rendered possible by having a large country that was involuted in outlook. To take a small example, Japanese intellectual life is notable for the massive influx of foreign ideas and books, but few Japanese make efforts to export their ideas and books. The relative isolation is sustained by the existence of a large domestic readership and a sustainable market. Whereas Norwegian or South Korean academics and writers, who believe their domestic audiences to be small, seek to export their intellectual products, the same urgency is utterly lacking in the case of their Japanese counterparts. In turn, very few non-Japanese know literary Japanese well enough, or care enough, to intervene in domestic debates, which are perforce conducted in Japanese, by and for Japanese people. Cultural involution, though ethnocentrism is a cultural universal, became a powerful tendency in Japanese life.

Thirdly, after its pretensions of imperial grandeur had collapsed completely in 1945, Japan went on an upward trajectory that reached its apogee in the boom or "bubble" years of the 1980s. In 1979 Ezra Vogel, a Harvard sociologist, published a bestselling book, which was taken to mean that Japan was "number one". Hyperbolic claims about Japan proliferated, such as the notion that the total real estate value of Tokyo exceeded that of the United States. The high tide of Japanese economic growth not surprisingly also saw the expansion of Japanese uniqueness discourse [*nihonjinron*]. Understandably, theories of Japanese uniqueness and greatness flooded the intellectual marketplace. Aided by intellectual isolation, untenable propositions about Japanese uniqueness were disseminated, such as: Japan is unique because it is an island nation (but what about the UK or Iceland?); its language is unique (which language isn't in some ways?). Because of Japan's relative cultural isolation and involution, few outsiders challenged fantastic propositions about the Japanese people themselves, or about other nations and cultures proposed by blinkered and myopic Japanese pundits. When Japan ceased to be "number one", what remained was the conviction of Japanese uniqueness, and bits and pieces of this discourse that became part of Japanese commonsense.

Homogeneous, isolated, and unique, contemporary Japanese society harbours a mythical understanding of itself. One idea that is almost never mooted is the idea of Japan as an ordinary society, not substantively different from France or Germany, or Taiwan or South Korea. What is crucial here is that what makes various discourses of Japaneseness possible is the notion that there is something different about the Japanese people, who are all basically similar. To be sure, concrete predicates of Japaneseness have differed across the postwar period and among various Japanese people: some highlight older virtues, such as solidarity and harmony, while others stress their propensity toward punctuality and peacefulness. What is almost never challenged is the category of Japan or Japaneseness, which is assumed to be homogeneous, isolated, and unique.

★

The 1980s witnessed an expansion and deepening of the Japanese uniqueness discourse, but the bursting of the property bubble deflated it. It is difficult to find people today who will trumpet Japanese greatness in terms of its economic might, and certainly no one will brag about its geopolitical or military strength. The shift is undeniable, and since the mid-2010s, there are two widely disseminated perspectives on the state of Japanese society: the idea that Japan is stagnant and even diseased, and the notion that Japan is a wonderful place to live. The former is much more widely articulated, especially by politicians and pundits.

A map of the imperial powers
of the Pacific, 1939.

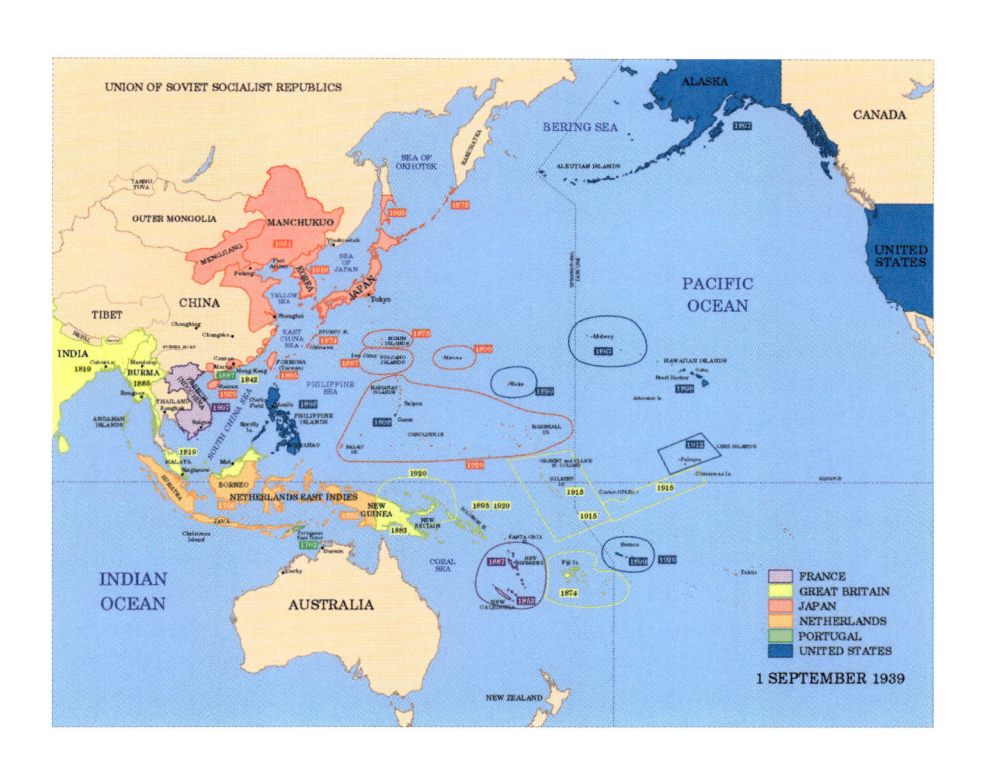

The "Japanese disease" discourse is essentially an effort to make sense of the end of rapid economic growth. Once an economic colossus about to take over the world, the Japanese economy hardly registers in global consciousness in the 2010s. In 1985 when I interviewed senior executives at Sony – at the time at its zenith of global brand recognition and perceived innovativeness and coolness – and asked them about Samsung Electronics, founded that year, the normally taciturn men could barely suppress laughter. Presumably none of them were laughing as the upstart quickly superseded the technologically path-breaking and fashion-leading Japanese company. Indeed, Sony and other once mighty firms are struggling in the brave new world of global competition. According to one influential strand of thought, we can see in their fate the state of Japanese society today: lacking leadership or innovation, and therefore becoming stationary or stagnant. The undeniable decline of the postwar Japanese economic system supposedly built on lifetime employment, the seniority-wage system, and enterprise unionism finds ready reminders in macroeconomic statistics, such as deflation. Even more troubling is the look ahead to an ageing society of declining population. Japan appears to be on a path of permanent decline.

The most common characterisation of the period after the property bubble burst in 1990 is as the "lost decades". Initially pundits talked of the lost decade in the early 2000s, but by the early 2010s they began to talk of the lost two decades. They may well be talking about the lost three decades soon. The same mindset fuels the idea of the "Japanese disease". Although diagnoses vary, there is a widespread sense that the Japanese body politic is ill: senescent or sclerotic. Academics Masaru Kaneko and Tatsuhiko Kodama point to systematic weaknesses in dealing with economic stagnation, an ageing population, and other potential threats to the wellbeing of the Japanese economy and society. In contrast, Shichihei Yamamoto and Shū Kishida stress the Japanese propensity to eschew principles and to rely on "common illusions" as the source of Japanese malaise. Expressed as system or culture, presumably the same attributes were responsible in part for the Japanese economic miracle, but they are said to be vitiating contemporary Japan.

Not surprisingly, the Japanese disease discourse has an inevitable addendum: cure or prescription. Perhaps the loudest call for cure is to restore past glories: the rapid economic growth of the 1950s–80s. Abenomics is in many ways a return of the infrastructural state that bulldozed and built postwar Japan: constructing roads, railroads, and bridges to everywhere and nowhere. It is warmed-over Keynesianism, and in its essence is something of a throwback to the rapid economic growth period of the immediate postwar decades. The attendant desire to "normalise" Japan by revising the war-renouncing Article 9 of the Constitution is another effort to regain national normality and vitality. At its most ideological, it seeks to revive older, presumably more "traditional", virtues, including those associated with prewar Japan such as martial valour, which has long been taboo in the postwar period. What makes revanchist nationalism and militarism less of a threat than casual outside observers might think is the curious consensus among right-wing and conservative politicians about the supremacy of the United States in global and regional affairs. Japan remains a client state of the United States, a persistent and possibly permanent loser of World War II. Instead of anti-Americanism, frustration or insecurity manifests itself as anti-Korean or anti-Chinese sentiment. Unable to stand up to the global superpower, articulation of impotence or aspiration appears as irrational hatred of neighbouring countries and peoples. Be that as it may, another striking feature of contemporary Japan is the relative quiescence of progressive voices. In part this may be a consequence of the generally liberal tenor of intellectual life and even the mass media in contemporary Japan. Yet few make a cogent case for an alternative direction for Japan beyond the tired old leftist platitudes or criticisms.

There is another, equally popular take on contemporary Japanese society. It is the belief that – whatever its checkered past, such as the tragic Pacific War – Japan has become a land of peace and prosperity, even if it is no longer number one. Foremost in this mindset is the sheer efficiency and comfort of everyday life in Japan. It is not that Japan is free from all problems – inequality [*kakusa*] and poverty, natural disasters and social problems undoubtedly exist – but they pale in significance compared to the worse situations of crime and terrorism, hunger and war facing the rest of the world. In spite of the Fukushima nuclear disaster – usually called 3/11 in Japan – or economic stagnation, the regnant conservative outlook – the general satisfaction with Japanese life – accounts in part for the parliamentary electoral victory of the Liberal Democratic Party (LDP) in 2016, and the generally conservative tenor of Japanese life. Put differently, even as the reigning Liberal Democratic Party seeks to restore the glorious past (either the high-growth period of the 1960s or possibly the imperial-militarist glory of the 1930s) and is therefore reactionary, its status as the party of order and therefore of conservatism renders it as a party of choice for people enjoying security and prosperity, however modest. As there is no compelling vision of a better future, it is not surprising that, contrary to the OECD norm, young Japanese people tend to support the LDP and express more stridently nationalist sentiments.

Contemporary Japanese conservatism in fact articulates well with the idea of the Japanese disease. Put simply, Japan may not be the most powerful country in the world, but it is a blessed land of peace and security, democracy and human rights, great food and beautiful nature, and advanced technology and vibrant popular culture. It is not "number one" but it is nevertheless a great place. As Professor Sukehiro Hirakawa of Tokyo University writes: "it was of course good to be born in Japan."[1] Symptomatic is the popularity of books that extoll the country, in which titles say all: *Living in Europe: Nine Wins and One Loss for Japan* (Mahn Emiko Kawaguchi, 2014) or *My Conclusion After Living in England, France, Japan, and the United States: Japan Is the Best Country to Live in* (Yumiko Autier, 2014). Never mind that for most people their country of birth – with family and friends, native language and culture – is the best place to live in. If proof were needed, however, foreign witnesses seem ready to assure Japanese people that indeed Japan is an "amazing" country.

The idea of Japan as a blessed land becomes at times a model for other nations and peoples. Professor Takao Suzuki of Keio University argues that, after the failures of Western civilisation, Japanese culture should play "the leading role in the period of globalism" and recommends the international spread of the Japanese language. There is only a short step from the generalised satisfaction with Japanese life to a new articulation of Japan as number one. The generally hyperbolic nature of the emergent discourse points even to the revival of Japanese economic might.

What unites these competing views of contemporary Japan – undoubtedly there are many other perspectives – is the unreconstructed belief in the integrity and relative homogeneity of Japanese people and culture. Few, if any, Japanese people would deny the existence of status differences [*kakusa*] and wealth inequality, as well as gender, generational, regional, religious, political, and other sources of diversity. Nevertheless, one of the fundamental axes of social life remains the almost unbridgeable chasm between insiders (Japanese) and outsiders (non-Japanese or foreigners). The relative strength of the boundary waxes and wanes, and the meaning or attributes of Japaneseness (and, residually, of non-Japaneseness) fluctuate. Yet, in spite of considerable challenges to the presumption of Japanese integrity and homogeneity, there is a remarkable robustness to the boundary of Japaneseness. Precisely because Japanese people and culture are thought be an integral, independent, isolated, and homogeneous entity, it becomes easy to generalise and theorise about Japanese people and culture: hence the enduring popularity of the theory of Japaneseness [*nihonjinron*]. Again, many cultures have similar discourses – all nations are alike in some ways – but contemporary Japan is notable for the popularity of this genre. Its source, as I have suggested, lies in intellectual isolation and cultural involution, thinking that Japan is at once homogenous, isolated, and unique.

Many Japanese people are reasonably well informed and reflective about the present state of, and prospects for, Japanese society. Few expect the return of rapid economic growth. Many more are acutely anxious about the future, if only from the 3/11 earthquake, tsunami and the near meltdown of the Japanese nation, but often more from the rise of China or the North Korean nuclear threat. At the same time, in spite of sluggish economic growth, it remains the case that Japan has been remarkably successful in dealing with the challenges facing OECD countries. Certainly, foreign news – wars and refugees, terrorism and fanaticism – seem much worse than the problems of contemporary Japanese society. Whatever the sources of insecurity, structural or contingent, short term or long term, they seem in recent years to have deepened the chasm between domestic Japan and the rest of the world. Cultural and intellectual involution becomes the silent background for all discussions of the present and future of Japan.

★

Is Japan exceptional or unique? There's a simple truth that all countries are rugged individualists, claiming some sort of differences or even uniqueness. The South Koreans and the Japanese may seem similar to external observers in the same way that the Belgians and the French seem similar to Japanese people, but rarely do people deny their differences from others.

After all, there are diagnoses similar to the notion of Japanese disease in other countries. Most famously, there was the British disease, much mooted during the 1970s thanks to the industrial and imperial decline of the former superpower. France has a bevy of commentators who thrive on the idea of French exceptionalism, and increasingly on its putative decline.

The idea of ethnic or national uniqueness is merely a permutation of ethnocentrism, surely something of a cultural and historical universal among human collectivities. And the idea of decline, as much as that of progress, can be found everywhere. But the proximate reality is that a period of rapid economic growth was at once historically aberrant and widespread among all the OECD countries. And no OECD country has experienced anything remotely approaching the rate of rapid economic growth from the golden age of the 1950s and 1960s. In this sense, Japanese economic stagnation makes Japan a normal or ordinary country among OECD nation states. And while some Japanese politicians and pundits clamour for the glory days of rapid economic growth, not only is the return to sustained high growth unlikely, but it is also almost certainly undesirable, based as the earlier period was on labour exploitation and environmental destruction. Curious, too, is the postwar focus on mass industrialisation – as some of the strongest sectors of contemporary Japan are smaller firms and craft industries. There is widespread recognition of the value of crafts in Japan today – especially in the food and related industries – but it is not something that was feted during the high tide of rapid growth.

There is one dimension, however, in which Japan seems very much an outlier from other OECD societies. Japan appears to have resisted the surge of right-wing populism that has swept through many advanced industrial societies in the past decade. This, however, needs some clarification: there is a highly influential group of quasi-racist nationalists, usually called the "internet right wing" [*netto uyoku*]. One of its principal grievances is the special privilege given to the ethnic Korean minority, which is surely an implausible proposition given the history and persistence of ethnic discrimination. It would be facile to characterise it as a subspecies of a generic populist, anti-immigration movement, as there are several ways in which Japan departs strikingly from France or Austria.

One is political convulsion, especially populism. The general conditions I have delineated above have at once prevented a large influx of foreign migrant workers common in other OECD countries – thereby making the claim of "protecting" one's country and culture somewhat unconvincing – and sustained a generally conservative tenor in Japanese life. Populist racism is unnecessary in Japan because it is well articulated by leading politicians and systematically practised by bureaucrats. It is precisely their isolation and involution that leads politicians to make one incredible gaffe after another – in a way that makes Donald J. Trump seem like a model of probity. The former Tokyo governor, Shintarō Ishihara, is well-known for his insensitive remarks, and his xenophobia seems to respect few boundaries. He often employs imperialist and derogatory terms to refer to Koreans and Chinese, for example. In a similar vein, the deputy prime minister, Tarō Asō, suggested learning from the Nazi regime. What would immediately lead to resignation in any European polity hardly harms the status of leading politicians in Japan. All the same, there are people who insist that Japan is free of xenophobia and racism. The more general point is the irresponsible, and at times extremist, character of political discourse in Japan that obviates the populism and anti-immigrant racism common in OECD countries.

It would be problematic to dismiss Japan as a land of xenophobia and racism, however. There are deep-seated principles, such as freedom of expression, that tolerate seemingly xenophobic utterances. I was on a plane that landed precisely when the 3/11 earthquake struck. Amid the chaos, there was a long line for taxis, one of the few viable modes of transportation. Noticing that the line moved slowly, I was shocked to see that a taxi would often only take one passenger at a time. I suggested to the person in charge that perhaps several people going in the same direction might ride together. The immediate and unequivocal response was that "we must respect people's rights". In a similar spirit, many anti-racist Japanese intellectuals resist rules and legislation against hate speech precisely because it would violate the cherished principle of freedom of expression. Formalistic understanding – perhaps befitting a learning culture that stresses memorisation – belies the facile claims of Japanese national character but contributes in turn to protecting and even nourishing irrational and xenophobic elements in Japanese life. Indeed, because there is very little participation in foreign discussions about Japan, the predominant tenor of foreign writings on Japan – far from being triumphalist, like bestselling Japanese titles claiming how adoring foreigners are about Japan – tend to be vaguely orientalist and mildly negative.[2]

The ongoing Japanese discourse about Japanese people and culture is important because it affects how the people and society operate. It is difficult to imagine the near-suicidal warfare of seventy-odd years ago without a widespread acceptance of militarism and imperialism. Similarly, the pervasive belief in peace and security serves as a powerful check on the Abe regime's efforts to renounce Article 9 of the Constitution and potentially put Japan on a path toward revived militarism.

Contemporary Japan is of global significance because it is facing many of the problems afflicting advanced industrial countries, such as a rapidly ageing society with impending problems with pension and welfare benefits, or environmental and human constraints on economic growth. These and other challenges expose the limits of the modus operandi of the extant political economy and call for more viable and sustainable solutions. In many ways, then, Japan is more important as a model now than it was in the 1980s, when it was still largely following the examples of other advanced industrial societies. Today, it's not clear that it makes sense for Japan to continue to do so, as it is about as mature and advanced a society as there is in the world.

Here the conservative, and even xenophobic, discourse offers more than a glimmer of truth. It may very well be that Japan provides a good model for interactions between civilisation and the natural world, given the traditional regard for nature and environment (but why the insistence on nuclear power after Fukushima?). The persistence of egalitarian instincts that limit sky-high executive salaries found in the US and elsewhere is surely one viable solution to the question of permissible economic inequality. Perhaps rapid immigration needs to be curbed to prevent the existence of an underclass? There is a strong strand of post-materialist, post-consumption culture in Japanese life, exemplified by the "tidying" queen Marie Kondō. The persistence of craft industries in Japan may show a way beyond the mass-produced, mediocre products of consumer society. And innovation in popular culture is surely worth our attention. There is, then, much that is attractive in Japan, diseased or stationary as some claim it to be. It remains unclear, however, whether these putatively positive impulses in contemporary Japanese life will survive the ongoing effort to resurrect the older political-economic model, and possibly even an older, prewar one that led to its auto-destruction over seven decades ago.

It would behove not just Japanese people to track how Japan deals with the myriad problems facing it, but the world at large. And in this regard how Japanese people see themselves and their country has considerable significance. The powerful persistence of the belief in, and sometimes the reality of, homogeneity, isolation, and uniqueness may very well undermine the desire and the effort to sustain an environmentally friendly, egalitarian, and peaceful country.

1. In Hirakawa's book, the title was modified as "pretty good" but in a later article he writes that it was "of course good" to be born in Japan. The special issue of the journal *Shinchō 45* (July 2016) in which the articles by Hirakawa and Suzuki appear is entitled "The plan to 'Japanize' the world".
2. Having published a book on multi-ethnic Japan, I am at times asked about Japanese attitudes and actions against non-Japanese peoples. I am struck how the prevailing presumptions seem to be that Japanese people are xenophobic and possibly racist.

REFERENCES

Asahi Shinbun Shuzaihan, *Kono kuni wo yurugasu otoko*, (Tokyo: Asahi Shinbunsha, 2016).
Autier, Yumiko, *Igirisu, Furansu, Nihon, Amerika, zenbu sundemita watashi no ketsuron: Nihon ga ichiban kurashiyasui kuni deshita*, (Tokyo: Tainbunshō, 2014).
Baldwin, Frank and Anne Allison (eds.), *Japan*, (New York: NYU Press, 2015).
Fujii, Satoshi, *"Sūpā shinkansen" ga Nihon wo sukuu*, (Tokyo: Bungei Shunjūsha, 2016).
Gamble, Andrew, *Britain in Decline*, (London: Macmillan, 1981).
Hirakawa, Sukehiro, *Nihonjin ni umarete, maa yokatta*, (Tokyo: Shinchōsha, 2014).
"Nihon ni umarete yahari yokatta", *Shinchō 45*, July 2016, pp.66–70.
Ise, Masaomi, *Sekai ga shōsan suru Nipponjin ga shiranai Nippon*, (Tokyo: Fusōsha, 2016).
Kaneko, Masaru and Tatsuhiko Kodama, *Nihonbyō*, (Tokyo: Iwanami Shoten, 2016).
Kawaguchi-Mahn, Emiko, *Sundemita Yōroppa: kyūshō ippai de Nihon no kachi* (Tokyo: Kōdansha, 2014).
Kondō, Marie, *Jinsei ga tokimeku katazuke no mahō*, (Tokyo: Sanmāku, 2010).
Lie, John, *Multiethnic Japan,* (Cambridge: Harvard University Press, 2001).
Lie, John, *Modern Peoplehood*, (Cambridge: Harvard University Press, 2004).
Lie, John, *Zainichi (Koreans in Japan),* (Berkeley: University of California Press, 2008).
Lie, John, *Sustainable Society, Japan,* (New York: Oxford University Press, 2020).
Mitsuhashi, Takaaki, *Dai 4-ji sangyō kakumei*, (Tokyo: Tokuma Shoten, 2016).
Moffitt, Benjamin, *The Global Rise of Populism*, (Stanford: Stanford University Press, 2016).
Mōgenroku, Kenkyūkai, *Ishihara Shintarō Mōgenroku*, (Tokyo: Tīōentateinmento, 2012).
Müller, Jan-Werner, *Was Ist Populismus?* (Frankfurt am Main: Suhrkamp, 2016).
Pilling, David, *Bending Adversity*, (New York: Penguin Press, 2014).
Saitō Taka, *Sensō no dekiru kuni e*, (Tokyo: Asahi Shinbunsha, 2013).
Samuels, Richard J., *3.11: Disaster and Change in Japan*, (Ithaca: Cornell University Press, 2013).
Shirai, Satoshi, *Eikyū haisenron*, (Tokyo: Ōta Shoten, 2013).
Suzuki, Takao, "Nihongo to Nihonbunka ga sekai wo heiwa ni suru." *Shinchō 45*, July 2016, pp.19–26.

Takeda, Tomohiro, *Sekaiichi jiyū de sabetsu no nai kuni*, (Tokyo: Besutoserāzu, 2016).

Tokuyama, Yoshio, *Abe Shinzō "meigen" roku,* (Tokyo: Heibonsha, 2016).

Yamamoto, Shichihei, and Shū Kishida, *Nihonjin to "Nihonbyō",* (Tokyo: Bungei Shunjūsha, 2015) [1992].

Yasuda, Kōichi, *Netto to aikoku*, (Tokyo: Kōdansha, 2012).

Zemmour, Éric, *Le suicide français*, (Paris: Albin Michel, 2014).

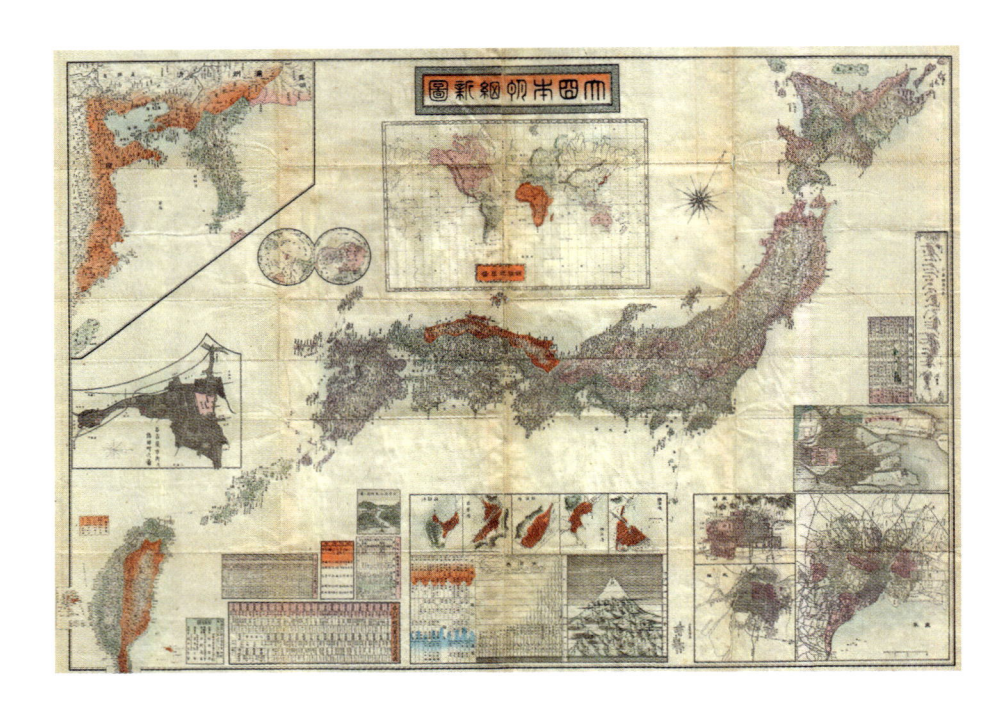

Japanese map of imperial Japan with Taiwan, 1895.

FROM CHINESE WORLD ORDER TO JAPAN'S MODERN MINDSET

Dick Stegewerns

This essay will endeavour to provide an overview of Japanese views of the outside world and Japanese self-images from the early modern period up until the present day.[1] I will stress the revolution in Japanese views of the outside world, as the country at the time of the Meiji Revolution shifted from a Chinese type of world order to a Western world order. Equally, I will emphasise the continuity of what I term "Japan's modern mindset" from this same Meiji Revolution until the present day, in which Japan tends to position itself between East and West, looking up to 'the best of the West' while looking down upon 'the Asian rest', and accordingly not including itself in Asia.

First of all, we need to ascertain that in the Tokugawa or Edo period (1603–1868), this uniquely long era of peace and stability in Japanese and world history, there was no Japan and there were no Japanese. The inhabitants of those isles that we nowadays call Japan did not have a Japanese identity, and accordingly no views of the outside world.

Many overviews of Japanese history tend to stress the pacification and unification of the Japanese isles, and thus tend to focus on the central military government [*bakufu*] in the shogunal capital of Edo (present-day Tokyo). Compared to previous periods in Japanese history, it indeed must be acknowledged that the authority of central power on the various outlying regions was greater than before. However, the fundamental division in more than 250 feudal domains [*han*] remained, and things we nowadays consider pre-eminently central government tasks such as tax, justice, police, and army were their concern.

 Central entities like the *shōgun* – the hereditary leader of the *bakufu* – and the emperor did not mean anything to most people. In case they were *samurai*, the military class that had turned into civil bureaucrats, their ties of loyalty, dependence and identity ended at the level of the domainal lord [*daimyō*]. But early modern society was still overwhelmingly rural, and for the majority of people life in an isolated community was their

海軍大臣 西郷従道公

逓信大臣 榎本武揚公

大蔵大臣 松方正義公

農商務大臣 谷干城公

文部大臣 森有礼公

Japanese Ministers of the Meiji period, 1886.

daily experience: their identity would not transcend beyond family and village. This prevailing early modern structure was much more important in circumscribing a Japanese national identity than the central government's so-called isolationist foreign policy [*sakoku*], which completely forbade travel abroad, strictly controlled foreign trade and severely limited the influx of foreigners.

★

However, even in this early modern, fractured and isolationist setting some people, especially an elite minority employed by the central government, needed some sort of a view of the outside world. For instance, when constructing and implementing the *bakufu* prerogative of a foreign policy, whether isolationist or not, and when dealing with foreign merchants in Nagasaki, the only port open to trade with the Chinese and the Dutch.

And there were also some, not in service of the shogunal bureaucracy, but whose exceptional occupations linked them in an immaterial way to the outside world, such as Buddhist and Confucianist scholars, and even a few intellectual adventurers indulging in "Dutch studies" [*rangaku*]. Still, we can hardly call these exceptional men with a view of the outside world as "Japanese". Even if their bodies were firmly linked to the Japanese soil, their minds had been formatted in a Chinese way. In a situation where classical Chinese served as the Latin of East Asia, education was to a large extent based on the Confucianist classics, and neo-Confucianism was all but the state ideology – adopting the Chinese view of the outside world was merely a form of going through the motions.

The Chinese world order is Sinocentric, dependent on place, and retrogressive. Its criterion is the level of Chinese civilisation, mainly defined in Confucianist terms. The zenith of Confucianism was considered to have taken place a few thousand years ago, and since China had provided the venue for this Confucianist paradise, China was, is, and will always be the number one and centre of the world. Entities within the scope of China's civilisational power, which had adopted Chinese civilisation – most easily signified by the use of Chinese script – and who were willing to pay tribute to the Chinese emperor, were included in the Chinese world order as countries with kings. All other entities were discarded as mere barbarians, for which the Chinese were so inventive as to use different characters representing the direction where they came from.

The inhabitants of the isles that we nowadays call Japan could handle the idea of being inferior to the Chinese. They had been very willingly borrowing and adapting almost everything from the so-called "realm of the middle" for some one thousand years. Moreover, the Chinese were so self-centred that – somewhat in contrast to their tendency to categorise various types of barbarians – they never took the pains to rank the countries partaking in their civilisational sphere. Accordingly, the Japanese, the Koreans and the Vietnamese were free to think of themselves as the number two in the world, and without exception, this is exactly what they did. And things were facilitated in the case of Japan by the fact that the country occupied a unique, autonomous position within the Chinese world order, which gave it the freedom to choose what to take and what to leave. The Japan Sea up until the modern period functioned as an insurmountable obstacle for the various Chinese imperial dynasties, whereas they had found it relatively easy to interfere politically or militarily in the countries that were connected by land to China.

This relative freedom also made for slight Japanese deviations in handling the Chinese world order during the Tokugawa period. After the Tokugawa victory in the Battle of Sekigahara in 1600, a rigid political order and class-based society came into being. These were primarily aimed at the suppression of all potential destabilising forces, whether central, regional or foreign, military, political, social or economic. Not

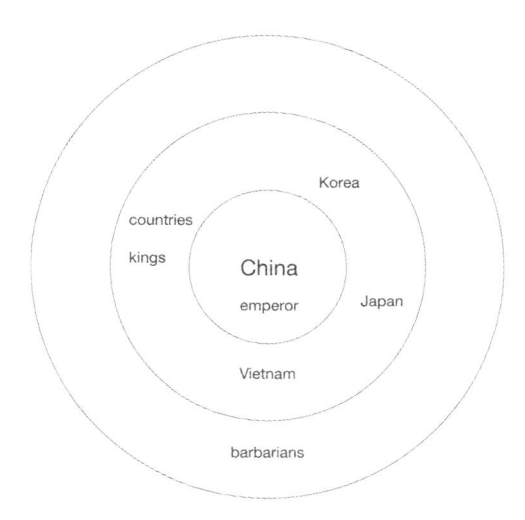

The Chinese World Order.

long after the Tokugawa settlement was implemented, armed resistance to the new internal order became impossible, making for the almost 250-year "long peace" of the Edo period, stimulating a huge increase in population, agricultural production, and inter-regional trade.

However, in the same century, the Ming dynasty in China was militarily ousted by the Ching dynasty, making for half a century of war and turmoil. Peace, stability and prosperity are signs that a realm is ruled in a moral Confucianist way. In that sense, 17th century Japan was doing remarkably better than the leader of the Chinese world order itself. Moreover, the dynastic revolution presented an unignorable internal contradiction concerning China's superior position within this system. The problematic thing was that the entity that had overtaken the centre of the world order was not ethnically Chinese. The half-nomadic Manchu hordes that now occupied China were ranked as semi-barbarians or complete barbarians by the same world order they were now supposed to be leading. Korean or Vietnamese opposition to this uncivilised situation could easily be crushed by the use of sheer force, but the Japanese elite minority that was bestowed with the luxury of a view of the outside world had the freedom to debate this anomaly. On the basis of their newfound superior peaceful and stable internal setting, they could only conclude that, for the moment, their country was the Confucianist number one or, slightly more humbly, the number two in the temporary absence of number one.

★

However, as time passed, and the situation of Japanese Confucianist superiority and Chinese Confucianist inferiority continued for generations, Japanese views of the outside world became bolder. On the basis of their ongoing superiority and a concomitant lack of hope that China would pull itself together once again, a Japanese elite minority was not loath to project their superiority into the future. And by the time this abnormal situation had lasted for more than one-and-a-half centuries, they had become so self-confident they were no longer satisfied with superiority in the present and the future: they started craving a uniquely Japanese superior past as well. This is nothing special in itself, and many forms of ethnic nationalism have walked the same path of more or less imagined communities creating a national past and identity. However, in the case of Japan there was the somewhat problematic fact of more than a thousand years of "national history" in which they had been importing and imitating almost everything from the China-dominated East Asian continent.

Still, arduous nationalists are not easily stopped in their tracks, and also in this case adherents to the new school of *kokugaku* [often rendered as national learning, nativism or proto-nationalism, but I have a strong liking for the more modern concept of "Japanese studies"] had no qualms about finding a truly unique Japanese brilliance in their special emotional ties with nature as expressed in the *Man'yōshū*, a collection of 7th-8th century poetry. One may wonder how they covered the problematic fact that the Japanese did not have their own script: in order to have written historical sources in which to find their own brilliance, they had to make do with documents written in Chinese script. But at least they could argue that at this stage the Chinese characters were merely used as instruments to transcribe the Japanese language, not to convey their meaning, and thus unfolded a truly Japanese spirit as yet uncontaminated by Chinese influence.

The first *kokugakusha*, adherents to this new nationalist trend, can also be termed the first Japanese. They transcended the limitations of their feudal domains and their social status – often samurai – and started upon the arduous task of creating a unified Japanese past, spirit, and identity. In other words, while not born Japanese, in the process of creating Japan, they recreated themselves as Japanese. However, in many cases it was not difficult to see that they had started out with Chinese minds. They had all been trained and educated in a Confucianist way, and although the message they preached increasingly became anti-Chinese, the way they expressed themselves, structured their arguments, and created a new mission for themselves was often steeped in Chinese precedents.

★

These Chinese roots are also very notable in the new view of the outside world the *kokugakusha* professed. It will be clear that the creation of a Japanese world order was anything but revolutionary, as it was an exact copy of the Chinese world order. The superficial changes were limited to taking China and its emperor out of the world's centre and putting Japan and its emperor in it. Although this of course involved changing the criterion for ranking countries from Chinese civilisation to something "uniquely Japanese", whether that was culture, the eternal lineage of the imperial institution and its direct descent from the sun goddess, a brave male spirit [*Yamatodamashii*], or a more melancholy awareness of the transience of things [*mono no aware*].

However, the real problem lay in populating this new world order. It could not make do with mere vocal support from inside. Rather, it needed to be upheld and legitimised by foreign entities willing to partake in this game of Japaneseness, making the trip to the shogunal capital of Edo – not the imperial capital of Kyoto – to bow before Japanese superiority and pay tribute. It was clear that neither neighbouring China nor Korea could be expected to pay their respects, and accordingly give content to this second layer, encircling and legitimising the pure Japanese centre. This is where the Ryukyuans and Ainu, heterogeneous ethnicities in the south and the north of the Japanese archipelago, were mobilised. Whereas they had been the object of compulsory forms of homogenising Japanification for many centuries, they now once again were told to retreat to their peripheral position and be as heterogeneous as possible in order to function as indispensable foreign entities. Therefore the Japanese world order ended up as an even more arrogant construction and bigger lie than the Chinese world order. An island empire almost equal to Japan's present-day territory is termed "the world" and the rest of the globe is turned into a barbarian wasteland.

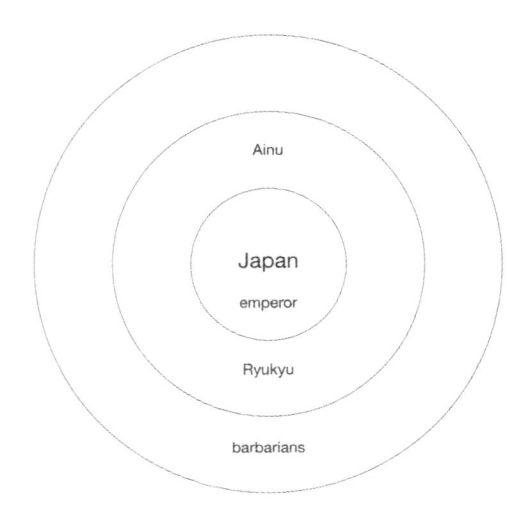

The Japanese World Order.

That, at least, is the way it seems at first sight. However, the few representatives of the elite minority who were still hiding Chinese underclothes under their new Japanese kimonos were not yet capable of terming their former Confucianist brothers "barbarians". Thus, they had no choice but to act as if China and Korea did not exist. There was nowhere, within this clone of the Chinese world order, to position civilised entities who did not bow before envisioned Japanese superiority. It will be evident that the *kokugakusha,* in an extreme form of indulging in their newfound superior identity, had created a world order so shaky and irrational that it could only exist as long as the rest of the world paid no attention whatsoever to Japan.

★

The house of cards that was the Japanese world order immediately came crashing down when the outside world started taking notice. Not that the West was inherently terribly interested in Japan. The US, which made the strongest unified effort to include Japan in its game, was not motivated by anything more than the use of a stop-over harbour, for its ships on the way to China or visiting adjacent waters while hunting whales, no matter how far away from Japan's political or economic centres. But this minuscule motivation, backed up by a little push in terms of a parade of a few state-of-the-art steamships and, more importantly, unconsciously timed at a moment of profound *bakufu* weakness and indecisiveness, was sufficient to make the Japanese world order implode. When a *bakufu* official signed the first so-called "unequal" treaty with the West, signalling Western superiority and Japanese inferiority, a world order based upon Japanese superiority could no longer be.

By the way, the same signature could also be explained as "the barbarian-quelling grand general" – the official title of the shogun – not fulfilling the task bestowed upon him by the emperor. Accordingly, it gave a pretext and some legitimacy to those willing to use the authority of the emperor in rebelling against the shogunate, eventually bringing about the Meiji Revolution and, although unplanned at the outset, completely changing the whole of Japan.

The story of the Meiji Revolution is impossible to render briefly and, moreover, the more detail one obtains the more mind-boggling the inception of this unique minimum-scale maximum-impact palace revolution is. In a similar vein, it is not easy to understand how the mindset of a person from one day to another can switch from propagating Japanese superiority to going out in the streets and joyously shouting "we are inferior! Let's become civilised!" (which is my somewhat free rendering of the early Meiji period slogan *bunmei kaika*). Or in other words, how a person's views of the outside world and Japan's position in it can be completely reformatted from a Japanese world order to a Western one.

It would take way more space than allotted here to explain this in detail, but let me simply stress the fact that in order to accomplish this volte-face, it was crucial that Japan was confronted by a world order inherently different from the Chinese one it had been used to. The latter was, for instance, Sinocentric, dependent on place, and retrogressive. The Western world order, at least in theory, was universal, dependent on time, and progressive. The Chinese focused on a past period of brilliance, and told all non-Chinese that they would always be inferior to China; never able to become number one or fully partake in the highest level of Chinese civilisation. The Western world order told Japan that it was inferior at present, but provided the hope that just like any other (non-colonised) country it could join them on the road to universal civilisation, and become equal to a select group of civilised countries. In other words, the lines temporarily dividing the groups in three different stages of civilisation were porous, and there was no spatial criterion that formed an

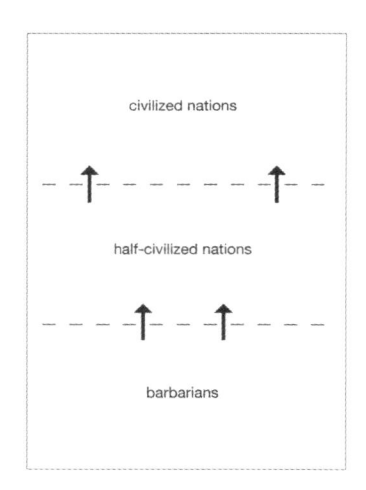

```
              civilized nations

          - -↑- - - - - -↑- -

             half-civilized nations

          - - - -↑- -↑- - - -

                 barbarians
```

The (Western) World Order.

obstacle to Japan rising to the highest level of civilisation. If this narrative of universality, progress and hope had been absent, Japan most likely would have fought and tried to resist foreign powers, just like Korea did. And things were decisively facilitated by the fact that the Japanese were ranked by the West as "merely" half-civilised, not uncivilised like the Koreans.

★

The abstract universal structure of the Western world order is given a more concrete content that may fluctuate from one period to another and from one's geographical position in this world. First of all, one is never aware of the whole world out there. The scope of our views of the outside world is limited by our awareness, sometimes gathered on the basis of our own lived experience, but more often conditioned by the mass media. This is evident from so-called psychological maps of the world, based on the awareness of various parts of the world, where from a West-European point of view Europe and the US are many times their actual size, whereas Africa and large parts of Asia are miniscule. When we limit ourselves here to the case of Japan in the Meiji period, we should acknowledge that the number of countries that made up Japan's outside world were few. In hierarchical order, it was aware of: England, the then leader of the Western world; Germany, as the up-and-coming representative of continental Europe; its Western neighbours the US and Russia; and its Asian neighbours China and Korea. Other entities were well-nigh invisible from a Japanese point of view.

These countries had to be grouped in a way that was in line with the dictates of the world order. Accordingly, England, Germany, the US and Russia were categorised as civilised, Japan itself and China as half-civilised, and Korea as an uncivilised non-entity. The ranking of individual countries from a Japanese perspective was no different from the perspective of another country partaking in the same Western world order, although of course a different location makes for some minor countries becoming invisible and others visible. The only liberty the Japanese gave themselves was to rank themselves above China, a tendency which, in the period before the first Sino-Japanese War of 1894–95, would probably not have been shared by any other country.

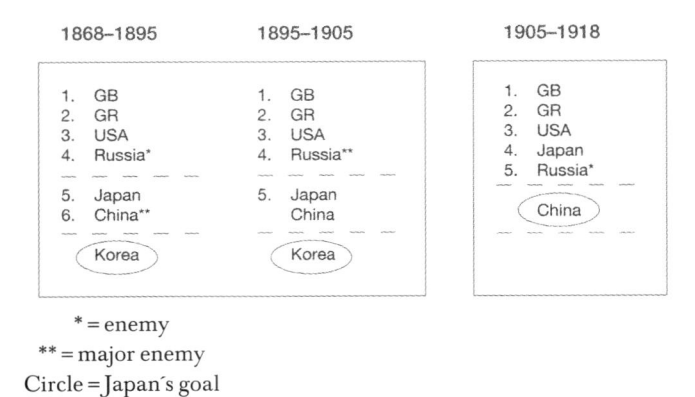

```
1868–1895              1895–1905              1905–1918

1. GB                  1. GB                  1. GB
2. GR                  2. GR                  2. GR
3. USA                 3. USA                 3. USA
4. Russia*             4. Russia**            4. Japan
                                              5. Russia*
5. Japan               5. Japan
6. China**                China                  (China)

  (Korea)                (Korea)
```

* = enemy
** = major enemy
Circle = Japan's goal

However, our views of the outside world often are not as neutral as described above, where visible countries are judged on the basis of their civilisational stage and rank. Many countries tend to be characterised as allies or enemies. During the Cold War for example, the map of the world was, to a large extent, divided between a blue capitalist camp and a red communist/socialist camp. In the case of Meiji Japan, we need to ascertain the country's main foreign policy priority in order to find out which of the visible countries, from a Japanese point of view, are considered enemies, and which allies.

I hope that a look at the structure of Japan's views of the outside world will make clear that the ambition to do away with the so-called unequal treaties could not function as that dominant foreign policy priority. This would have turned all countries in the group of civilised nations into Japan's enemies, an impossible situation when one takes into account that, due to the wide civilisational gap between the three groups in the Western world order, Japan could not even take on one of these countries. Doing away with humiliating unequal treaties could only function as a long-term dream, not as a short-term pragmatic policy.

Just like the model countries of its day, Japan prioritised an expansionist foreign policy. Even before the Meiji Revolution there had been a drive among some leaders to conquer the Korean peninsula. In the Meiji period this rather irrational notion acquired a more solid Western and modern footing by means of the imported set of terms of the line of sovereignty [*shukensen*] and the line of interest [*riekisen*]. It was most prominently advocated by the most powerful man of the late Meiji period, Yamagata Aritomo, and subsequently was supported almost universally by the Japanese political and military leadership, the oppositional forces, the media, and the common people. The proposition is that a country cannot be truly independent when it merely defends its line of sovereignty: it depends on the support of third parties, and thus is not autonomous. Accordingly, one needs to go beyond this line, and occupy and defend a strategically advantageous line of interest, so one no longer needs to depend on the goodwill of a third party. And in the case of Japan, prime minister and army general Yamagata publicly announced in the first prime minister's speech in Japanese parliamentary history that this line of interest incorporated the whole of the Korean peninsula.

★

The occupation of Korea, and thus the establishment of a Japanese sphere of influence on the Asian continent, dominated the Meiji mind. It overshadowed all other policies. The Japanese were willing to spend a staggeringly high percentage of their national budget on the expansion and modernisation of their army and navy, and for this same purpose fought two bloody wars.

The so-called First Sino-Japanese War of 1894–95, and the Russo-Japanese War of 1904–05 are better termed the two Korea wars, because this was, first and foremost, what they were about. And whereas the first war was a calculated total victory over a weakened China, but a dismal failure in the sense that it did not result in Japanese rule over Korea, the second war can be characterised as a form of Russian roulette to the same degree as Pearl Harbor.

Japan recklessly gambled its autonomy and independence, most likely the northern island of Hokkaido, as well as the lives of tens of thousands of its young men and all the money it had and could borrow, on a war that it was destined to lose. The Japanese came out victorious only because revolutionary circumstances on the home front meant that the Russian tsarist regime had to sue for peace. This shows us the dangerous and horrible extent to which an expansionist goal blinded the whole of the Japanese nation – although this time around, the war led to the occupation of Korea. Regrettably, the attainment of this long-cherished objective did not lead to a halt in Japanese expansionism. Korea was now seen as part of the Japanese empire, and accordingly became part of its line of sovereignty, thus making the line of interest shift to the northeastern part of China – the occupation of which turned into Japan's national obsession up until 1945.

★

In all of this it should be clear that there was no room whatsoever for any Asianist policy. On the one hand, because of Western fears of a "yellow peril", the Japanese government made sure to censor all Asianist content from its official statements. However, much more important was the mere fact that Japan's main goal was to turn Korea into a Japanese sphere of influence, and accordingly, Japan had to first oust Chinese influence from the peninsula. Within such a framework, any call upon Asian brotherhood could only sound hollow.

Moreover, the Japanese could only conceive of neighbouring Korea as an empty stage for others to occupy (and rather the Japanese than the Russians). A war against the Koreans was never considered. They were a non-entity, in the lowest-ranking group of uncivilised countries: one need not communicate with them and, moreover, one definitely did not want to be identified with them. Just like the elite minority of the Edo period had Chinese-formatted minds, their Meiji period counterparts boasted a West European mindset, with which they had no problem looking down upon their fellow countrymen.

But even stronger was the shuddering awareness of the Western tendency to sweep Japan into one heap together with China and Korea. The utter humiliation of being treated in this manner informed an urge to stand out and be treated as superior, if possible as part of the group of Western civilised nations. It was this strongly felt motivation that inspired the famous 1885 article *Datsu-A ron* [Stepping Out of Asia], which was published in the *Jiji Shimpō* [Current Events] newspaper by Japan's most famous moderniser, Fukuzawa Yukichi. At the time, the editorial did not stand out, and was forgotten for almost a century, but in hindsight it functions as the canonical text that briefly, but poignantly, reveals the Japanese modern mindset ever since the Meiji period.

Although there are some fluctuations over time, in line with changes in the world order, this mindset can be depicted by a scheme such as on page 68, which represents Japanese views of the outside world from the end of the Russo-Japanese War. Japan positions itself between East and West, looking up to the West European or American leaders of civilisation, and looking down upon Russia and the Asian entities China and Korea. Just as the English can define Europe as "the continent" and, every once in a while, forget to include themselves, the Japanese very consciously did not include themselves in "Asia". As the author of *Datsu-A ron* concluded: "in spirit we break with our evil friends of Eastern Asia".

★

Japan was in a league of its own and, moreover, it felt it was equipped with a special mission on this planet, on behalf of civilisation. Given the combined credentials of having Asian roots and being the most diligent and successful non-Western disciple of the West, some opinion leaders advocated that the country should function as a bridge, bringing about understanding between the two civilisations – although this was mostly seen as "teaching Asians". Some even went wild and conceived of a unique Japanese role in attaining the amalgamation of Eastern and Western civilisation [*tōzai bunmeiron*], taking it to a higher level of one united world civilisation, with their country assuming the superior role of leading it, as some kind of "slightly yellow white man's burden". However, although many Japanese political and intellectual leaders cannot help but attribute their country with a unique mission, they tend to place it more humbly within the "normal" Japanese mindset, in-between the best of the West and the Asian rest.

Neither should one be fooled by propaganda at the time of the Asia-Pacific War, in which the Japanese were touted as "the chosen people", with their country becoming the world leader, either because of its special link with the sun goddess or because of its invincible Yamato spirit. For their part, England and America were dehumanised as "devils and beasts" [*kichiku Ei-Bei*].

The reality of the wartime so-called "comfort stations" – military brothels – in Japanese occupied territories presented a much more realistic depiction of the continuing Japanese modern mind-set: Japanese "comfort women" were relatively expensive, Korean ("annexed Japanese") somewhat cheaper, Chinese considerably cheaper, and native women the cheapest deal you could get. White Western women were *hors catégorie*, a special privilege only for officers.

Neither Japan's defeat in the Asia Pacific War or its postwar experience changed its mindset. First within the framework of the American occupation of Japan, but before long within the Cold War structure, the country had to settle itself in an inferior position, subservient towards the US. And although its high-speed economic growth gradually outdid the European players and even attained number two rank, the Old World continued to outshine Japan in non-economic fields – it was both the cradle and zenith of culture, art, music, fashion, cuisine, and sports, and remained an object of veneration.

Postwar Japan's spectacular economic growth also widened the gap between itself and other Asian nations. Japan's GNP on its own was easily several times bigger than the whole of Asia combined. Forays into other Asian markets only made Japanese businessmen and engineers aware that "out there" was a world that in some cases was not completely unfamiliar to them, but which they had left behind many decades ago. Accordingly, an increasing economic involvement in various east Asian and southeast Asian countries did not lead to stronger feelings of proximity and togetherness. On the contrary, it merely underlined the Japanese modern mindset of the country as a non-Asian entity in a league of its own.

And all this was further emphasised by Japan's unique status as the only non-Western country represented in the G7 and many other eminent institutions. But, most of all, one should be aware of the Cold War superstructure, in which everything was about two opposing ideologies and contradictory political economic systems, and where things like (supranational) region did not mean a thing. The largest part of East Asia was communist and thus enemy territory. The Cold War structure was very instrumental in sustaining Japan's modern mindset, so Japan could continue thinking of itself without any problem as the world's number two and Asia's number one – although in the latter case, Asia was merely a geographic term and did not imply anything like an identity.

★

Whereas the Cold War period was predominantly benign to Japan, the post-Cold War period has been tough. And this is not merely in terms of familiar phrases such as "the burst bubble", "the lost decade(s)" and "economic crisis". Japan's modern mindset, which has survived relatively intact for almost 150 years since the Meiji period, is now in danger.

Japan's Prime Minister Shinzō Abe reaches
out to shake hands with Chinese President
Xi Jinping during a regional economic
meeting in Yanqi Lake, Beijing, 2014.

The country is no longer the world's number two, but has been downgraded to number four. Moreover, it has been usurped by Asian entities, namely China and India, meaning that Japan can no longer hold on to the number one position in Asia. One may assume that this new situation, which looks to be further consolidated in the near future, will inevitably result in the implosion of Japan's superior self-identity.

Although some opinion leaders have reacted pragmatically to the changed hierarchy by proposing an updated version of Japan's special mission in this world – the country is uniquely qualified to bridge the gap between the US and China – it is hard to deny that a considerable part of Japanese commentary regarding China's rise has been couched in terms of "fear China" [*kyō-Chū ron*].

This can only be natural when we consider the fact that present-day generations only know the Japanese modern mindset: this has accordingly been functioning as part of their identity. However, it may very well be inevitable that they adjust to a more humble mindset – namely that of a peripheral position within a Chinese regional order.

From a historical, long-term perspective, such a return to the elite minority Japanese mindset of the 7th century up until the 18th century may one day be termed "back to normal", and Japan's modern mindset characterised as a mere historical anomaly of less than 150 years.

1. Due to the wide scope and long timeframe but limited size of this chapter, along with the objective of this publication, my essay is relatively rough, brief, and radical. Instead of the usual academic detail and grey zone, a clear choice has been made between either white or black. For the same reasons I have hardly mentioned any sources. Although my first forays into this field were stimulated to some extent by Tessa Morris-Suzuki's *Re-Inventing Japan – Time, Space, Nation* (M.E. Sharpe, 1998) and articles by Yamamuro Shinichi, the essay rather is the distillation of four decades of watching Japanese films, three decades of reading Japanese historical sources and the daily Japanese newspaper, almost two decades of living in Japan and being on the receiving side of various Japanese media (although I also had the privilege of working as a foreign correspondent in Japan for foreign media) and, most gratefully, twenty-five years of being forced to bring all my insights down to a structured overview of Japanese views of the outside world and the national self for a student audience.

The Galapagos Syndrome.
Will it work outside of Japan?

EDUCATION AND THE CONSTRUCTION OF JAPANESE NATIONAL IDENTITY

Roger Goodman

During the late 1970s and throughout the whole of the 1980s, foreign coverage of Japanese education was almost completely positive. It was taken for granted that there was a link between Japan's education system and its extraordinary economic growth. It seems a long time ago now, but by the end of the 1980s it was thought possible that Japan would be the largest economy in the world by the end of the following decade. Foreign experts flocked to Japan to learn the "secrets" of its education system and found it in the emphasis on basic skills, a centralised curriculum, and highly-qualified, respected and well-remunerated teachers. Japanese school children were depicted as exceptionally hard working, disciplined and respectful of authority. Commentators were intrigued by the focus on teaching in groups rather than concentrating on the individual child. Indeed, individualism was seen as getting in the way of good learning and appeared to be viewed negatively. All of this was seen as in direct opposition to the basis of educational philosophy in "Western" (seemingly any country outside Asia) education. The fact that the economies of North America, Latin America, Europe and Oceania were all faring so much worse than those of Japan (and by the end of the 1980s many of its neighbours) was seen as reason enough to "learn from Japan".

This view changed dramatically with the bursting of the Japanese economic bubble in 1991. Indeed, many of the reasons which had been given for how the education system was, at least in part, responsible for Japanese economic success in the 1980s were given as reasons for its demise in the 1990s. In particular, the education system was seen as stifling individual talent and an entrepreneurial spirit. Japanese children were believed to lack creativity because of the over-emphasis on conformity. The system was criticised for its lack of diversity and choice. The new buzzwords were *tayōka* [diversification] and *jiyūka* [liberalisation].

In the 1990s, a second theme became apparent. This was the notion that the education system was increasingly being turned into a vehicle for nationalist ideology. The word "nationalism" can carry many connotations, from patriotism at the positive end to racism and xenophobia at the negative end. The reports on Japan's education system becoming more nationalistic were clearly pitched towards the negative end of the spectrum, and frequently compared the situation with the role of education in the 1930s and 1940s. To understand the current debates, therefore, we need first to look at the history of Japanese education more generally in the development of modern Japan.

★

The history of the Japanese education system is well covered in English language literature on Japan. Education as a concept has been given great respect in Japan since at least the introduction of Chinese writing in the 4th century. This is not surprising given the fact that, in resource-scarce Japan, human beings have always been the country's most important natural resource.

By the 18th century, Japan already had, by global standards, a very well-established education system. Education in schools for the upper classes, in particular, already had many of the features of the contemporary system. By the first half of the 19th century, more than 40 per cent of boys and 10 per cent of girls had obtained education outside the home. This comparatively high rate of education provided an excellent basis for rapid economic, social and political reforms during the Meiji period. The Meiji oligarchs believed that the education system was the key to the successful modernisation of the country, and that modernisation was the key to avoid colonisation (a lesson lost on Japan's neighbour Korea which, ironically, ended up being colonised by a modernised Japan). The Meiji leaders added to the existing system elements of other education models which they had picked up on intensive fact-finding trips overseas: the French system of a centralised authority; the German model of an elite higher education system; the importance of character-building from the British; and, practical pedagogical techniques and a focus on vocational education from the United States. In 1875, at the beginning of the Meiji period, around 35 per cent of children were receiving elementary education. By 1905, 30 years later, it was over 95 per cent.

Japanese schoolchildren.

With Japan's defeat in 1945, the US occupation forces tried to dismantle Japan's prewar and wartime education system: they saw it as having played a major role in disseminating ultra nationalist ideologies among the younger generation. This process was curtailed considerably due to the greater fear of the spread of Communist ideology to Japan via the education system in the late 1940s. The result was that, according to many commentators, Japan was left with an education system that may have had a new structure but whose content and beliefs were little changed. It remained essentially a Japanese system with Western elements added to it. It was a system designed to serve the interests of the nation rather than those of the individual citizen, even if its focus now was on developing a workforce for economic growth rather than soldiers for territorial expansion.

The postwar Japanese education system was designed to turn out male workers who would conform to the company ideology, work hard and put the firm before their personal wellbeing. They would persevere and always strive to do better; and, of course, they would be literate, numerate and able to understand new ideas and apply them quickly. When it came to female workers, they would not only contribute to the work effort but also cheer up workplaces by their presence [known as *shokuba no hana*]; they would leave when they got married and become the ideal homemakers for the male workers and the ideal mothers for the next generation of workers. These gendered ideologies of the normative expectations of what it meant to be Japanese in the postwar period were powerfully reinforced by a widespread literature which was grouped under a catch-all phrase of *nihonjinron* [theories of Japaneseness] and widely disseminated via the media. While these ideologies were critiqued, they were little challenged until the Japanese economy came to a juddering halt at the beginning of the 1990s.

The post-bubble period in Japan has often been depicted as an era of introspection. The first decade has been written off by many commentators as "the lost decade" [*ushinawareta jūnen*] even though unemployment never even reached 6 per cent and GDP only declined in two of those ten years. The following fifteen years have seen a more robust determination by political leaders to regain a sense of pride in what it means to be Japanese, and instil this in what is seen by many political commentators as an increasingly rootless, some would say feckless, younger generation. It is this desire to instil Japaneseness that many commentators have described as a form of growing nationalism. The purpose of the rest of this essay is to examine the rhetoric and the reality of this external perception in three areas that have often been picked out in the media (both inside and outside Japan) as typical of a Japan which is turning inwards and rightwards.

★

The Japanese media has a penchant for summarising complex social phenomenon in simple phrases and expressions. The "Galapagos syndrome" is one such. It originally referred to an isolated branch of a globally available product, in the way that Charles Darwin encountered isolated flora and fauna on the Galapagos Islands that had developed unique characteristics. As technology moved towards adopting worldwide standards and specifications, Japanese companies were increasingly seen as being out of step by focusing only on their domestic markets. Well-known examples include 3G phones that cannot be used outside Japan, and the difficulty of using foreign cash cards in the country. In Japan, the expression has more recently become associated with the perceived reluctance of the Japanese, especially the young, to spend time overseas. In 2010, one survey suggested that two-thirds of white collar workers would not want to work abroad.[1] Japanese academia has also been widely criticised for becoming isolated from the outside world. This is sometimes described as the "curse of Japan", in that Japan has just enough universities (1,200 of them in total) and academics to constitute an intellectually satisfying self-contained community.

It is the apparent lack of interest among young Japanese in seeking overseas education that has caught the headlines the most. Whereas in the 1980s, the younger generation, especially young women, were seen as adventurous and outward-looking, the current widely held perception is that they are afraid to leave the shores of Japan. There was a lot of coverage of the trip to Japan by Harvard President Drew Faust to encourage more Japanese students to study there. It was widely reported that only five Japanese students attended Harvard as undergraduates in 2009, and only one of them matriculated as a freshman. Japanese enrolment at Harvard has been declining for fifteen years while enrolment from China and India has more than doubled. More broadly, Japan – which has in terms of spending the second largest higher education sector in the world after only the US – *sends* less than 1 per cent (32,000) of all internationally mobile students abroad, of whom 55 per cent go to the US and 10 per cent to the UK, and *receives* less than 3.5 per cent (135,000) of all foreign higher education students, of whom 66 per cent are from China and 12 per cent from Korea.

While the rhetoric generated around the idea of Japan becoming increasingly isolated from the outside world has been growing ever louder in recent years, the reality is somewhat different and more nuanced. The decline in the number of Japanese students overseas must be seen in the light of the decline in the absolute number of young Japanese in the population. Japan's demography is changing – and facing further change – more dramatically than any recorded population changes outside either war or plague. To take one pertinent example, in the 18-year period between 1992 and 2010, Japan saw a 40 per cent drop in the number of 18 and 19-year-olds in the population. Since this is the cohort that constitutes over 95 per cent of all university entrants, it has had a major impact on higher education and forced Japanese universities at all levels to invest huge resources in recruitment – something they did not even need to think about in the 1980s when demand for university places far outstripped supply. A very large amount of the decline in the numbers of young Japanese going overseas, therefore, can simply be explained by demographic factors.

In the light of the pressure on domestic institutions to retain student numbers, the investment by the government in encouraging overseas study is particularly notable. In 2013, the ministry of education and science (MEXT) launched a programme entitled *Tobitate! Ryūgaku Japan* [Go Abroad! Study Overseas, Japan] with the target of sending 120,000 university and 60,000 high school students abroad by 2020. The ministry has invested even more effort in attracting foreign staff to come and work in Japanese institutions. The government has set a target to have the International Baccalaureate taught in 200 high schools by 2018; it has designated and funded a programme of fifty-six Super Global High Schools and thirty-seven Super Global Universities, which have all been set tough targets for demonstrating lasting internationalisation among their staff, students and curricula; perhaps most impressively, central and local government remain fully committed to the Japan Exchange and Teaching (JET) programme which is in its twentieth year. The JET programme currently employs (on very good salaries) over 4,500 recent graduates from over forty countries who work in Japanese schools and boards of education. Over the past twenty years, it has employed well over 60,000 participants in total. The JET programme is the largest single graduate employer in the world. It is fully funded by the Japanese taxpayer to the tune of over US$400 million a year. Holders of Japanese passports can only participate in the programme if they renounce their citizenship. It is surprising how little coverage this programme has been given in the light of the perception that Japan is increasingly isolating itself from the rest of the world. (For a fascinating account of the development and philosophy of the JET programme, see David McConnell's *Importing Diversity: Inside Japan's JET Programme*, 2000). Ironically, there has been a huge decline in interest in the programme from UK applicants in recent years. The UK had more than 1,400 graduates on the programme in 2001 but fewer than 400 by 2013. There has been no suggestion that this reflects a Galapagos syndrome among UK youth.

★

Few subjects have exercised Japan's neighbours, especially China and South Korea, so consistently over the past two decades than the perceived revisions to Japan's history textbooks. All Japanese textbooks have been regulated by the ministry of education since 1948, including social studies textbooks which are used to teach schoolchildren Japanese history. This system was introduced to take control over the content of textbooks away from the government – they had exercised this assiduously during the wartime period – and to give the responsibility to independent publishers. Local education boards can only choose between government-approved textbooks for use in their schools. The role of the ministry is to ensure that the textbooks are impartial and free from errors. Increasingly, however, the ministry has been accused of interfering with the content of textbooks and thus of being responsible for their presentations of worldviews more in accordance with the wishes of the government of the day. As governments have become more right wing so, some have argued, have the textbooks. Several issues in particular have become sites for contestation and complaint from both inside and outside Japan. These include: depictions of Japanese colonialism and its "war of aggression" on the Asian mainland in the 1930s; the "Rape of Nanjing" in the winter of 1937; the treatment of the euphemistically-named Korean "comfort women" [*ianfu*] who served the sexual needs of Japanese soldiers throughout the war; and the mass suicide of civilians in Okinawa at the very end

Members of far-right revisionist group Japanese Society for History Textbook Reform with banner saying "(Give) children accurate history textbooks".

of the war. Other issues which have stimulated debate include the accounts of the treatment of the Ainu in Hokkaido in the Meiji period; the abuse of Koreans in Tokyo during the 1923 Kanto earthquake; and, more recently, the ownership of the so-called Northern Territories, as well as the Takeshima and Senkaku islands.

The contents of the textbooks have been subject to protest and litigation inside Japan since the 1950s, the most famous objections being raised by a Tokyo University of Education professor, Saburo Ienaga, over almost thirty years of court battles. In 1982, however, the textbook authorisation system became a major diplomatic issue for the first time when the ministry of education was reported to have demanded a particular textbook publisher use the phrase "*advanced* [進出] into" rather than "*invaded*" [侵略] in relation to Japanese actions in northern China in the 1930s. The Chinese government strongly protested the change and the Japanese government quickly apologised for any misunderstanding, although it was not clear that the ministry had ever recommended the change in the first place. More clearly antagonistic to Japan's neighbours was the publication in 2000 of the *New History Textbook* [*Atarashii Rekishi Kyokasho*] by a group of conservative scholars called the Japanese Society for History Textbook Reform, which was unambiguously intended to promote a revisionist view of Japanese history. The society's core stated objective was to "avoid the dissemination of masochistic history" and it set out to offer a less negative version of Japan's annexation of Korea in 1910, Japan's role in China in the 1930s and Japan's role in World War II. When the textbook was approved by the ministry of education in 2001, it caused huge controversy in Japan, China and Korea.

While the accounts of Japanese history textbooks have been strong on political rhetoric, they have often been weak on the reality of what has happened during both the screening process, and when it comes to the actual impact of the textbooks in schools. While the textbook screening process has generally been depicted as a force for conservatism, in some ways it is better seen as a force for liberalism. There are many publishers of social science textbooks in Japan (the potential profits from the market are huge) and most of them consistently set out to submit the most liberal versions of history they can, and argue long and hard with the ministry to have their versions accepted. The final versions are the result of long negotiations. The *New History Textbook* was unusual in that the Japanese Society for History Textbook Reform wanted to present the most conservative version of history that it could. It too, however, was subject to demands from the ministry for numerous revisions before it was finally made available for boards of education to adopt.

It is at this stage that the story becomes interesting but has scarcely been reported at all. It is important to note that there are thirty unique textbooks for social studies (from five different publishers) for use in Japanese primary schools; there are eight textbooks for the study of history as part of the Japanese social studies curriculum from eight different publishers for use in junior high schools; and there are at least fifty textbook editions available for teaching Japanese and world history in Japanese senior high schools. When the *New History Textbook* was published in 2001 and made available for use in junior high schools, hardly any boards of education and individual schools adopted it. According to the Japanese Society for History Textbook Reform, which had hoped to see the textbook used in up to 10 per cent of schools, in 2005 it was only being used by 0.039 per cent of junior high schools across Japan: eight private junior high schools and one public school for the disabled in Tokyo, and three public junior high schools and four public schools for the disabled in Ehime Prefecture.

Moreover, we do not know how the textbook was delivered and received in some of the schools where it was adopted. Japanese teachers are not only among some of the best educated and best paid in the world (their salaries are higher than the average among those with similar educational backgrounds, which is unusual in a global perspective), but they also have tended to be left-of-centre in their political outlook. The only national trade union of any potency in Japan since the general purges of national, as opposed to company, unions at the end of the 1940s has been the Japan National Teachers' Union which has long lobbied and protested against perceived nationalist policies such as raising the national flag and singing the national anthem at entry and graduation ceremonies. It is possible that some teachers might use the right-wing textbooks as an exemplar of the dangers of government curriculum reform and the revision of national history. Japanese schoolchildren in turn are the most literate population of schoolchildren in the world – despite the immense challenges of learning to read and write in Japanese – and would be as open to such sophisticated teaching as schoolchildren anywhere else.

The nuances of the adoption and classroom usage of the history textbooks has never been addressed in Chinese and Korean criticisms of

Japanese textbook revisions over the past two decades. Perhaps most ironic though is that in both China and South Korea there is only one history textbook available for teaching in school in each country, and in both cases that textbook is produced directly by the ministry of education.

★

The current Abe administration in Japan has generally been characterised as asserting a stronger image of Japan and its role in the world than its predecessors. With the opposition weakened by factionalism and charged with incompetence for their handling of the fallout from the Fukushima nuclear accident, the administration is in as strong a position as any Japanese government for the past two decades. It is widely reported that Abe is manoeuvring himself for a third term in office. It is in this light that the re-introduction of moral education as an official subject in elementary and junior high schools from 2018 and 2019 respectively has been viewed with concern by some commentators.[2]

The ostensible explanations for the new moral education programmes are rising rates of bullying, drop-outs and juvenile delinquency in Japanese schools which are ascribed to the poor moral codes of young people that could be remedied by strengthening the children's "normative consciousness" [*kihan ishiki*] and awareness of their national identity. While the evidence of a rise in bullying in particular is hard to measure, and juvenile delinquency rates have actually fallen considerably in recent decades while crime by the elderly has grown very rapidly, few commentators can disagree with the idea that anything that reduces bullying in schools and juvenile delinquency must be a good policy. Similarly, few can disagree with most of the proposed curriculum with its focus on key-words such as gratitude, courtesy, public-mindedness, honesty and sincerity and topics such as information morality, sustainable development and bioethics. The contentious areas of the curriculum relate to expressions which could be perceived as nationalistic in tone – "love of one's country" and "respect for tradition and culture and native religion" – and the fact that textbooks might be imposed on teachers whereas previously they could, and did, develop their own materials.

As Kristoffer Hornburg Bolton[3] points out, much of the negative reporting of the introduction of the new curriculum is based on at best a misunderstanding and at worse a wilful distortion of a number of important facts. Many of the elements of the new curriculum which the Abe administration is accused of introducing have been part of the school programme for more than thirty years, since the era of Prime Minister Nakasone Yasuhiro and his major educational reforms of the 1980s. Nakasone was of the view that in an increasingly globalised world, it was more important than ever for children to have a strong sense of their national identity and cultural background. Many of the current issues surrounding the new moral education agenda relate to this tension between international and national identity and how to build a bridge between them. In this light, the moral education curriculum reforms look considerably less threatening, not least when the goals of the new curriculum also clearly include the need for "nurturing children who can think how to live and act on the basis of autonomous judgment". Moreover, many of the icons selected as exemplars for children to learn from are Japanese figures associated with international perspectives such as the so-called "father of the Japanese navy" Sakamoto Ryōma, the bacteriologist Noguchi Hideyō, even the marathon runner Takahashi Naoko. Many of the others are Western figures such as Abraham Lincoln, Marie Curie and Mother Teresa. It is conspicuous though, as Marie Roesgaard[4] points out, that there are no non-Japanese Asian icons in any of the ministry approved textbooks.

As with the history textbooks, the most significant qualitative research question that needs to be answered is "how are the approved textbooks actually used in schools?" The answer from the work of both Bolton and Roesgaard seems to be that they are not used in the ways that the ministry of education had hoped. Bolton observed moral education teaching in thirty-two classes in an elementary school, which accounted for all of the teaching on the subject delivered in that semester. This, importantly, was a school which had already publicly committed to taking moral education seriously. Yet the teachers in the school only used the officially-mandated textbook in 15 per cent of the lessons, preferring other non-mandated texts or simply their own materials. Bolton's explanation is that "media framing has succeeded, to a certain degree…and the textbook is being treated as an extension of the Abe cabinet's will". In short, teachers are not passive in Japan, and the fact that politically they tend to be left-of-centre makes them reluctant, even in a school committed to moral education, to use the official textbook, which they view as overly ideological, as their focus. Even when they did use it, they would, according to Bolton, "contextualise it with personal stories and moral lessons of their own". Perhaps most significantly, in this school as in many others, when teachers needed catch-up time for classes, moral education classes were dropped. Indeed, Bolton estimated that in the school where he was researching only about half of the allotted hours were delivered – even though the topic already had the fewest hours assigned to it in the curriculum. This is largely because, while the classes are part of the official curriculum, they are not tested, and hence unimportant for the students' career prospects. Although this is not mentioned by Bolton, one suspects that in those classes which do take place, the level of student effort is likely to be less than in the subjects they need to master in order to get into a good university. Japanese pupils are sensitised from a very early age to invest time and effort at school in an extremely instrumental manner.

★

As we have seen above, there is a great deal of rhetoric that insinuates the Japanese government is imposing a more nationalistic curriculum on the school system. Abe Shinzō is one of the most powerful Japanese prime ministers in a generation, and he has espoused political views which are seen by Japan's neighbours, especially China and Korea, as right wing and provocative. He has been particularly keen to create a more positive image of Japan's recent history for schoolchildren and to move away from the "masochistic history" that he believes has been dominant for most of the postwar period. Many ascribe his strong feelings on the subject to the fact that his grandfather was Kishi Nobusuke, who was prime minister between 1957–60. Kishi had been a member of the Tōjō Cabinet during the Second World War and was sentenced to serve a spell in Sugamo Prison by the American occupation forces after the war. He was released as the Americans switched their attention to the rise of communism. In his book *Utsukushii Kuni e* [Towards a Beautiful Country], Abe himself has written: "Some people used to say that my grandfather was a 'Class-A war criminal suspect' which was something I found very objectionable (when I was growing up). It is because of that experience, I believe, that I have become so emotionally attached to the ideas of 'conservatism'." There is no doubt that there has been a move to the right in Japanese politics in recent years with Abe as its figurehead. In most cases there has been very little political opposition. There is also some evidence that young Japanese themselves have become less enthusiastic in exploring the world outside Japan and have become increasingly politically apathetic, especially compared to their student predecessors of the 1960s and 1970s.

As I hope the cases explored in this essay have shown, however, this is far from the only story that can be told about Japanese education today. The government itself is worried about the inward-looking nature of its youth, and has invested very large amounts of taxpayers' money on schemes to encourage students to go overseas and young foreigners to come to Japan, not only to teach English but also to expose Japanese people to different ways of thinking. Even if there is a move to make the curriculum more conservative, we have seen that teachers in Japan do not passively accept these changes but engage with, moderate and in some ways often subvert them. Japanese pupils themselves are also not inert recipients of knowledge, but sophisticated consumers who know when and where to invest their efforts.

Japan is a complex, multifaceted, pluralist society containing many viewpoints among its population which, it is important to remember, is the most widely read and best-informed not only in Japan's history but arguably in the history of the whole world. The puzzle is why the rest of the world has such a simplistic view of the Japanese as a homogenous, conformist population. The answer is clearly complex. It has something to do with the Yoshida Doctrine of the postwar period when the Japanese state followed a policy of economic growth and political disengagement. It has something to do with the "curse of Japan", which is just big enough not to need to interact, except economically, with the outside world. The Japanese government itself, though, must take a large measure of the responsibility for not articulating a more nuanced and up-to-date account of Japanese society today.

1. *Wall Street Journal*, September 16, 2010.
2. (See, for example, *Japan Times* editorials, "Moral Education's Slippery Slope", October 26, 2014, and "Moral Education Raises Risks", February 10, 2015).
3. Hornburg Bolton, Kristoffer, *Moral Education in Japan: The Coming of a New Dawn, Abe's New Moral Education*, Master's thesis, University of Oslo, 2015.
4. Roesgaard, Marie H., "Globalization in Japan: The Case of Moral Education". Conference paper: Rethinking "Japanese Studies" from Practices in the Nordic Region, University of Copenhagen, August 22–24, 2012.

Mother with baby working at home.

FINDING ONE'S PLACE

Anne E. Imamura

The family is important as a locus where the balance between individual rights and the emphasis on institutional commitment plays out. In Japan, the family system has also been used as a symbol of Japan's uniqueness.

In 1958, British sociologist Ronald Dore wrote that "all societies have a family system, but few are as consciously aware of their family system as the Japanese."[1] This was almost sixty years ago, and one might well ask if, and in what ways, the Japanese today are "consciously aware of their family system", and the relevance of that system going forward.

The family system to which Dore referred was legally significantly changed from the system that had existed until the end of World War II. However, norms and expectations do not necessarily change because the laws do. In this essay, I would like to examine the Japanese family system today in the context of the changing structure of Japanese society. I will touch on issues around demographics and gender roles and raise a few questions for future consideration.

The 1947 Constitution formally declared equality between the sexes; revisions to the civil code adopted that year abolished the *ie* [household] structure that was multigenerational and based on a single, patriarchal head. However, the importance of the family as an institution was maintained in the revised registration system [*koseki*] based on the nuclear, rather than the extended, family.

Thus, the tension between individual rights and aspirations and the importance of belonging (in this case to a family), have been imbedded in and reinforced by the legal system since 1947.

In spite of many legal changes and the development of economic opportunities that make it possible, at least in theory, for individuals to support themselves financially, the issue of belonging continues to be extremely important in Japan, and is supported by both laws and societal expectations.

In this context, it is relevant to note that the term *kazoku* [family] means the members of the house – those who belong, and that the *koseki* Family Registration System clearly shows who belongs, who does not and how each individual member entered or left the family. Indeed, one way of referring to legal marriage is to be entered into the spouse's *koseki*. By law, spouses must have the same family name, and by custom, family members would share a family grave. This custom has led to a number of challenges in recent years: some women do not want to be buried in their husband's family grave; people without children may have problems purchasing a family grave because of the need to hold a family member responsible for various memorials in the future. With the declining birth rate, there are concerns among the elderly about whether their heirs will maintain the grave, and concerns among the young about shouldering that responsibility.

The current *koseki* system is based on a two-generation family. However, both social practice and the law expect children to care for their dependent parents. The difference is that social practice places this responsibility on the eldest son, whose wife will do the actual care giving, while according to the law, all children inherit equally and have equal responsibility for care giving.

This postwar family model was a hybrid of the focus on male lineage, and the aspirations for a loving home and a private space for parents to raise their children.[2] Modernisation was marked by a change in gender roles that meant most married women were expected to assume the role of full-time housekeepers. The Japanese family sociologist Ochiai Emiko used the term *shufu-ka* ["housewifisation"] to refer to the process by which the ideal role for Japanese women became that of a full-time "professional" housewife.[3]

At a time when stability and uniformity were highly valued in Japan as a means to collective and individual success, Japanese corporations could expect that their male employees would work long hours because their wives were managing the home and focusing on the couple's children. The family, education and employment systems provided security for individuals who did well in them, a goal for all Japanese because attainment of this security was, in theory, based on hard work and merit, not class or patronage. Ideal marriage ages were based on the calculation of the time needed to raise two children before the husband reached retirement age and the family income declined. This uniformity also provided a strong foundation on which society could build its economy and compete in the international arena.

The Japanese government has campaigned for men to be more involved in childcare, but resistance from companies makes it difficult for them to take paternity leave.

Over the almost sixty years since Dore put forward his ideas, a number of changes have impacted this picture: among them, an ageing society and increased opportunities for women. (Issues I do not discuss in detail in this essay include the ups and downs of the Japanese economy; the recognition by the Japanese that even though access to the "best" education, and hence best jobs, or lifestyle, was in principle open to all, it was in fact the children of fathers who had graduated from top universities who were most likely to attend top universities, and subsequently reap the benefits; and, since the 1990s, the questioning of whether the Japanese state is able to provide the security that its citizens "purchased" by focusing on their social roles rather than their individual desires and rights.)

An issue of particular importance to the *koseki*-based family system is membership – who belongs? In addition to marriage and birth, people may join a family by adoption. In Japan today, the majority of adoptions continue to be of adult men who are adopted into a family to take over the family business. This reinforces the family as something more than a unit based on affection.

In addition, marriage must be between one man and one woman. Gay marriage and domestic partnership are not legally recognised in Japan. There are cases in which one partner in a same sex couple adopts the other (adding them to their *koseki*) so that for a variety of legal purposes they may be considered family members.

This *koseki* system has been described as 1 + 1 = 1 meaning that the unit is the family, not the individual. If a man and woman marry, they are in the same *koseki*. If they have children, these children are in their *koseki*. If an unmarried woman has a child, that child is entered into her *koseki*. In case of divorce, the children are in the custodial parent's *koseki* and currently there is no joint custody.[4]

In spite of the challenges this system raises when it comes to the emphasis on the individual in the Japanese Constitution and other laws, it was generally accepted as a core component of the stability of Japanese society; and the role of the mother was seen as a key factor in the socialisation of Japanese children who became productive members of that society.

★

In the late 20th century the birth rate began to decline. For decades, the Japanese government had been trying to deal with an ageing society by encouraging people to marry and have children. However, the average age at marriage continues to increase, and although there have been some ups and downs, the birth rate remains low. By the middle of the 21st century, the overall population is expected to fall by 20 per cent compared to the 1999 population, and one in three Japanese people will be aged 65 or over.

In the context of this demographic transition, gender roles and care giving are major concerns of the Japanese state and the Japanese family. As the population shrinks and ages, dominant questions arise: who will be the workers in the Japanese economy and who will care for the aged? The answer, more than forty years ago, was gender based: women filled part-time or temporary roles, or did work that could fit with their family responsibilities. But men were the financial support of the family and made it possible for (or required) women to be responsible for nurturing. This picture is not unique to Japan, but the employment system – primarily one could argue, the lack of lateral hiring which leads to the near impossibility of returning to a high-paying job after taking time out – reinforced this separation to an extent that can be argued to be detrimental to both the individual and to the economy/state.

In grappling with this challenge, issues related to individual rights and excessive individualism versus collective responsibilities remain. Government white papers may discuss the need to develop policies to deal with declining birth rates focusing on men's and women's roles, or how to balance childcare and work. These simultaneously raise the question of whether, with economic growth, the lives of the majority of people and the structure of society have become too individualised, and thus whether the dream of marriage and child rearing has been lost. This in turn reflects the continued influence of, or nostalgia for, the gender-based norms of the family system and its role as a foundation of a stable, predictable society.

Since the mid-1980s, Japanese laws and advisory documents have supported equal employment opportunities for women and men. In practice, there is still a significant deficit of women in managerial positions, and increasing these as well as expanding opportunities is one of the major focuses of the current Abe government. Over the thirty-year period since the first equal employment opportunity law went into effect, most doors have been opened for women in theory, yet they are not proportionally represented in senior positions. One reason for this is the Japanese employment system, which in principle is seniority based: and women,

Older Japanese people maintain their independence by keeping fit physically and mentally.

like men, have to work their way up over years in a company. Other reasons include the lack of role models. The life of a salaryman is not necessarily appealing (long hours, overwork, and the possibility of uncompensated overtime). If a woman wishes to have children, there are good laws to support maternity (and paternity) leave, but inadequate childcare options, and lingering social expectations may make an individual feel guilty for being unable to work the long hours of her colleagues. In recent years, the term "maternity harassment" [*mata hara*] has been coined to refer to the way women are treated by their bosses when they announce they are pregnant.

There are also economic reasons. If one parent takes childcare leave, it is economically more advantageous for the lower paid spouse to do so, and wives typically earn less than their husbands. In addition, the current tax law makes it economically challenging for a wife to continue working if she earns over 1.3 million yen a year. Thus, unless she either has a high income or good future prospects, the combination of income loss and the cost of childcare may make it "logical" for the wife to become the full-time parent.

Data clearly illustrates the gendered impact of raising children. According to the 2016 White Paper on Gender Equality, 10.3 per cent of women and 7.6 per cent of men are raising pre-school aged children. But men's labour force participation rate is 98.5 per cent, and women's is 52.3 per cent. Whereas there are no major changes in the participation rate of men over the peak child rearing years, for women aged 25–29 it is 47.7 per cent, increasing to 56.7 per cent when they are aged 40–44. In addition, men are four times more likely than women to work 60 hours a week or more – a percentage that increases when they are in their thirties and forties, the age they are most likely to have small children at home. Moreover, 60 per cent of women quit work at the birth of their first child.

The Japanese clearly recognise the cost of having children. When asked, as part of Cabinet Office research, why they want fewer children, wives in full-time employment chose 'fears for negative impact on the job' more frequently than other groups.[5]

A major barrier to employment while raising children is the lack of public childcare. As more families depend on two incomes, the number of children on waiting lists for nurseries is a national problem.

Government data shows that 24,825 children nationwide were denied day care in 2012. Tokyo led by far with 7,257 cases. The health ministry has set up a special fund to provide support to municipal governments to ease the problem. However, supply and demand issues continue, based on locality, and low wages are a barrier to attracting and retaining qualified childcare professionals.

The government has campaigned for men to be more involved in childcare, coining the term *ikumen* (*iku* from the word for childcare) around 2010. Whereas the law (paternity leave) supports this, and younger men express their willingness, pressures in the workplace (similar to *mata hara*) make the reality difficult. Japan's long-held corporate culture of long working hours must change in order to realise Abe's much-touted society "where all women can shine". And in spite of the rhetoric about increasing the birth rate, women who try to combine full-time work and child rearing still encounter criticism and lack institutional support. For example, on February 21, 2016, Yutaro Tanaka, an elected Liberal Democrat Party member for the Suginami ward in Tokyo wrote a blog post critical of a group of mothers who had held a protest demanding more childcare facilities. The unmarried, childless Tanaka argued that the responsibility for raising children lies first with each household, and that while "woman power" is necessary to revitalise the economy, mothers should not force child rearing on society, and demand or expect nursery places. Rather, they should ask "please help us raise our children". His blog was met with extensive criticism, including the fact that people with views such as his are one of the reasons for Japan's low birth rate.

★

In spite of policies such as mandatory long-term care insurance and the development of many services, care giving – primarily for the elderly, but also for those with mental or physical challenges – continues to be primarily a family and gender-based responsibility. In some cases, families engage in "double care": care for pre-school children or grandchildren along with care for parents or grandparents.

In this ageing society, the challenge of caring for the elderly is huge. The Japanese family system assumed this responsibility would be taken on by the son, with the day to day care done by his wife. Today, the responsibility still clearly falls on the shoulders of women. Approximately 80 per cent of the 90,000 people who leave work to provide care (to senior citizens) are women. However, in spite of normative assumptions, approximately one third of caretakers of the infirm elderly are men. There were about 250,000 caregivers in 2012 (85,000 men and 168,000 women).[6]

Among the reasons for this change are that there are fewer children to care for their elderly parents; a daughter-in-law might not live close, or she may have work or responsibilities of her own. In 1968, 49.6 per cent of caregivers were daughters-in-law. By 2010, this figure had dropped to 16.1 per cent, and today there is less consensus as to who should provide care.

Caregivers face different challenges related to their gender. For women, care giving is seen as calling on skills they already possess – or are supposed to. For men, it is uncharted territory that not only requires new skills, but also the potential loss of a job, along with contact with former colleagues and friends, or a reduction in working hours.

Almost 60 years after Dore questioned whether the Japanese were aware of their family system, the question is still relevant. Here are some areas where it is in evidence.

Corporations still rely on the family system model, at least implicitly, given the lack of support provided for caregivers. If women or men leave or reduce work to care for others, it is almost impossible to return to a good, secure, full-time job and thus make a contribution to the Japanese economy. The majority of caregivers impacted by this have been women. A question for the future is whether an increase in male caregivers will lead to changes.

For a variety of reasons, including external pressure and domestic demand, several laws protecting the rights of individuals were enacted in the late 20th and early 21st centuries. These laws lessened the authority and autonomy of the family, or rather the family head, and both made it possible for family members to seek protection and for the state to provide this in areas that once had been considered domestic matters. Domestic violence legislation lessened the normative authority of husbands over wives and increased acceptance for wives seeking protection from abuse. It also made it possible for abused husbands to seek protection.

A recent focus is on the rights of the child. In the 21st century, legislation was enacted protecting children from abuse. This includes exclusion from pornography – both participation in and being subject to – and the recent declaration that children have the right to be raised in a family rather than in an institution, a point to which I will return.

Child poverty and the economic challenges faced by single mother households provide a further illustration of the importance of the family

Japanese mother with her child.

system today. Around one in six children lives below the poverty line. These figures put Japan at tenth place among the thirty-four member countries of the Organisation for Economic Co-operation and Development in terms of child poverty.

A major reason for this is the legal and social status of single-parent families. The employment rate for single mothers in Japan is 81 per cent – also the highest in the OECD. However, only 39 per cent of these women have regular employment, meaning jobs that offer benefits and a chance of promotion – the more likely scenario as a single parent is working two or three jobs to make ends meet.

The fact that any couple can end a marriage by mutual consent simply by going to a local government office and filling out a form illustrates the rights of the individual within the family. The vast majority of Japanese divorces are by mutual consent. However, this option does not provide legal support for the rights of children. Child support and alimony can only be mandated if the couple divorce through a court or mediator – but there is no legal enforcement if the divorce was by mutual consent. In reality only about 20 per cent of divorced single mothers, regardless of how they carried out their divorce, receive any sort of money from their ex-husbands. The rest have to make do with job income, family support and government assistance. If the child is born out of wedlock, the mother needs an affidavit signed by the father recognising paternity and agreeing to pay support. Without this, the court has nothing to enforce. Getting this can be both challenging and expensive if lawyers and other legal professionals are involved.[7]

The issue of family versus individual rights also applies to children who cannot live with their families. The social norm is that it is better for a child to remain connected to a biological family than be raised by strangers, or in an institution. This prioritises family and raises questions of what is better for the individual.[8]

In May 2014, Human Rights Watch released the report, *Without Dreams: Children in alternative childcare in Japan* which criticised over-institutionalisation. In response, the Ministry of Health, Labour and Welfare established a special council on child welfare in September 2015. In May 2016 the Child Welfare Act was revised to focus on the "principle of family-based care" guaranteeing life in a family-setting including adoption and foster care, for all children. Institutionalisation is limited only to cases whereby family-based care is "not appropriate", and even in such cases the act obligates the placement of children into institutions that can provide "the best possible family-like settings".

★

In Japan today there are questions of where an individual belongs. Anne Allison discusses the concept of not having a place where one belongs [*ibasho ga nai*], writing that this is a slippage from a time when home meant security based on the breadwinner's stable job and steady income, and a sense of the future through one's children.[9] In Japan today, home no longer provides this.

Prime Minister Abe talks about the importance of women contributing to Japan's economic growth and instituting policies and programmes so that women can "shine". These include targets for the number of women in management positions by a given year. So far, there have been no penalties for companies that fail to reach these targets, although it has been announced that businesses that make great strides in hiring and promoting women will be given preferential treatment in contracts for public works.

One recent development is that the ministry of internal affairs and communications is to adapt its systems to allow married women to print their maiden name alongside their legal family name on new identification cards and residence cards. This is part of an effort to encourage women to stay in the labour force, and to encourage companies to allow married women to include their maiden names. The law will still require married couples to use a single surname, however.

On the individual level, a recently coined term reflecting good places to work while raising children is *ikubosu* (*iku* from childcare, and the English word boss). This mostly refers to small businesses in which the boss is very supportive of childrearing responsibilities.

And on the national level, in March 2015, Prime Minister Abe launched the *Sankyuu* Papa Project to support and encourage fathers to take paternity leave. The concept includes being thankful to wives for giving birth, and to the children who have come into the world [*umarete kite kureta waga ko*]. At the project launch it was stated that the goal was for 80 per cent of fathers to take a day or half day of leave within two months of their child's birth. Not much, perhaps, but a start.

A major issue is where the state will allocate resources. How much will it contribute to increasing childcare facilities? Will it develop more policies encouraging grandparents to live with their children, and thus strengthen family based care? Currently, the government gives tax breaks to families who want to build larger houses so that older people can live with their grandchildren. Since April 2013, it has cut inheritance taxes for people who contribute to their grandchildren's education or even their weddings and child-rearing activities.

A second issue is whether the labour shortage will lead more companies in the private sector to develop new ways of reincorporating workers who have temporarily left the labour force to care for family members, and provide support systems to enable single mothers to work full time. In some localities and employment sectors with labour shortages, such programmes are already developing. For example, Goshen, a social welfare corporation in Machida, western Tokyo, has built a dormitory where single parents who work in one of their care homes can live – with fixed rent, set shift times and childcare facilities. Outside Tokyo, some local governments, including in Hamada, Shimane Prefecture, provide subsidies to single-parent families who wish to move to the area.

★

Both policymakers and ordinary Japanese people are very aware of the Japanese family system, and institutions have not (yet?) changed to become more closely aligned with the individual. Some responses to this are to avoid or postpone the responsibilities that go with marriage and child rearing and with care for the aged (or one's own care when elderly). The recently coined term *sotsukon* [graduate from marriage] refers to a couple who stay together but live apart, pursuing individual goals. This is an option that requires economic or other resources.

As individual responses increase, the challenge for the state continues to be how to develop policies that nurture both the individual and the family, and lead to the continued development of Japan.

1. Dore, Ronald P., *City Life in Japan: A Study of a Tokyo Ward*. (Berkeley and Los Angeles: University of California Press, 1958).
2. Hashimoto, Akiko and John W. Traphagan (eds.), *Imagined Families, Lived Families: Culture and Kinship in Contemporary Japan*, (Albany: SUNY Press, 2008).
3. Goldstein-Gidoni, Ofra, *Housewives of Japan: An Ethnography of Real Lives and Consumerized Domesticity*, (New York: Palgrave Macmillan, 2012).
4. Jones, Colin P.A., "Hague jars with Japan's family law, a zero-sum game with only one outcome", *The Japan Times,* April 16, 2014.
5. Cabinet Office, Gender Equality Bureau, (Naikakufu, Danjo Kyōdō Sankakukyoku) White Paper on Gender Equality, "Males' Work and Life in Transition", June 2014. http://www.gender.go.jp/about_danjo/whitepaper/h28/gaiyou/index.html
6. Cabinet Office, Gender Equality Bureau (Naikakufu, Danjo Kyōdō Sankakukyoku) Heisei 28 Ban, Danjo Kyōdō Sankaku Hakusho, White Paper on Gender Equality, May 2016.
http://www.gender.go.jp/about_danjo/whitepaper/h26/zentai/pdf/h26_tokusyu1.pdf
http://www.gender.go.jp/english_contents/about_danjo/whitepaper/pdf/ewp2014.pdf
7. See, for example, Hertog, Ekaterina, *Tough Choices: Bearing an Illegitimate Child in Contemporary Japan*, (Stanford, California: Stanford University Press, 2009).
8. See for example, the discussion in Bamba, Sachiko and Wendy L. Haight, *Child Welfare and Development: A Japanese Case Study,* (Cambridge: Cambridge University Press, 2011).
9. Allison, Anne, *Precarious Japan,* (Durham and London: Duke University Press, 2013).

Japanese business ethics.

JAPANESE WORK IDENTITY IN INTERNATIONAL ENCOUNTERS
Pia Moberg

In my experience as a cross-cultural trainer and consultant, the average Japanese person in the workplace is seen by many foreigners as focused on quality, and people oriented, but also committed to their processes in regard to team work, communication and meeting structures. The Japanese, on the other hand, sometimes tell me that it is hard to cooperate with foreigners since they do not focus on details – for example, setting up meetings without a clear agenda. Even worse, they say that many foreign companies lack sufficient protocols for root-cause analysis when problems appear. They feel there is a lack of ability to share best practices in a constructive way.

So how do we share experiences and processes across cultures in a fruitful way in the globalised world? The first step is to acknowledge different cultures have different assumptions and expectations about, for example, problem solving, building trust, conducting meetings and giving presentations.

Japan opened its domestic markets and became an international economic superpower during the postwar period. The term *kokusaika* [internationalisation] was interpreted and discussed among policymakers as well as by scholars and corporate representatives. But did this economic miracle really make the Japanese – so closely connected to their work – more international in their working identity?

Mergers and acquisitions are common in the corporate world, and Japan is no exception. Statistics show, however, that Japan has lost market share in many areas during the last few decades. What is the explanation for this? The question is too complex to solve in this essay, but I will provide some thoughts from an intercultural perspective.

Many Japanese companies are monocultural, and are still not comfortable with English as the corporate language in international interactions. Adopting a global language policy can be an important step towards growth, as in the case of the e-commerce company Rakuten, which successfully implemented an English-only policy in 2010. All meetings, presentations and emails inside the company are entirely in English. In 2015, the chief executive Mikitani Hiroshi announced that the average employee's score on the Test of English for International Communication had reached 803 points (compared with an average of 526 in 2010). Other companies such as Nissan and the fashion retailer Uniqlo have also adopted an English-only policy, and in 2015 Honda announced its intention to follow suit. Since the English education system in Japan focuses on passing entrance exams, students do not become familiar with the English language as an efficient and necessary tool for international interaction. But finding an identity in the global business market is, of course, not only about language. It is also about communication.

★

Situations that seem to be problematic for many Japanese people are virtual international meetings, particularly telephone conferences when you cannot see other participants' gestures and expressions. With the help of some intercultural models, I will explain some of the reasons why these can pose challenges.

The Lewis Model is a triangle, which categorises cultures as linear-active, multi-active and reactive.[1] Those in linear-active cultures are decisive planners, logical and favour proactivity (for example, in North America and Western Europe). People from multi-active cultures are more emotional and impulsive. They talk fast, and show their feelings openly (for example, in South America and Africa). Reactive cultures, such as Japan, are composed of good listeners, who are courteous, polite and indirect. This model helps us to understand Japanese reactivity in contrast to a need for proactivity in many global business situations. The linear-active and multi-active view assumes that you speak up if something is wrong or you disagree, but the reactive tendency is the opposite: usually silence. In a virtual meeting, the Japanese never disagree openly unless they have a high level of trust in each other. When something is at stake – a decision to be made or a problem to be solved – you benefit from a good relationship and an established communication protocol.

A crucial area in all global meetings is the way in which people communicate. Multi-actives use overlapping speech as a norm: the listener is supposed to interrupt the speaker. You speak at the same time! Linear-actives,

The Lewis Model.

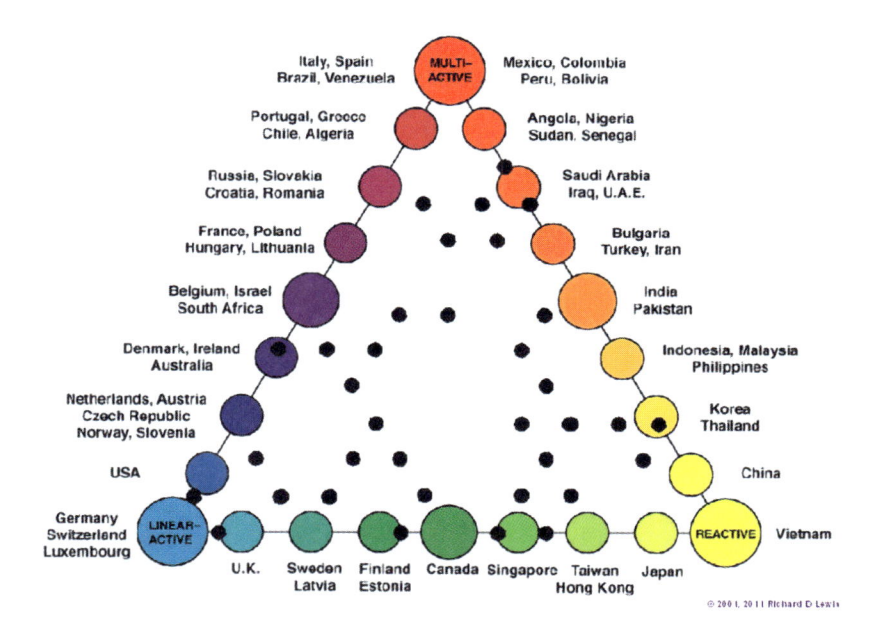

on the other hand, speak one at a time, with a speaker stopping to let listeners respond, while in reactive cultures, there is more silence – often, silence is used as turn-taking tool. They also stop speaking to let listeners respond.

The differences in communication styles cause problems in virtual meetings, especially with Japanese team members who are waiting for their turn to speak. In workshops in Japan, we practised interrupting techniques in order to allow the Japanese to enter discussions with French and Latin American people. Most of the Japanese participants felt exhausted afterwards – the need to interrupt and be "rude" was a challenge. French people, on the other hand, said they forgot their points and lost momentum when they had to wait for their turn to speak. In the discussion afterwards, the Japanese told us that they thought the French people on their team had been angry with them for the last year, since they interrupted all the time, whereas the French interpreted the Japanese silence as a sign of disinterest and a lack of expertise.

In her book, *The Culture Map*, Erin Meyer presents a number of useful scales.[2] Each scale shows a different dimension in which many intercultural clashes occur. The concept of high-context and low-context defines the communications scale. Japan is as high-context as one can be. This means that the Japanese are very formal and indirect. Messages are implied rather than directly expressed. To say "no" is very rude, and would not happen during a meeting in a high context culture.

In Japan it is a virtue to "read the air" [*kuuki o yomu*] and to listen between the lines. Those who do not pick up the implied messages – what is not said is as important as what is said – are *kuuki o yomenai hito* [people who cannot read the air]. They are viewed as insensitive. This communication pattern works fine among Japanese colleagues, but becomes problematic if applied in a virtual global business meeting when there are many low-context cultures participating (for example, the US, northern Europe, or Australia). If we then add those from talkative multi-active cultures who might violate any time schedule, we can clearly see the need for an established communication protocol.

One key feature in Japanese society is the acceptance of hierarchical power. Working with international colleagues and customers, the Japanese sensitivity towards hierarchical structures, in combination with a need for consensus in decision-making, is a challenging combination for many. This goes especially for informal meetings and brainstorming sessions with members of a more egalitarian organisation. According to

Meyer's Leading Scale, which measures the degree of respect and deference shown to authority figures, placing countries on a spectrum from egalitarian to hierarchical, Japan is the most hierarchical country in the world, and Sweden the most egalitarian. At the same time, they are the two most consensus-oriented countries, where unanimous agreement is the norm, in contrast to top-down decision-making processes (for example, in China, India and many Latin American countries).

These characteristic features lead to some consequences in virtual meetings for the Japanese. It is very difficult to have spontaneous discussions, since communication follows hierarchical chains, and all decisions have to be prepared and decided prior to official meetings. Therefore, they can never count on on-the-spot-decisions. If someone higher up is present at the meeting, the people lower down will simply not express their opinion – especially if it differs from their bosses. This must also be considered if the chairman of the meeting is Japanese. So how do you then have a fruitful informal session with Japanese clients in cyberspace? In my experience, it is better for the boss not to participate in informal meetings or brainstorming sessions at all in order to enable creative discussions.

On Meyer's scales of evaluating and disagreeing, Japan is one of the top countries when it comes to indirect negative feedback and avoiding confrontation. If the Japanese want to give negative feedback or complain about someone or something – or they simply have a different view – they would never express this in front of a group, and definitely not during a formal meeting. Negative statements are rather made in informal, face-to-face situations, and then in a diplomatic way. The negative information is wrapped in a positive framework. During a formal, virtual meeting, asking questions about a presentation and its data, for example, is appropriate, but asking questions outside the agenda or criticising the presenter is very inappropriate and might even damage relationships.

This is closely linked to the art of persuasion. The Japanese way to build a reliable ethos and become trustworthy is not by complex and theoretical reasoning, but by providing facts and figures. A hypothesis without supporting facts is simply not valid, and showing reams of data is seen as scrupulous and character building. The characteristic Japanese feature of being focused on details and data, and at the same time, seeing the whole context creates a specific mindset. This is illustrated by a series of experiments Professor Richard Nisbett and Masuda Takahiko carried out. In one of these, American and Japanese participants were asked to take a photo of a person. The Americans took a picture of a face, while the Japanese took a picture of a person sitting in a room, showing them in their environment. When asked about their choice, the Japanese said they thought the Americans had just taken a picture of a face, not a person, and the Americans thought the picture the Japanese people took was of a room, not a person.

In problem solving, the key is root-cause analysis, where you take the whole picture and all the details into account. For the Japanese, it is also crucial to build trust. Japan is a relationship-based society where a good relationship is more important than the task in hand.

To sum up the information in the scales, we can see that the Japanese favour formal and indirect communication where attention is paid to hierarchical status. It is crucial to save face, and open debate involving negative statements should be avoided. Discussions should have a point of departure in empirical data, and at the same time, participants should have trust in their relationships. Spontaneous discussions involving assumptions are not favoured. This makes it hard for foreigners to enter the Japanese work process.

Apart from these models, one concept that I found extremely useful when explaining Japanese patterns of behaviour is *kata* [form].[3] The correct form – doing things in the right way – permeates all practices in Japan, be they art, manufacturing or business etiquette. The body's movement in martial arts, the worker's manual at the assembly line or the way a name card is handed over are all examples of best practice. The form creates the content, or at least the form is a prerequisite for the content to be perfect. The advantage of this approach is the result: the team works to find the best practice in any given area, which creates a very high standard. One example is the *Shinkansen* which has carried more than ten billion passengers in the last fifty years: the average delay across all of Japan's bullet trains is thirty-six seconds a day. The drawback is inflexibility. Not only does the process determine the right *kata*, and thus which rules are to be followed, but it also limits the options not chosen.

Even though the *kata* mindset is omnipresent in Japan, Toyota has been a representative for introducing the concept to the Western business community. *Lean* and *kaizen* are other examples of concepts closely linked to the *kata* concept. *Lean* means to reduce waste in all ways possible in manufacturing and processes, and *kaizen* means "continuous improvement".

Japanese educational, societal and corporate institutions have one thing in common: they impose rules – *katas* – to be followed and leave very little room for improvisation and independence. Thus the Japanese corporate worker might feel uncomfortable in an international environment, and his patterns of behaviour might be questioned when working in a global team. When Rakuten decided to implement an English-only policy, they changed the communication *kata* in the company. The language became the form, which step by step, changed the content, i.e. the mindset, of their employees.

The expression *sanpoyoshi* from the traditional business world of the Edo and Meiji periods means satisfaction in three parts: vendors, buyers and society. The idea is that the ultimate business climate is a win-win situation where no one loses and society prospers. This system was made for Japan and worked very well in the domestic market, even during the postwar period. Every part had its own *kata*, to optimise processes. To translate *sanpoyoshi* (and other concepts such as *kaizen*) for a foreign business partner is not always easy. This is not necessarily because it is hard to understand, but rather because of an unconscious assumption that Japanese models and culture traits are for the Japanese, not foreigners.

In many areas in Japan, such as in higher education and the corporate world, there is a fear of becoming too "unJapanese". Last year, I gave a keynote address about Japanese female leadership at a university in Tokyo. Afterwards, a student came up to me with her biggest worry: losing her Japanese identity during a ten-day stay in the US that summer.

This fear is also reflected in the amended version of the curriculum for compulsory education, where the study of patriotism and morality are enforced. Your identity as Japanese includes bringing out Japanese values, cultures and traditions. In the civic curriculum it is clearly expressed that you should view foreign ideas from the horizon of Japanese ways of thinking.

An important part of being a trustworthy member of society and a good citizen – *shakaijin* – is joining the labour force as soon as possible after graduation. First-class citizenry is thus only for men – not women – who manage to get "a real job" and contribute to society in a productive way. This view is deeply rooted, and even if contemporary Japan is very different from this norm (most of the workforce will not be permanent employees; women work; there is a declining birth rate) it may take some time to change the mindset.

During a workshop I facilitated in Japan some years ago, I saw the need for a tool which could measure consensus, risk and consequence in cross-cultural interactions. After some years of research and trial and error, I will now present the result: the Chadberg scale[4]. I will introduce the model and its parts and then explain how this can be useful in the case of Japan.

The Chadberg scale is a model consisting of five parts in a circular diagram. Borrowing terminology and inspiration from weather prediction, the Chadberg scale is modelled on the barometer which measures pressure. In the same way that sunshine, cloud, fog and rain are mutually interdependent for our existence and wellbeing, so are the parts in the model.

A higher level equals higher pressure, and higher pressure results in a more serious degree of potential risk and consequence. Most projects – be they producing a truck engine, writing a doctoral thesis or composing a piece of music – involve all five parts, each part representing a different stage in their process. All parts are equally important. The Chadberg scale can be applied to meetings, project management, risk mitigation, and international encounters.

I will explain the model using meetings as an example. A level-one meeting can be any social interaction with no consequences or commitments involved; there should be no pressure to come to any conclusion. It is creative, informal and free.

At a level-two meeting there is a purpose with a possible – but not fixed – outcome. For example, a brainstorming meeting where you gather around a table, pen and paper in hand, but with no written agenda.

Level three is the first step towards an organised meeting. An agenda is sent out, along with, occasionally, instructions, although these may not necessarily be strictly enforced. The agenda can also be handed out at the beginning of the meeting, meaning there is no time for preparation. A characteristic feature of this meeting is that topics not on the agenda may be brought up.

A high-pressure meeting – level four – is strict and formalised – a board meeting, for example. All participants have made necessary preparations beforehand, and the meeting is carried out according to schedule. Someone is responsible for sending out an agenda and prepared material in advance. At this level, agreements on next actions written in the minutes are carried out. As we can see, the big difference between a medium-pressure meeting and a high-pressure meeting is that the latter

The Chadberg Model.

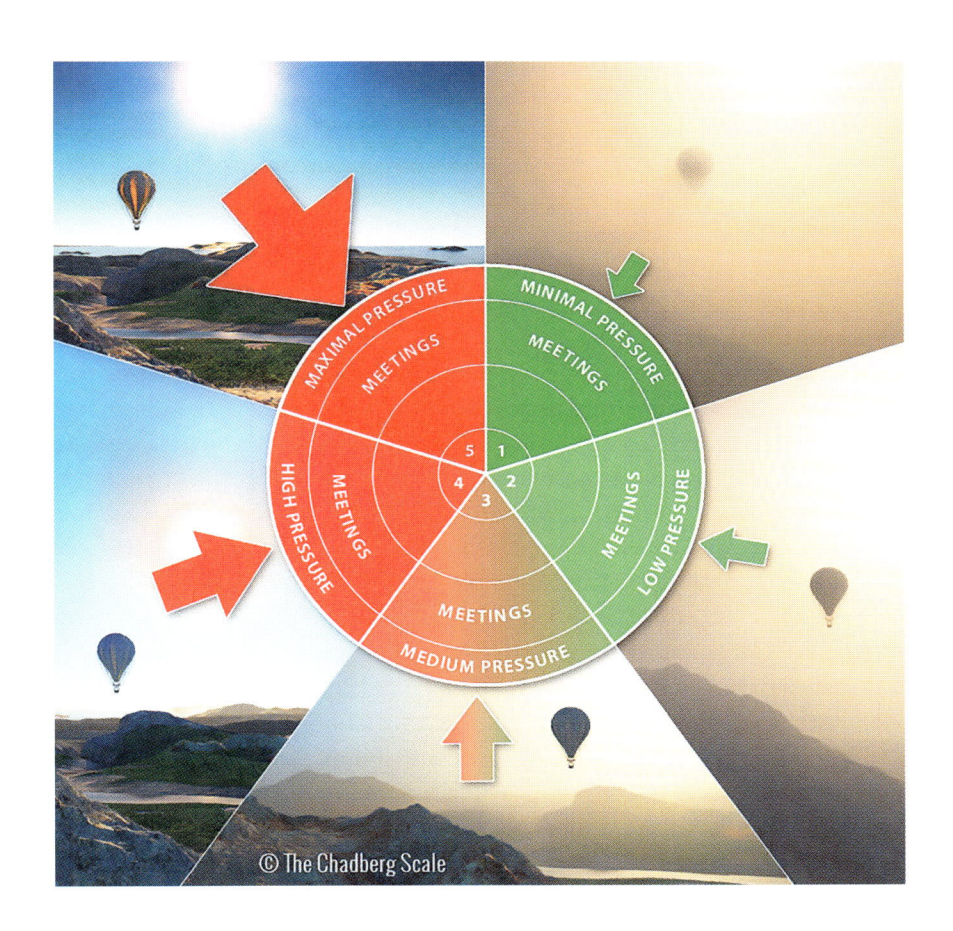

is defined by a structured process in three steps: before, during, and after.

At a maximal-pressure meeting – level five – there are no surprises and everything is very well prepared. The three-step process described for level four is carried out with precision. There is no room for spontaneity or unprepared questions. Annual board meetings and other formal events are such meetings.

So how can this be useful in understanding identity in Japan? For the Japanese, a meeting with an outlined agenda is formal, and at level four or five by default. It is the result of an in-house decision-making process at level one or two. In a formal meeting there are no revelations, only presentations of results. Since virtual communication is standard in international projects, many companies only communicate with each other through cyberspace and thus the meeting format becomes formal. The need for informal working meetings in global teams is obvious, so the trick is to have informal creative working meetings in a formal setting. The first step is to recognise the Japanese way of conducting various kinds of meetings and establish their level on the Chadberg scale: for example, informal consensus building on a two-three level, the level one after work sessions at a local pub, and formal meetings at level four-five.

Another key question is how you establish a safe and encouraging virtual environment with people from another culture whom you have never met before. Those from linear-active cultures do not need too much relationship-building prior to entering a joint project – sometimes an ice-breaking activity is enough. People from multi-active cultures often feel they need to build relationships prior to doing business, and might express this verbally. But being part of a reactive culture, Japanese people need to understand the context and all persons related to the project. Meeting each other face to face is always the best option here, but if this is not possible, the second-best approach is to establish an informal platform fifteen minutes or so prior to the real meeting. I recommend a small number of participants, no more than a handful. Here you can share pictures, personal experiences or simply introduce yourself. Using the Chadberg scale, you first establish a level-one meeting, and then jump directly into a level-four meeting.

A Japanese friend working as a secretary in Sweden told me that the global company she works for often calls for meetings at level four-five, but never reaches beyond level three meetings in practice: Swedish

JAPANESE WORK IDENTITY

participants do not prepare enough beforehand, and do not make an effort to follow up decisions made.

If we apply the scale to communication in the working environment, the Japanese worker is usually aiming for level four-five in the workplace, where there is a high pressure to perform, but jumps to level one when leaving the office for a drink. If applied to a project, the Japanese wish to spend longer on informal discussion and empirical tests – level two or three – before finalising results. Once at roll out – level five – there is no way back.

If Japanese companies wish to be more integrated in the global market, the big challenge is to allow foreign colleagues to share their work processes on a more informal level. This involves being comfortable speaking English. The Japanese have historically been more comfortable at levels one, and then four and five, with foreigners. There is now a need to go farther and develop new *katas* for teamwork and group efforts with non-Japanese colleagues.

From the examples above, we can see that often differences in perception about, for example, a meeting could be more about definition than simply "Japanese business practices". Using the Chadberg scale, along with other models, can help people to align expectations. In doing so, the Japanese will better understand their own patterns of behaviour, and hopefully also those of their foreign colleagues.

★

In the documentary *Jiro Dreams of Sushi* (2011), David Gelb portrays the sushi chef Ono Jiro and the staff at his ten-seat, three-star Michelin restaurant in Tokyo. A restaurant reviewer is asked for his opinion. He praises Jiro's sushi as the best in the world, and lists five attributes of master chefs. First, he says, they take their work very seriously and consistently perform at the highest level. Secondly, they aspire to improve their skills all the time. Thirdly, the environment must be clean. If the restaurant doesn't feel clean, the food isn't going to taste good. The fourth attribute is impatience: they're stubborn, will never give up, and insist on having things their way. The final attribute is passion: great chefs are passionate about their work. The reviewer says Jiro has all five attributes. Constantly, without deviating even the slightest from the path, Jiro has put the reviewer's theory into practice. He is the ultimate role model for the diligent Japanese *shakaijin*, devoting his whole life to his work, following the *kata* to perfection. On the Chadberg scale, Jiro is performing at level five from morning to night.

In my training as a leadership coach in Sweden, I learned about the importance of work-life balance and how you should distribute your time as an employee and leader between your work, family, personal interests and friends. Does Jiro have a work-life balance?

If Japan wishes to become global, is it possible to keep its traditional mindset while at the same time speaking English in meetings, sharing practices with colleagues and clients from all over the world and retaining high levels of performance? I believe so. Japanese people have an outstanding ability to adapt and refine processes, as long as they understand why and how they must do so. Only then can a new *kata* be created.

1. For more information about the Lewis Model see www.crossculture.com and Lewis, Richard D., *When Teams Collide: Managing the International Team Successfully*, (Nicholas Brealey International, 2012); Lewis, Richard D., *When Cultures Collide: Leading Across Cultures*, (Nicholas Brealey International, 2005).
2. Meyer, Erin, *The Culture Map: Decoding How People Think, Lead and Get Things Done Across Cultures*, (Public Affairs, 2014).
3. I first read about this in *Kata: The Key to Understanding and Dealing with the Japanese* by Boyé Lafayette De Mente, (Tuttle Publishing, 2003).
4. *Meeting Sense: The Chadberg Model – a guide to efficient meetings, on all levels, in any culture by Pia Moberg and Peter Chadwich (Japco Publishing House, 2018).*

Suzuki Teitaro Daisetsu,
Buddhist thinker and scholar.

RELIGIONS IN JAPAN

Inken Prohl

This essay gives a very brief account of the religious traditions of Japan, mainly Buddhism and Shinto. It shows that these two broad traditions have, from ancient times to the present day, provided a framework for a variety of practices, including rituals performed both for ancestors and for this-worldly benefits.

Japanese religiosity is predicated on the search for this-worldly benefits, but this search has little to do with the ways the Japanese conceive of themselves as members of a distinct nation or culture. In order to understand Japanese conceptions of what makes Japan special, we need to look, not at the practice of religion, but rather at the way religion is understood in Japan.

In this essay, I will demonstrate that what we know as Buddhism and Shinto are, like the very term "religion", best understood as products of transcultural flows. This term will first be introduced and defined, and then will be used to ground an illustration of how the concept benefits those of us who want to know more about religion and culture in Japan.

Focusing particularly on the cases of Christianity in Japan and on Zen, I will show how categorisations like Shinto, Zen, and Christian do not necessarily reflect any homogenous systems of religious notions and practices. Rather, it is the reflection on these terms that serves as the basis of national identity. This essay will reveal some of the ways in which this dynamic works out.

★

For much of Japanese history, people have venerated gods, goddesses, ancestors and other transcendental entities. Following the introduction of Buddhism to Japan, Buddhas and Bodhisattvas joined this list of the venerated. The main goal of this veneration was – and remains – the pursuit of this-worldly benefits, such as protection of the nation and its rulers,

Next pages: Graveyard at Shitennōji temple in Osaka.

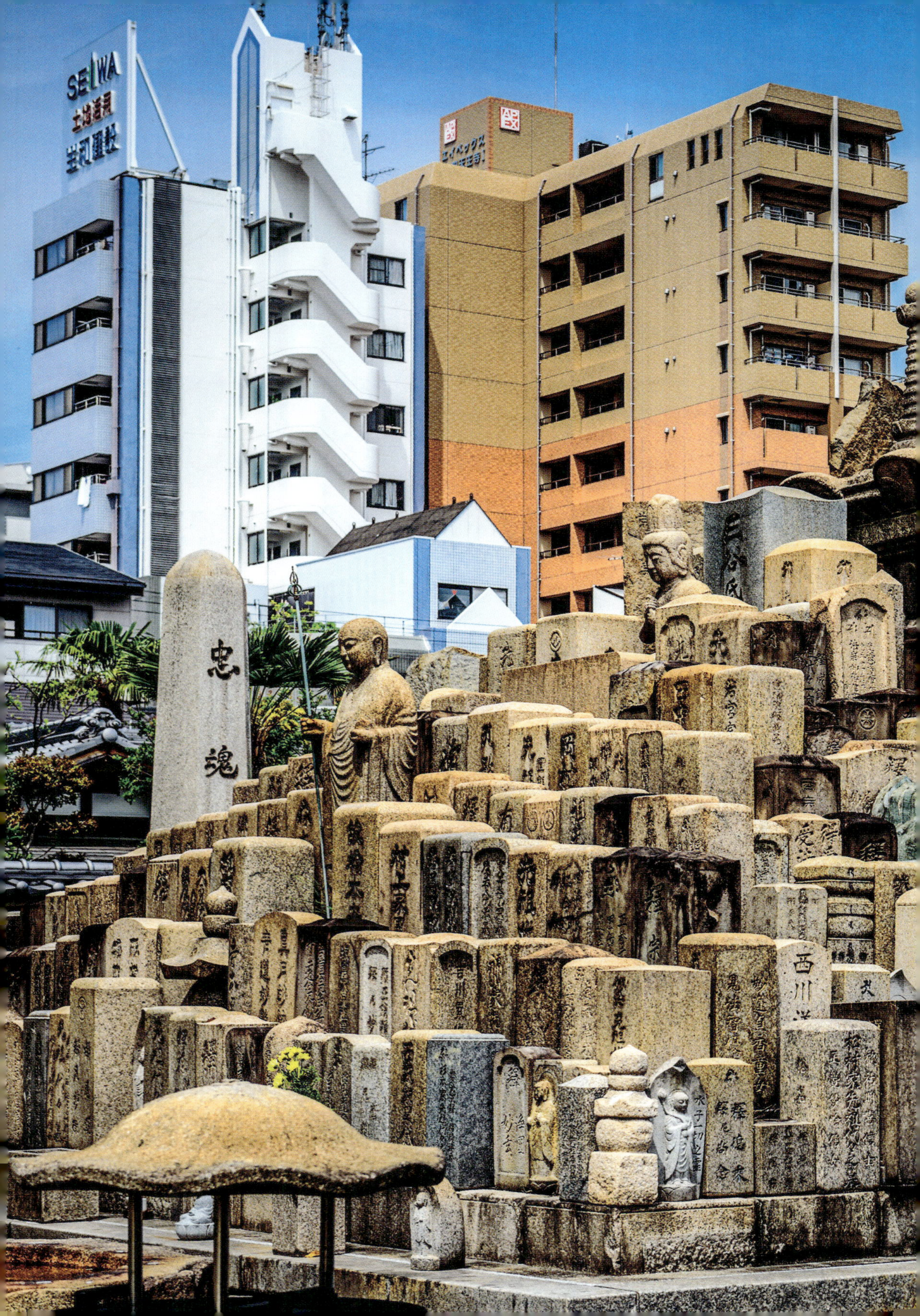
SEIWA
APEX
忠
魂

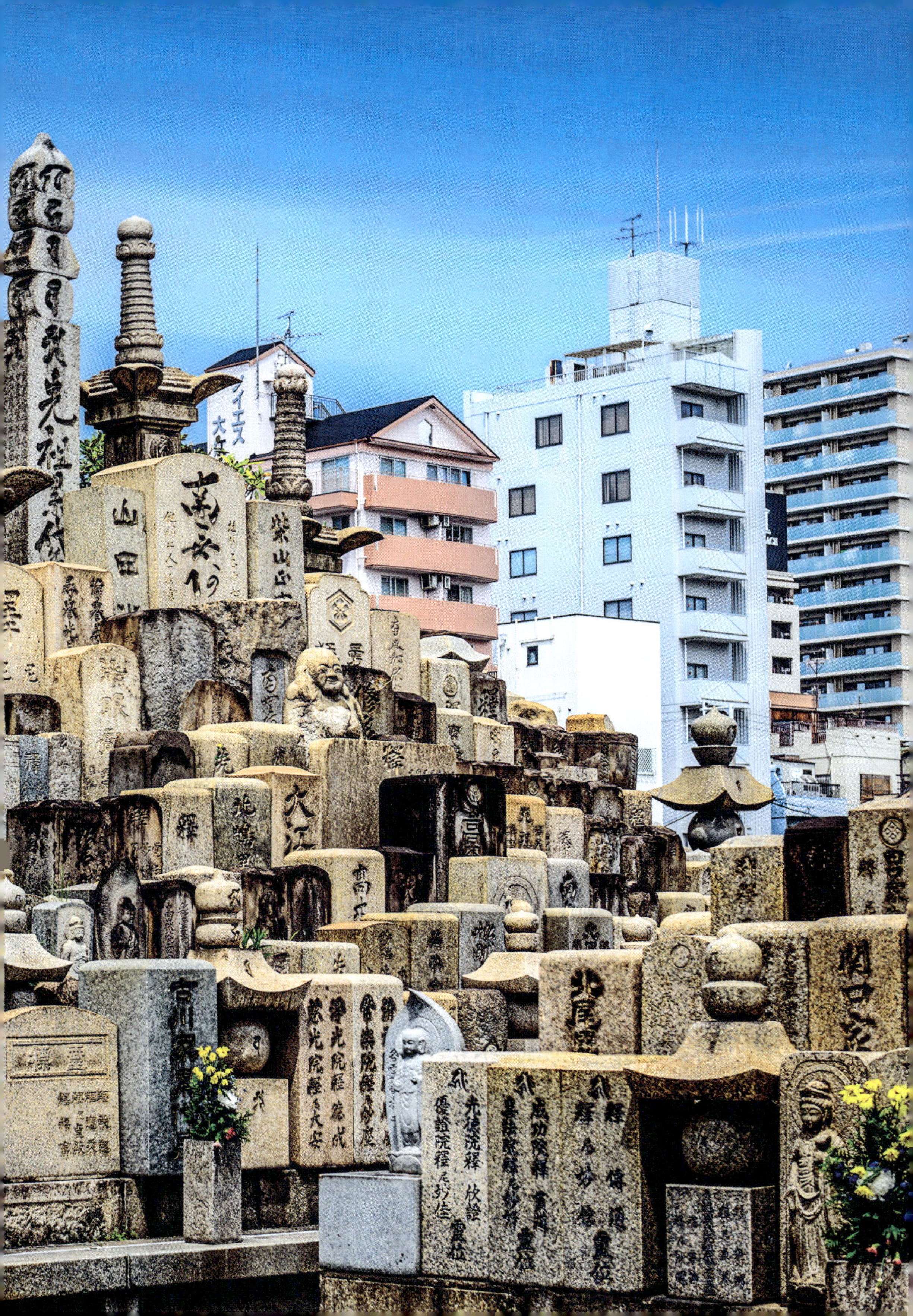

bountiful harvests, good health or healing, success and, now, personal advancement. These entities are believed to have supernatural powers at their disposal, including the power to grant these benefits, and people have sought by prayer and ritual to obtain access to them.

Following its introduction in the 6th century from mainland Asia, Buddhism became the official state religion. Like the local deities, Buddhist gods became the objects of veneration and potential sources of this-worldly benefits. Both the priests of the local gods and the priests of Buddhism started to reflect on the relation between the different types of deities. Over the centuries, this reflection became the basis of what we nowadays know as Buddhism and Shinto. The practices and ideas of what we now call Taoism and Confucianism, imported from China during the succeeding centuries, and later the practices and ideas of Christianity, introduced to Japan in the 15th century, were mingled into the various religious practices as well as into the process of reflection.

Elaborate rituals and religious scholarship took place in temples and shrines all over the country; these were built at state expense. Priests of Buddhism and of the local gods served together at these sites and conducted rituals for collective as well as individual benefit. One important function fulfilled particularly by Buddhist priests was asking for assistance in delivering the dead safely into the otherworld. For this reason, the majority of local Japanese temples remain places of rituals performed for ancestors and the recently deceased. In these rituals, and in those seeking more immediate, practical benefits, what matters to the practitioners is not specific doctrines or adherence to particular institutions, but rather the powers of the entities. Indeed, were we to ask people in Japan which school of Buddhism they belong to, we would likely be told they do not know, because – thanks to the gods – no one in their family has recently died.

As practitioners and scholars continued to reflect on the traditions of which they were a part, various theories arose concerning the relationship between the native gods and Buddhist deities. The theory of *honji suijaku* [original ground, manifest traces] became especially influential. According to this theory, Buddhist deities choose to appear in Japan as local gods to more easily convert and save the Japanese. On the flip-side, the theory also holds that native gods are manifestations of Buddhist deities. Some have argued that these two entities form an indivisible whole that should merit equal standing, while others have claimed that either Buddhist gods or native deities are superior. Relatively undisturbed by the lively debates on this relationship, the intermixture of Buddhist and local gods became very successful. Places of worship evolved from wayside sites to small temples to monasteries, and became places of power guarded by the gods and known for the benefits they could confer. For the majority of Japanese people, the efficiency of these sites became much more important than the names of the gods and their respective places in some abstract religious system.

Thus, when looking into religion in Japan, it is necessary to distinguish between the level of practice and the level of discourse. On the level of practice, the principal feature of Japanese religiosity is seeking the help of the gods in the pursuit of this-worldly and otherworldly benefits, as we can see at temples and shrines all over Japan.

★

The lively scenery of Japanese religious practice can be understood as a product of various transcultural flows. These transcultural flows – contact with, and the importing of, ideas and practices from other cultures – can be understood as the engine of cultural development. These flows enrich cultures while initiating reflection and change. In the Japanese case, the worship of local gods was augmented by the introduction of Buddhist gods; more gods and their various powers became available via the importing of other traditions, such as Confucianism and Taoism. Further religious thoughts and practices were introduced in the 15th century when Catholic missionary activities began in Japan. Although they first enjoyed the favour of the Japanese military leaders, suspicions became aroused against the missionaries, and Christians were persecuted in the early decades of the 17th century.

In contrast to Japanese religious traditions, Christian belief demanded absolute loyalty to God. In the Japanese context, where the gods used their supernatural powers on behalf of the living, and where a strict social hierarchy was in place, Japanese military leaders felt threatened by the Christian demand that all obedience and allegiance belong to God. They thus forbade not only Christianity, but all foreign influences in Japan and decreed that everyone register at a Buddhist temple. Buddhist temples consequently proliferated all over the country, gaining wealth and power and remaining largely unchallenged while the country remained all but closed to any contact with the outside world. In this case, transcultural flows in the form of Christian missions to Japan had a profound influence on the history of Japanese religion as well as the nation as a whole.

The power of transcultural flows was even more intense after the so-called Meiji Restoration in 1867. Up to the first half of the 19th century, the term "religion" [*shūkyō*] did not exist in Japan. In 1853, Japan was forced by Commander Perry's "black ships" to allow international commerce and cooperation. This enforced change in attitude brought not only Western goods and merchants into Japan, but also the word "religion", the arrival of which led to the coining of *shūkyō*. The word is notorious for its ambiguity. As we know from religious and cultural studies, the century-old attempt to define it necessarily cannot lead to a conclusive result: religion as such will never be fully defined because its distinct trademark lies in its usability as a free-floating signifier, which is to say, a term that can take on different meanings, depending on context and how it is used. The term is forever in need of a definition, which happened to suit the Japanese elite. Following its introduction, Japanese state officials, scientists, and intellectuals realised that the strong discursive force of the word could be of great use in different processes of negotiation and governance. For example, Japanese religion was presented as a world religion, the equal of Christianity, thus underscoring Japan's claim to standing as a modern nation. The essentially Japanese characteristics of Japanese religion were stressed, while, at the same time, certain practices were disregarded or diminished as superstition, thus ostensibly proving Japan to be a modern, rationalist country. In the wake of the importation of the term, manifold transformations took place in the local religious scenery as well as at the level of reflection on religion in Japan.

One of these transformations was the unrolling of freedom of religion, an idea that could only make sense once a world had been made for religion as such. In response, Catholic, Protestant, and Orthodox churches sent their clergy on missions, and Christian communities gained the legal right to exist and to preach. Today, since less than 1 per cent of the Japanese population claims Christian belief or affiliation, the influence of Christianity as practised is low. Although the practice was, and is, insignificant, the ideas brought into Japan were profoundly transformative among the Japanese religious elite and intelligentsia.

The invention of the term "religion", together with the introduction of Christian ideas and practices, stimulated a complete rethinking of Japan's conception of its own history and ways of dealing with the gods. This history was reframed step-by-step with the help of categories taken over from Christianity, like "doctrine", "truth", "monotheism", and "spiritual". The adherents of the different Buddhist schools developed a concept of thinking about the gods and the truth in terms of teachings that were distinguishable from each other. These schools gave themselves distinctive doctrines, rules of practice, and codes of behaviour. The newly defined Buddhist schools also adopted Christian practices of conversion and charity work.

Little by little, people became conscious of being "Buddhist", and it was during this process that the very term "Buddhism" arose as a religious entity comparable to Christianity.

The pre-modern importation of Buddhist practices and thought – as well as those of other Asian traditions – added to the variety of religious practice, while at the same time forcing intellectuals to think about the relationship between the transcendental entities of various origins. The encounter with Christianity added slightly to the religious marketplace, while stimulating a profound reorientation of what was perceived as religion in Japan. Following the Meiji Restoration, the winning party – the leaders around the Japanese emperor – observed that the strength of the Western powers was their grounding in the Christian faith. Among the elite, the need for a comparable spiritual support was felt, and it was decided that this support should be based on the power of the native gods of Japan. This was the birth of what we now know as Shinto.

Shinto, very often proclaimed to be the native religion of Japan, is best described as a set of rituals, institutions, and teachings invented at the end of the 19th century and oriented around the veneration of local gods. These practices had taken place in Japan since ancient times, but until the end of the 19th century were intermingled with Buddhist practice and thought.

An important feature of this newly invented tradition, the Yasukuni shrine, was established in the heart of Tokyo. The site enshrines the souls of the Japanese killed in the Sino-Japanese Wars (1894–95; 1937–45), the Russo-Japanese War (1904–05), and the Second World War (1939–45) and has long been a symbol of nationalism. While the shrine and visits to it by Japanese politicians are frequently the subject of heavy criticism, particularly from Japan's Asian neighbours, it plays a rather minor role in terms of generating affect on the individual level.

Buddha figures lining the pathways of Daishō-in temple grounds on the island of Miyajima, near Hiroshima.

As we have seen, Japan has borne drastic interventions into its religious landscape during the past 150 years. As a result, religion became the subject of an elaborate discourse characterised by highly individual interpretations. These interpretations are formulated by scholars of religion, individuals and journalists. Their ideas about religion are very influential and therefore need to be taken into account if one wishes to see the relationship between religion and national identity in contemporary Japan.

The discourse on religion is mostly expressed in a body of literature known as *nihonjinron* [Japan theory]. This is best described as "defining Japaneseness" and attempts to do so have become a huge intellectual enterprise, responsible for thousands of books, articles, TV programmes, radio shows and websites. The key word in this quest is "uniqueness". This essential uniqueness of Japaneseness is thought to be beyond the ken of Westerners. The debate is devoted to such questions as: who are we Japanese? What makes the Japanese unique? Why are the Japanese so successful? What makes the Japanese spirit so special? And, more recently: which characteristics of Japanese religion form the basis for the superiority of Japanese spirituality? As scholars have shown, most Japanese people seem to be affected by the images generated by Japan theory. Searching for Japanese identity is clearly a national pastime in Japan.

★

Suzuki Teitar Daisetsu (1870–1966), who is famous for introducing Zen Buddhism to the wider world, was one of the first promoters of *nihonjinron,* launching the idea of the uniqueness of the Japanese spirit based on his version of Zen Buddhism. Suzuki was a lay Buddhist who lived for a long time in the United States, where he became familiar with Christian thought, Western notions of religion, and Western forms of mysticisms, particularly the work of Emanuel Swedenborg (1688–1772), the famous Swedish mystic. Combining his knowledge of Buddhism with his familiarity with Western thought, Suzuki created a completely new form of Zen Buddhism that stresses pure experience as the centrepiece of awakening.

The concept of pure experience cannot be found in the traditional writings of Zen Buddhism. It is therefore very likely that the newly invented "Suzuki Zen" owes much more to Western religious thought than to the tradition of Zen Buddhism – or, at least, a great deal. Be that as it may, Suzuki became famous for introducing the world to the spirituality of Zen Buddhism. His best-selling books became very influential not only in the West, but also in Japan. His writings are very popular in Japan because he stresses not only the uniqueness, but also the superiority of Japanese spirituality. In a way, Suzuki may be dubbed a master of "othering", which is to say, deriving one's own identity through demarcating the "other", in this case, institutional Christianity and the West in general. The other, however, is needed to apophatically constitute one's identity, a point beautifully illustrated by a recent advertisement for Suzuki's books for the Japanese market, which praises them as "the Bible of Steve Jobs".

★

In the mid-1990s, books on the uniqueness of Japanese religion became hugely popular in Japan. These books portray Shinto as Japan's native religion and claim that practising it will bring about purification and give practitioners a "mystical" experience. Modern Japan is said to have lost touch with this tradition, partly due to "aggressive" Christian thought, as expressed, for example, by religious scholars and philosophers such as Umehara Takeshi and Nakazawa Shin'ichi. These books depict Japanese religion as animist and polytheist; they claim that worship of the gods of nature is important to the tradition, adding that this, along with the idea of the coexistence of all beings, has allegedly been preserved in Japanese Shinto and Buddhism up to the present. Because of this, it is argued, Japan is able to make an important contribution to solving problems afflicting modern society. The authors stress that Asia, and particularly Japan, will save the world because of its religious traditions. Japanese religion is contrasted with the putatively Christian tradition of the West, in which the "germ of destructive thinking" is supposedly to be discovered.

With the help of highly controversial terms like animism, polytheism, or mystical – designations that lack clear definition and serve ideological purposes – the popular literature on Japanese religion effectively re-reads the Japanese religious tradition. The visions of Shinto and Buddhism presented here imply Japanese superiority. In this discourse, Christianity serves as the negative other that is criticised. At the same time, however, Christianity serves as an *Abgrenzungsfolie* – a foil used to identify and articulate the positive features of what is seen as Japanese religion.

Additionally, scholars like Saeki Sho'ichi, Yuasa Yasuo, Kamata Tōji, Yamaori Tetsuo and many others engage in this kind of discourse by attributing the superiority of Japan to Japanese religion. Strolling around a Japanese bookshop, you'll notice hundreds of books on the characteristics of Japanese religions on offer, often with glossy pictures and messages that promise to explain the mystery of the Japanese spirit. Again, we need to stress that the assumptions about Japanese religion found in these publications are highly speculative at best. One could also name authors like Ōhashi Rōysuke, Ueda Shizuteru, or Sonoda Minoru, who not only publish their books in Japanese, but also act as representatives of Japanese culture for a foreign audience. Their descriptions of Japanese religion are often freshened up with titbits borrowed from new age thought, such as a focus on the powers of nature or the use of the word spirituality, in order to advance their claims about the superiority of Japanese religion.

The apologetics of the "superior" Japanese religion are not located on the fringes of society. Rather, they occupy prominent positions in the cultural mainstream. They are highly visible in the Japanese media; powerful publishers publish their books. As with the Japan theorists themselves, these writings on religion have become part of mass culture and are in fact sometimes described as commercialised articulations of contemporary Japanese nationalism. One could even argue that the *nihonjinron* functions as a Japanese civil religion, the main tasks of which are the generation of national purpose, symbolic self-defence, and consensus around essential values.

It could also be contended that some of the authors of self-assertive discourses on Japanese religion act like priests in a cult – the cult of the superiority of the Japanese nation. Like a religious cult, the ideas formulated affect the resolution of social conflicts. Religion helps to balance these conflicts by dislocating their solutions into the transcendental sphere. The quest for harmony with nature, for example, can be construed as a criticism of such negative aspects of modernisation as alienation and rationalisation.

★

Terms like "group building" or "group identity" have long served as keywords for understanding Japanese society. At the beginning of the 21st century, however, the Japanese are in search of meaning and identity in a mainly secularised society. In this sense, Japan bears many similarities to societies in the Western world. But in contrast to cultures like the German

The Fushimi Inari Taisha Shrine in Fushimi-ku, Kyoto.

or the Swedish, Japanese national identity still plays a very important role in the individual's search for identity. Participating in annual events and festivals at local shrines or temples, particularly New Year rituals, offers a kind of belonging and conveys some idea of what it means to be Japanese.

If not in the form of traditional religions, religion nevertheless remains important in contemporary Japan in the form of the so-called New Religions that have emerged in Japan since the late 19th century. Research suggests that between 15 and 25 per cent of the Japanese population claims membership of one of these New Religions, of which Sōka Gakkai is best known. This organisation is also present in Sweden as Svenska Soka Gakkai International.

The teachings of these new religious organisations are able to adapt to changing needs and are oriented especially to the needs of the individual. At the same time, they integrate what they call elements of the traditional religions of Japan, and very often bestow new meaning on what physically remains of those traditions – the shrines and the temples. The New Religions contribute to the general trend of nostalgia by organising festivals and pilgrimages. Provoked by a dissatisfaction with the present, nostalgia, which can at best be grasped through the Japanese term *furusato* [old village, home, or native place] is widespread in contemporary Japan and is used by politicians, city planners, and advertisers. The pilgrimages organised by the New Religions are designed to convey feelings of belonging to a great cultural and religious tradition.

Some of the New Religions link their rhetoric of nostalgia with assertions that they teach a new form of Buddhism, a form that will bring about universal salvation. Thus the claim that Japan possesses a special potential for saving the world is found not only in the literature of Japan theory, but also in the writings of the New Religions. An example: *Agonshū* [Agama-School] or *Kôfuku no Kagaku* [The Institute for Research in Human Happiness] have been widely regarded as appealing especially to urban-based, younger, well-educated Japanese who are often dissatisfied with modern scientific rationalism and materialism. Some of the older New Religions also link particularistic and universal themes underpinned by a potent nationalist agenda, as for instance, *Mahikari* [True Light].

On the other side, you have groups like the *Byakko Shinkokai* [True and Large Society of the White Light], another older New Religion that expresses its aspiration towards world peace through its rituals and prayers. This links to another strain in contemporary Japanese self-identity: a feeling of being called to act as prophets of peace. Stressing Japan's special mission for peace helps, as some commentators point out, to enable some Japanese people to adjust to the fact that they are not the only human beings on earth.

★

More important than the practice of religion to the engendering of some feeling of national identity are the ascriptions of "religion" and "spirituality" in Japan theory and in the omnipresent media. The pervasive reflections on the so-called "Japanese spirit" within the media not only bestow upon its audience the feeling that they learn something new, but also makes for good entertainment. The Japanese audience is assured that whatever problems the 21st century and globalisation may hold, Japan will deal with them because of its unique religion, which has a salvific potential not only for the Japanese people, but for the whole human race.

Japanese advertisers, meanwhile, make extensive use of religious architecture, art, and ritual to generate images and feelings of nostalgia. Advertisers try to sell green tea, soft drinks, or noodle soups with the help of religious and traditional symbols like the image of Mount Fuji and pictures of Zen gardens. Japan Railways used pictures of temples and shrines in its Discover Japan and Exotic Japan advertising campaigns. A television advertisement in the 1990s showed a Buddha statue, the roof of a temple, the silhouette of a pagoda, and *tatami* – a traditional straw mat – in the red light of the evening sun, above which a gentle voice intoned, "Kyoto: here you can find the key to esoteric Buddhism". The aesthetics of religion are used to create expectations of tradition and reassure people that such aspects still remain in Japan. These expressions denote a sense of belonging, a cultural and emotional home intrinsic to the Japanese experience. Together, the use of religious symbols in the media contributes to a nostalgic zeitgeist that idealises Japan's past, including, and perhaps especially, its religious history as read through this nostalgia.

This idealised view of Japanese religious history, as well as a proclaimed Japanese spirituality, helps to conceal its problematic aspects. Japan's theory of religion, along with nostalgic images of religious symbols, promise some kind of salvation on the basis of a self-proclaimed superior Japanese spirituality.

However nicely it is phrased, this promise implies the inferiority of other religious worldviews, and is thus liable to promote or give voice to a kind of religious nationalism. At the same time, the rhetoric of religious superiority can also be seen as a counterbalance to Western claims of the universality of their own values and worldviews, and thus as a reaction to the historical and cultural impact of the transcultural flows discussed above.

In summary, even if national identity seems to have relatively little to do with institutional religion in contemporary Japan, religion in form of *nihonjinron*, and as used in the media, remains fundamental to Japanese identity. Reflection on religion continues to be used to bear witness to the alleged uniqueness of Japanese spirituality, be this either Buddhist or Shinto spirituality – or some mix of both. To feel a sense of belonging, to learn something about what it means to be Japanese, to understand the meaning of life, or to get in touch with what the future might bring, it is no longer necessary to enter a New Religion, visit a shrine or temple or, for that matter, talk to family members or friends. It is simply a matter of buying a book, watching a television programme, or looking on the web for an article that contains an appraisal of the uniqueness of Japanese culture and the superiority of the Japanese spirit.

The cover of Åsa Ekström's book
Hokuo Joshi (Nordic Girl), 2015.

MANGA AS JAPANESE

Jaqueline Berndt

Manga – that is, comics or graphic narratives – have been attracting critical attention as a part of Japanese culture with an extraordinary suitability for transcultural flows. But not all manga are popular with global audiences, and not all manga exhibit the traits which people perceive as "Japanese". Both "manga proper" and "Japaneseness" are a matter of perspective, and as such they call for address in the plural form.

While different actors identify different kinds of manga as Japanese, inside as well as outside of Japan, a felt recognisability as Japanese is one common thread running through recent discourses, as Stevie Suan, for example, discusses with regard to anime. Against this backdrop, tracking down *what* exactly it is which makes manga Japanese appears to be less reasonable than pursuing *how* manga is Japanese – that is, which aspects of manga distinguish it from other kinds of comics.

This essay focuses on three: industry, that is, Japan as the initial site of manga production and the extraordinarily inventive business model of combining magazines as market makers with subsequent book editions as profit generators; mediality, which ranges from the materiality of the magazine format to the cultural and aesthetic interrelations supported by it; and representation, especially insofar as it applies to what linguist and cognitive scientist Neil Cohn has called "Japanese Visual Language", a modular symbol system, highly consistent across artists and easy to share. As the three aspects are closely interrelated, they will partly overlap in the sections below.

1. *Industry*

In Japan, the word *manga* has had a broad semantic range since the 19th century when pictorial reference books flourished under that name, such as the *Hokusai Manga* (1814–78). Later the word was employed as a label for newspaper caricatures and comic strips and subsequently for animated cartoons on TV (that is, before the term *anime* gained currency in the 1970s). During the postwar period, however, *manga* has come to signify primarily entertaining graphic narratives, whose representational devices and consumption practices are grounded in magazine serialisation. This is what the Japanese word *manga* evokes today in the first place, whereas book editions [*tankōbon*], which follow the serialisation of successful works, have been circulating mainly under the name of *komikkusu* – from English *comics*. Evolved under the specific conditions of postwar Japan, the publication format of the magazine distinguishes manga – as an industry, medium and form of representation – from other kinds of comics, in the eyes of both Japanese and non-Japanese members of the manga camp. The very fact that all attempts at transplanting this format to other markets have failed may attest to its particularity, or Japaneseness.

The Republic of Korea had come closest to the Japanese market until the 1997 financial crisis affected their publication industry to the extent that most *manhwa* magazines were discontinued and efforts turned to online comics, so-called webtoons, a domain in which Korea is much more advanced than Japan, as Park in-Soo describes. Thus, the first thing which makes manga culturally distinctive is not an illustration style or representational substance, but a specific publication format and the related business model.

Tankōbon volumes, running to approximately two hundred pages, made the cheaply produced, low-price and highly volatile manga magazine contents commercially viable. Japan has been one of the few countries in the world where comics artists can make a living, thanks to the close interrelation between magazines and *tankōbon*, which has formed the core of the manga industry. But since 2005, the initially subsidiary book edition has become paramount, generating approximately two thirds of the annual sales of all printed manga, and major manga magazines now have an eye on so-called media mix from the very beginning of drafting a series.

Due to the rapid ageing of Japan's society, the prime target group for the magazines – teenagers – is shrinking, and they prefer smartphone and games to printed matter (as visual as it may be) anyway. Accordingly, the industry's commercial heyday, exemplified by the magazine *Shōnen Jump* and its 6.53 million copies a week in 1995, has entered the realm of nostalgia:

in 2015, *Shōnen Jump* had a weekly print run of less than 2.4 million copies.

Thanks to the wide circulation of manga magazines, a significant proportion of the Japanese population is manga-literate by now. But this situation is about to regress due to the landslide changes in media usage induced by digitalisation. These gained momentum when the northeastern paper mills became inoperative after the triple disaster of March 11, 2011: the tsunami and the subsequent meltdown at the Fukushima Daiichi power plant triggered by a major earthquake.

Even if classic manga content reformatted for mobile devices or video games is the entry point for young consumers, manga in the sense of printed, monochrome and mute graphic narratives, is becoming a old medium. This transformation manifests itself in a new indifference towards medium specificity. In Japan, fans and critics had been distinguishing printed comics from animated TV series since the 1970s, not least because of the prevalence of the magazine format. But outside Japan, where the broad reception of both media set in decades later, the word *manga* has more often than not been used in a non-medium specific way, namely in reference to a whole range of subcultural phenomena, stretching from fan communities and their activities to character design, illustration style, and narrative conventions.

2. *Mediality*

One of manga's major properties is networking, something which takes its departure from the magazine's mediating between characters and readers, artists and readers, and also readers and readers. Once specialised magazines were established (beginning in the 1950s), their pages had to be filled and the consumers kept hooked. This was accomplished not only by extended serialised narratives, but also through paratextual elements which usually do not reappear in the later book edition; for example, short comments by the manga artist addressed directly to readers, or announcements by the editors in the magazine's page margins. In addition, survey postcards and special pages reserved for letters and fan art helped to involve readers in quasi-virtual communities. With respect to mediality, the magazine format seems to have anticipated what was materialised fully by the internet, which in turn has proved to be vital for manga's global spread. In other words, the fact that manga's globalisation gained momentum around 2000, in parallel with the rise in popularity of the internet, cannot only be traced back to the historical disinterest of major Japanese publishing houses in foreign markets. Apparently, the manga medium itself – its participatory and community-building potential – has matched the phase of transition from the culture of the Gutenberg galaxy to the mediascape of the information society.

Forming the backbone of the manga industry from the late 1950s to the early 2000s, the publication format of the magazine also gave rise to another one of manga's most salient characteristics: gender-specific genres. From the 1970s onwards, the gendering encompassed both artists and readers (not magazine editors though). But while series targeted at men are not necessarily being read only by men, feminine-looking page layouts and linework are less likely to cross borders of gendered taste. Down to the present day, the public "standard" of manga manifests itself in the male genres.

Symptomatic in that regard is the inclination of politicians and civil servants to privilege male artists who employ a generically masculine style. For its 2015 free brochure, *Tokyo Bōsai* [Disaster Preparedness Tokyo], the Tokyo metropolitan government commissioned Kawaguchi Kaiji to create the fourteen-page manga supplement *Tokyo 'X' Day*. And deputy prime-minister Asō Tarō, who has been promoting "Cool Japan" since the early 2000s, is known to be in favour of Saitō Takao and his hard-boiled action series *Golgo 13* (running since 1968). While works by artists like these are mainly popular with elderly [salary]men, the online fan community shows an inclination to ascribe to them "an outdated style called gekiga", as Takeuchi Miho observes.

Serialised graphic narratives targeted at girls and women [*shōjo, josei*] have led female readers worldwide not only to consume, but also to create manga. Although stylistically close to Japanese manga, their publication is not necessarily linked to the Japanese market anymore. To cite two Swedish examples, Åsa Ekström is now successfully publishing in Japanese – an originally produced collection of comic strips titled *Nordic Girl Åsa Discovers the Mysteries of Japan* (2015–16), and a Japanese translation of her Swedish publication *Sayonara September* (2015). In contrast, Nosebleed Studio, now formed by Natalia and Catarina Batista, Elise Rosberg, Joakim Waller and Alice Engström, relies mainly on a domestic fan-base rather than Japanese corporate support for producing manga.

Manga book shop in Osaka.

Excerpt from Åsa Ekström's book Hokuo Joshi.

Two differences between manga beyond Japan and in Japan are noteworthy though. First, the generic gendering is less possible abroad where manga readership forms a minority anyway; many non-Japanese readers who are not familiar with manga still assume this medium to be "childish" and, in the case of female styles, even perpetuating conservative gender roles in part due to its non-realistic and highly conventional visual rendering.

Second, manga has come to be appreciated inside and outside Japan as an apparently inexhaustible reservoir of narratives. This again rests on the magazine format. The available space allows not only for dynamic, rapid-fire action sequences, but also for lengthy pursuit of affective states and emotional changes – one dialogue may fill many pages, in which the plot does not progress much – and a more visual rather than verbal storytelling. Manga artists and their editors have developed sophisticated techniques of paneling, guiding the reader's gaze across pages and double-page spreads.

The mode of magazine serialisation has given rise to an interplay of page and panel as well as an aesthetic awareness of the double-page spread. These did not have an equivalent in western comics until recent exchanges and attempts to create something which can be called a fusion style. In general, printed graphic narratives hold the potential to unsettle the reader who incessantly has to decide whether to privilege the single panel or the entire page, if not the double-page spread: the page may push itself to the fore of the reader's attention, and then again, the page may go unnoticed, and characters may stay within borders, within "shots" or frozen moments to be visually scanned in sequence. While the two variants assume different weight in different works, a high degree of interrelatedness remains characteristic of manga. If it does not apply to the relation between panel and page, it applies certainly to the relation between panels on a page: cut out, few manga panels are strong enough to convince by themselves, as autonomous images.

3. *Representation*

Reaching beyond the actual publication format and related business model, genre-specific magazines have shaped the local as well as global identity of manga as a highly codified and participatory media, suiting (and structurally anticipating) the age of digital networks and virtual reality. Back in the 1980s, European comic critics still agreed that manga were culturally too particular, and therefore too exclusive, for Europeans to enjoy easily. Thirty years later, manga has become, according to cognitive linguist Neil Cohn, "one of the most recognisable styles of representation". This characteristic is usually traced back to Tezuka Osamu (1928–89), the pioneer of graphic narratives in postwar Japan, who defined his drawing style famously as "hieroglyphic"; a tool for storytelling. Adopting these hieroglyphs – or modules – has proven to be socially rewarding for younger people worldwide as it allows them to enter a community and to acquire social identity as one of its members. Thus, many non-Japanese people have become "manga-literate". They know that a so-called *chibi* – a diminutive creature – may be a different manifestation of the same character, relating, for example, an inner self-image and not just an inner voice; they are familiar with the manga-specific device of layering perspectives within one and the same panel, for example, when the object at which a character gazes appears behind this very character as if they could gaze with the back of their head; and they are able to process abundant modifiers and decode pictograms or visual "morphems" (as Cohn calls them), like wordless speech balloons containing only three dots as a sign of speechlessness, cruciform popping veins as a sign of anger, and nosebleeds as an indication of lust.

This manga literacy has been one factor in spurring the global popularity of a recent series whose protagonist lacks the infamous manga-esque saucer eyes, namely Nakama Ryō's *The Story of Isobe Isobee: Life Is Hard in the Floating World*, serialised in *Weekly Shōnen Jump* and related magazines since 2013. Protagonist Isobe Isobee has a face reminiscent of *kabuki* actors depicted in *ukiyo-e* woodcut prints, and as such he may appear very Japanese to those who are familiar with this form of traditional visual art, but for manga consumers, his look took getting used to. What makes the series appear Japanese in a manga-specific sense is not necessarily character design. On the industrial and media side, it is the publication site – the flagship manga magazine – and this magazine's recent engagement in developing globally successful media franchises. Isobee has proven his aptitude for crossing media from magazine serialisation to bound book edition (sixteen *tankōbon* volumes in total), to Flash and web anime, and even a stage version, not forgetting related fan production, primarily online via social networking sites. On the representational side, it is the use of abundant modifiers, including a nosebleed when reading erotic books, the varying page layouts, and also verbal elements such as humorous dialogue, but most important is the overall setting and tone of the narrative.

Set in Edo in the early 19th century, the series features a lazy slacker who lives with his mother although he is of marriageable age. In front of her he pretends to be devoted to the way of the samurai, but actually he is more like a contemporary *hikikomori*, a reclusive young man who withdraws from social life. Similarly, he is not good at communicating with women (whom he desires) and consumes pornography instead. Thus, the success of Nakama's series suggests that the key to a popular manga lies less in an apparently "Japanese" look than in accessible, and by now globally shared, cultural references as well as playfulness, which is not necessarily in line with straight, content-oriented readings. What Isobee offers is neither historical realism nor a serious approach to contemporary social issues, but a parody of cultural nostalgia for a time long gone and, for male readers, the opportunity to laugh at the *hikikomori* in themselves.

The identification of Japaneseness is usually focused on visible traits. One of them is the visual representation of ethnicity in manga. Isobee, for example, looks Japanese, from his small eyes to his hairstyle and attire. The fact that he enjoys popularity among Japanese and non-Japanese consumers alike may be related by some critics to the latter's indulging in Orientalist desire, but it also points in a different direction, one beyond representationalist readings. Manga's way of conventionalising representations (for example, of ethnicity) distracts from the initial reference, and thereby entails the possibility of moving beyond segregation altogether. As is widely known among fans, whether manga faces are ethnically specified differs according to genre. While *shōjo* [girls'] manga shows a particularly strong penchant towards Westernisation and employs Japanese faces mostly for the characterisation of supporting characters (to indicate sneakiness or other flaws), manga for men, especially realist ones for non-infant readers [*seinen* and *gekiga*], feature Japanese or Asian faces occasionally, as do Ōtomo Katsuhiro's *AKIRA* (1982–90), Urasawa Naoki's *Billy Bat* (2008–12) and Kawaguchi Kaiji's *Eagle: The Making of an Asian-American President* (1998–2001). But they also exhibit a penchant to deracialise, and thereby universalise, their protagonist, in contrast to some of his female partners.

In female genres, Caucasian-looking Japanese characters are mostly signifiers without Caucasian signifieds. Precisely this makes them available to both consumerist play and post-ethnic projections, for example by non-Japanese fans of various ethnicities and races. While Caucasian as conventionalised, and as such allegedly neutral, faces may be related to a utopia beyond race altogether, representational readings can become a barrier for easily investing imagery with fantastic visions or experiences of one's own everyday life. Yet, manga balks at being subjected to either representation or use-related analysis. It calls for both, just as manga-esque faces can pass as both ethnically neutral and specified, depending on context and the viewer's experience.

★

In the late 1980s, when manga started to attract critical attention inside and outside of Japan, its Japaneseness was not of much interest to Japanese manga critics. Their battlefield was limited to the domestic public sphere – and they did not know much about non-Japanese comics anyway. Today, manga is inclined to be identified as Japanese by completely different actors, despite the key role of intercultural exchange during its formative years and recent transcultural flows that have already given rise to a significant number of non-Japanese productions.

For most of its history, manga has been flying not only above the radar of national identity, but also below it, belonging to the domain of subcultures, and as such being prone to attempts at regulation (first and foremost with respect to sexual representation).

This essay did not aim to dismantle discourses of nationalisation, or expose the contribution of popular media to a homogenised notion of Japanese culture. It rather foregrounded distinctive features of manga as comics. It goes without saying that these are always informed by discourses, and these discourses suggest that manga can stand in for "Japan" and go beyond it at the same time. It is local enough to be recognisable as a brand which conjoins attempts at nation branding, and it is sufficiently global, appearing as a local variant of globally shared affects, demands and media experiences. With respect to critical engagement, especially outside Japan, a hope remains that manga gains acknowledgment in its own right, and is not limited to being a representation of Japaneseness.

REFERENCES

Andrew Targowski, Juri Abe & Hisanori Katō (eds), *Japanese Civilization in the 21st Century*, (New York: Nova Science Publishers, 2016).

Berndt, Jaqueline, "*SKIM* as *GIRL*: Reading a Japanese American Graphic Novel through Manga Lenses", in Monica Chiu (ed.) *Drawing New Color Lines: Transnational Asian American Graphic Narratives*, (Hong Kong University Press, 2014), pp.257–278.

Berndt, Jaqueline, "Manga, which Manga? Publication Formats, Genres, Users", in Andrew Targowski, Juri Abe & Hisanori Katō (eds), *Japanese Civilization in the 21st Century*, (New York: Nova Science Publishers, 2016).

Berndt, Enno & Jaqueline, "Magazines and Books: Changes in the Manga Market", in Jaqueline Berndt, *Manga: Medium, Art and Material*, (Leipzig: Leipzig University Press, 2015), pp.227–239.

Brienza, Casey (ed.), *Global Manga: "Japanese Comics" without Japan?* (Farnham, Surrey & Burlington, VT: Ashgate, 2015).

Cohn, Neil, *The Visual Language of Comics: Introduction to the structure and cognition of sequential images*, (London: Bloomsbury, 2013).

Galbraith, Patrick W. and Jason G. Karlin (eds.), *Media Convergence in Japan*, (Kinema Club, 2016). http://creativecommons.org/licenses/by-nc-sa/4.0/, accessed October 10, 2016.

Park, Soo-in/パク・スイン(朴秀寅)「韓国のウェブトゥーン」、『日韓漫画研 [*Japanese-Korean Manga/Manhwa Studies*], Jaqueline Berndt, Yamanaka Chie & Leem Hye Jeong (eds.), (Kyoto International Manga Research Center, 2013), pp.227–242. http://imrc.jp/images/upload/lecture/data/11_パク・スイン.pdf, accessed October 10, 2016.

Suan, Stevie, "Performing Differently: Convention, Medium, and Globality from Manga (Studies) to Anime (Studies)", in *Comicology* (online conference proceedings), Jaqueline Berndt (ed.), (Kyoto International Manga Museum, 2016), p12.

Takeuchi, Miho/竹内美帆「線から捉え直す「劇画」—さいとう・たかをを中心に」 ["Reconsidering *gekiga* from the perspective of the line: The case of Saitō Takao"] 、『日韓漫画研究』[*Japanese-Korean Manga/Manhwa Studies*] Jaqueline Berndt, Yamanaka Chie & Leem Hye Jeong (eds.), (Kyoto International Manga Research Center, 2013), p.180 [157–199]. http://imrc.jp/lecture/2011/10/3.html, accessed October 10, 2016.

JAPANESE ARCHITECTURE: TRADITION AND MODERNITY

BILLET-DOUX

Japanese woman writing a letter on
paper scroll with ink brush, 1911.

FROM CONCRETE TO ABSTRACT

Elisabet Yanagisawa Avén

The quality we call beauty...
must always grow from the realities of life.

JUNICHIRO TANIZAKI
In Praise of Shadows

Japanese aesthetics is a rich field of sensuous knowledge. In this essay I focus on the essence and achievement of Japanese aesthetics; its main features, its sources, and the genealogy of philosophical and religious concepts, along with metaphysical concepts, all of which have been the point of departure for Japanese art and aesthetics for around a thousand years.

Even if today we do not want to consolidate differences between cultures, but rather strengthen the similarities between them, we have to consider that the aesthetical cultures of East and West have different processes of development. In short, the development of aesthetic processes in the East has gone from expression in pre-modern times to representation in modern times. In the West, the development of aesthetics has gone the opposite way; from representation towards individualistic expression. This why we must pass through a threshold if we want to approach a Japanese way of thinking and perceiving aesthetics – first and foremost, this is done through intuition. We have to perceive using our own bodies and senses, rather than by thinking conceptually. This means that there is a need for intimacy by perceiving sensibilities, by being affected by the essence of the material: the sensuous properties of matter as colours, nuances, consistencies, scent and textures. Japanese aesthetics has a dimension preceding reason and cognitive knowledge. Intuitive knowledge is direct, without any need for analyses, arguments or logical reasoning. It is about feeling joy, care and love for an object, and affinity

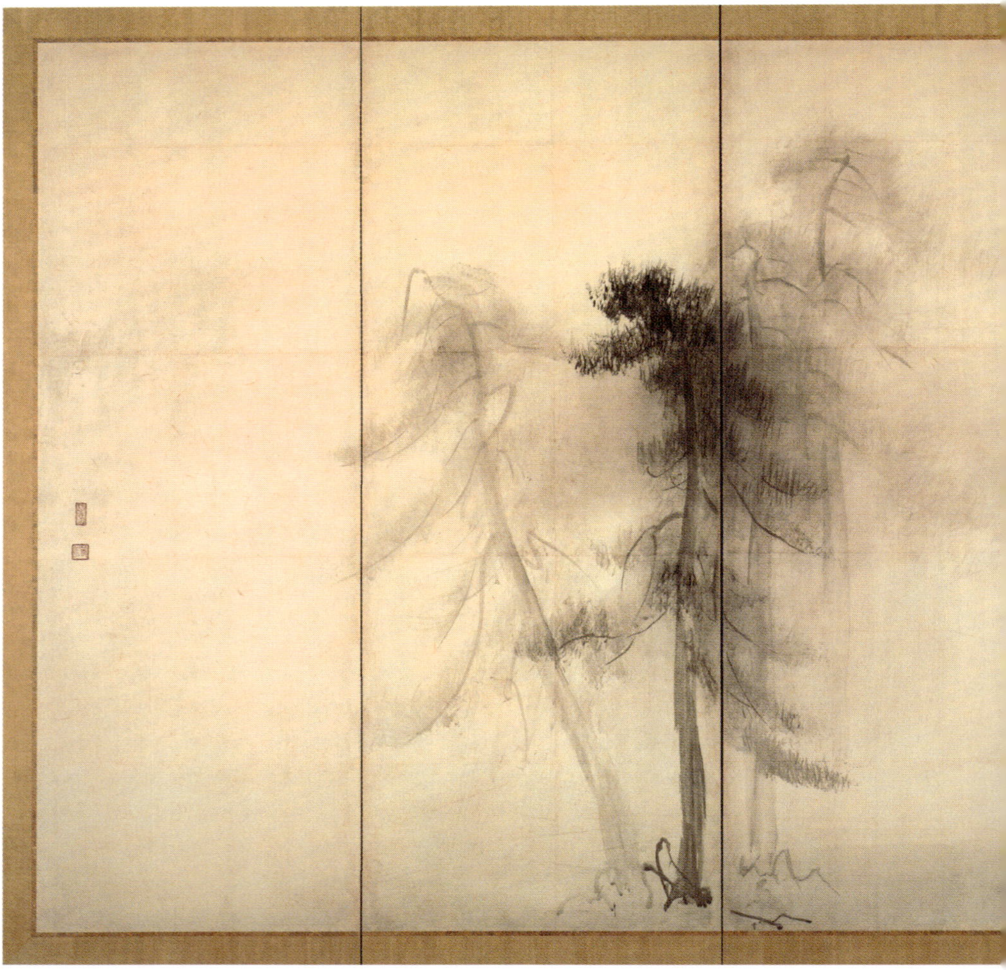

Pine Trees by the painter Hasegawa Tohaku (1539–1610).

to matter and things. But this interconnectedness with matter is not materialistic, rather, it is a way of feeling an intimate relation to the subtleness of it, how it is perceived, and how we listen and discern our ability to become attuned to certain affects of reality.

To fully comprehend advanced, developed aesthetical language, we must also understand animism. Animism is the worldview that perceives all things – including objects, places and creatures – as animate and alive. Part of this belief is the idea that non-human powers of different kinds, and to different degrees, also affect human beings and human conditions. Microcosmos, that is, the human being, and the macrocosmic universe are interrelated. Humans are forms of life in-between cosmic and earthly. In Japanese metaphysics, the body-mind is the place where divine intimacy can be activated and experienced, through different practices. This is why the physical senses and sensuous perceptions are the base for the human experience: to perceive matter through the senses makes it possible for *kami*, the deities or gods, to enter into matter through the human body and mind. This is the point of departure we must comprehend when we investigate the meaning of Japanese aesthetics – and how it is practised rather than theorised. This animistic perspective also views nature as the process, source and power of life. It sees an "aliveness" or a sense of motion as the most crucial aspect in the evaluation of artistic qualities. All things in nature are in a changing process, in cyclical orbits of different length. Animism relates to Shinto, the oldest Japanese religion. In Shinto, nature is the power, source and process of everything, and a very important aspect of the continuous changing nature of things is an appreciation of the seasons.

According to Chinese philosophy, everything we experience in reality derives from the interplay between the differentiated forces of *yin qi* and *yang qi*, as a tension between complementary forces. To have *qi* is to be alive and the dead are those without *qi*. *Qi* and *dao* are related in this way: *qi* is the force and *dao* is the way. Motion and strength were highly valued in the artwork of ancient China and Japan. But *qi,* or *ki* in Japanese, is related to many things other than artwork: it is a crucial notion in philosophy, the arts, medicine, martial arts and in *qi gong*. This gives us an idea of *ki* as a force of life, also physically transmitted invisibly through the air, through smells and vapours. But there is no abstraction in the understanding of *ki*. It is an immanent force of a spiritual aspect that is manifested in bodies as well as in material objects: spirit in matter.

FROM CONCRETE TO ABSTRACT

According to the critic and writer Donald Richie, elegance is a kind of refinement, "of beauty in movement, appearance, or manners; a tasteful opulence in form, decoration, or presentation; a restraint and grace of style. Most of the components of Japanese aesthetics carry this connotation of elegance".[1]

Many kinds of elegance exist. Each kind expresses something specific. It is a language of aesthetics and the sensuous that has its own grammar. Elegance is socially derived, and therefore aesthetic notions in Japan are theories of taste. Historically, refined tastes developed among the aristocracy and the wealthy. The Heian Court culture in the 11th century was a highly "modern" community, with developed tastes, poetic refinements, elegance in gestures and behaviour, and with rich articulations in language of these aesthetical sensations. The writer Murasaki Shikibu (973–1014 AD) who wrote *Genji monogatari* [The Tale of Genji][2] is a great source for getting a concrete idea of this sensibility, and she lived over a thousand years before Marcel Proust. In the same class is Sei Shonagon (966–1017 AD) author of *The Pillow Book*. This text is quite contemporary in its style of writing; lists of what is beautiful or ugly, delightful and funny, as well as descriptions of characters and atmospheres. In the 20th century, the neo-sensualists[3] Yasunari Kawabata and Junichiro Tanizaki followed up the sensibility of female writers from the Heian era. Yukio Mishima's writings also give the reader an idea of what Japanese aesthetics is about, in terms of affect, sensibility, restrained passion and the relationship between the concrete and the abstract.

The sensibility to things is visible in everyday activities and objects; flowers, gardens, clothing, food, crafts, architecture and design. The everyday aspect derives from Shinto, which embraces life in its all affirmed aspects. The boundaries between fine art and craft in Japan are porous. Craft is valued as highly as fine art, sometimes more, considering, for instance, the prices of utensils for tea ceremonies and vessels for *ikebana* [flower arrangement]. The commonplace also derives from Daoism, a philosophy of earthly life, where the art of artlessness is the highest value, and the art of life is the way. An important person for *mingei*, the folk craft movement in the 1920s–30s in Japan, was Soetsu Yanagi (1889–1961), a Japanese philosopher.

Tao or *dao* means "the way", and this is a method – not a theory, but a practice for life and for art. It is a practice with no doctrines or rules, and no texts to interpret or analyse. *Tao* is an activity that takes place in the

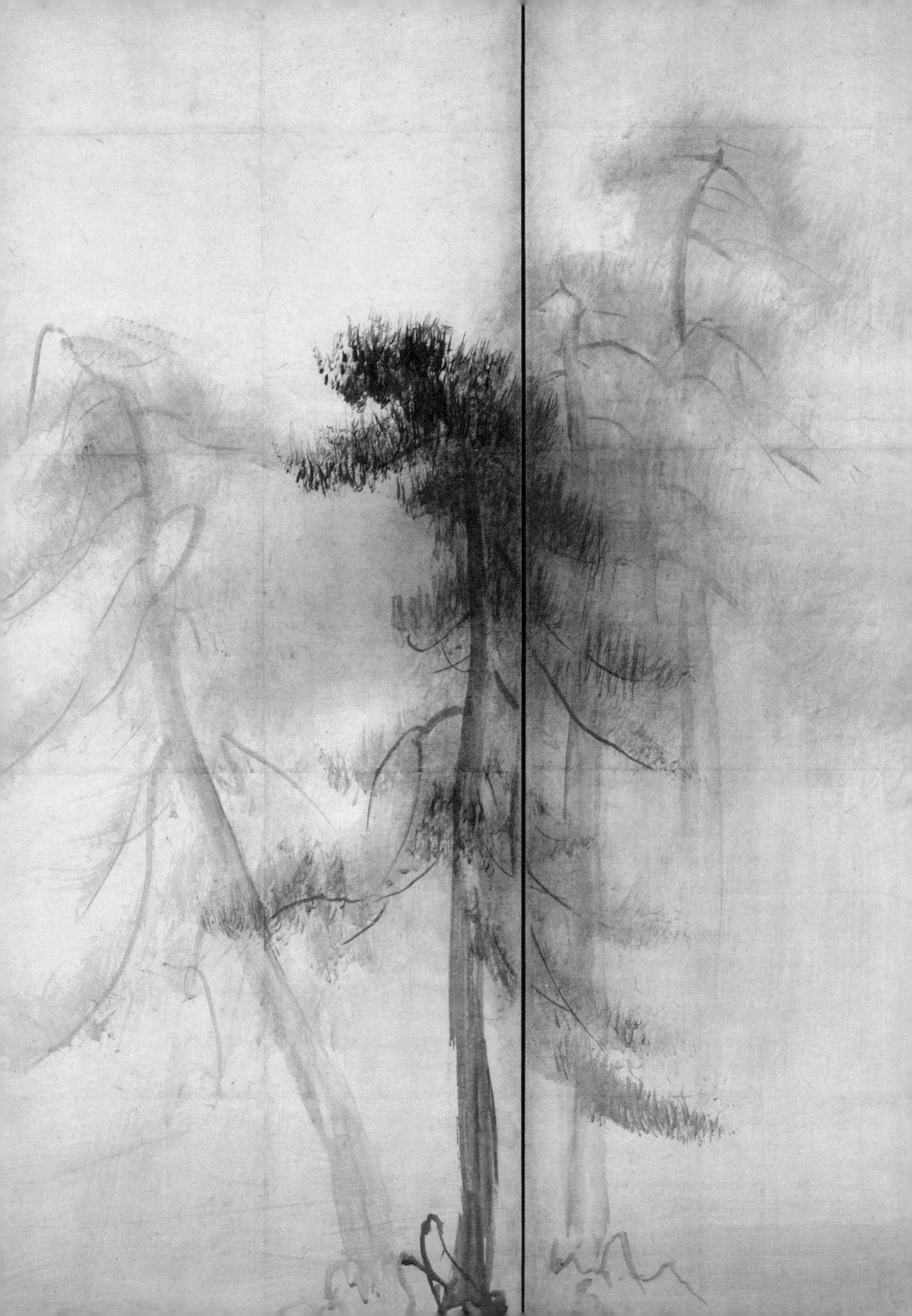

body and mind, transforming the practitioner. The idea of *tao* is that it can be almost anything: a way of art, music, craft, garden design, flower arrangement, pottery, scent, calligraphy or martial arts. It can be a way of searching for enlightenment through introspection. But, nevertheless, *tao* can also be a way of affirming desire, love and pleasure according to Taoism, which has affected the Japanese way of thinking and acting through the centuries. *Tao* is a body-mind practice that emphasises the body and the senses. It is an affirmative way of embracing life, and its multiple expressions. All ways are different aspects of immanent life, and are used to explore life and to develop oneself and one's soul. Thus, the divine and the earthy are tightly entangled in East Asian cosmology.

★

Calligraphy, *origami*, pottery, silk textiles, *kaiseki ryori* [gastronomic food in the setting of tea ceremony], *kōdo* [the art of fragrance], and *ikebana*, [flower arrangement] are all examples of ephemeral and perishing art forms, highly valued in Japan because of their momentary aspect. *Aware* is a literary and aesthetic ideal cultivated during the Heian period (794–1185). It often describes the bitter-sweetness of brief and fading moments: "At its core is a deep, emphatic appreciation of the ephemeral beauty manifest in nature and human life, and is therefore tinged with a hint of sadness; under certain circumstances it can be accompanied by admiration, awe, or even joy".[4] The notion of *aware* was revived by the doctor and scholar Motoori Norinaga (1730–1801). As the anthology *Keys To Japanese Heart and Soul* puts it: "According to Norinaga, *aware* is a combination of two interjections *a* and *hare*, each of them was uttered spontaneously when one's heart was profoundly moved". Norinaga studied literature, and in particular Murasaki Shikibu's *Genji monogatari*. He arrived at the conclusion that in pre-modern Japanese aesthetics *aware* was an important ideal. He coined the notion *mono no aware*, translated as "a deep feeling of things", or "the pathos of things". In Norinaga's view, *mono no aware* is a "purified and exalted feeling, close to the innermost heart of man and nature. It tends to focus on the beauty of impermanence and on the sensitive heart capable of appreciating that beauty".[5]

Aware refers back to *Manyōshū*, the oldest collection of Japanese poetry in existence, compiled from 759 AD during the Nara period. The meaning of the word is akin to "a colour or a perfume to a sentence. It bespoke

Detail from Pine Trees by
Hasegawa Tohaku (1539–1610).

the sensitive poet's awareness of a sight or a sound, of its beauty and its perishability".[6] While its meaning has changed over time, the genealogy of *aware* is to be found in the *Kojiki,* (711–12) an ancient Shintoist collection of myths, and the Nihongi, the oldest text of Japanese history, completed in 797 AD. *Mono no aware,* as Norinaga explains it, has a double meaning: the "sorrow, grief and sadness" is in tandem with "happy events" and "funny situations", and "excitement"– and thus *aware* takes a first step as "aesthetic feeling".[7] The "pathos of things" means, according to professor of aesthetics Ōnishi Yoshinori, "the aesthetic excitement and by intuition to the very metaphysical bottom of the 'universal thing' and the 'universal Being'".

★

We have certainly paid attention to the organisation of space in traditional and contemporary Japanese compositions, whether it is the arrangement of food on small plates, or how to make use of the *tokonoma* – the niche in the wall for displaying *ikebana* artwork in the *tatami* room. We are now facing the concept of void and its importance in Japanese aesthetics. *Ku* means emptiness, but not in the sense of poverty and lack, it means rather a state of latent, or unactivated, virtual power; a potential for being filled. The negative void of emptiness is always in tension with the positive concreteness of materiality and form. This tension between form and emptiness, matter and void is a law of nature, one that enables a natural and living balance. *Ku* is a Buddhist concept that also connotes a kind of asceticism. Parallel to *ku* is the notion of *mu* – "nothingness". Nothingness is not the same as emptiness; *mu* is a *daoist* metaphysical notion that means both nothingness and fullness. The metaphysical enigma is that these states imply the same condition, a great thought to reflect on. The symbol of *mu* is the circle, *enso*.

In contemporary Japanese aesthetics we find a kind of refined simplicity. This simplicity is often related to purity, or a sense of sacred cleanliness. Purity is a strong element in Japanese aesthetics, deriving from Shinto practices, namely purification rituals of four different, but related fields: body; matter; mind; and soul. These Shinto rituals of purification have a strong relevance in Japanese secular society today: they are the basis for simplicity and minimalism – in gestures and deportments, organisation of space and arrangement of items, all these visible things

Detail from Pine Trees by
Hasegawa Tohaku (1539–1610).

have concealed aspects of metaphysical aesthetics. A visible composition includes an invisible aspect, such as attitudes and ideological content, deriving from purification.

★

Oneness is the point of departure. The source is One, it is eternal, abstract and potential. It is nothingness and fullness at the same time. Darkness is its abode. The *Tao Te Ching*, in chapter forty-two, describes how *tao* is related to duality, in Chinese *yin yang*:

> The Tao gives birth to One.
> One gives birth to Two.
> Two gives birth to Three.
> Three gives birth to all things.

This depicts how oneness and duality are two sides of the process. The source divides itself and becomes two forces; *yin* and *yang,* female and male. A tension arises between the positive and negative poles, and this is three – the power of desire. *Yin* and *yang* can be comprehended in many symbolic ways – as warm and cold, soft and hard, dark and light.

> All things have their backs to the female.
> And stand facing the male.
> When male and female combine,
> All things achieve harmony.

There is a bit of *yin* in *yang*, and vice versa. These are metaphorical notions, which give us images of metaphysical laws. Desire is the fundament of everything created. All things are related to this bipolarity, and this gives force to development. Desire is the driving force for achieving harmony, and harmony means to be in tune with *tao*. The states of *yin* and *yang* are always in motion. Nothing is fixed, all is continuously changing in different rhythms, and turns from the extreme state of *yin* to the extreme state of *yang* and back again. The philosophy of change conveys that motion is the basis for being alive. If things become fixed, they die. Motion generates new energy, including new ideas and the desire to realise them. This is the dynamic process of creation, the development of nature. Thus *tao* teaches that life is a recycling process. Birth and death lead to rebirth. And rebirth is always as a new figure. Matter is rebirthing as well as beings, and all are interrelated to *tao*. This is the metaphysical base for all aesthetics. Art forms in Japan are a combination of a strict organised form [*kata*] and spontaneity of making and of movement. There is a tension and a motion between the fixed and the changeable. Oneness and duality are not contradicting.

★

In pre-modern times – i.e. from medieval times – many aesthetic practices were related to both personal and collective transformations of mind and body. Thus, teachings were held in communities, between master and disciples, and were secret teachings. One example of these are those of Zeami Motokiyo. These are based on his experiences of, and thoughts about, the performance art *Noh*, founded by Motokiyo and his father Kan'ami Kiyotsugu. His most well-known text, *Fushikaden* [Transmission of Style and the Flower] was written around 1400–18 AD[8] but was only rediscovered in 1908 in a secondhand bookstore in Japan. Deeply related to the art of *Noh* is the notion of *yūgen* – profound, mysterious, cosmic beauty. It derives from Chinese Taoism, with roots as far back as the 10th century. The first symbol *yū* connotes darkness and confinement; a spiritual relation to ghosts and spirits and other worlds, along with: imprisonment; mystery; quiet places; solitude and secluded things; deep water; cosmos; and a cosmic sublime. The same dictionary notes that *gen* originally described a dark, profound, tranquil colour of the universe. *Yūgen* is linked to the feminine *yin* in the *yin-yang*-philosophy. *Yin* is receptivity and openness, but is also a closure, a spatial womb, and an inner cosmic realm. As we have seen previously, the *yin-yang* philosophy is about interrelated opposing forces that are continuously changing. Neither force dominates the other; they are reciprocally, fluidly interconnected. Thus, *yin-yang* thinking does not enhance static ideals; it signifies reversal, stillness as death, and animation as life.

Today the character *yūgen,* as it is used in Japanese aesthetics, encompasses a meaning close to "the beautiful sublime", one that is defined as dim, weak, faint, and indistinct. It is an immanent notion that departs from the real concreteness of physicality, while sliding from invisibility to visibility as a layered transversal in the between-ness of the real and the phantasmagorical.

★

The Way of Tea - *chado* - expresses a view of art as life. It concerns everyday movements, everyday objects. In the art of tea we see how attention is given to proximity values – small scales, ephemeral experiences and hapticity. An aesthetical ideal is the tea master Sen no Rikyu's (1522–91) taste for the subtle, understated and the subdued. Japanese taste was early on divided into a number of different preferences, or particular aesthetic types. We will look deeper into the notions of *shibui, wabi* and *sabi*. The latter expresses a refined natural style that is imperfect, asymmetrical and austere. This is the taste of the way of tea. *Shibui* means understated and astringent, and is a medieval notion applied to colour, design, taste, and voice as well as human behaviour. *Shibui* is an adjective designating "a subtle, unobtrusive and deeply moving beauty"[9] that is austere, subdued, and restrained. The Japanese philosopher Kuki Shuūzo describes *shibumi* as signifying "understated, astringent" that signifies an inactive relation to the other. He likened it to the tannins of unripe persimmons, or the astringent inner skin of chestnuts. But the connotations in Japanese also include quietness, depth, simplicity and purity. The antonyms are gaudy, showy, boastful and vulgar.

The anthology *Keys to the Japanese Heart and Soul* outlines the meaning of *wabi*: "an aesthetic and moral principle advocating the enjoyment of a quiet, leisurely life free from worldly concerns. Originating with medieval hermits, it emphasizes a simple, austere type of beauty and a serene, transcendental frame of mind".

As we see, *wabi* is not only about material properties, but also ethical values related to a life of self-cultivation – and it has a metaphysical meaning. *Wabi* is a central concept in the aesthetics of the tea ceremony, and is also manifested in poetry as *haiku* and *waka*. Sometimes *wabi* is reduced to being translated as "raw", "rough" or "rustic", which is inadequate – it only depicts its surface. Thus, we have to confront the notion of *wabi* as something that has both internal and external features. The three parts of *wabi* are first, simple, unpretentious beauty; secondly, imperfect, irregular beauty, and thirdly, austere, stark beauty.

1. Simple, unpretentious beauty
According to tea master Jakuan Sotaku: "*wabi* means lacking things, having things run entirely contrary to desires, being frustrated in our wishes".[10] The original sense of *wabi*, then, embraces disappointment, frustration, and poverty.

> Always bear in mind that *wabi* involves not regarding incapacities as incapacitating, not feeling that lacking something is deprivation, not thinking that what is not provided is deficiency. To regard incapacity as incapacitating, to feel that lack is deprivation, or to believe that not being provided for is poverty is not *wabi* but rather the spirit of the pauper.[11]

This means the transformation of material insufficiency so that one discovers a world of spiritual freedom unbounded by material things. This feature gives matter an artless, *wabi* beauty.

Here is a famous image to recall by the tea master Murata Shūkō, in Kisho Kurokawa's *Intercultural Architecture, The Philosophy of Symbiosis*. "A prize horse looks best hitched to a thatched hut".[12] This means that the unexpected combination of an exclusive horse in conjunction with a very simple hut gives another kind of uncommon and guileless beauty ideal, rather than a general and common view of beauty. It is about artlessness.

2. Imperfect, irregular beauty
Shūko also said: "The moon is not pleasing unless partly obscured by a cloud". Cracks and tears, if properly mended, are not disliked in *chado*. Utensils do not need to be perfect. There is a famous story about the tea master Sen no Rikyu, prizing a cracked vase at the temple Onjōji. And the Seppo tea bowl is particularly admired because it has been repaired.

3. Austere, stark beauty
This third aspect is about a tranquil, austere beauty, a cool, stark beauty, colourless, and non-vivid, more like an ink wash monochrome. This was Sen no Rikyu's ideal of "spring of grass amid the snow". At first, this is the extreme of *yin*, a cold withered beauty; but as there is sign of "aliveness" under the snow "it is the merest tinge of *yang* at the extremity of *yin*".

Sabi is a term that is used in conjunction with *wabi*, to form the well-known notion of *wabi-sabi*, often used in terms of Japanese aesthetics and minimalism. "*Sabi* points toward a medieval aesthetics combining elements of old age, loneliness, resignation, and tranquility, yet the colorful and plebeian qualities of Edo-period culture are also present".[13] This quality is interrelated to *wabi,* through the viewpoint of simplicity and austerity. The deliberate selection of the simple is a choice to withdraw from the glamour of things. Poverty is not emphasised, but rather, *sabi* is a conscious decision based on an instinct; a refined taste and the ability to value simplicity because of its elegance, and not from the point of view of status.

The word was originally a verb, *sabu,* meaning "to decay, to fall into ruin". *Sabi* can be traced to the poetry of *Man'yōshū*[14] where the adjective *sabushi* – "lonesome" – is used.

In medieval poetry, *sabi* comes to mean "withering", and is thus related to images of winter, colourlessness and bare nature. The poet Basho (1644–94) found *sabi* in this *haiku* by his disciple:

Two blossom-watchmen
With their white heads together
Having a chat.

Leonard Koren, the author of *Wabi-sabi: for Artists, Designers, Poets and Philosophers,* describes *sabi* with the nuanced keywords: "fragility, imperfection, impermanence, incompletion, irregularity (odd, misshappen, awkward, ugly forms), unpretentiousness (unstudied and unassuming), things modest and humble, things unconventional, and anonymity" – in other words, "a fragile aesthetic ideology".[15] Moreover, *sabi* implies a temporal aspect; the word also means "rust". Thus it depicts the metallic patina of rust and the tarnished patina of things used or old. Koren is very precise in his descriptions of how *sabi* is embodied in matter: "discoloration, rust, tarnish, stain, warping, shrinking, shriveling and cracking. *Sabi* comes with nicks, chips, bruises, scars, dents, peeling, and other forms of attrition that are testament to histories of use and misuse".[16]

★

Iki is a traditional Japanese aesthetical notion; more of a kind of refined taste. The word is still in use, but its meaning today is reduced to the informal word for "cool". *Iki* is composed of internal and external modalities. It is related to an external trait that is tangible and has a real nuance, texture and body. The internal aspects of *iki* deal with ethical codes that derive from two sources of self-cultivation; *bushidō* [the way of the warrior, the *samurai*], and Buddhism. The internal features of *iki* give it a profound and noble character that cannot be expressed only by means of tangible matter (that also includes the body and its appearance). *Iki* has developed in an amalgamated, abundant culture, and embodies paradoxical contradictions between ethical codes of behaviour from the codes of *bushidō;* an urban secular lifestyle of "the floating world" based on pleasure[17]; and the meditative Zen-consciousness of renunciation.

"A living philosophy must be able to understand reality"[18] begins the philosopher Shūzo Kuki (1888–1941), who was the main interpreter of the notion of *iki* in Japan. *Iki* is composed of internal and external modalities. *Iki* is recognized by certain sparse, tangible and haptic material qualities or atmospheres. *Iki* is not a general taste – things that are said to be *iki* are quite rare – but it is about a certain style. According to Kuki, the intentional structures of *iki* are three: the basic tonality of *iki* is *bitai,* which means a "coquetry" directed at a person of the opposite sex. Kuki claims that *"iki na koto"* [things *iki*] connote relationships that are out of the ordinary. It aims to convey a dualistic attitude, a slight erotic tension. This hint at desire is just this – it is not a realisation. And as such, it is "protecting a possibility as a possibility".[19] The second aspect of *iki* is *ikiji,* an idealistic mindset: "pride and honour". This sprightly ideal derives from a code of conduct from the moral ideal in Edo culture, the samurai life-style *bushidō*. The third feature of the intentional structure of *iki* is *akirame*, a Buddhist concept that means "renunciation", "resignation", and "acceptance".

Forms of postures, gestures and manners are important aspects of aesthetics in Japan. *Kata* means form, and bodily form, for those who are acquainted with martial arts. Daily gestures such as pouring tea, rising up from the floor, closing a door, or bowing are made with an awareness of form. *Iki* can be seen, according to Kuki, in a "bending of the perpendicular line through the center of the body to form a curve".

"It is no coincidence that striped designs are considered *iki*", he continues. Vertical stripes represent light rain. Parallel lines express lightness. Stripes in an umbrella formation, or converging to one point, are not expressing *iki,* according to Kuki: "In order to express *iki,* a design must be visually disinterested and purposeless. Radiating stripes having a center, have achieved their goal". And complex patterns do not represent *iki* either. Patterns containing curves do not normally become a pure expression of *iki*, and representational design, as opposed to geometric design, never characterizes *iki*, according to Kuki.

Iki is expressed in spatiality as well; when it comes to architecture, *iki* is distinctly expressed in a dual relationship to forms or material, not in a plurality of mixed forms. The *sukiya*-style teahouse, which is the simple teahouse in the style of *wabi*, is the best example of *iki* architecture, according to Kuki. It is an intimate room of four and a half *tatami* mats, and invites a contemplative spatiality. The choice of duality in material and form express the *iki* taste, or awareness: in other words, it is a cultural creation, a construction. The creation of a dual contrast in material structures and textures is an expression of *iki*. Kuki guides us to look at the ceiling, which has two different textures, and the floor, which has two different materials, *tatami* and wood. This kind of simple, refined and strict composition are expressions of *iki*. *Iki* taste cannot succumb to complexity; it is simple and dualistic, avoiding curved lines. In pattern design *iki* is expressed through texture and non-figural pattern, and the scale is small.

The genealogy of *iki* derives from the Edo era[20] in the 17th century, and depicts the urban taste of connoisseurs, who visited the pleasure quarters, which were strictly regulated in closed areas. At that time, female artists and entertainers of different social grades worked in these areas. "The floating world" was a subversive subculture, almost totally confined in its own realm, and not accessible for the general population. The highest ranked *geisha*, the *tayu*, in the demi-monde, was a goddess of art and beauty, akin to a non-human creature embodying the essence of *shibumi* and *sabi*. *Tayus* can be compared to the *hetaerae* in ancient Greece – highly educated courtesans, not simple prostitutes. Their lifestyles were like an embodiment of Nietzsche's *amor fati* – a fate that one has to accept, making the most of its potential. They were not depraved women; rather rare artists of the highest rank; musicians, dancers and singers. *Gei-sha* literally means arts person. They embodied a suprasensuous ideal.

Daoism, Confucianism, Shintoism and Buddhism are the main thinking styles that have affected Japanese aesthetics. Metaphysics explores the fundamental nature of reality; life and its existence and relationship with natural laws. This is expressed in the form of "arts of self-cultivation", unique in East Asian art. Arts of self-cultivation in Japan are pottery, calligraphy, *ikebana,* gardening, *Noh* and many kinds of crafts, and also martial arts. The self-cultivation aspect derives from both Buddhism and Shinto, and implies many different ways – *dō* – to go in order to seek enlightenment. It is about the process, not the outcome; the object as a result. This means that the aesthetical value lies not in a product, but its values are higher, perishable and ephemeral. In the West, ethics is detached from aesthetics, ever since the philosopher Immanuel Kant divided ethics from aesthetics, leaving aesthetics today to stand independently. Before Kant, the two were interrelated. Things that were beautiful, it was implied, were also true or good. Today we need to rediscover many aesthetical and ethical interrelationships, but we are in need of another way of talking about aesthetics and ethics, beyond the older paradigms. To explore in what ways aesthetics and ethics are related is a new and important issue.

"Ethics" in this context means not moral dogma, but individual values and a contextualizing of the aesthetic in a broader view than only the field of the arts. This is the main difference between Japanese and Western aesthetics today, regarding the different development of cultural histories. We also have to be reminded that in Japan, there exist two parallel paths of aesthetics: pre-modern Japanese and modernism from the West. Japanese culture is an amalgamation of many different periods of culture, mostly adopted from China's different dynasties, along with some different religions, philosophies, and thinking styles, and recently, Western modernism.

★

Japanese intuitions are notions of powers, and express affects. Japanese intuitive notions are compounds of complex codes, which serve as keys to various aesthetic tastes. However, these tastes are not subjective, but operate as collective aesthetical agreements between people, a confirmation of the relevance of these different kinds of purely existing tastes. Reality is described through multiple sets of sensory moods, tastes or compilations of properties of matter. These differ from each other through careful shifts of nuances, and operate as key words, images of taste, or styles.

The delicate articulated notions of beauty and refinement derive from metaphysics, and deal with profound and complex ethical meanings. We can comprehend this adequately only by practice, and through developing an individual discernibility to sensations. Sharing using language; developing a grammar for aesthetical relationships, becomes a collective communication of aesthetical values concerning life and the art of life. This is a way of practice through whatever art form one is inclined to. Only by immersing oneself with one's body and mind can a transformation take place. The body-mind is the passage. By exploring ways of self-cultivation one is continuously open to change in the thinking and reassessment of one's own life.

1. Richie, Donald, *A Tractate on Japanese Aesthetics*, (Berkeley: Stonebridge Press, 2007), p.25.
2. *The Tale of Genji* is compared with the works of Shakespeare and Proust, and is a great source of inspiration and influence on many other art forms in Japanese culture.
3. *Shinkankaku* [neo-sensualism] is a literary genre, founded by Kawabata, as opposed to the realistic school.
4. *Keys to the Japanese Heart and Soul*, (Kodansha Bilingual Books, 1996), a bilingual collection of articles selected from *Japan: An Illustrated Encyclopedia*, p.29.
5. Ibid. p.31.
6. de Bary, Theodore in *Japanese Aesthetics and Culture*, edited by Nancy G. Hume, (Albany: SUNY Press, 1995) p. 4.
7. "Ōnishi Yoshinori", in *Modern Japanese Aesthetics*, edited by Michel Marra, (University of Hawaii Press, 1999) p.135.
8. *The Flowering Spirit, Classic Teachings on the Art of Noh*, by Zeami, with an introduction by William Scott Wilson, (Kodansha International, 2006).
9. *Keys to the Japanese Heart and Soul*, p.37.
10. Sotaku, Jakuan and Roku, Zen-cha, in Sen Sōshishitsu, ed., Chado Koten Zenshū, vol. 10 (Kyoto: Tankōsha, 1961), pp. 296–97.
11. Ibid.
12. Yamanoue Sōji Ki.
13. *Keys to the Japanese Heart and Soul*, p.35.
14. *Man'yōshū* means "Collection of Ten Thousand Leaves", a compilation of poetry made in 759 AD during the Nara period. The collection contains poems from 347 AD. The word *sabi* is mentioned in a poem by Kawabe no Miyahito (711 AD).
15. *Wabi-Sabi for Artists, Designers, Poets and Philosophers,* pp. 9, 68, 71–72.
16. Ibid., p.62.
17. "The floating world" refers to the urban culture during the Edo era, especially the closed pleasure quarters in Edo (present-day Tokyo).
18. Shūzo, Kuki, *The Structure of Iki,* translated by John Clark (Sydney: Power Publications, 2011), p.13.
19. Ibid., Kuki, p.19.
20. The Edo era began in the Tokugawa shogunate in 1603 and ended in 1868.

Shisen-dō, established as a residence in the 17th century. Today, the villa is a Buddhist temple for the Sōtō Zen sect.

EN – INTERACTING SPACES IN JAPANESE ARCHITECTURE

Kristina Fridh

When I visited the Venice Architecture Biennale in 2016, the theme for the Japanese pavilion was focused on the Japanese term *en* (縁), interpreted from various perspectives of today. *En* denotes interactional, dynamic processes and originates from ancient Buddhism and the law of karma as being the bridge between cause and effect in the process of actions. *En* is also part of Japan today, in everyday life, and is the bond in social relations between people that we meet, unexpectedly or as planned. The text from the introduction of the exhibition told me:

> *En* corresponds to the belief that the world is filled with multitudinous unexpected meetings, or the feeling that we should appreciate those meetings and live together. It is the grace to accept the ongoing flood of encounters and events, no matter how unpredictable they would seem to be.
>   *En* also means 'edge' or 'margin'. It implies an ambiguous boundary that not only surrounds multiple kinds of living spaces but makes them interrelate and interpenetrate. The nature of those *En* boundaries and the resulting interpenetrative areas encourage humans to act and to encounter each other.

The exhibition pointed at the connection of how *en* is used both in contexts of social bonds as well as architectural boundaries, and brings out the positive potential in these encounters, describing "*en* architects" as forming spaces that can make people live in a positive way. In our relations we are dependent on each other, and this reliance is part of the social structure – *en* refers to our bonds and our dynamic interrelations. In architecture, *en* is the link bridging inside and outside, building and landscape, a mutual relationship. This relation is dynamic and continuously changing, connecting and separating spaces, just as the bonds between people are constantly in flux, as we connect and separate from each other.

    These are inspiring thoughts, and make me, in the role of architectural researcher, further reflect on my experiences of space and spatial interrelations in Japan – architecture and buildings not being merely objects, but mental experiences and encounters. *En* is an invisible force, and is part of the mental process in perceiving and conceiving space. One strong architectural encounter I had was with a building designed by the Japanese architect Ito Toyo, a crematorium called Meiso no Mori [Forest of Meditation]. In the building, I could strongly feel and sense *en* in a modern version, translated into today's architecture. There was a bridge between me and the architecture in a staged experience, where I, the surrounding landscape, and the building met in the perception of a white, undulating and hovering cloud.

    I will come back to this experience, but first I want to explore how space is conceived in the Japanese tradition, which will also explain the background and different meanings of *en*.

★

In Japan, space is conceived as a changeable process, as experience in time, and as a subjective perception; that is, space is in a person's mind, and not an external object. *Ma* is one of several characters for space, and sometimes has been explained through *Noh*, traditional Japanese theatre. *Noh* has been called "the art of *ma*" by Komparu Kunio, author of *The Noh Theater – Principles and Perspectives*, as it is often referred to when it comes to this form of theatre. According to Komparu, *ma* could be translated to also mean "spacing", "interval", "gap", "blank", "room", "pause", "rest", "time", "timing", or "opening".[1] *Ma* could then be described as a continuum over space and time, and as courses of events and processes. *Ma* is in our minds and is related to our experiences. In *Noh* theatre, time and space change in the mind of the audience. The actor's mask and costume give a dreamlike impression, and the stage design or decor is simple and not altered. In the story, the actor makes suggestions and indications while the mind has to fill in; it is the audience who have the task of completing the actor's role and changing the scene. The story is transferred into the world of imagination – a connection is evoked with the audience, involving them in the performance.

The character *ma*, in kanji (間), first showed the moon through an open gate, but this was later changed for the character signifying the sun. What is illustrated is an image of a changing, ongoing process connected to the interplay of light and time.

The conception of *ma* originates from the Japanese indigenous religion Shinto. *Ma* was a temporary place where the deities, *kami*, could descend to earth and animate the place they came to with their power and spiritual energy, *ki*. In springtime, the gods could be brought to the village and the rice fields to encourage a good harvest, and in the winter, the gods were sent back to the mountains. These ceremonies of fetching the gods, connected to the cultivation of rice, could be described as ritual renewals of spaces. Similar rituals are still performed in Japan today.[2]

A branch of the sakaki tree could become a temporary abode for the gods, and was installed like a pillar, centred and encircled by four trees or posts, and a rope, *shime-nawa*, with stripes of paper symbolising the rays of the sun. *Ma* is then the empty space where the gods descend, and fill and charge this place, *himorogi*, with their spiritual power. The ground of this place was sometimes covered by gravel, and, as such, contributed to the archetype of the traditional Japanese dry landscape garden, *kare-sansui*, as seen in the well-known garden of the temple Ryōan-ji in Kyoto, where three compositions of stones are grouped on raked gravel.

This tells us that *ma* is not related to physical form, but to a person's experience of space at a particular time. Space is changeable and changing and is not defined by permanent walls. One has to imagine the boundaries of the space, actually temporarily visualised by the rope and the four trees or posts. Space is defined as a field of tension around and in the pillar, symbolised by the branch. The pillar then is central in traditional Japanese architecture.

★

Traditional Japanese architecture is based on open structures and floating spaces between horizontal planes – the floor and the roof, which is held up by the pillars. This reminds us of modern, open beam and post constructions. The open space in between these horizontal planes is not defined by spatial, visual borders, such as walls – but you have to imagine where the boundaries of spaces are. The floating, ambiguous spaces are continuously interacting with the garden and the landscape in an ongoing continuous interplay, where a dynamic balance is taking place. It may not even be clear what is inside or outside – this experience of space is changeable, both in terms of the actual space, and in terms of time.

The transactional, changeable zone between inside and outside is called *en-gawa*, which can be translated to veranda, and *en* is the intermediary link between inside and outside. *En* connects the rooms in the house and the movements between them, as a kind of corridor, and also separates the spaces from each other, and makes it possible to move outside the rooms. In this transactional zone, *en-gawa*, the building can be transformed into other forms through changeable, movable building units, which form vertical layers. The villa Shisen-dō [The Poet's Hermitage] in Kyoto, built in the so-called *sukiya* style, which is characterised by simplicity and unpretentiousness, is a good example where the horizontal planes as well as the *en-gawa* are clearly visible. The borders of space are set through movable modules, space then changes over time – and this is also a way to adapt the building to climate conditions and different seasons.

During the hot and humid summer in Japan you need to open the house to allow air to circulate – at the same time as obtaining shade under the eaves of the roof and protection from strong sunlight. In the winter, you need shelter from cold weather; the house is then closed to the garden. There are also movable units inside, such as *fusuma* – sliding doors, opaque and covered with paper, in order to make the rooms smaller and therefore easier to heat during wintertime.

In his book *From Shinto to Ando*, Günter Nitschke makes these interactional processes between outside and inside clear through defining the vertical layers. He uses two examples from Kyoto, one describing the interaction between the building and the garden, *shake*, and the other between the building and the street, the Japanese town house *machiya*.[3]

The Nishimura Villa, also built in the *sukiya* style, is a so-called *shake*, a dwelling for Shinto priests, and is located close to Kamigamo Shrine in the northern part of Kyoto. These dwellings were built during the Edo period (1600–1868), but the Nishimura Villa was built approximately 100 years ago, although the garden goes back 800 years.

Light and air are transmitted into the Nishimura Villa through the vertical, movable layers. From inside to outside they can be described as first *shoji* – sliding doors with translucent paper as well as wooden lattice work and wood used as filling at the base. The paper is *washi* made from the bark of mulberry trees. The next layer comprises sliding doors of

Top: Shisen-dō. Interacting spaces – view of the garden and the en-gawa.

Bottom: The Nishimura Villa. The movable vertical layers in the en-gawa are visible from inside and out.

glass, which have been added as a climate protection in the 20th century. They sometimes have window bars of wood, and are placed at the far edge of the *en-gawa*. Shutters for protecting the interior from rain, so-called *amado*, are often found, also visible in the next example, the town house *machiya*, and they can be inserted in solid boxes on the sides of the openings, and have slits to facilitate ventilation. To get protection from the sun, there are blinds made of reeds or bamboo, *sudare*, hanging from the eaves of the roof, which form the last layer.

These changeable vertical layers are also found in other types of buildings, both in *minka*, the commoners' houses, and in the architecture of the ruling class, for example, the Imperial Katsura villa in Kyoto.

★

The other example is, as mentioned before, the Japanese town house *machiya*, where there are interacting spaces between the street and the house. The houses are a combination of dwelling places to live and places to work, shops or workshops, and the life in the *machiya* and the town districts is vividly illustrated in 18th and 19th-century woodblock prints, *ukiyo-e*. The examples here are from the Shinbashi-dori neighbourhood, the Gion district in Kyoto.

In the *machiya*, merchants and craftsmen could open up their shops and workshops to the street, the public space, in the morning, and close their business in the evening, in order to get privacy behind the wooden lattice windows. These houses are deep and narrow, and spaces for one's private life are located at the back of the house and on the second floor, where you find the same layers as between the house and garden in the Nishimura Villa. Here you also find *amado*, the shutters that protect from rain.

The *machiya* is continuously interacting and balancing with the street through the intermediary link *en*. The changeable layers between inside and outside are also movable modules, but here they are wooden lattice windows, which let air into the house and create shade during the hot summer period. They also act to prevent people seeing inside, and a little curtain, *noren*, at eye level at the entrance, protects from a direct view from the street. Again, we can say that *en* is both connection and separation. Unfortunately, today you seldom find these houses open to the street.

Light plays an important part. The interplay between the light and shadows on the surfaces of the layers gives the facades changeable

Machiya, the Gion district in Kyoto.

The play of light on the wooden lattice work.
Sudare, blinds made of reeds or bamboo.

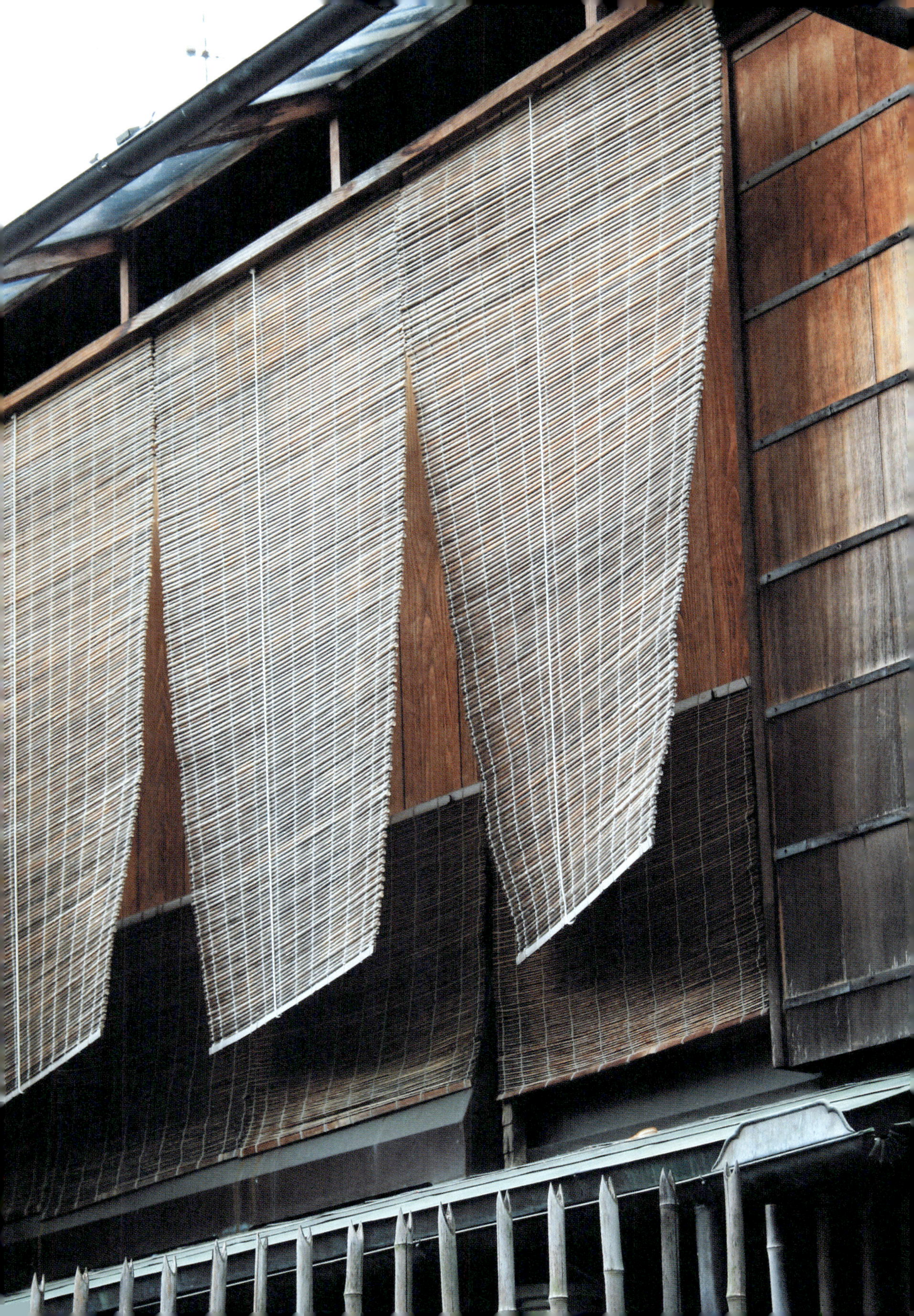

appearances during the course of the day – and the facades also change when you look at them from different angles.

The imperial villa and garden of Katsura in Kyoto was designed in the 17th century, an era when Japanese culture was deeply influenced by Zen Buddhism. Katsura comprises the palace called Katsura Rikyū or the Katsura villa, as well as the garden where teahouses and rest pavilions are found. The garden is described as a garden for strolling or as an extended tea garden, and the buildings were built in the *sukiya* style, the rustic ideals of which were modesty and simplicity and were taken from the folk houses, *minka*, and the peasant culture. The Katsura villa has become an icon for Japanese as well as foreign architects, not least because it visually resembles Western modernism.[4]

However, I would like to focus on how the villa and garden are joined in dynamic interaction – the spaces balancing, inside and outside, in continuous movement. The buildings here are strongly linked to the garden through *en*, and you find the same vertical, movable layers as I have described before, such as *shoji* and *amado*. Katsura, which includes both the buildings and the garden, is built up of different sceneries, like a stage-setting, and the buildings and the pavilions are continuously interacting with the garden creating a processual, changeable experience.

These experiences are based on the movement through the garden, a kind of "movement space", which is the opposite to, for example, the gardens of Versailles, which are based on predetermined, axial perspectives of overall views. To experience Katsura, you have to move around in the buildings and in the garden. From the buildings and pavilions you discover staged sceneries, some of which have literary allusions, for example, *The Tale of Genji*. The movable layers can be arranged to show different views of the garden and, depending on light and shadow, the vertical layers change during the course of the day and the degree of transparency varies. Mental processes are evoked where *en*, as intermediary link in the dynamic balance with the surrounding landscape, has the leading part, and there is focus on the directing and the stage-setting of changeable architectonic experiences. The ongoing, dynamic interaction between the buildings and the garden is a very good example of how space is experienced as a changeable, mental process, and not as a permanent object.

EN – INTERACTING SPACES IN JAPANESE ARCHITECTURE

Let us move on to contemporary architecture and look at some buildings where the vertical layers and the changing facades, interacting with light and shadow, are easily recognisable. In the Bato-machi Hiroshige Museum, for example, you find similarities with the wooden lattice work of the *machiya*. This is a museum mainly based on a collection of drawings and woodblock prints, *ukiyo-e*, by Utagawa (Ando) Hiroshige, and the prints, which are exhibited here, also show ways of creating space in layers, like a collage, where the forms together with the experience of colours create the depth in the picture, unlike using a central perspective construction.

The museum, which was completed in 2000, is one of the early works by the architect Kuma Kengo. A graphic pattern is staged by the play of shadows on the facade, formed by repeated louvres of wood, and their appearance changes during the course of the day. The shifting, partly transparent facade creates the link between inside and outside, *en*, and the interacting, continuously changing process starts where building, human being and landscape interrelate, meeting in a mutual reunion. Kuma is using his method called "particlizing" where the facade, divided into smaller parts – "particles" – with empty spaces in between, is part of a stage-setting, with the play of light creating a changing scenery that the visitor takes part in, and in this mental process becomes one with the architecture – the boundaries are erased, and the building is not experienced as an external object.[5]

In Tokyo, on the avenue Omotesando-dori in Shibuya-ku, the architectural office SANAA designed a store, Dior Omotesando, completed in 2003. Here also, layers are used between inside and outside; one outside envelope made of transparent glass, and an inner layer of curved plastic screens of acrylic with a thin, printed linear pattern, which reflects light. The illusion is of a textile curtain, undulating and changing in character during the course of the day, and the building has another appearance in the evening. The interior is protected from the lively, urban environment outside by the changing, half-transparent layer, but the movements of people inside can still be perceived through the play of shadows on the facade. This is also a stage-setting, with light and material interacting with the urban landscape, which forms the link *en* and evokes mental processes in line with the changing facades.

Another example from contemporary architecture where you strongly experience the intermediary link, *en*, is, as mentioned, Meiso no Mori

Next pages: Facade, Bato-machi Hiroshige Museum designed by the architect Kuma Kengo.

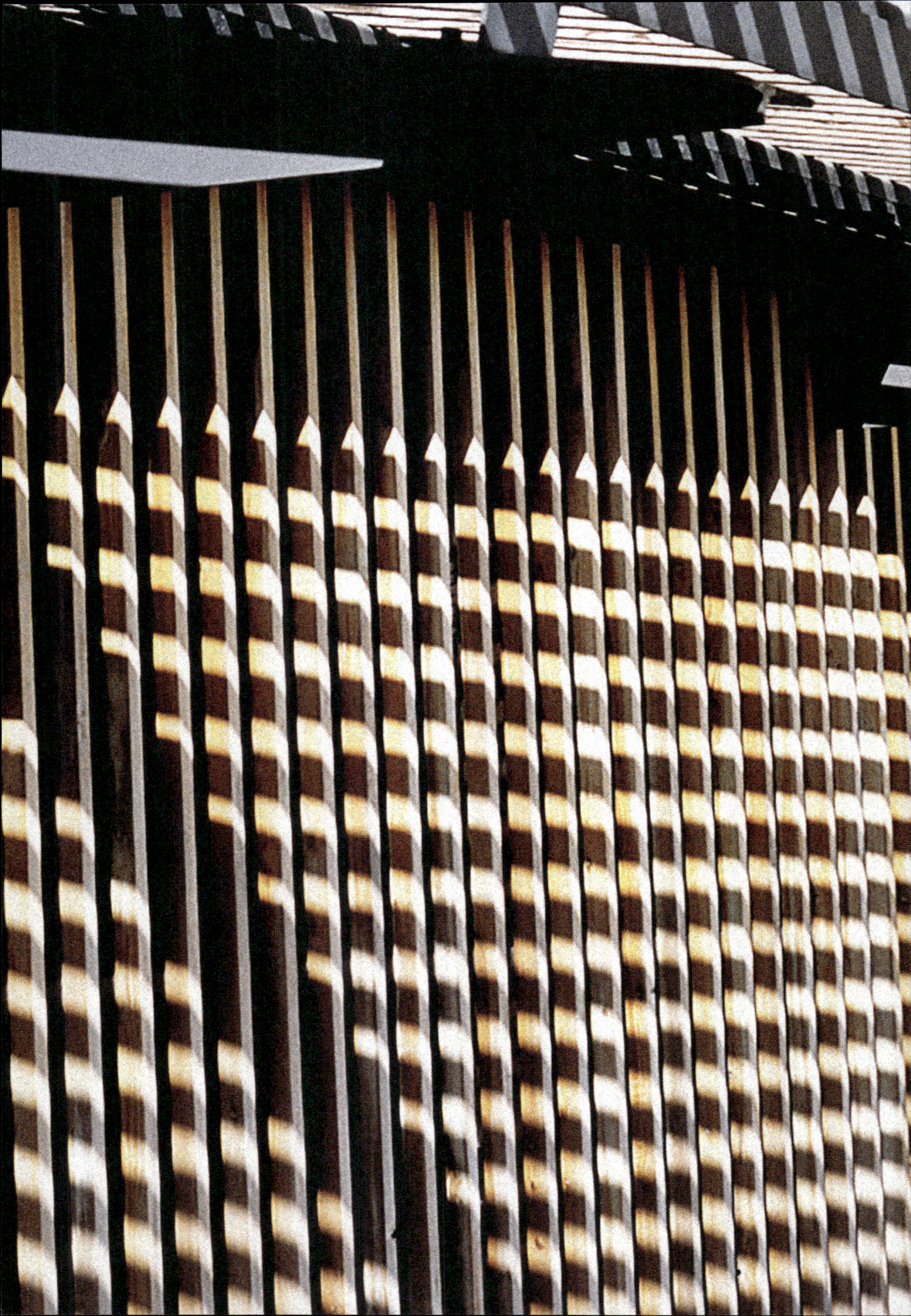

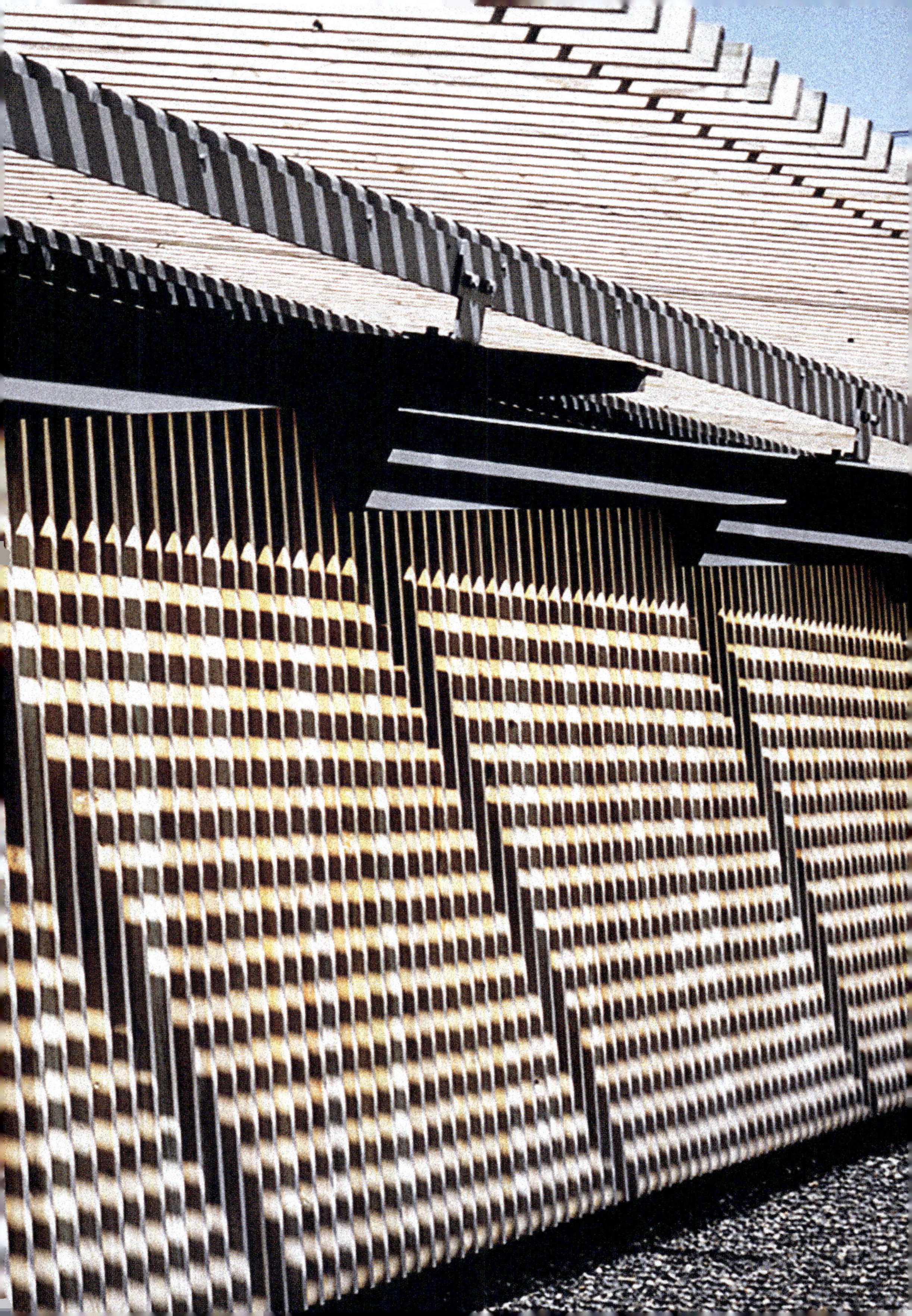

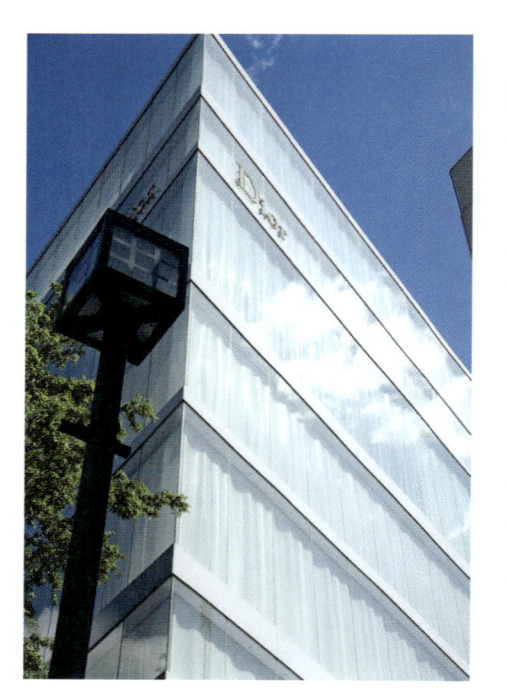

Dior Omotesando by the architectural office SANAA in Shibuya-ku, Tokyo. The building changes appearance in the evening.

Next pages: Meiso no Mori, designed by Toyo Ito & Associates, Architects.

[Forest of Meditation], a municipal funeral hall outside a small village, Kakamigahara, in the Gifu region. The crematorium, completed in 2006, was designed by the architect Ito Toyo. In the building, a white, soft and undulating roof of concrete is supported by curved columns, placed as floating elements, "melting" down to the floor. The columns are not positioned in relation to a rigid, framed grid, but to the organic roof. When you enter, you experience *en* in the spacious entrance hall, that is, in the ambiguous, floating space between horizontal, undulating planes, a space which could be either inside or outside. The space resembles a huge *en-gawa* [veranda] and the scale is bigger than in the traditional examples.

The vertical layers are here transformed into glass and interior screens, interacting and balancing with the landscape and the cemetery outside. The whole building as a volume, with the white undulating roof, is continuously in interplay with its surroundings in a dynamic, balancing flow that the visitor both takes part in and is part of. The interior is waving, and indirect light forms the spaces, and sculpts the building's materials. The play of light on surfaces evokes the sensuous connections to material and materiality, which intensifies the physical experience of the stage-setting in the building.

Outside, a dynamic interplay has been staged with the landscape: the visitor discovers that the whole building is having a conversation with a pond, in which reflections from the white undulating roof can be seen. In the interior, the mirror-like surface of the pond recurs in the glossy materials of stone, whose surfaces reflect the dynamic landscape outside. There is an ongoing organic flow of space between inside and outside, which is strengthened by the rounded floor socles, the columns and the undulating ceiling. The white roof is integrated in the surrounding landscape, the woodland and the mountain scenery, forming a soft, white field that has settled in the dynamic, undulating surroundings. The stated intention is that the roof is white clouds, slowly drifting in the sky, creating a gentle, soft atmosphere at the site.[6] Changing, dynamic interplay is staged, as well as spatial experiences and perceptions of changeability, and a mental process is evoked while the link, *en*, builds bridges between consciousness and matter – building, landscape and human being.

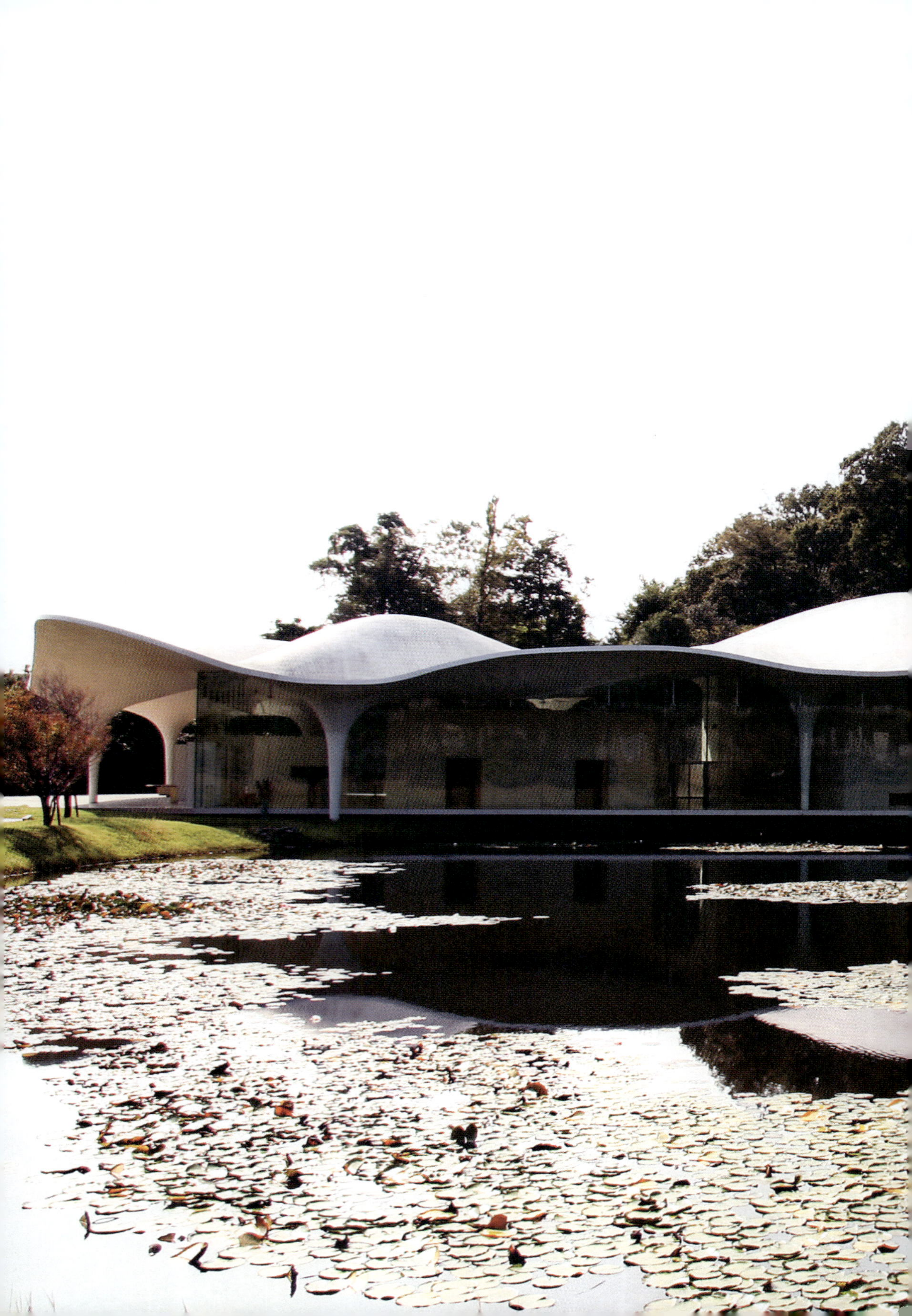

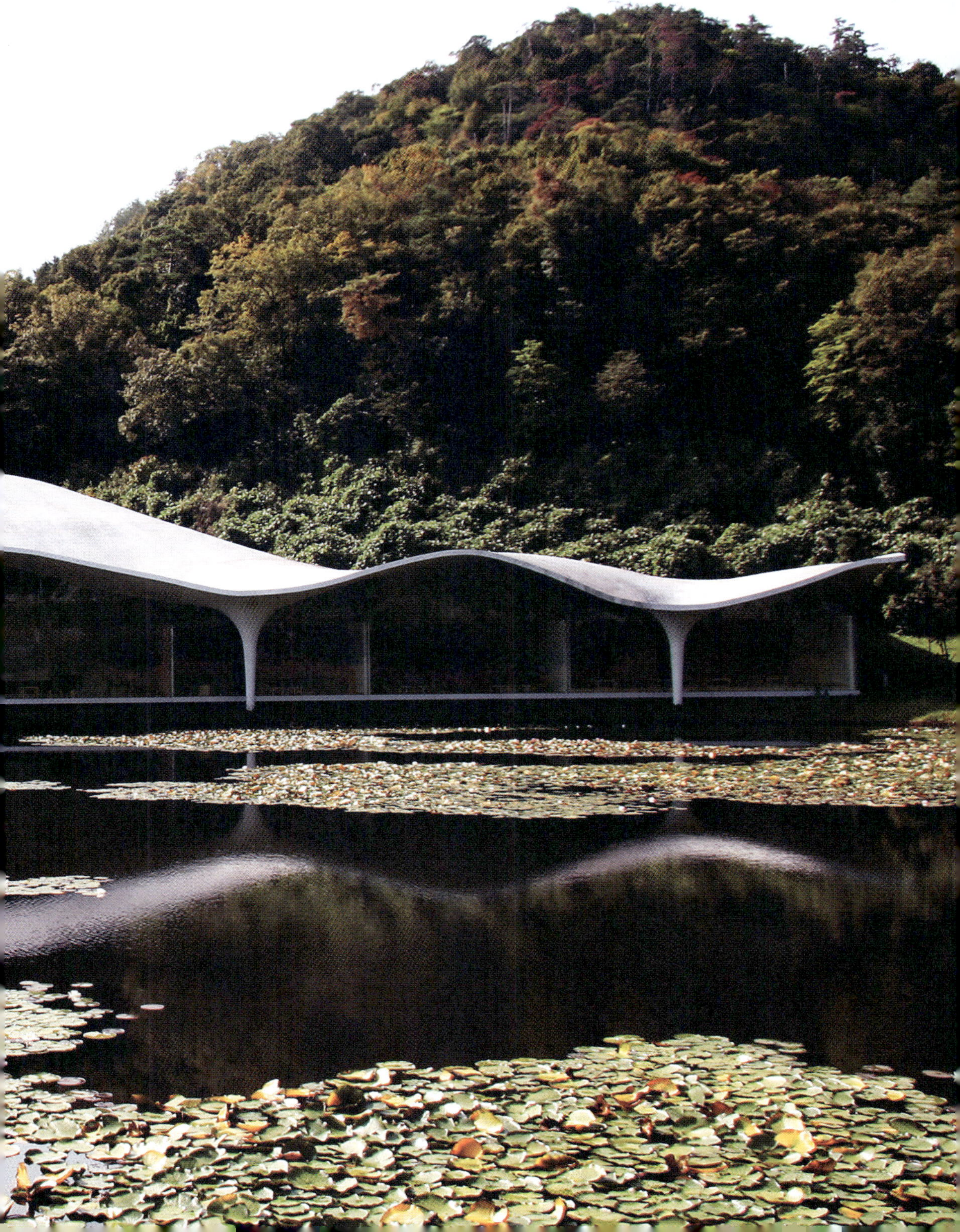

Top: View from the entrance hall. Floating spaces between horizontal, undulating planes interact with the surroundings.

Bottom: The vertical layers, the glass and the interior screens, interact and balance with the landscape outside.

1. Komparu, Kunio, *The Noh Theater. Principles and Perspectives* (New York/Tokyo: Weatherhill/Tankosha, 1983), p.70.
2. Thompson, Fred, "A Comparison between Japanese Exterior Space and Western Common Place", in *Nordic Journal of Architectural Research*, no. 1/2 (1998), 115–136.
3. Nitschke, Günter, *From Shinto to Ando. Studies in Architectural Anthropology in Japan* (London: Academy Editions, 1993), pp. 84–93.
4. Itō, Teiji et al. (ed. Baba, Shozo), *Katsura* (Tokyo: Shinkenchiku-sha, 1991).
5. Kuma, Kengo, *Materials, Structures, Details* (Basel: Birkhäuser, 2004).
6. "Toyo Ito 2005–2009", *El Croquis*, no. 147 (2009), 70–87 (p.72).

For the original source for "The Forest of Meditation", see Fridh, Kristina, "From Japanese Tradition towards New Subjectivity in the Architecture of Kengo Kuma and Toyo Ito", in *arq: Architectural Research Quarterly*, Vol. 21, no. 2 (2017), 113–130.

Tadao Ando, Ando Museum, Naoshima.

EVOKING IHYOU

Blaine Brownell

Japanese architecture has captivated the imagination of the Western world since the latter half of the 19th century, when the Meiji era ended centuries of isolationism and Japan became a willing participant on the world stage. After the initiation of the Meiji Restoration in 1868, Japan's ensuing rush to modernise, and to a great extent Westernise, led to radical changes in approaches to architectural design and construction. The following decades brought about a tumultuous and far-reaching transformation in Japan's built environment in which the destructive forces of modernisation, major seismic disasters such as the Great Kanto earthquake of 1923, and finally the massive devastation from World War II led to extensive rebuilding. Throughout the 20th century, much of what replaced traditional Japanese structures represented a copy of Western designs, from prewar European-style municipal buildings to the postmodern edifices of the 1980s.

However, with the approach of a new millennium, Japanese architects began to chart a new course for their craft. Radically contemporary and increasingly independent from Western styles and methods, Japanese architecture has once again found its identity. In many respects, this new quality represents a compelling future for architects worldwide, as evidenced by the fact that, since 2010, half of the architects to win the Pritzker Prize – the highest honour for architects internationally – have been Japanese.[1] Although contemporary Japanese architecture can often be identified due to its attention to material craft, conceptual purity, and spatial resourcefulness, no particular or overarching style guides its development. Nevertheless, there is a singular quality that pervades these works – a fundamental aspect that is as omnipresent as it is curious – which is the element of surprise.

In Japanese, one word for surprise is *ihyou* (pronounced "ee-hyoh"), which means something unexpected. This nuance is important for a term that guides contemporary Japanese design, which rarely seems gratuitous or shocking. Rather, surprise, in this case, refers to the subtle yet powerful manipulation of expectations in the mind of the beholder. By raising the user's consciousness and inviting interrogation, today's Japanese designs leave an indelible impression. There are various methods employed to achieve this phenomenon regardless of a building's size, programme, or construction type. In this essay, I will describe three fundamental approaches for *ihyou*, named after what Japanese architects aim to express in each case: impossibility, incongruity, and totality.

★

Impossibility might seem an odd aspiration for architecture, but this is just what some of the most influential Japanese architects today aim to embody in their work. The impossible is that which defies natural physical laws. Walls that appear to float, materials that seem incomprehensibly thin, or entire sections of building that are devoid of visible load-carrying structure are all manifestations of impossibility.

"I have a deep interest in what is fictional," says architect Kengo Kuma. "What I like is when something real is hovering just a little bit".[2] Kuma bases his pursuit of impossible architectural strategies on the desire to awaken the user's consciousness, and this connection between awareness and reality defines his work. When asked why reality is somehow authenticated by the unreal, he responds: "If it is a little unreal, there is a little bit of a surprise. If there is no surprise with something, it is not real, because it goes unnoticed".[3]

One of the architectural champions of the unreal is Tadao Ando. Many of his admirers appreciate his attention to the interplay between light and shadow, the thoughtful assembly of platonic volumes, and the relentless drive towards material perfection. An equally important, although little discussed, objective in many of his works is the apparent defiance of natural laws. Specifically, Ando incorporates details that intentionally express an uncanny lightness, as if gravity is not a governing force. This seeming implausibility is enhanced by the heaviness of a predominant material language of reinforced concrete.

One example can be seen in Ando's Chichu Art Museum in Naoshima, Japan. This "art museum in the earth", as its name translates from the Japanese, is built underground, with a series of courtyards and skylights designed to bring daylight in from above. These spaces are defined by

Ando's signature architectural "fair faced" concrete, which serves dual functions of façade and structure – including retaining the large mass of earth above the museum. In one three-storey tall courtyard, Ando designed an uninterrupted diagonal slit on an otherwise solid wall that frames two sides of the volume. This narrow void cuts across the surface, notably continuous at the corner, and no columns or other vertical supports are visible. This strategy is a clear expression of "gravitational escapism" on Ando's part – as if the architect is daring visitors to imagine a weightless earth.

Another example may be seen in the Ando Museum. Located on the east side of the same island, this is a gallery of the architect's own work. A small subterranean chamber is illuminated solely by natural daylight that enters via a conical skylight above. The skylight itself is not visible from within this room, however, for the ceiling consists of an expansive concrete disc. Sunlight reaches the space around the perimeter of the disc, creating an optical effect akin to a solar eclipse. The viewer gradually becomes aware of that which is absent: an indication of structure. If the ring of light – which emanates from a single, central source – is uninterrupted, where are the shadows cast by the disc's supports? In short, how does this heavy slab seemingly hover in mid-air, without any physical attachment?

As indicated above, Kengo Kuma is similarly enamoured with the subversion of physical laws in architecture. In the 1990s, at an early phase of his career, Kuma became focused on the development of material details as a way to celebrate the refinement of craft while also critiquing standard practices. His obsession with bringing natural light indoors led him to declare his wish to "erase" architecture, not in the sense of razing buildings but in dematerialising facades. A conceptual approach based on so-called "particles" of light motivated the design of porous, light-transmitting skins in a variety of materials. Like Ando, Kuma's material selections often amplify a sense of the unreal.

A case in point is the Lotus House located in a remote, mountainous region of eastern Japan. The linear structure, which flanks a lotus pond, is clad in a chequerboard facade of small panels. At first glance, the materiality is not evident, and in broad daylight appears to be a surface of white and black tiles. On close inspection, however, the dark tiles are revealed as voids in between the white tiles which, because of their incredible thinness, belie any sense of physical depth. Are these made of a stretched

Tadao Ando, Chichu Art Museum, Naoshima, 2004.

textile or paper, perhaps? No, they are composed of stone! The wall surfaces were conceived "as countless holes", the architect explains. "I have wished to create light walls that the wind would sweep through, using the massive material that is the stone".[4] This impossibly thin detail is composed of 30mm thick travertine sheets suspended from barely visible 18 × 6 mm flat bars of stainless steel. For a material that has historically been employed because of its sturdy, load-bearing capabilities, its use as an ephemeral curtain here is startling.

The agility with which Kuma and Ando approach concepts of solid and void in architecture is connected to a deeper understanding of traditional Japanese architectural principles. Western architecture is largely defined by walls and windows – also known as "punched openings", as if literally punched out of the wall. The frame that results creates a static boundary between subject and object. In contrast, the predominant framing elements in Japanese architecture are the floor and ceiling, not the wall. As a result, the subject and object commingle in a single space, despite the fact that the interior portion is protected from the elements. "In such a case, the main concern of planning is the introduction of a sequence and speed into a continuous space", claims Kuma. "One cannot help but introduce into the building the parameter of time as well as the parameter of space. As a result, space takes on the character of a dynamic image, and space and time become inextricably entwined".[5]

The aperture thus enables a significant function in Japanese architecture that is distinct from its role in the Western tradition: it is a spatial connector. Architects Takaharu and Yui Tezuka embrace this capacity of the aperture as a defining element of their work. Their projects seek to eradicate conventional boundaries between inside and outside, as evident in the names of buildings like House to Catch the Sky and Temple to Catch the Forest. In their Echigo-Matsunoyama Natural Science Museum, for example, the architects designed one aperture out of an immense sheet of submarine-grade acrylic capable of withstanding the loads from the heavy snowpack that the region regularly experiences.

Whenever possible, they seek to make the aperture operable. Entire sides of their buildings can slide away, creating a continuous space between interior and exterior. In their Wall-Less House, for example, three sides of a rectangular building can be made completely open, from floor to ceiling, as retractable windows slide into a core wall on one side. In a contemporary manifestation of traditional Japanese design, walls are truly transitory. Even the columns that keep the upper floors from collapsing are barely visible. According to Takaharu Tezuka "... we always feel that to open a window has a stronger meaning, and makes better architecture. And so I think our projects are really dependent on the window. The window must be open".[6]

★

Most buildings today are surprisingly predictable. Through the standardisation and homogenisation of the constructed environment, we have come to anticipate many building cues without being conscious of this expectation. We regularly look for tell-tale signs of an edifice's use, floor locations, structural load paths, entrances, circulation sequences, and material logics without an awareness of this ongoing analysis.

Thus, another approach pertains to the development of intentionally incongruous means of expression in the built environment. Incongruity refers to something that is out of harmony with its context or out of keeping with conventional practices. One way Japanese architects achieve this result is by questioning everything: materials, construction techniques, programme, spatial configuration, massing, and so on. Tezuka Architects identify technology as a fertile area for interrogation: "... we think that technology is the key to expanding the boundaries of architecture", says Takaharu Tezuka. "Otherwise, if one always sticks to the same parameters, one can expect the same results".[7]

One way architect Toyo Ito commonly achieves the unexpected is by undermining preconceptions of structural behaviour. For lay audiences, the results are not impossible so much as nonsensical. For example, a series of Ito's works focuses on the use of diagrids, or diagonally framed structures. Buildings that eschew vertical columns are rare; however, Ito's unusual approaches, which incorporate irregular spacing and member sizes, set his projects even farther apart from conventional practice.

Ito's temporary 2002 Serpentine Pavilion in London, designed in collaboration with engineer Cecil Balmond, was a single-volume building whose facade and structure were completely integrated. Conceived as the manifestation of a series of intersecting lines placed at different angles, the resulting envelope – composed of an intricate pattern of trapezoidal and triangular shapes – readily accommodated the binary functions of transparency and solidity. All structural loads were conveyed through

Toyo Ito, Mikimoto Ginza 2, Tokyo, 2005.

this interdependent frame, without the separate vertical columns that would be a standard feature. The memorable result received many accolades, with *The Guardian* architecture critic Jonathan Glancey calling it "one of the most exquisite and revolutionary buildings of recent times".[8]

Ito's design for a stand-alone store for Tod's in Tokyo in 2004 continued this structural approach, in this case utilising an irregular diagrid of reinforced concrete reminiscent of the Zelkova trees lining Omotesando Avenue. In 2005, construction was completed on the architect's Mikimoto 2 store in Ginza, a nine-storey rectangular building exhibiting yet another investigation of this concept. In the case of Mikimoto 2, Ito treated the facade as a structural tube composed of two layers of plate steel with concrete poured in-between. Like the other projects, the building is otherwise column-free. By softening the edges of the apertures with rounded corners, Ito further disguised the presence of an internal diagrid. The finished project is visually striking due to its departure from several norms of high-rise construction: there are no continuous vertical load pathways, the solidity of the corners is repeatedly violated, there are no discernible floor lines in the solid portions of the envelope, and there are no perceivable construction joints that indicate boundaries between individual steel plates. Together, the absence of these common visual cues of structure and construction results in an extremely curious, and unforgettable, edifice.

Other methods of achieving incongruity focus on the smaller scale of material details. Architect Jun Aoki approaches material applications as the fundamental means to undermine traditional expectations in buildings. His Aomori Museum of Art employs two primary material languages: brown earthen construction that rises from the ground and white volumes that descend from the sky. In the latter case, Aoki uses brick in a highly unconventional way. The brick wraps all surfaces, including the undersides of cantilevered volumes – something one never sees except in the case of vault structures, which are not present here. Upon closer inspection, the visitor realises that the soffit bricks are not dimensional modules but thin sheets applied like ceramic tiles. Although the effect is subtle, particularly given that the surface is painted a homogeneous white colour, the use of brick (as opposed to stucco) lends an uncanny quality to the hovering masses.

"A material is perceived according to a code – a social code. And so we can manipulate the code itself", says Aoki. "This is a very interesting idea

Jun Aoki, Aomori Museum of Art,
Aomori, 2006.

for us. If we make a new kind of code through the realisation of our architecture, the people's code will transform accordingly. The material will therefore be recoded".[9] This reconceptualisation can be seen in his Louis Vuitton Ginza Namiki store in Tokyo. Aoki sought to create a facade of engineered stone that would convey an unanticipated lightness. The final design employs glass-fibre reinforced concrete panels that incorporate inset pieces of translucent marble. The concrete and marble are similar in colour and finish, so the facade appears homogeneous during the daytime. However, at night the interior lighting glows through the stone, revealing a previously undetected visual porosity. The architect conceives such material details as experiential transformations. Discussing a similar integration of fibre optics and limestone in the Louis Vuitton Roppongi interior, he says "...you might be held in suspense by the question of whether it is a stone or an image; however, it is actually not a stone, nor an image. It is just a transition".[10]

Incongruity is also attained by rethinking the relationship between a building's programme and its physical form. This connection is a fertile territory for reimagination precisely because it has become so predictable. We can look at the Grace Farms designed by SANAA in New Canaan, Connecticut as one example of this reconceptualisation. The project's programme consists of a variety of different uses including an auditorium, cafe, library, and gymnasium, all set within a rolling landscape. The typical approach would be to create several small independent structures, each with its own grade level – similar to Philip Johnson's estate located in the same town. However, SANAA decided to create a single structure that unites the disparate activities under one roof. The building assumes a serpentine form that traces the ridges of the landscape like a river, its open colonnades providing views of the surrounding forests beyond. According to urbanist Sam Holleran, the unexpected manifestation is akin to "an ant farm – channeling through the earth, popping up from below, and dropping down into the folds of hillside".[11]

Ryue Nishizawa, one of the two principals of SANAA, adopted the opposite strategy in the design of a house for Yasuo Moriyama in Tokyo. In this case, the standard approach for a residence in a suburban block would be to create a single detached structure. However, Nishizawa created a series of standalone structures, one for each activity, with a network of exterior spaces in-between. These structures include private spaces for the client as well as rental units for on-site tenants. "In this house, the

SANAA, Grace Farms, New Canaan, Connecticut, 2015.

Kengo Kuma, Sunny Hills Minami-Aoyama, Tokyo, 2013.

client is given the freedom to decide which part of this cluster of rooms is to be used as a residence or as rental rooms", states Nishizawa. "He may switch among the series of living and dining rooms or use several rooms at a time according to the season or other circumstances. The domain of the residence changes after his own life".[12]

★

One of the most effective means of making an indelible impression is to treat architecture as a totalising experience. This goal is attained by maximising architecture's signal-to-noise ratio, which is to say by emphasising meaningful material and spatial cues, while minimising superfluous aspects of design and construction. This strategy entails reducing the material palette to as few products and systems as feasible, while hiding or eliminating extraneous elements. In this way, architects maximise the experiential stories conveyed by their projects.

A common theme in contemporary Japanese architecture pertains to the aggregation of many similar material units. Both Kuma and Aoki are well-known for this approach. Kuma's Sunny Hills store in Tokyo, for example, is a veritable cloud of timber slats that constitutes a kind of thickened, borderless facade. Inspired by the construction of bamboo baskets, the thin wooden members form a micro-diagrid that is several layers deep. The timber thicket is also reminiscent of a congested forest through which dappled sunlight enters during the day. Another noteworthy project is Kuma's Folk Art Museum at the China Academy of Arts in Hangzhou, China. Designed as a set of terraced volumes set against the hillside, the museum features a facade that blends with its tiled roofs. Just outside floor-to-ceiling glass walls, thousands of repurposed roof tiles are suspended with stainless steel cables. The result is a field of hovering ceramic elements that not only bring shade to interior spaces, but also visually connect with the building's predominant roof material.

Jun Aoki's White Chapel in Osaka takes a similar approach to creating a multilayered envelope. In this case, the facade is composed of steel rings assembled to form truncated tetrahedrons. The rings' different angles cast intricate patterns of shadows against white interior curtains, diffusing direct sunlight while generating visual interest. The facade of Aoki's Louis Vuitton store in Roppongi Hills has a similar circle motif, but in this case, the architect uses glass tubes instead of steel rings. Specifically, nearly 30,000 10cm-diameter clear glass cylinders are encapsulated between two plates of glass to create a facade that is over 30cm deep. Despite the transparency of all the glass used, this layered composition amplifies reflected light to create a shimmering field of optical distortions.

In addition to material refinement, a related and characteristically Japanese approach to creating an immersive experience is to unite a building's interior with its exterior. Like Kuma's discussion of the window above, bridging indoor and outdoor spaces creates continuity and establishes a more dynamic condition than that of a fixed window frame. For example, SANAA's Glass Pavilion at the Toledo Museum of Art is a single-storey gallery (with additional subterranean spaces) that is composed primarily of floor-to-ceiling glass walls sandwiched between the roof and ground planes. The tall panels of low-reflectivity glazing emphasise the visual connections between the building and its lush site.

The Glass Pavilion is an example of literal continuity; however, Japanese architects also design figurative connections between architecture and landscape. For example, the same firm's Rolex Learning Center at the Ecole Polytechnique Fédérale de Lausanne in Switzerland functions more as a site than a building. Its expansive floor plate undulates extensively in sections, creating a sheltered field of artificially rolling terrain. Junya Ishigami's KAIT Workshop at the Kanagawa Institute of Technology houses a single, rectilinear volume of space surrounded by glass. The roof is supported by over 300 thin steel columns that vary in spacing and orientation. In this case, the floor is entirely level, but the number and placement of the columns impart the feeling of a forest. By varying the density of the columns, Ishigami was able to suggest spatial hierarchies and different functional uses without building physical walls. Another project makes both literal and figurative connections: Sou Fujimoto's Naoshima Pavilion is a visually permeable structure composed of triangulated steel mesh panels. The porosity of the single-volume folly enhances relationships with its context; meanwhile, the mesh panels also form an artificial topography near the base, inviting visitors to climb the constructed ground plane.

A related totalising strategy seeks minimalism in the extreme. When visual noise is eliminated, the visitor's sensory impact is maximised. Artist and designer Tokujin Yoshioka understands the potency of rarified material experiences. His installations and structures are often inspired

SANAA, Glass Pavilion at the Toledo Museum of
Art, Toledo, Ohio, 2006.

by ephemeral natural phenomena that he seeks to capture in inert physical form. For example, his Lexus L-Finesse exhibition at the Museo Della Permanente in Milan consisted of 700km-worth of transparent fibres that were suspended from the ceiling in a white room. The density of the fibres, which barely touched the floor, conjured up the sense of a thick fog. Artist Shinji Ohmaki's Liminal Air installations are similar works, although the fibres are hung at different heights to suggest a topographic surface underneath the dense material.

Ryue Nishizawa's Teshima Art Museum, which he designed in collaboration with artist Rei Naito, is an exemplary work of totalising experience. Located on Teshima Island, the gallery is a single volume of space contained within an oblong, flattened dome structure. The roof consists of a 25cm-thick structural shell of white concrete and is punctured by two oculi – both open to the air – and one at each end. The absence of columns and lack of control joints, form ties, or other signs of construction give the impression that the roof is impossibly light. What is even stranger is the floor: water slowly percolates up from nearly invisible holes in the jointless concrete. Over time, as the water gradually beads up on the hydrophobic concrete surface, it gathers with nearby droplets, and small rivulets run down imperceptible slopes into an undetectable drain. As visitors sit quietly within the large, resonant chamber, they become conscious of the slow passage of time – focusing on the movement of water, the soft shuffle of feet, and the birdsong that enters through the open portals.

★

The three strategies of impossibility, incongruity, and totality all seek to induce a state of *ihyou* in audiences by generating novel experiences. Obviously, novelty is a relative state defined by some departure from ordinary circumstances. According to Japanese designer Kenya Hara, the key to understanding a baseline condition is to gain an appreciation for the sum of experiences and habits each individual has formed related to the built environment. The designer can then manipulate fundamental aspects of this set of experiences. "A designer creates an architecture of information within the mind of the recipient of his work", states Hara.[13]

The approaches employed by contemporary Japanese architects to evoke surprise relate to theories of cognitive science. Philosopher Ludwig Wittgenstein argued that much of visual perception is "half visual experience, half thought".[14] In the article "Imagination and Perception", philosopher P.F. Strawson discusses Wittgenstein's scrutiny of the viewer's moment of surprise: "He is particularly impressed by the case where they [visual contents] undergo a change of aspects under one's very eyes, as it were, the case where one is suddenly struck by a new aspect", he writes.[15] This *ihyou* phenomenon is enhanced when approached with sophistication and nuance. "I always try to convey the surprising moments of my designs with a degree of subtlety," says designer Oki Sato of Nendo. "Large surprises are quite easy, like saying 'Boo!' I'd like to make the surprises as small as possible, in order to enhance the process of discovery".[16]

In short, *ihyou* is about making the common uncommon. By manipulating the everyday fabric of experience, today's Japanese architects recalibrate their audiences' expectations of what is possible within the built environment. At the same time, they infuse the user's daily activities with delight, intrigue, and even awe. In the best cases, the work blurs distinctions between what is real and what is fictional. "Experiencing [new buildings in Japan] is a process of suspending architecture in a perpetually evanescent and temporary state of 'in-between' where becoming and fading away, growth and decay, presence and absence, reality and fiction, silence and speech take place simultaneously – or perhaps are one and the same thing", writes architectural historian Botond Bognar. "It is in this sense that many of these designs evoke the images of elusive phenomena, of twilight, shadows, clouds, or mirage, and gain a certain ephemeral or fictive quality".[17]

1. Since 2010, the following Japanese architects have received the Pritzker Architecture Prize: Kazuyo Sejima and Ryue Nishizawa (2010), Toyo Ito (2013), and Shigeru Ban (2014).
2. Kengo Kuma quoted in Brownell, Blaine, *Matter in the Floating World: Conversations with Leading Japanese Architects and Designers,* (New York: Princeton Architectural Press, 2011), p.42.
3. Ibid.
4. Kuma, Kengo "Lotus House," June 2005, https://kkaa.co.jp/works/architecture/lotus-house
5. Kuma, Kengo "Particle on Horizontal Plane" in *The Japan Architect* 38 (Summer 2000): 120.
6. Takaharu Tezuka quoted in Brownell, Blaine, *Matter in the Floating World*, p.32.
7. Ibid., p.28.
8. Glancey, Jonathan, "They said it couldn't be done", *The Guardian* (July 23, 2007).
9. Jun Aoki quoted in *Matter in the Floating World*, p.158.
10. Ibid., p.150.
11. Holleran, Sam, "Estate of Grace: Confronting Privilege and Possibility at SANAA's Grace Farms," *The Avery Review* (February 2016).
12. Nishizawa, Ryue, "SANAA (Sejima + Nishizawa) 1998–2004," *El Croquis* 121/122 (2004).
13. Hara, Kenya, *Designing Design,* (Baden, Switzerland: Lars Müller Publishers, 2007), p.156.
14. Reboul, Anne, *Mind, Values, and Metaphysics,* Volume 2 (New York: Springer, 2014), p.11.
15. Strawson, P. F., "Imagination and Perception", in Lawrence Foster, Joe Swanson, (eds.), *Experience and Theory*, (Amherst: University of Massachusetts Press, 1970).
16. Oki Sato quoted in *Matter in the Floating World*, p.67.
17. Bognar, Botond, *The New Japanese Architecture,* (New York: Rizzoli, 1990), p.21.

JAPAN'S CHRISTIAN CENTURY AND THE KAKURE KIRISHITAN

Great Genna Martyrdom of Nagasaki (1622).

EARLY JESUIT ENCOUNTERS WITH 'WARRING STATES' JAPAN

M. Antoni J. Ucerler, S.J.

In this short essay, I shall endeavour to provide a historical sketch of the early encounters of the Japanese in Japan with members of the Society of Jesus, a Roman Catholic religious order of men founded in 1540 to propagate the Christian faith. The founding of the Jesuits, as members of the Society of Jesus are referred to, overlapped with a momentous period in world history. This was the era of European maritime exploration and expansion around the globe. It could, in fact, be referred to as the first great 'age of globalisation' – for better and for worse. It was also an era when Christian missionaries embarked on missionary enterprises on multiple continents, from Mexico, Colombia, and Paraguay to India and Indonesia, from the Malay Peninsula to Macau in China, and further east to Yamaguchi, Kyoto, and Nagasaki in Japan.

Each of these countries and cultures presented unique challenges for the missionaries who arrived on their shores. Japan, the furthest missionary 'outpost' of the European Jesuits, was a unique civilisation, with a complex language and culture that did not easily lend itself to mastery, or even initial comprehension. What then were some of the cultural and religious issues that the missionaries and their Japanese interlocutors faced when they first encountered each other? Before answering this question, we need to clarify how Europeans first learned about the existence of Japan.

Our story begins with Marco Polo's journeys overland across the Silk Road to the court of the Mongols in the 13th century. In his famous diaries, which were dictated sometime between 1295 and 1298, we find a curious reference to a land that we now know represents the Japanese archipelago. In subsequent editions of the early illuminated manuscripts, which were produced in the Republic of Venice not long after the invention of the Gutenberg handpress, there are references to 'Zipangu' or 'Cyampagu', i.e. to a fabled group of islands lying to the east of the Chinese empire. Polo heard reports of such isles full of silver and gold, but he was never able to reach them.

Europeans thus continued to be ignorant of the exact location of Japan for another 250 years, until finally one day in 1543, a group of Portuguese vessels sailing in the South China Sea were blown off course by a storm, and unexpectedly landed on the shores of Tanegashima, a small island off the southern tip of Kyushu. The Portuguese had begun exploring the western coast of Africa in the early 15th century. By the 1480s, they finally succeeded in rounding the 'Cape of Storms', known today as the Cape of Good Hope, a treacherous sea route through the currents where the Atlantic and Indian Oceans come together over razor-sharp jagged rocks not far below the surface.

As they continued their explorations along the eastern coast of Africa, they established several safe ports, including the strategically located Mozambique Island, where they could winter and wait for the winds that would allow them to sail farther east. This eventually led to the conquest of Goa in 1510 and of Malacca the following year. With these footholds secured, the passage was open to the South China Sea. The lease of Macau along the Pearl River Delta in 1557 from the Ming court made it possible for the Portuguese to act as intermediaries in the trade between China and Japan. In fact, the Europeans quickly developed a thriving market in silk and other rare and coveted commodities, including spices and porcelain. The Portuguese were quick to take advantage of the official ban on Japanese vessels sailing into Chinese ports. The Ming coastguard was trying to prevent the frequent raids carried out by the *wakō*, a group of Japanese pirates, who were often working hand-in-hand with Chinese shipmen looking to make a quick profit.

Japan was thus integrated into the international hub of trading outposts of the so-called East Indies under the system of Royal Patronage [*Padroado Real*] of the Portuguese court in Lisbon. This sphere of influence included places and cultures as diverse and distant from each other as Mozambique, Goa, Malacca (Melaka), Macau, and Nagasaki.

These commercial and diplomatic developments set the scene for the arrival in Japan of Francis Xavier (1506–52), one of the founders, together with Ignatius of Loyola, of the Society of Jesus. Having landed in Kagoshima on August 15, 1549, he soon set about establishing the first Christian communities in that country. He accomplished this despite the immense difficulties of communication and the dangers that came with

Japanese painting of St. Francis Xavier.

arriving in a country of sixty-six kingdoms governed by rival samurai engaged in war with each other. After he had secured permission from several local warlords to preach his faith, he was able to spend approximately two years in the country. With his activities in India, the Malay Peninsula, and Indonesia, Xavier soon became the idealised prototype of the Roman Catholic missionary who captured the imagination of his fellow Europeans and inspired them to follow in his footsteps. This was reflected in the many works of art that represented his life and the books that were written about his endeavours. The latter were printed in numerous editions and in a variety of languages all across Europe, from Lisbon to Paris and from Rome to Augsburg.

One curious volume, which recounts the story of the Japanese martyrdoms of 1622, printed in Polish in Poznań in 1625, includes a unique engraving of Xavier as a pilgrim carrying a staff and a rucksack. The inscription in Polish and Latin, reads as follows: '*S. Franciszek Xawier–Societatis Iesu–do Japoniejęsię pieszo wyprawujący*' [St. Francis Xavier, of the Society of Jesus, setting off on foot to Japan]. This image is symbolic rather than literal, for it expressed the idea of the Christian mission as an urgent pilgrimage to the ends of the known world. This ideal would inspire generations of Jesuits as well as other religious orders of Catholic Europe to make their way to Japan.

What specific role did the Jesuits play in these encounters with the civilisations of East Asia in the aftermath of Xavier's foundation of Christian communities in that part of the world? And what did they hope to accomplish, as they left Europe thousands of miles behind them, many never to return to their native shores? Their peculiar approach to other cultures becomes evident from the way they came to understand the Jesuit missionary enterprise (or *empresa*, as they often referred to it in Spanish and Portuguese) and the means they employed to introduce Christianity to an ancient civilisation that had very different religious traditions and cultural norms.

The most influential among Xavier's successors was an Italian nobleman by the name of Alessandro Valignano, who arrived in Japan in 1579, after having first spent several years in India and the Portuguese enclave of Macau. Valignano had been appointed 'Visitor', i.e. delegate, of the Jesuit Superior General in Rome, Everard Mercurian (1514–80), to all the missions of the East Indies. This gave him the authority to formulate a new policy of 'cultural accommodation'. This approach differed greatly from the European model of conquest in the Americas, where the sword and the cross arrived together on the same ship, and often worked in tandem to further the colonial interests of the Portuguese and Spanish. But how and why did he come to conclude that missionaries needed to adapt, rather than try to impose their own ways upon the people of Japan?

In a letter penned in 1595 to Claudio Acquaviva (1543–1615), the Jesuit superior general who succeeded Mercurian, Valignano reflects upon his more than 20 years of experience in Asia. He recounts in detail what he had been told soon after his arrival in Japan by Ōtomo Sōrin (1530–87), a Japanese *daimyō* [lord] who was known as Don Francisco, or King Francisco after his baptism. This powerful warlord of the kingdom of Bungo in eastern Kyushu had met Francis Xavier two decades earlier, and in the 1580s became the Jesuits' great benefactor and protector.

During their lively conversations Sōrin and several other Japanese Christian samurai, including Arima Harunobu (1567–1612) and Ōmura Sumitada (1533–87), had told Valignano in no uncertain terms that the Jesuits had to learn to understand and respect Japanese customs. Valignano reports the following about their conversations:

> Lord Francisco of Bungo [...] told me that if we wanted to attempt to convert Japan, we would have to master the language and live according to [Japanese] norms of civility (*policía*). Moreover, [he noted that] it could only be taken as a sign of diminished intelligence to imagine that a handful of foreigners could possibly induce the samurai and their lords to abandon their own time-honored customs and civilized forms of courtesy in order to accommodate themselves to our foreign ways [...] which appeared to the Japanese to be most barbaric and lacking in civility.
>
> He also said that if I could in some way find a remedy to this sad state of affairs, he would consider me an angel sent from God so that His Holy Law could spread throughout Japan with honor and esteem [...] It is for these reasons that I convoked our first general consultation in Japan in the year 1580.

This letter is a valuable source, because it offers us a rare opportunity to hear – at least indirectly – the voices of influential members of the Japanese samurai elite, as they speak candidly with Valignano about the

Christian mission and express their frustrations. The Jesuit Visitor took to heart what he had heard and soon enacted major changes.

Just before his departure in 1582, after two years of intense deliberations, the Jesuit Visitor wrote a long report to Rome to inform the General of the *Resolutions* he had compiled for the proper governance of the mission. In the opinion of the majority of missionaries, the only way to ensure the survival and development of the church in Japan was to promote the formation of a native clergy with the admittance of Japanese young men into the Order. These candidates needed, moreover, to be given proper training in both religious subjects as well as the humanities. This represented a major shift from the previous decade, during which the Christian community had continued to grow but had also been hindered by the strict and uncompromisingly negative view of the Japanese people adopted by the Portuguese Jesuit, Francisco Cabral (1529–1609). A former soldier, Cabral had expressed his contempt for the Japanese as unreliable and untrustworthy. As a result, he concluded that they could never become priests or Jesuits; and he insisted that they should be completely subordinate to their European superiors. But Valignano did not accept his view of Japan or the Japanese.

Valignano was well aware of the fact that the admission of native candidates into the Society of Jesus was a novel and a controversial idea in Europe. He thus felt the need to justify his new policy and provide a rebuttal to Cabral's criticisms. In another letter penned to Rome, Valignano noted that:

> If the [Japanese] are treated properly, go through the novitiate experiments, and acquire the requisite learning, we may confidently hope they will become able workers in no whit inferior to European subjects. They are truly a very capable people endowed with talents of a high order [...] They are very courageous and patient in meeting adversity and hardship, and persevering and meticulous in their studies.

Having persuaded Acquaviva in Rome, Valignano decided in 1580 to establish a Jesuit novitiate (a house for initial religious training), two secondary schools or *seminarios*, and a college of higher learning. In the case of the College of Funai, which became the first Jesuit college in East Asia, it was the *daimyō* Ōtomo Sōrin, who gave the Jesuits the land to build it in his kingdom. The aim of the *collegio*, which was later transferred to Nagasaki, was to provide a higher level of studies in both the European and Japanese humanities, as well as in philosophy and theology for those who were training for the priesthood and had already completed their basic studies at the *seminario*.

But what did the Jesuits teach at this college, which was attended by young European as well as Japanese Jesuits in training? Valignano wrote to Rome in 1583 and again in 1592 requesting that Jesuit scholars in Europe compile a summary of philosophy and theology for use in Japan, but this textbook never materialised. To remedy the situation, he assigned this crucial task to a Spanish Jesuit theologian in Japan. This was Pedro Gómez (1535–1600), who had taught the full curriculum of the *studia humanitatis* at the University of Coimbra before embarking for Asia, proving himself to be an able scholar. While in Portugal he had worked under Pedro da Fonseca (1528–99), a Portuguese Jesuit who was widely known in Europe as the 'Aristotle of Portugal'.

Gómez's compendium for the college in Japan included three parts: a treatise on astronomy; a partial translation of Aristotle's *De anima*; and an adapted version of the *Roman Catechism of the Council of Trent,* which was first published in Rome in 1566. Gómez initially composed the compendium in Latin, but the students found it difficult to read in view of their limited mastery of the ancient language of Rome. To remedy this problem, he sought the help of two erudite former Buddhist monks, Paulo Yōhō and Vicente Hōin, who had converted to Christianity and become Jesuits, and his fellow Spaniard, Pedro Ramón. Together they produced a Japanese translation, with many revisions and additions that reflected a Japanese mindset, between 1594 and 1595.

It is interesting to note that the only surviving manuscript copy of the original Latin version of 1593, preserved in the Vatican Library, was a gift of Queen Christina of Sweden (1626–89), who was living in Rome after abdicating the throne. She was an avid collector of rare books and manuscripts and a scholar in her own right. In 1995, I discovered the long-lost Japanese translation of this work, produced exactly 400 years earlier in 1595, in the archives of Magdalen College at the University of Oxford.

Soon after Valignano had succeeded in putting the mission on a new and more solid footing, he decided that it was time for Christian Europe to see at first hand the fruits of the Jesuit efforts in Japan. To achieve this goal, Valignano chose four boys and formed an 'embassy' to Europe.

Jesuit missionary Alessandro Valignano (1539–1606).

His purpose was both to recruit new missionaries for the mission and to find funding in Japan: the Jesuits were constantly on the verge of bankruptcy on account of the poverty of the majority of converts, who were unable to support them. The four young men embarked on what would become a sensational journey of encounter between East and West with a life of its own.

Among the great and the powerful who honoured them in Europe were Philip II of Spain, the Regent of Portugal, the Duke of Tuscany, the Doge and Senate of Venice, as well as the Dukes of both Milan and Mantua. Itō Mancio (1569–1612), one of the four boys, has been represented in numerous sketches, manuscripts, and works of art. Recently, a painting of Mancio produced in 1585 by Domenico Tintoretto (1560–1635) was discovered in Milan, where it is preserved by the Trivulzio Foundation.

While in Rome, the boys met two popes, beginning with the great benefactor of the Society of Jesus, Gregory XIII, who supported many colleges, including the four institutions founded by Valignano in Japan. After Gregory's death they also met several times with his successor, Sixtus V. Their travels and very public audiences were widely reported and illustrated in several dozen editions about their journeys printed in Europe, including a German broadsheet newspaper that appeared in colour in Augsburg in 1586.

Upon their return to Japan after a voyage that had taken them across Asia to Europe and back over a period of eight years, between 1582 and 1590, the boys, now young men, were received in Kyoto by the Japanese regent, Toyotomi Hideyoshi (1537–98). After his subjugation of Kyushu, he had issued a decree in 1587 expelling the Jesuits. This development complicated matters for the delegation and for the future of the mission. Valignano was thus able to accompany the young men on their journey back to Japan only in his capacity as ambassador of the viceroy in India. Hideyoshi knew that the Jesuits remained in the country, but decided for a time to turn a blind eye to their missionary work and to their defiance of his decree.

Meanwhile, the embassy to Europe had brought back with them a Gutenberg handpress, which they used twice en route to print two works in Latin, one in Goa in 1587 and another in Macau the following year. The arrival of the press marked the beginning of a short-lived but very productive period of printing of devotional works, as well as a variety of educational materials, between 1590 and 1614. Curiously, the missionaries' first use of movable metal type to print texts in Japanese script overlapped with the introduction of Korean metal type to Japan. Hideyoshi acquired this printing technology during his first invasion of Korea in 1590. The Korean casting of metal type predates Gutenberg by at least 150 years.

The Jesuits began by printing works in Japanese transliterated phonetically with Roman letters. The first such work to come off the press was an abridged edition of the *Golden Legend* (or *Legenda aurea*), that is, excerpts from the *Lives of the Saints* by Jacobo da Voragine (1228–98). Only two copies of this exceedingly rare Jesuit translation into Japanese from the original Latin survive to this day. One is preserved in the Bodleian Library in Oxford and the other in the Biblioteca Marciana of Venice.

These initial successes led the Jesuits to experiment with the casting of metal type in cursive Japanese script, including several characters on a single piece of type, which resulted in elegant masterpieces of early Japanese printing. Previously, works printed to resemble calligraphic brush-strokes had only been produced on individually hand-carved wooden blocks – a Chinese technique that dominated East Asian printing until the 19th century. Once they mastered these techniques, perhaps the greatest work the Jesuits produced, both in terms of the quality of translation as well as the creation of cursive metal type for printing, was the *Giya do pekadoru* or *Guide of Sinners*. This devotional book was composed by one of Catholic Europe's most famous writers of the 16th century, Luis de Granada (1505–88), a Spanish Dominican. It is noteworthy that the four boys had the chance to meet him on their journeys throughout the Iberian Peninsula.

Other important works that came off the Jesuits' mission press included the very first grammars of the Japanese language compiled between 1604 and 1608 by the Portuguese Jesuit, João Rodrigues (1562?–1633), who was known as *Tçuzu* or 'Interpreter'. Rodrigues had arrived as a young boy in Asia and later worked as an interpreter for both Toyotomi Hideyoshi and Tokugawa Ieyasu before being exiled to China after the missionaries fell out of favour with the shogunate.

It is noteworthy that these grammars and dictionaries still serve today as key references for the historical study of the Japanese. Rodrigues's careful analysis of the complex epistolary style, used for official documents and correspondence, and variations in dialects and vocabulary usage offer insight into a linguistic world that remains otherwise difficult to master.

Important innovations also took place in the arts. Instead of relying solely on imports from Europe, many devotional images were produced in Japan. Around 1590, the Italian Jesuit, Giovanni Niccolò (1560–1626) founded a painting academy in Nagasaki, where he instructed his Japanese, Chinese, and European pupils in the art of European oil and watercolour painting, as well as in the production of etchings. Among the most famous images produced in Japan and later venerated by the Christians who went into hiding during the persecutions of the 17th century is a painting by an anonymous artist, *Our Lady of the Snows*, preserved in Nagasaki. Other images of the Madonna, as well as of Christ as Saviour, the *Salvator Mundi*, were prevalent among works produced by his school. These paintings were in high demand by Japanese Christians and missionaries alike, and some of them survived among the 'hidden Christians' in Nagasaki, Hirado, and the Gotō Islands, where they used them for the purposes of worship. Other hybrid works of Namban, or 'Southern Barbarian' art (a term the Japanese coined to refer to all things Portuguese and Spanish), such as liturgical objects and coffers, intricately decorated with inlaid mother of pearl and lacquer, were also popular.

In later decades, Japanese artists worked in Macau, where they had been exiled in 1639 in the aftermath of the closing of Japan to the Europeans – with the notable exception of Dutch traders, who occupied the trading post of Dejima in Nagasaki until the 18th century. Among these artists was a group of sculptors who carved the famous façade of the Church of St Paul in Macau, which includes both saints and mythical creatures from East Asian lore.

As part of his strategy of cultural accommodation, Valignano also insisted on the pursuit of traditional Japanese arts, such as the tea ceremony or *cha no yu*. The Jesuit *Rules for the Japanese Province*, compiled in 1590, also mention a set of *Rules for the Master of Tea*. These included a meticulously compiled list of traditional utensils used during the ceremony that all Jesuit houses should obtain. Every Jesuit residence was to have a tearoom, where distinguished guests could be properly entertained. And special tea bowls with Christian motifs, including crosses, were produced for this specific purpose.

In this way, the Jesuits in Japan began a process of creating a hybrid Japanese-Christian culture. Valignano's key insight and inspiration was that the evangelisation of Japan was not to be interpreted as a civilised Europe bringing the Christian faith to a barbaric or foreign land. Rather, the missionaries' work was to reflect that of the primitive church of apostolic times, when St Paul preached to the Greeks on the Areopagus. Valignano chose to apply the same principle to China and Chinese culture. Thus, Ancient Greece and Rome, which had become Christian, could serve as models for China and Japan.

Even after the persecution in Japan began in earnest, with the official ban on the Christian faith issued by shogun Tokugawa Ieyasu (1543–1616) in 1614, curiosity and interest in Christian books persisted throughout the Edo period. It is interesting to note that the main conduit of information about Christianity became the publications in classical Chinese compiled and published by the Jesuits in China.

The first Jesuit missionary in China to gain wide acceptance among the literati of the Ming dynasty was Matteo Ricci (1552–1610), whom Valignano had sent to Macau to begin his study of the Chinese language. Ricci would become the first westerner to master classical Chinese and compose both Christian, philosophical, and scientific works in that language. He was also the first to gain regular access to the Forbidden City, following his admittance to Beijing in 1601.

The missionaries in the Middle Kingdom were engaged at the imperial court as scientists – mathematicians, astronomers, and engineers. Their endeavours included activities as wide-ranging as the reform of the calendar based on astronomical observations and calculations, the production of maps (of the world and of China), hydraulics, and the building of military defences, including the design of cannons. But they did not forget that their main purpose for being in China was to propagate the Christian faith; and to that end they composed many works explaining the tenets of Christianity, beginning with basic summaries or catechisms, as well as treatises on vices, virtues, and the Ten Commandments, to name but a few.

Ricci noted the importance of these books not only for China but also for Japan in a letter he wrote to Rome from Beijing:

> It gave us great consolation to know that many of our works written in Chinese characters were useful in Japan because of their use of the same characters. For this reason, Fr. Valignano reprinted [my] Catechism [*The True Meaning of the Lord of Heaven*] in Canton and arranged for it to be sent to Japan; and Fr. Francesco Pasio has requested that I send him many of these books, for they have great authority in Japan insofar as they come from China [...]

Japanese Christian painting of *Our Lady of the Snows*.

The importance of these books is also confirmed by Diogo de Mesquita (1551–1614), who had accompanied the four boys to Rome and had acquired a Gutenberg handpress in Lisbon. In a letter written to Rome in 1613, shortly before his own death at a time when exile was imminent, he informs the Jesuit Superior General that:

> During these persecutions, especially when priests cannot travel freely through the territories of Christians whose lords are pagans, it is impossible to exaggerate the wonderful results obtained by these books [...] for they serve as preachers to the Christians. With this help both the persecuted and non-persecuted are confirmed in their faith and their customs.

Most of these books were strictly banned in Japan following the expulsion of the Jesuits, because of their suspect connection with Christianity. The inspection of books was first carried out in Nagasaki in 1630 at Shuntokuji Temple with the explicit purpose of ferreting out any volumes being imported from China that may have been composed by the foreign missionaries at the imperial court in Beijing. This was further formalised with the establishment of the Inspectorate of Books, also in Nagasaki, in 1639. The shogunate appointed the Confucian physician and botanist, Mukai Genshō (1609–77), to lead the new office. Besides his function as a censor of forbidden imported publications, Mukai's mandate included the selection of Chinese books for the shogun's library in Edo, the Momijiyama Bunko. He also dealt with orders from Edo of Chinese books that the shogun and his officials had explicitly requested.

Yet so concerned were the Japanese authorities about the possible dissemination of Christian-tainted books among the populace that even a passing mention of the names of a Jesuit missionary – particularly those of Matteo Ricci or Giulio Aleni (1582–1649) – would warrant a book being put on the index of prohibited items. On several occasions, such books were found among the cargo of the Chinese merchants. In each instance, the authorities immediately launched a thorough investigation into the importer's background and ultimate intentions, which included the interrogation and torture of all the sailors.

Despite this strict censorship, manuscript copies of these publications, including Jesuit books on Christian doctrine, such as Alfonso Vagnone's (1566–1640) *Exposition of the Ten Commandments*, escaped the vigilance of the authorities and circulated illegally among scholars. Other works on science, such a copy of Johann Adam Schall von Bell's *Treatise on the Telescope*, were also known to Edo scholars. Some of these works had been brought into Japan before the expulsion of missionaries, but others were imported through the Chinese merchants of Nagasaki. Of foremost interest to Edo scholars was Matteo Ricci's famous 1602 world map, of which numerous manuscript copies survive in Japan. On some copies, to avoid censorship, the seal of the Society of Jesus, the name of Ricci, and any references to Christianity, were carefully erased. Restrictions on scientific books would be eased in 1720, when Kyoto mathematician and scientist, Nakane Genkei (1662–1733) convinced Tokugawa Yoshimune (1684–1751) that they needed to refer to Jesuit works on astronomy published in China to carry out their own reforms of the Japanese calendar. Permission was granted, provided that the work otherwise contained no references to the 'evil teaching' of Christianity.

A detailed exposition of the reasons for the expulsion of the missionaries and the persecution of Christianity in Japan remain beyond the limited scope of this essay. The tumultuous times during which these events took place are not easily characterised. As missionaries were captured, executed, or forced to apostatise, native Japanese Christians had no choice but to go underground, where they maintained secret rituals and continued to worship to the best of their ability. While arguably imperfect and incomplete, Jesuit missionary efforts to adapt the Christian faith to Japanese culture rather than to import a fully grown 'foreign tree' and forcibly transplant it into Japanese soil had somehow succeeded.

The survival of the hidden Christians beyond the collapse of the shogunate in 1868 bears eloquent witness to this fact. It is remarkable to note how a group of Nagasaki Christians who had come out of hiding in 1865, when French priests were first allowed to build a church in Nagasaki for the foreign community, willingly underwent arrest, exile, torture, and – in some cases – death. The story of their courage in suffering and dying for their faith in the first years of the Meiji Restoration led to the declaration of conditional religious freedom in 1873, after their plight became known in Europe and North America. Thus, as the shogunate and the early Meiji government both discovered in their own way, a seed had indeed been planted; and it would not be easy to uproot or eradicate.

REFERENCES

Alden, Dauril, *The Making of an Enterprise: The Society of Jesus in Portugal, its Empire, and Beyond, 1540-1750* (Stanford University Press, 1996).

Bailey, Gauvin A., *Art on the Jesuit Missions in Asia and Latin America, 1540-1773* (University of Toronto Press, 1999).

Boscaro, Adriana, *Sixteenth-Century European Printed Works on the First Japanese Mission to Europe: A Descriptive Bibliography* (Brill, 1973).

Boxer, Charles R., *The Christian Century in Japan (1549-1650)* (Cambridge University Press, 1951; rpt Carcanet Press, 1993).

Cooper, Michael, *The Japanese Mission to Europe, 1582-1590: The Journey of Four Samurai Boys through Portugal, Spain and Italy* (Global Oriental, 2005).

Rodrigues the Interpreter: An Early Jesuit in Japan and China, (Weatherhill, 1974; rpt 1994).

Elisonas, Jurgis (George Elison), "Christianity and the Daimyō", in John Whitney Hall ed, *The Cambridge History of Japan*, vol 4, *Early Modern Japan* (Cambridge University Press, 1991), pp 301-72.

Deus Destroyed: The Image of Christianity in Early Modern Japan (Harvard University Press, 1991).

[Fróis, Luís], *História de Japam*, ed. Josef Wicki, 5 vols, (Biblioteca Nacional de Lisboa, 1976-1984).

Tratado em que se contêm muito sucinta e abreviadamente algumas contradições e diferenças de costumes entre a gente de Europa e esta província de Japão (...), published as *Europa-Japão. Um Diálogo civilizacional no Século XVI*, ed. Raffaella D'Intino (Comissão Nacional para as Comemorações dos Descobrimentos Portugueses, 1993).

[Gómez, Pedro], *Iezusu-kai Nihon Korejiyo no Kōgi yōkō* [The Compendium of the Jesuit College in Japan], ed Obara Satoru, 3 vols (Kyōbunkan, 1997-99).

Higashibaba, Ikuo, *Christianity in Early Modern Japan: Kirishitan belief and practice* (Brill, 2001).

Lach, Donald F. and Edwin J. Van Kley, *Asia in the Making of Europe*, 9 vols, (University of Chicago Press, 1965-93).

Moran, Joseph F., *The Japanese and the Jesuit:. Alessandro Valignano in Sixteenth-Century Japan* (Routledge, 1993).

Pacheco Diego, "Diego de Mesquita, S.J. and the Jesuit Mission Press", *Monumenta Nipponica*, 26 (1971), 431-43.

Ucerler, M. Antoni J., "Alessandro Valignano: Man, Missionary, and Writer", in *Asian Travel in the Renaissance*, ed Daniel Carey (Blackwell, 2004), pp 12-41.

"Jesuit Humanist Education in Sixteenth-Century Japan: The Latin and Japanese MSS of Pedro Gómez's Compendia on Astronomy, Philosophy, and Theology (1593-95)", in *The Latin and Japanese MSS of Pedro Gómez's Compendia*, ed Kirishitan Bunko, Sophia University, 3 vols, (Ōzorasha, 1997), vol 3, pp 11-60.

[Valignano, Alessandro], *Sumario de las cosas de Japón (1583). Adiciones del sumario de Japón (1592)*, ed José Luis Álvarez-Taladriz, Monumenta Nipponica Monographs: 9, I (Sophia University, 1954).

Yamamoto, Hirofumi, "The Edo Shogunate's View of Christianity in the Seventeenth Century", in *Christianity and Cultures: Japan & China in Comparison, 1540–1644*, ed M. Antoni J. Ucerler (Institutum Historicum Societatis Iesu, 2009), pp 255–67.

Ward, Haruko Nawata, *Women Religious Leaders in Japan's Christian Century, 1549–1650* (Ashgate, 2009).

Ōtomo Sōrin (1530–1587).

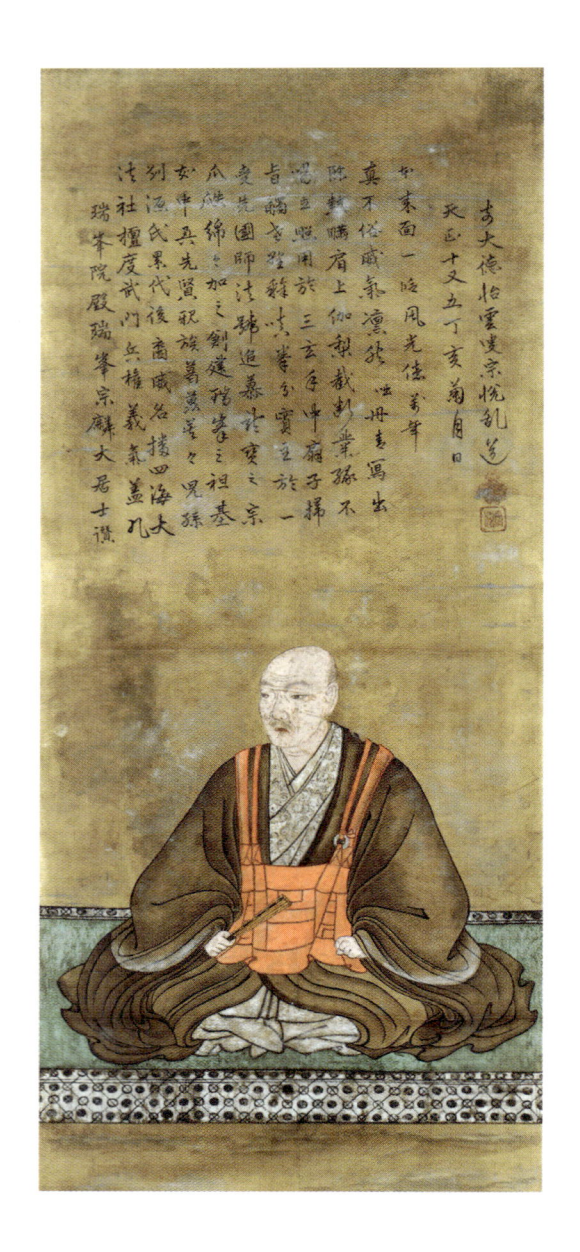

THE CHRISTIAN THREAT TO JAPAN
Stephen Turnbull

Within half a century of the arrival of Christianity in Japan the faith became subject to increasingly severe persecution. Shūsaku Endō's book, *Silence,* and its subsequent film adaptation, portrays very well the belief of those in power that the Christian message had no place in the 'mud-swamp' of Japan, and that its missionaries spread sedition and encouraged disobedience. Yet underlying this fear was a much deeper suspicion that the Spanish in the Philippines intended to invade Japan in conjunction with an uprising by a fifth column of Japanese Christian *daimyō* [lords]. In fact, the Spanish never developed any such plans. This idea was only ever expressed by over-enthusiastic European priests and boastful foreign merchants. Nevertheless, it was a possibility that was always taken seriously by Japanese leaders – and because their primary concern was the internal 'Christian problem' their reaction was expressed at a level verging on paranoia, resulting in the persecution of Christianity and its supposed elimination.

★

The earliest written reference to fears of a Christian uprising in Japan supported by an invasion from abroad is contained within a letter from the Jesuit Luis Frois dated the October 16, 1578. In it, he reports widely believed rumours circulating in Bungo Province (modern Ōita Prefecture) that the Jesuits – who were supported by the Portuguese – were waiting until they had sufficient converts to form an army, at which point a Portuguese armada would set sail and help them turn their spiritual conquests into military ones. Even Ōtomo Sōrin (1530–87), the Christian *daimyō* of Bungo, laughed off that suggestion,[1] but Alessandro Valignano (the Italian who oversaw the entire Jesuit missionary effort in China and Japan from 1574 until 1606) revisited the topic in 1583 and noted that several non-Christian *daimyō* and Buddhist priests had surmised that they could not understand why the Spanish monarch would spend such vast sums on the mission if the end was not to conquer Japan.[2]

That possibility, remote though it may have been, would remain an underlying obsession among Japan's rulers for decades, and in its initial stages no individual did more to keep those fears alive than Father Gaspar Coelho (1530–90), the Portuguese-born Jesuit leader in Japan from 1581 onwards. Coelho's fault was to regard the Jesuit order in Japan as the church militant, which is perhaps not so surprising when all he saw around him was war. He was naturally a great supporter of the Christian *daimyō*, particularly Ōmura Sumitada (1532–87), whose domain of Hizen Province (modern Nagasaki Prefecture) was to become vital to the Christian effort. In 1574, with Coelho's full support, four Portuguese ships came to the rescue of Sumitada when he was attacked by his anti-Christian neighbour, Ryūzōji Takanobu (1530–85). The grateful Sumitada undertook the conversion to Christianity of his entire domain. Unfortunately, this did not immediately guarantee Sumitada's security: Takanobu invaded Sumitada's lands again in 1577 and in 1578. Faced with losing their great ally to vassalage under a pagan lord, the Jesuits helped him once more, and in recompense Sumitada ceded to them the port of Nagasaki, which became a Jesuit colony in all but name.

Takanobu then threatened another Christian *daimyō*, Arima Harunobu (1567–1612). By this time Coelho had become vice-principal, and on the March 3, 1584, in a dramatic escalation of European involvement, he made the first of three visits to Manila to ask for armed help from the Spanish.[3] He requested four ships laden with men, artillery and food to be sent "to succour the Christians of Japan that are pressed by the heathen" – Takanobu being the heathen he had in mind. Coelho's request fell on deaf ears, but even though no Spanish help arrived, Ryūzōji Takanobu was defeated and killed in April 1584. During the battle, the Christian Harunobu bombarded the Ryūzōji clan from the sea using two European artillery pieces supplied by Coelho. Their salvation must have seemed like divine intervention because Takanobu had made it known that his first act after gaining a victory would have been to crucify Coelho and sack Nagasaki.[4] In truth, the removal of Takanobu was due more to an alliance the desperate Arima had made with the pagan Shimazu clan of Satsuma (modern Kagoshima Prefecture). Unfortunately for Coelho and the Jesuit mission, the Shimazu were now poised to fill the vacuum left by the Ryūzōji, so Coelho returned to the Philippines with requests for

The Nagasaki Martyrs, painting from the 18th or 19th century.

armed intervention against the Shimazu on November 11, 1584 and January 24, 1585.⁵

Again, no positive response was made, so Coelho's fellow Christians had to make do with whatever European military support could be provided from within Japan itself. Yet in undertaking these diplomatic missions Coelho had crossed a line by raising the possibility that Spain could intervene militarily in wars between rival *daimyō*. It was a scenario that attracted little comment in 1585, but in a few years' time the situation would change dramatically. The geographically limited wars between the *daimyō* of Kyushu were taking place against a national backdrop of Toyotomi Hideyoshi's unstoppable rise to power. Hideyoshi (1536–98) had begun his military career as a foot soldier in the army of Oda Nobunaga. Following the latter's death, a series of military victories transformed his position from a *daimyō* to someone who had a very real chance of bringing about national hegemony – something he would achieve in 1591.

In May 1586 Father Coelho travelled to Osaka to seek Hideyoshi's support against the Shimazu, who now looked certain to conquer the whole of Kyushu, taking the Christian *daimyō* and Nagasaki along with it. As a veteran of diplomatic trips to Manila to seek military support, Coelho knew exactly what to ask of a ruler, but was highly incautious over what he had to offer in return. Hideyoshi was already entertaining thoughts about a conquest of China, so Coelho rashly suggested that the Jesuits would supply two ships for use in a future expedition. To launch an invasion of China via Korea (the most practical route), Hideyoshi would first have to conquer Kyushu and bring the Shimazu to heel, and for that Coelho impulsively promised to put all the Christian lords in Japan on Hideyoshi's side. In reality, he lacked the influence to deliver on the latter pledge, nor did he realise that many of the Christian *daimyō* were loyal to Hideyoshi already.

Hideyoshi appeared to be in agreement, however, and sent Coelho on his way with encouraging carte blanche for the gospel to be preached throughout Japan. The grateful Coelho began a diplomatic offensive among the Christian *daimyō* of Honshu and Shikoku to create a Christian alliance in support of Hideyoshi, but he returned to Nagasaki in December 1586 having failed utterly in his task. That a union of Christian *daimyō* was impossible even on Kyushu had been illustrated while Coelho was away, because Ōmura and Arima had disgraced themselves by fighting a war with each other.⁶

THE CHRISTIAN THREAT TO JAPAN

Hideyoshi's invasion of Kyushu took place in 1587 and was satisfactorily completed without Coelho's help, so instead of leading a crusader army in Hideyoshi's service, Coelho had to content himself with a trip from Nagasaki to congratulate Hideyoshi on his stunning victory. The meeting took place on Coelho's impressive private warship and was very cordial, so Coelho was completely unprepared for what followed a few days later. In apparent contradiction of all that he had said to Coelho in Osaka, Hideyoshi issued a decree expelling all Christian missionaries from Japan.

In his written explanation Hideyoshi said that Japan was "the land of the gods", and he compared the alien Jesuits to the leaders of the *Ikkō-ikki*, the "single minded league" of the Buddhist True Pure Land sect who had fought his predecessor for ten years, causing Hideyoshi many problems before he overcame them. In Hideyoshi's eyes the Jesuits were even more dangerous than the *Ikkō-ikki* because the Buddhist sectarians had mainly seduced the lower classes. The Jesuits, however, had seduced *daimyō*, whose numerous followers, sheepishly coerced into converting, went around destroying Buddhist temples.[7] Some of the Christian lords were loyal to Hideyoshi. Others were highly suspect, and it is very likely that Coelho, who combined the roles of religious leader and secular ruler, sailing from his fortress town of Nagasaki like a prince on his own warship, had contributed not a little to Hideyoshi's suspicions.

Coelho was not a man to take this lying down. Faced with the prospect of Nagasaki being confiscated and the Jesuits sent home, he went back to the Christian lords to persuade them to unite in armed resistance against Hideyoshi. He rashly offered to supply weapons and financial support, but the situation in Japan had changed radically in seven years. It was no longer a case of supporting one petty Christian *daimyō* against a petty pagan. It was instead a pledge of European support for a *coup d'état* against the man who now ruled half of Japan and looked certain to conquer the other half too. To make matters worse, most of the Christian *daimyō* whom Coelho approached had served Hideyoshi during the Kyushu campaign and been richly rewarded for their loyalty. Even Arima Harunobu flatly rejected the alarming proposal.

Within days Nagasaki was confiscated by Hideyoshi. The 'Jesuit colony' had lasted only seven years. Abandoned by the Christian *daimyō*, the increasingly desperate Coelho turned again to the Philippines and sent a letter to Manila, suggesting that 300 Spanish soldiers should invade Japan

St Francis Xavier arriving in Japan in 1549.

and overthrow Hideyoshi. The secular Spanish authorities sent his request on to Madrid (which was equivalent to ignoring it), while his Jesuit superior wrote back severely criticising him for his inflammatory suggestions. In 1589, Coelho approached Macao instead, sending Father Belchior de Mora to ask for 200 Portuguese soldiers. That request produced some weapons but no troops, and an alarmed Father Valignano took de Mora back to Japan with him in 1590. Hoping against hope that the matter had not reached the ears of Hideyoshi, Valignano arranged for the personal armaments to be secretly sold and for the larger cannon to be sent back to Macao. Valignano then turned his attentions towards punishing Coelho, a fate he avoided by dying in May 1590.[8]

Hideyoshi may not have known anything about Coelho's plans, but all that he had feared about the Spanish seemed to be revealed as a real and present danger following the wreck in 1596 of the Manila galleon *San Felipe*. Japanese attempts to requisition the cargo were met by defiance from the ship's pilot, who bragged about his country's power and claimed that the advance of the Spanish Empire was customarily preceded and facilitated by missionaries. The statement came to the ears of Hideyoshi, who realised that his edict of 1587 expelling the missionaries, which he had never properly enacted, had been the right one. A real persecution of Christians followed, and Japan's first martyrs died in February 1597. As for the existence of a fifth column, Coelho's dreams of an uprising were still being expressed. Not long before his martyrdom, Friar Martin of the Ascension wrote to the Spanish court criticising the Jesuits for their lack of loyalty to the Spanish crown:

> In Nagasaki alone they could have armed thirty thousand trustworthy musketeers, all of them Christians from the villages possessed by the fathers around Nagasaki, and they could have trusted these men as much as Spaniards, because they dare not disobey what the fathers lay down and order. And with these Christians and with the Spaniards they could, with the help of God and with Spanish industry and military discipline, conquer and pacify all of Japan.[9]

He ends with the belief that through these means, Konishi Yukinaga, the Christian *daimyō* of Higo Province (modern Kumamoto Prefecture) could become the ruler of the whole of Japan.[10] It was the Coelho situation all over again, and Alessandro Valignano's reaction was one of similar contempt for the young friar's failure to understand the true situation. He was determined to crush this alarmist talk before it got out of hand. For all his genuine devotion to Christianity, wrote Valignano, Konishi Yukinaga (who had led the Korean invasion) was the loyal servant of Hideyoshi, and if Konishi believed that the Jesuits were planning to hand Japan over to Spain he would be the first to raise his sword against them.[11]

★

Toyotomi Hideyoshi died – an inevitability that all dictators dread – leaving a five-year-old son and heir, and the questions over his regency threatened to plunge Japan back into the chaos from which he had rescued it. The result was the displacing of Hideyoshi's heir by Tokugawa Ieyasu (1542–1616), whose family were destined to rule Japan until 1868.

The Jesuits held their breath when Ieyasu assumed the role of shogun in 1603. He proved to be as suspicious of Christianity as his predecessor, so not wishing to endanger the Japanese Christians any further, the authorities in Manila took steps to control the flow of priests and stated quite clearly in 1606 that "no religious shall pass to the provinces of Japan through these kingdoms".[12] It was a prohibition ignored by the Jesuits with religious zeal, and the Philippines remained the main conduit for missionaries to enter Japan, much to Ieyasu's annoyance.

Japan was also a different place in terms of its rulers' understanding of Europeans. The seamless robe of Catholic Christianity as presented by the Jesuits had been exposed as a sham by the arrival in Japan in 1600 of Dutch and English Protestants. Richard Cocks, head of the East India Company's trading post on the island of Hirado (modern Nagasaki Prefecture), missed no opportunity to denounce his Catholic rivals in front of the Japanese, and to play cynically upon the regime's deepest fears. In October 1615, for example, he wrote to his colleague Richard Wickham advising him to state before the Japanese authorities that King Philip of Spain had usurped Portugal and would do the same in Japan if he could, with his priests acting as his instruments of rebellion. Cocks even suggested that two Spanish ships bound for the Philippines but unexpectedly driven to Japan by wind had not arrived by accident:

> ... they were sent on purpose by the King of Spain having knowledge of the death of the old emperor, thinking some Papist lord might rise

and rebel, and so draw all the Papists to flock to them and take part, by which means they might suddenly seize some strong place and keep it till more succours came, they not wanting money for men for the accomplishing of such a stratagem.[13]

By 1615, however, such comments were merely adding fuel to the flames that had started burning on January 27, 1614, the date of the issuance of Ieyasu's expulsion edict. Unlike Hideyoshi's orders of 1587, this one was acted upon and, in Boxer's well-chosen words, 'sounded the death knell for Christianity in Japan for two and a half centuries'.[14] Richard Cocks mentions it in a letter written a month later and concludes ruefully that the news about the expulsion of Papists was too good to be true.[15] He would see it come true over the next few years, and in 1621 Cocks himself would inform the Japanese authorities about a priest hiding in Hirado.[16]

In preparation for their expulsion, set for October 27, 1614, the missionaries stripped their churches and even went to the length of reburying bodies in secret so they could not be profaned. Forty-seven brave priests stayed behind to lay the foundations of the underground church which would characterise the remnants of Christianity. In that same year some very high profile Christian exiles, including the *daimyō* Takayama Ukon (1553–1615), arrived in Manila.[17] The much smaller reverse flow of secret priests to Japan also continued. It may have been only a trickle but it was enough evidence of a self-renewing Christian problem for Japan to provoke the most extreme solution of all: Japan should invade the Philippines. It would cut off the supply of priests, wipe out Christianity, and destroy forever the Spanish threat to Japan.

The idea of an invasion had in fact been entertained by Hideyoshi, and was revisited twice under the Tokugawa before the idea was given serious attention in 1637.[18] The instigator of the plan was not the shogun, even though the Dutch East India Company was convinced that he was to blame.[19] Instead it appears to have been the brainchild of the two *bugyō* [magistrates] of Nagasaki, who hoped to curry favour with their superiors. The matter was raised at a meeting held towards the end of September 1637 with François Caron of the Dutch East India Company.[20] Caron wanted trade to be shifted from the Portuguese to the Dutch. He contrasted the Portuguese willingness to flout Japanese laws by bringing priests into the country with the Dutch attitude of docile obedience as 'the Shogun's loyal vassals'.[21] The two *bugyō* wanted to destroy the three

Iberian bases of Manila, Macao and Keelung on Taiwan.[22] In their eyes, Manila was the most important of the three because the chance of closing down forever the supply of Catholic priests was regarded as a good bargaining chip with the *bugyō's* superiors in Edo when the time came to gain official permission to invade. The army would have to be supplied either by the shogun or by a *daimyō* acting on the shogun's behalf, such as the enthusiastic local persecutor of Christians, Matsukura Katsuie (1598–1638) of Shimabara. Yet the plan had a great weakness: Japan's lack of naval power. A guarantee of Dutch naval support would ensure that the army could be transported to Manila. It also promised a low-cost operation, which was another positive point to place before the shogun.

Manila was by then one of the most heavily fortified places in East Asia. Caron had neither the desire to assault it nor even to transport samurai to do so, and suggested meekly that the Dutch were now more merchants than soldiers. One of the *bugyō* seemed to accept Caron's excuses, while the other kept shaking his head, but neither of them was inclined to give up. The next day they presented a document addressed to the shogun's council for their "loyal vassals" to sign that would commit the Dutch in no uncertain terms to supporting and supplying an invasion:

> Recently we have understood that the people of Manila are breaking the emperor's prohibitions and are sending priests, who are forbidden in Japan. As a result, they are viewed as criminals by Your Honours. If the High Authorities decide to destroy this place, the Hollanders, who bring a good number of ships to Japan every year, are always ready, in time or opportunity, to present our ships and cannon for your service. We ask that Your Honours trust and believe that we are, in all matters without exception, ready to serve Japan.[23]

The choice was clear. The Dutch had to decide between abandoning their reputation as servants of the shogun, with all the implications for their trade that such a move would have, and the huge dangers of committing men and resources to an overseas military expedition against a formidable enemy that could result in the destruction of the company's entire fleet.

The Dutch chose danger, and agreed to support and partly convey the Japanese army of invasion on six ships. The shogun, who had just been informed, to his great annoyance, of the arrival of Father Marcello Mastrilli with some other missionaries from Manila, agreed that the

Portrait of Toyotomi Hideyoshi, ca 1600.

invasion should go ahead.[24] He envisaged an army of 10,000 men to be supplied by Matsukura Katsuie of Shimabara, but the shogun's chosen commander soon become involved in a serious development that would sound a death knell for the plans.

An uprising against another *daimyō's* tyrannical rule on the Amakusa Islands had quickly spread to the Matsukura territory. The rebels, who were predominantly Christian, sacked Katsuie's property and barricaded themselves inside Hara Castle, a dilapidated fortress on the Shimabara peninsula. The quelling of what became known as the Shimabara Rebellion would require all the military resources of the Tokugawa Shogunate for almost two years. There was no spare capacity for an invasion of the Philippines, and even less of a stomach for one. The Dutch naval support promised so loyally for the expedition was used instead for a bombardment of the Christian rebels' castle.

The shock caused by the Shimabara Rebellion realised the worst fears for the remaining Portuguese in Japan when the shogun decided that they should follow the Jesuits in being deported. With the Sakoku Edict of 1639 all contact was cut off from Catholic Europe, and even the loyal Dutch were confined to the artificial island of Dejima in Nagasaki Bay. One or two European priests would slip into Japan over the next half century. The last of the line, the Italian Father Sidotti, arrived in Japan from Manila in 1708. All were apprehended, and none of course sailed with a Spanish invasion fleet. The country was now secure and Christianity, the pernicious creed behind all the threats to Japan for over a century, had been completely eliminated.

---

1. Boxer, C.R. The Christian Century in Japan: 1549–1650 (University of California Press, 1951), p 151.
2. Ibid., p 158.
3. Bernard, Henri and Tientsin, S.J. 'Les Débuts des Relations Diplomatiques Entre le Japon at les Espagnols des Iles Philippines' (1571–1594), Monumenta Nipponica 1,1 (1938), p 113.

4. Murdoch, James, A History of Japan, vol 2 (Kobe, 1903), p 220.
5. Bernard, Henri and Tientsin, S.J., 'Les Débuts des Relations Diplomatiques Entre le Japon at les Espagnols des Iles Philippines' (1571–1594) Monumenta Nipponica 1,1 (1938), p. 113.
6. Elisonas, Jurgis, 'Christianity and the daimyō' in John Whitney Hall and James L. McLain, eds, The Cambridge History of Japan, vol 4 Early Modern Japan (Cambridge University Press, 1991), p 352.
7. Boxer, C.R. The Christian Century in Japan: 1549–1650 (University of California Press, 1951), p. 147.
8. Ibid., p 149; Moran, J.F. The Japanese and the Jesuits: Alessandro Valignano in sixteenth-century Japan (Routledge, 1993), p 73.
9. Cooper, Michael, Rodrigues the Interpreter: An Early Jesuit in Japan and China (Weatherhill, 1974), p 160.
10. Ibid., p 161.
11. Moran, J.F, The Japanese and the Jesuits: Alessandro Valignano in sixteenth-century Japan (Routledge, 1993), p 54.
12. B&R Part 14, p 218.
13. Boxer, C.R., The Christian Century in Japan: 1549–1650 (University of California Press, 1951), pp 310–311. The spelling has been modernised.
14. Ibid., p 318.
15. Farrington 134
16. Cocks, Richard, Diary of Richard Cocks; Cape Merchant in the English Factory in Japan 1615–1622 with correspondence (London, 1883), Volume II p 207.
17. Paske-Smith, T.R. 'Japanese Trade and Residence in the Philippines' Transactions of the Asiatic Society of Japan XLII (2) (1914), p 703.
18. Turnbull, Stephen, 'Wars and Rumours of Wars: Japanese Plans to invade the Philippines, 1593–1637',Naval War College Review Autumn 2016, vol. 69, no, 4, 107–120.
19. Yamamoto, Hirofumi Kanei Jidai (Nihon Rekishi Sōsho vol. 39) (Tokyo, 1989), pp 54–55.
20. Caron, François and Schouten, Joost A True Description of the Mighty Kingdoms of Japan and Siam. Reprinted from the English edition of 1663 with Introduction, Notes and Appendices by C.R.Boxer (London, 1935), pp. xlii-xlv.
21. Clulow, Adam, The Company and the Shogun: the Dutch encounter with Tokugawa Japan (Columbia University, 2014), p 122.
22. Caron, François and Schouten, Joost A True Description of the Mighty Kingdoms of Japan and Siam. Reprinted from the English edition of 1663 with Introduction, Notes and Appendices by C.R.Boxer (London, 1935), p. xliv.
23. Clulow, Adam The Company and the Shogun: the Dutch encounter with Tokugawa Japan (Columbia University, 2014), pp 123–124.
24. Boxer, C.R. The Christian Century in Japan: 1549–1650 (University of California Press, 1951), p. 151.

Liam Neeson in Martin Scorsese´s
Silence, 2016.

JAPAN'S HIDDEN CHRISTIANS
IN LIGHT OF MARTIN SCORSESE'S *SILENCE*

Christal Whelan

Martin Scorsese's latest and most epic film – *Silence* – deals with the prolonged and horrific persecution of Christianity in Japan during the 17th century. Paradoxically, the film's debut in Boston, my hometown, on Christmas Eve, 2016, though pregnant with symbolism, was unlikely to attract its most Christian audience. I, along with a coterie of admirers of Catholic novelist Endō Shūsaku's novel *Silence* (from which the film was adapted), had waited with impatience for over twenty years for Scorsese to produce this film after numerous interruptions and postponements. The novel's English-language translator, the Irish Jesuit and long-term Tokyo resident, William Johnston, was the first to inform me that the distinguished Italian-American director had acquired the film rights to the novel and that Scorsese's film was not the first but the second stab at its cinematic adaptation. Scorsese's precursor, the versatile Japanese director Shinoda Masahiro had produced *Chinmoku* [Silence] in 1971 with the screenwriting assistance of Endō himself. It was a successful and masterful period drama, but one whose ending skimped on the author's deep sense of religiosity and left Endō chagrined.

My excitement to see Scorsese's *Silence* was countered in equal measure by my own apprehension. Even if better aligned with Endō's own interiority, would the cultural and temporal remoteness of premodern Japan be too great to bridge, even for a director as legendary as Scorsese? And the question did matter, insofar as cinema enjoys a privileged status of communication for a vast segment of the contemporary public that eschews literature in favour of swifter and more spectacular modalities. Scorsese's film would therefore be the most likely version of the story to live on in the popular American imagination, and probably far beyond that in its global reach. I could not pretend to be a disinterested party since I had spent a decade of my personal and professional life in the early 1990s dedicated to understanding Japan's hidden Christians. Passionate to the point of an obsession, I had finally moved out of my apartment in

Dōzaki Catholic Church on
Fukejima, Gotō Islands.

Tokyo and gone to live in the remote Gotō Islands (a key area around which much of *Silence* revolves), seeking the company of contemporary hidden Christians, the descendants of Japan's first converts to Christianity in the 16th century. At the time, I was perplexed as to why these Christians had remained underground even in the present day, despite constitutional changes guaranteeing religious freedom in the 19th century and again, more liberally, in its postwar revisions.

To understand how a scantly known minority group such as the hidden Christians came into existence at all requires dipping into a chapter of Japanese history that few outside a handful of academic specialists and Japanophiles even know exists. The story begins with the arrival in Japan in 1549 of Portuguese Catholic missionaries with Francis Xavier at the helm. The original mission was Jesuit, although Dominicans, Franciscans, and Augustinians eventually joined them. While the Japanese were curious about everything Western from eye-glasses to Latin, the country's rulers, increasingly fearing divided loyalties and the compromise to their own power and governance, began a serious crackdown on missionary activity. In 1597, the supreme ruler of Japan – Toyotomi Hideyoshi – ordered the crucifixion of all Christians in Kyoto. From hundreds on the list, sympathetic officials allowed the number to be reduced to twenty-six people who were taken to Nagasaki and publicly crucified. They were: three Jesuits, six Franciscans, and seventeen laymen. In 1614, the government issued an edict outlawing the Christian religion and described Japan as "the country of gods, and of Buddha", and in no uncertain terms condemned the Christian religion as the opponent of Confucian morality, Buddhist law, and the Shinto way – that amalgam that uniquely constitutes the Japanese religious temperament. In 1636, even non-missionaries, that is, Portuguese merchants, were added to the watchlist and made to take up residence on a small fan-shaped island called Dejima, connected to Nagasaki by a bridge. But after a massive peasant revolt – the Shimabara rebellion – revealed the depth of Christianity's roots in Kyushu, even a permanent quarantine station such as Dejima was seen as providing a dangerous loophole to the outside world. The best solution then was to completely sever all relations with the Portuguese, even including a ban on the desired trade. Thus, by 1639 Japan's contact with the West consisted solely of traders from the Dutch East India Company – no Portuguese, no Spaniards, no Catholics – confined to the premises of the tiny artificial island.

This historical moment marks Japan's entry into a long period of self-imposed national isolation where the government forbade its own citizens from leaving the country, and strictly controlled and confined those who entered Dejima. But obviously there were covert Christians in the country, mostly on Kyushu and the offshore islands. An estimated 150,000 Christians had gone underground around this time and continued to practise their religion in secret, since it had now become a crime punishable by death.

Aware that there were still Christians in spite of the edicts, the government came up with some cruelly innovative methods to ferret them out. One of these, the annual ritual known as *e-fumi,* took place at local Buddhist temple complexes where all villagers were required to trample on a sacred Christian image. To recoil from this act, or blatantly refuse to do it, led to one's arrest. Christians would then be tortured rather than summarily killed, since the goal was to promote apostasy, that is, renunciation of their faith. If that did not come to pass, execution would follow swiftly. The practice of *e-fumi* had actually begun a decade earlier in Japan, but became systematised with the establishment in 1640 of the Religious Inquisition Office, which made it an integral part of the new year's celebrations across Kyushu.

Another method to discover Christians in hiding made use of the five-family group system of mutual responsibility, whereby the misdeeds of a single family member would have consequences not only for them and his or her family, but for everyone in all five families. It was meant to provide an incentive not to be selfish by practising an outlawed religion since it would have consequences beyond both yourself and your family. However, an irony of this system was that it could also work in the Christians' favour if all five families were Christian. After all, during the era when Christianity flourished, the Franciscans, Dominicans and the Jesuits had all established Third Orders or confraternities – small monastic bands of laymen and women who led lives of devotion without taking vows.

Japanese Christians lived within this severe social climate, under constant threat of persecution, in which harassment and torture were considered successful if they could induce apostasy, which remained the goal. Some punishments designed for this purpose were the retraction of employment leading to begging or starvation, dismemberment, branding, dousing with boiling water, lowering the victim's body into the boiling sulfur springs of Unzen, a volcanic mountain near Nagasaki, and

Bible class (1909).

ana-tsurushi, or headfirst suspension in a pit of excrement for hours or days until the person either recanted or died. Even the *kanji* characters for the word 'Christian' (in Japanese, *kirishitan*), based on the Portuguese *Cristão*, were changed from a meaningless phonetical grouping to one that could be translated as "to cut the limbs until they bleed".

But a crucial problem for the underground Christians remained a lack of knowledge about their newfound faith. The Bible had never been translated into Japanese. There were once devotional books that contained all the major Catholic prayers in Japanese with many Latin and Portuguese words sprinkled throughout. These were the *orassho* (in Portuguese, *oração*) or prayers. What knowledge these Christians had of their new faith remains questionable, given the chronic shortage of priests. Their number never exceeded 137 – to administer to a congregation of 300,000 at its height. The method of spreading their message that the missionaries had adopted was predicated on a growth paradigm. Believing that salvation was not possible without baptism, they baptised as many people as possible with the bare minimum of indoctrination. The missionaries intended to help deepen the faith of these new converts at a later date when the mission had grown stronger and was better staffed. But the persecutions rendered this future scenario impossible. The newly converted were left to their own devices to understand as best they could their new religion. It is likely that whatever religious notions they had inherited from Buddhism, Shinto, and local folk practices were interwoven at an early stage into an amalgam of eclectic spirituality which they defined and defended as 'Christian'.

During the centuries of Japan's closure to the outside world, the hidden Christians remained concealed in order to survive. We do not really know what they were practising. But in 1854, an American, Commodore Matthew Perry, arrived in Yokohama to forcibly open Japan to the rest of the world. The following year the Treaty of Amity and Commerce permitted Americans to practise their religion in Japan. Similar agreements with other nations encouraged missionaries who were eager to enter Japan. To avoid rivalry among various missionary groups, the Catholic Church granted exclusive rights to the conversion of Japan to the Society of Foreign Missions of Paris. The Japanese authorities consented to the construction of Christian churches with the understanding that these were to minister only to the needs of foreign residents. The French missionaries established churches in Hakodate, Yokohama, Tokyo (then called Edo), and Nagasaki.

The first superior of the Society of Foreign Missions had heard rumours that there were Japanese Christians, the remnant of the church that Francis Xavier had founded, and that they lived in remote mountains. He also learned that only recently some had been put to death. The branch of the society working in the Nagasaki area, where Christianity had flourished in the 16th and 17th centuries, hoped to make contact with these hidden Christians. That encounter eventually occurred at the newly built Ōura Church in Nagasaki when the French priest Bernard Petitjean arrived one morning to find fifteen Japanese waiting at the door. Once inside, three women knelt beside him and said: "The heart of all of us here is the same as yours". One of them asked: "Where is the statue of Mary?"

From his diaries, we know that Father Petitjean clearly esteemed the hidden Christians, and wrote that they had some knowledge of Catholic theology: they knew of the Trinity, the Fall, the Incarnation, and the Ten Commandments. Although they were without books or priests to instruct them, they had transmitted a number of prayers orally over several hundred years. Many knew the Lord's Prayer, the Hail Mary, the Apostles' Creed, the Salve Regina, and the Act of Contrition. Some communities even kept treasured Christian objects passed down from their ancestors. Petitjean recounted a visit to Sotome, a region west of Nagasaki, where he was the overnight guest in the home of a family who had preserved a picture of the fifteen mysteries of the rosary, with images of St Francis of Assisi and St Anthony of Padua. He also learned of the basic structure of hidden Christian groups who could not risk having separate buildings dedicated to religion. They worshipped in their own homes and their leaders were two priestly officials: the *chōkata*, or calendar man, who could usually read and write and whose duty was to lead the Sunday prayers, determine the liturgical calendar, and minister to the dying. The other official – the *mizukata* – was the baptiser and saw to infant baptisms. A third man functioned as a liaison between these officials and the community.

From this point in time, knowledge about hidden Christianity began to emerge. Petitjean estimated the total population to be around 10,000, but the Society of Foreign Missionaries' Mission Report for 1878 lists 17,380 Catholics, and 30,000 schismatics. This latter category consisted of hidden Christians who did not identify with the Catholicism they encountered in the 19th century and kept aloof.

There is also good reason why many of these Christians in hiding may not have desired to come forward. Freedom of religion was first granted

Twenty-Six Martyrs Museum,
Nagasaki.

in 1890 by the Meiji Constitution, though its terms were still conditional and open to interpretation: Japanese could "within the limits not prejudicial to peace and order, and not antagonistic to their duties as subjects, enjoy religious freedom".

Not exactly an open invitation. Many hidden Christians evidently decided to remain just that, although others slowly emerged to join the Catholic Church. Presumably these were the 17,380 Catholics of the Mission Report. While the granting of religious freedom might seem the end of the story, as there was no longer any dire necessity to hide, oddly it was not the end at all. In the 1930s the work of Tagita Kōya uncovered the continued existence and perseverance of hidden Christian communities. He began his work on Iōjima, a small island off the coast of Nagasaki where 90 per cent of the population were descendants of the first converts to Christianity in the 16th century. From there he launched his zealous search for other communities, discovering them in Nagasaki, Sotome, the Gotō Islands (an archipelago in the East China Sea, west of Nagasaki), and in Ikitsuki and Hirado (islands off the coast of northwest Kyushu). These were heavily Christianised areas during the so-called Christian century. But there were outliers too. In places as far flung as Osaka and elsewhere, here and there, families cherished Christian heirlooms, keeping them hidden from generation to generation. Tagita had the rare and wonderful experience of meeting a 91-year-old man in Sotome who recited *The Beginning of Heaven and Earth*, a hybrid narrative of the *kakure kirishitan* of the Nagasaki area that melded together Buddhism, Christianity and folk stories into an imaginative whole. My investigations into the genealogy of this work led to my translation and annotation of this text, published by the University of Hawaii Press in 1996.

In 1949, Catholics in Japan gathered to commemorate the 400th anniversary of Francis Xavier's arrival in Japan. They chose as the site of festivities the spot where the Urakami Cathedral had once stood. Just four years prior to that celebration, on the morning of August 9, 1945, the United States Army Air Forces B-29 bomber Bock's Car dropped a plutonium atomic bomb over the munitions factories east of the Urakami River – but winds carried the bomb farther north. It exploded 500 metres above the cathedral, wiping out the district of Urakami, an area that had been populated for centuries by people of the Roman Catholic faith, both hidden and newly arisen. The centre of Catholicism in Japan, Urakami was also among the largest churches in Asia with some 16,000 members.

Amid the broken façade of the cathedral with its statuary blackened by heat flashes, Japanese Catholics and foreign and local clergy celebrated the arrival of Francis Xavier, known by the faithful as the 'Apostle of the East', and the seed of Christianity he planted in 1549.

From old photos of this event, one can see hundreds of women and girls wearing white mantillas, Christian clergy both Japanese and foreign mingling, and here and there a few hidden Christian guests, men with close-cropped hair dressed in kimono or *samue*, the casual wear of Buddhist monks. One of the activities was a colloquium held in the rectory of Ōura Church, the very place where in 1865 Father Petitjean had first encountered the tentatively emerging secret Christians. Now a delegation of priests, including Cardinal Gilroy, a proxy for the pope, waited there to meet the hidden Christians from the hills around Nagasaki, and hopefully even those from the distant Gotō Islands. The purpose of the gathering was to invite them back to the church, by reminding them of their historical continuity with Catholicism and of the unnatural rupture the persecutions had created. According to several of my informants, both Catholic and hidden Christian, no hidden Christian from the Gotō Islands attended that celebration. Nor was this event the last formal overture on the part of the Catholic Church to bring back to the body of Christ what increasingly appeared to be its wayward little toe.

Much later, in 1981, prior to Pope John Paul II's visit to Japan, the distinguished Jesuit historian of Japanese Christianity, Father Diego Yūki (a Spanish aristocrat who upon taking Japanese citizenship, assumed the name of a Japanese martyr), sent a briefing on the contemporary state of the hidden Christians to the office preparing the pope's visit. Yūki wrote the following: "Entrenched in their isolation the crypto-Christians have become a branch torn off the tree, slowly withering away. Their numbers are decreasing, and their Christian faith is on the wane too. In postwar Japan, when the youth deserted the villages *en masse* to find work in the cities, oral transmission of doctrine became an impossible task". Near the end of his statement, Yūki sums up his own position: "Theirs is not a case of acculturation but of disintegration of Christianity".

Local clergy in Nagasaki (including Father Yūki) had prepared for the pope's arrival by inviting the leaders of different groups of hidden Christians to meet him. Some declined, but others, namely from Ikitsuki island near Hirado, came to the welcoming site for the pope at Nishizaka where the Twenty-Six Martyrs Museum has stood since 1962. They were

Japanese Christians in Portuguese Costume, Japanese painting from the 16th–17th century.

carrying a huge white banner with a message in French reading: "Holy Father, Here are the Ancient Christians of Ikitsuki". Father Yūki personally introduced these hidden Christians to the pope who embraced those who stepped forward. Aside from this warm gesture, the pope evidently made no public statement about the hidden Christians. I asked Father Yūki whether the pope considered them Christians, heretics, schismatics, or something else, and he wrote the following in a letter to me dated January 11, 2000: "They are little people who under the pressure of the cruel persecution and lack of priests, books, and liberty for more than 250 years, changed little by little till they became a sort of animist religion. And that is not their fault".

Yūki's assessment of the situation suggests that even if the hidden Christians lacked core concepts of the Christian faith such as the resurrection, and in some cases may have stretched Catholicism beyond recognition, the Catholic Church continued to place the blame on horrifically coercive historical circumstances rather than on the volition of the hidden Christians themselves. Not everyone has been as generous in their estimation. In a memoir included in his collection *Stained Glass Elegies* (1969) Endō Shūsaku expresses his open disdain for the hidden Christians whose very faces he claims "reveal both craftiness and cowardice". The gist of his argument is that "…they were finally unable to rid themselves completely of the teachings of their ancestors [Christianity], while at the same time they still lacked the courage to make an open display of their faith as the martyrs had done". Endō clearly condemns their compromise, their secrecy, and their tendency to inhabit a grey zone where they are neither fish nor fowl. Perhaps Endō's deep ambivalence towards the hidden Christian may be considered a Rorschach test that reveals more about his own ongoing struggle as a Catholic in a country where Christianity of any stripe remains a minority religion.

The attempt in 1949 to bring the hidden Christians back to the Catholic Church was based on the idea that historical circumstances had coerced this group into abandoning Christianity; they merely needed to be reminded of their heritage in order to return to it. The Pope's visit in 1981 echoed the same theme. By 1999, the year that Japanese Catholics celebrated the 450th anniversary of Francis Xavier's arrival in Japan, the Portuguese Embassy in Japan honoured the occasion with a year-long calendar of events, but for the hidden Christians the year passed much like any other. In stark contrast to the celebration in 1949, by 1999 it appeared that no one seriously continued to hold the belief that the hidden Christians could be brought back to the church, their true heritage. The buzz about bringing them *back* anywhere had simply vanished.

When I first travelled to the Gotō Islands in search of hidden Christians, the question of why these people continued to hide perplexed me, and fuelled my inquiries about how this group of people viewed themselves and their own history. I soon discovered that their religious practices had grown tenuous over the centuries: they no longer observed much of their former liturgical calendar or disciplines, and the last baptism performed on the island of Narushima, where I lived, was that of a girl then in high school. In grappling with just what it was that still managed to hold these people together as a distinct faith group, I was compelled to ask the most embarrassingly elementary questions such as: what is religion? What is faith? Need they be yoked together? Then – how much can any religion stretch before it loses its core, and with that its meaning?

I witnessed contemporary hidden Christians expressing their religiosity in acts of worship: in the precise recitation of the *orassho* passed down from their ancestors; in their unique rendition of Holy Communion where bowls of saké are passed around and rice is received in the palm of the hand from the celebrant.

Each village has its own priests, its own congregation, and its own style of worship, an organisational structure that probably originated as a protective measure during an era when concealment of one's Christian identity was a matter of life or death.

Christians in Gotō typically possessed no explicit Christian artifacts such as rosaries, crosses, or the porcelain statues of the so-called hybrid Maria-Kannon (the Buddhist *bodhisattva* of compassion) common in museums throughout Kyushu. Or if they do own such objects, these are usually recent gifts from Catholic priests who have taken a pastoral interest in the hidden Christians. However, what one does find in the Buddhist family altars kept by all hidden Christians in Gotō are memorial tablets, or *ihai*, that express their hybridised Christian culture. On the front of these black tablets is the Buddhist name of the deceased painted in gold letters. If one removes the tiny lid from the tablet holder and slides out the slab, the Christian baptismal name is written in black ink on the unvarnished wooden back. These names, written in the script reserved for foreign words, are Japanised versions of Portuguese or Spanish names such as Isaberiya, Maria, Jiwan, or Paburo. The difference between the front and back expresses in concrete form the fracture of identity into the public persona as Buddhist and the private self as Christian. This ambiguous status, partly chosen and partly imposed, confuses a primary sense of belonging and brings to mind anthropologist Takie Sugiyama Lebra's observation about Japanese society: "ambiguity of belonging arouses suspicion and contempt".

This kind of vulnerability is compounded by the fact that hidden Christian religious ceremonies take place in people's private homes. There are typically no churches, temples, chapels, or shrines. The relegation of worship to the private sphere has led to the confinement of the religion to family and village groups. This also suggests what can happen when tangible representations of group identity, normally expressed publicly in architecture and the visual arts are no longer an available resource. What symbols of their tradition would be captivating enough to present day hidden Christian youth for them to want to carry on the tradition?

One of the two elderly hidden Christian priests I knew well lamented that the main problem with hidden Christianity was that it had no schools (i.e. public institutions) like the Catholics and Buddhists where they could train young people in their religion and produce priests for the future. Secrecy had evolved into privacy; they now had a merely private religion. Further, the absence of any system of recruitment had led to a systematic collapse, as young people migrated to the Japanese mainland in search of better work than the squid fishing of their fathers, or the tilling of small plots of daikon-radishes of their mothers.

Today, the groups that practise religion at all have whittled down the liturgical calendar. The primary event of the year is *Ōtaiya* meaning 'big evening' or Christmas Eve. *Kanashimi no agari* (a sort of Easter but without a resurrection), *Yuki no Santa Maria* (Our Lady of the Snows) which commemorates a 4th-century miracle in Italy, and *Kanashimi no hi*, the crucifixion of Christ, are irregularly celebrated holy days. Days of fasting have disappeared altogether, along with the prohibition against eating eggs and meat. Unlucky days for planting and needlework are also part of the past, and Sundays are no longer observed as holy days. Therefore, the times to congregate, renew community, and foster solidarity have grown scarce.

While persecution of the most physical sort had ended for contemporary hidden Christians, its disappearance has also left a distinctive legacy behind. Extreme violence assumed a new and modern face in the form of social suffering. Hidden Christians lived in their own homogenous villages; they married among themselves, or sought to escape their identity altogether by leaving the islands and embracing anonymity in one of Japan's great burgeoning metropolises. Until very recently, hidden Christians were arguably Japan's most invisible marginalised group. Yet in spite of various modes of oppression, over time they had created a solidarity and a hybrid religion opaque and inaccessible to an outsider. They continued to practise something they called 'Christian' even when it was not socially productive to perpetuate this ancestral tradition.

With these facts in mind, I watched Martin Scorsese's profound and nuanced adaptation of the novel *Silence* in which he captures with great sensitivity the depth of the Portuguese priests' dilemma, and recreates an epoch with exquisite and convincing detail. At the same time, it is quite clear that viewers would have no reason to leave the theatre with any impression other than that the truly extraordinary story they have just witnessed is safe in the remote past. But then perhaps it is unfair to expect viewers to think beyond the film when it tells one story beautifully – just not the *whole* story.

For me, one of the most wondrous features of the hidden Christians is that their lives demonstrated the possibility of practising two religions simultaneously, a situation in which the glass is neither half empty nor half full. Yet I also realise that I have the luxury of turning their situation – one coerced rather than chosen – into something positive and even inspirational. This queasy sentiment of my own is somehow also captured by the film in the last scene when viewers are given a privileged glimpse inside the cremation vat where the apparently renegade and apostate priest – Father Rodrigues – is just beginning his final journey. We are jolted from complacency and tossed headfirst into mystery by the sight of a small crucifix cradled in his hand just before the flames begin to roar.

Endō Shūsaku in Stockholm, 1985.

THE POWER OF *SILENCE*
Mark Williams

Born in Tokyo in 1923, but obliged to accompany his family, along with thousands of his fellow countrymen, to settle in Japanese-occupied Manchuria as tensions in the Asia Pacific intensified during the early 1930s, Japanese novelist, Endō Shūsaku's upbringing is never far beneath the surface of his fictional worlds. And when this upheaval was followed, a short time later, by his parents' divorce and the decision of his desperate mother to throw herself and her two young sons at the mercy of a sister living in the Kobe district of central Japan, the seeds of Endō's lifelong fascination with the question of personal identity were well and truly sown. More specifically, one incident from this period in particular – his aunt's insistence that the entire extended family attend Catholic mass on a regular basis and Endō's subsequent decision to embrace baptism into the Catholic tradition – was to have implications for his journey of self-discovery beyond his wildest dreams. And, however much he continued to argue that "I became a Catholic against my will", the fact remains, if his literary legacy, and indeed his personal testimony, is anything to go by, that his lifelong attempts to free himself from the clutches of his adopted faith were to serve as the wellspring for much of his literary oeuvre. As Philip Yancey acknowledges:

> [Endō] likens his faith to an arranged marriage, a forced union with a wife chosen by his mother. He tried to leave that wife – for Marxism, for atheism, for a time even contemplating suicide – but his attempts to escape always failed. He could not live with this arranged wife; he could not live without her. Meanwhile, she kept loving him, and to his surprise, eventually he grew to love her in return.[1]

The ensuing decade was to be equally formative for Endō. Spanning the period when Japan shifted from unbridled aggression in the Asia Pacific region to the need to confront a postwar reality in which the entire nation found itself on its knees and at the mercy of the US occupation, for Endō himself, this was a period of intense soul-searching and self-doubt. Saddled with the nickname 'Amen' during the war by so many of his peers on account of his affiliation with the 'enemy religion', it is hardly surprising that Endō spent much of this period, not so much questioning the motivation behind his decision to accept baptism, but, by his own admission, actively seeking to make his adopted faith into something more compatible with his Japanese identity – to refashion what he described as his "ill-fitting western suit" into a "Japanese kimono".

The challenge would remain with Endō for the rest of his life – and lies at the heart of *Silence* and so many of his acclaimed works. But, as the war in the Asia Pacific came to an end, and as Endō embarked on the quest for an appropriate focus for his philosophical and theological musings, it was to François Mauriac, George Bernanos and other French Catholic authors that his attention was drawn. There followed a nearly three-year interlude when Endō found himself among the first wave of postwar Japanese students sponsored to study abroad. And it was at the University of Lyon where his academic interest in the issues confronting the Catholic author was honed – and, indeed, where the seeds of a career as an author, as opposed to a critic, of fiction were sown.

The experience was by no means easy. Endō and his fellow travellers, some of whom, most notably the Carmelite priest Inoue Yōji, would remain friends for the rest of his life, arrived in France at a time when full diplomatic relations between the two countries were still to be restored. And Endō's literary oeuvre can be seen as testament to his perception of the ignominy of the belittled outsider. The frustration he experienced at his perceived inability to bridge the cultural divide – to scale the 'insurmountable wall' – he increasingly came to discern between East and West led to a gradual deterioration in his physical health and his eventual repatriation, on medical grounds, to his native Japan. The ensuing decade was punctuated by several periods of protracted hospitalisation – and the author's fictional portrayal of what amounts, in essence, to his own 'near death experience' is a constant refrain in his work, nowhere more so than in the, as yet untranslated, *Michishio no jikoku* [At Low Tide, 1965].

The decade 1955–65 was, however, by no means wasted on Endō. Not only did he succeed in securing the prestigious Akutagawa Prize for his early novellas *White Man* and *Yellow Man* (1955), he also penned a series of novels (including *The Sea and Poison, Wonderful Fool* and *The Girl I Left Behind*) that would secure his reputation as an artist in Japan and that laid the groundwork for his first internationally acclaimed novel, *Silence*. Endō also availed himself of this time alone with his thoughts to rework a series of early essays in which he had sought to delve deeper into some of the metaphysical questions that had been germinating since his childhood.[2]

One constant refrain in so many of these essays was the issue of Endō's Catholic faith and the role this exercised in his attempts at identity formulation. Defining the tension that he attributed to his decision to embrace baptism as a child in terms of a 'trichotomy', Endō portrayed his perception of a threefold opposition in his self-identity in the following terms:

> As a Christian, a Japanese and an author, I am constantly concerned with the relationship and conflict created by these three tensions. Unfortunately, I have yet to reconcile and create a certain unity between these three conditions in my mind and, for the most part, they continue to appear as contradictory.[3]

At first glance, the desire to identify and isolate various aspects of the human composite in this manner flies in the face of contemporary psychological theory. Why, one may well ask, was Endō so concerned with the need to posit a tension of conflicting forces in a manner that suggests mutual incompatibility, rather than representing these as a symbiosis of interrelated forces? For Endō, however, the depiction of such tension was essential – not as the basis of a fundamentally negative vision of human nature as representing an amalgam of ultimately irreconcilable forces, but as precursor of the attempt, integral to his literature, to highlight the essentially contradictory interdependence he increasingly came to discern as at work between various facets of the individual composite. The paradoxical attempt to forge a link between characteristics initially established as opposing forces of some binary tension represents a recurring theme in his oeuvre and, as we shall see, in *Silence* in particular.

For Endō, the attempt to somehow define his own personal identity was indivisible from the challenge he had earlier set himself to come to terms with the ramifications of a truly "Christian literature". Challenged by his extensive readings of Mauriac and others within the French Catholic literary community to address the perceived conflict between the "desire of the author to scrutinise human beings" and the "Christian yearning for purity", even before his sojourn in France, Endō had reached the conclusion that:

> Catholic literature involves not a literary portrayal of God and angels, but must limit itself to scrutiny of human beings. Besides, the Catholic writer is neither saint nor poet. The goal of the poet and saint is to focus all his attention on God and to sing his praises. But the Catholic writer must remember not only that he is a writer, but also his duty to scrutinise the individual ... If, for the sake of creating a truly 'Catholic literature', or for the purpose of preserving and propagating the Catholic doctrine, the personalities of the characters in a novel are subjected to artifice and distortion, then the work ceases to be literature in the true sense of the word.[4]

Challenged by this perceived pressure to forge his artistic world through consideration of the dramatic tension that ensues when religion and literature are placed in opposition (in a manner heavily reminiscent of Dostoevsky in *The Brothers Karamazov*, and many other of his classic works), Endō found himself, by the early 1960s, grappling with several of the themes that he would bring to literary maturity in the one novel, *Silence*. At the same time, granted respite from the more serious health concerns with which he had been struggling for so long, Endō took advantage of this opportunity to make several visits to Nagasaki. The city lay at the heart of the Japanese Catholic community and, with less than two decades having passed since its annihilation at the hands of a US atomic bomb (which inflicted disproportionate damage on the city's Catholic heritage), it was a poignant reminder of the tensions between East and West that had served to curtail his stay in France.

It was during the course of these visits that several incidents occurred that helped sharpen the focus of the outline for the novel that was germinating in Endō's mind. First and foremost of these was the visit to the wild and desolate shoreline north of Nagasaki. As he stood on the cliffs, Endō gazed out over the silent sea in the direction of the islands of Gotō and Hirado. He knew these to be the resting place of so many of the hidden [*kakure*] Christians who had been martyred for their faith centuries earlier – in addition to being home to the dwindling population of extant believers who had clung to the *kakure* tradition, eschewing the option to rejoin the Catholic fold following the return of the Christian missions in

Oura Catholic Church in Nagasaki.

the second half of the 19th century. As he stood there, Endō's artistic sensibilities took over. As a believer, he could not help asking himself how he would respond to the call, if necessary, to die for his faith – and he sought to comprehend the reluctance of the tiny *kakure* communities there to reconcile themselves with the more orthodox Catholic tradition into which their ancestors had bought. As he ruminated, Endō found himself formulating the figure of Kichijirō, the 'Judas' figure of *Silence*, who runs away at the first sign of danger – who even betrays the hapless missionary, Rodrigues, to the shogunal authorities – and yet who reappears, after every act of 'cowardice', begging for forgiveness and for the Christian sacrament of absolution. Endō was to invest considerable emotional energy into his depiction of this figure: here is the ultimate everyman, the man who incorporates into his very being that all too human tendency to mistake ego for belief, and of whom Endō was proud to declare on frequent occasions, "Kichijirō, that's me".

Two other chance encounters during his visits to southern Japan were crucial to the artistic process that had been set in motion by this landscape. First came the discovery of a *fumie* in a Nagasaki museum. As a Catholic, Endō would have been well acquainted with the *fumie* [literally, 'stepping on' and 'picture'] tradition used during the Tokugawa shogunate (1603–1867) in an attempt to ensure the total eradication of the Christian tradition in Japan. Comprising an image of Jesus, the Virgin Mary or some other Catholic icon, the *fumie* would be placed in front of anyone suspected of harbouring Christian sympathies – with the suspect obliged to trample on, or in another way defile, this symbol of faith. Stumbling across a *fumie* in the course of his travels, once more Endō found himself wondering how he would have reacted had he too been born in an age in which religious freedom was curtailed. Even more poignant, though, was his focus on the extent to which the bronze coating on this relic appeared shiny and worn away: as an author, Endō's interest would have been piqued by thoughts of the thousands who must have been involved in this process, and his sympathies would have immediately turned to that, admittedly small, minority who would have participated in this charade with a heavy heart.

The other discovery made by Endō at this time, crucial to his evolving narrative, comprised the references to the early missionaries, Giuseppe Chiara and Christavao Ferreira, that he found in the Jesuit archives. These figures emerged as the models for Rodrigues and Father Ferreira,

Endō's 'apostate priest', in *Silence*. The latter proved of particular fascination to Endō: the archives he consulted were full of praise concerning the early mission activities of Ferreira, and his letters back to the Jesuit headquarters in Europe were held up as a model of the unflinchingly 'strong' missionary. Of greater interest to Endō, however, was the fact that references to Ferreira's unstinting and self-sacrificial Christian service appeared to cease abruptly sometime in the 1630s, with all record of his subsequent activities seemingly excised from the Jesuit archives. To date, historians have struggled to piece together the details of what happened to Ferreira; as an author, however, Endō's interest was piqued. It did not require much by way of flights of artistic imagination to come up with the image of Ferreira as the 'fallen priest', broken, in all likelihood, by the psychological and/or physical torture that would doubtless have been inflicted upon him had he been captured, and consequently excommunicated from the Catholic fold as *persona non grata*. Historical 'truth' was of secondary importance to Endō; as an author, it was the very silence of the archives that inspired him to write, and he would have felt little compunction in sacrificing historical accuracy for the purpose of creating literary verisimilitude.

By the early 1960s the groundwork for *Silence* had been completed and Endō turned his attention to the finer details of composition. The challenge, however, remained: how to depict his protagonist struggling with what he perceives as the silence of God, and how to handle the crucial scene when, after all his trials and tribulations, Rodrigues finds himself confronted by the presence and the actual voice of God? Herein lies the genesis of the classic *fumie* scene of the novel in which Endō's protagonist is finally persuaded by his inquisitor, Inoue, and indeed by his erstwhile mentor Ferreira, that he should trample on the crucifix placed before him in order to save, not his own life, but those of the Japanese peasant converts, whose destiny is depicted as lying entirely in Rodrigues' hands, despite their previous apostasy. In the depiction of Rodrigues confronting the *fumie*, struggling against what he sees as the uncaring silence of God, Endō's narrative can be seen as following in a tradition, one that sees silence itself as the most eloquent testimony of divine presence. Indeed, the critic Mark Hughes has traced Kurt Vonnegut's portrayal in *Breakfast of Champions* of the "sudden silence" of the guns on Armistice Day in 1918 as indicative of the "voice of God".

Maria-Kannon, statue of the Buddhist Madonna, used for Christian worship in Japan.

The comparison is apt. For when, in Endō's novel, God does eventually break His silence to Rodrigues, authorising, if not actively encouraging, him to trample on the *fumie*, this can be seen as representing, not a complete reversal or abandonment of the protagonist's theological compass, but a deepening of his personal commitment to the one he now comes to acknowledge at a far more personal level.

The *fumie* scene is all too often cast as representing the climax of the novel. And, given the psychological rollercoaster that has been experienced by the protagonist – and indeed by the reader – throughout the preceding drama, the portrayal may be understandable. What such an interpretation fails to acknowledge, however, is the extent to which it is only following Rodrigues' outward show of apostasy that Endō's text comes to emphasise the protagonist's newfound oneness with God. Only now, as he seeks to come to terms with his revised status as 'fallen' in the eyes of the church, does he come to share an understanding, however limited that may be, of the extent of Christ's suffering for humankind.

In short, unlike his mentor, Rodrigues does not "live happily ever after". Instead, as the text appears at pains to stress in the concluding, post-*fumie* chapter – and perhaps even more so in the extracts from the "Diary of an Officer at the Christian Residence" that follow[5] – Rodrigues emerges from the experience of having his faith tested and of ultimately succumbing to the pressure to go through with his outward act of apostasy, as a man reborn, his faith renewed by the very experience of having been stripped of his pride. As the critic Dennis Washburn has noted, it is following his decision to defile the *fumie* that Rodrigues finds himself possessed of "a more self-reflective, critical consciousness that permits a new understanding of the nature of his faith".[6]

From a theological standpoint, therefore, there can be no justification for the Christ on the *fumie* to break his silence to the despairing Rodrigues by encouraging him to 'trample'. From a literary perspective, however, this is the moment of catharsis, the moment in which Rodrigues acknowledges his inner being, as if for the first time, and finds himself confronted with the light of God's grace. As an immediate consequence of this act, he finds himself released from detention and provided accommodation by the very authorities who had succeeded in inducing his apostasy. However, this dramatic change in his physical fortunes is nothing compared to the metamorphosis occasioned on his spiritual being. Far from depicting Rodrigues following in the footsteps of Ferreira, the narrative focus turns to a depiction of the protagonist paying much closer attention to the inner voice that has long sought to act as his guide along the road to self-discovery. Without that narrative shift, the protagonist's subsequent decision to agree to hear the confession of Kichijirō, the very man who had betrayed him to the authorities – to cling to the vestiges of priesthood even following his public act of renunciation by offering absolution to his betrayer – would appear contrived. Significantly, however, Rodrigues' journey of self-discovery has removed him from concerns for the reactions of the church and his former colleagues. Instead, he is now armed with a newfound confidence in his continuing and strengthened relationship with the being he now comes to refer to, not as God, but as "my Lord", leading him to conclude:

> No doubt his fellow priests would condemn his act as sacrilege; but even if he was betraying them, he was not betraying his Lord. He loved him now in a different way from before. Everything that had taken place until now had been necessary to bring him to this love. 'Even now I am the last priest in this land'.

Even this act, born not so much of defiance as of renewed conviction, however, does not mark the end of the novel. Indeed, it is left to the final diary section to underscore the extent to which the protagonist's newfound, more personal faith has taken root. By this stage, the action has moved on some twenty-five years, with the diary extracts recording events in the last decade of the life of Rodrigues, now living under the inherited name of Okada San'emon. The overriding focus of this brief concluding section is on a man, alone with his thoughts, yet still clinging to the fundamentals of the Christian faith he had purportedly long since renounced. Much of his time is occupied in writing. It is here, in the nature of the work in which his protagonist remains engaged, that Endō offers the clearest evidence that Rodrigues continues to vacillate: the desire to remain faithful to his creed remains in conflict with an acknowledgement of the need to adopt a more pragmatic approach towards the authorities.

During the course of this brief section, there are frequent references to Rodrigues/San'emon being engaged in writing a *shūmon no shomotsu* [literally, a book/document on religion]. The depiction has inspired considerable discussion among critics as to the provenance of this document; to some, the work was simply a "report on Christianity", an unequivocal denunciation of the core tenets of his erstwhile faith. Absent from such a reading, however is the crucial fact that this entire diary section has been reproduced, virtually verbatim – "extracted and adapted" in Endō's assessment – from a work entitled *Sayō Yoroku* [Miscellanies on the Search for Evil Religions]. This historical text, written by one of the clerks at the Christian residence in Edo in the mid-17th century, is a report on the movements of the foreign priests and others with strong earlier connections to the proscribed religion who were confined there under close surveillance.

In contrast to the *Yoroku*, which makes specific mention of the fact that this *shomotsu* was finished and signed by the following year, the diary in Endō's novel emphasises that this process is repeated on at least two further occasions. The modification is important, suggesting as it does that San'emon's ongoing writing is performed under duress; even some twenty-five years after his initial encounter with the *fumie*, he is still to be found penning a formal document, a "pledge of apostasy" disavowing all connection with his former faith. In short, even at the end of his life, San'emon continues to waver in his religious conviction, a consideration that adds poignancy to the final portrayal of San'emon, laid to rest in a Buddhist ceremony at Muryōin temple at Koishikawa and conferred the posthumous Buddhist name of Nyūsen Jōshin-shinshi.[7]

In the discussion to date, we have, of necessity, focused more on the interior monologue of the protagonist encapsulated within the short narrative section that follows the all-important *fumie* scene than on the psychological drama that precedes it. The emphasis is significant. For it is only here, in the carefully crafted portrayal of the protagonist standing in sharp contrast to the determined, unquestioning young priest who had first set foot in Japan, that the reader is drawn towards a sense of the depths of Rodrigues' humanity which, however flawed, nevertheless speaks to those around him.

Endō himself was to make much of his fascination with what he described as the "logic of the weakling". And it is only in the concluding, post-*fumie* chapter and the subsequent diary extracts – in the portrayal of the erosion of the protagonist's unshakeable belief in a division between "the strong" (embodied by Garrpe, Rodrigues' fellow priest, and the various Japanese converts and martyrs) and "the weak", including Rodrigues and Ferreira – that Endō's determination to call into question all such black and white divisions within some posited human duality is clearly articulated. Had it been uttered prior to his fall from grace, Rodrigues' consent to hearing Kichijirō's confession, the rhetorical question: "Can anyone say that the weak do not suffer more than the strong?" would lack potency. Coming as it does, however, following the protagonist's decision to cast off the vestiges of pride and self-grandeur – by defiling something that symbolised everything his life to date as a single-minded seminarian had stood for, the question seems more pertinent, Rodrigues' attempts at self-justification more nuanced.

By this stage, it should be noted, the uncompromising image of the "paternalistic" God who might have been expected to stand in judgement over Rodrigues' act of betrayal is gone. Instead, the diary focus is as much on the vacillating San'emon, and on Kichijirō who, in choosing – or rather finding himself drawn – to remain with San'emon, comes to stand, in many ways, as the physical embodiment of the protagonist's newfound image of a "maternal" God, seeking nothing else than to exist as his *dōhansha* [constant companion]. Endō himself was to make much of this image of Christ, the *dōhansha* figure of the New Testament. A far cry from the harsh, judgmental God of the Old Testament, Endō's focus here is on the light that penetrates the darkness of his protagonist's world, on the rays of hope and optimism that enable San'emon to keep debating with himself and with the authorities.

The image is stark – and leads to arguably the most concerted examination of the human composite in the author's entire oeuvre. In sharp distinction to the portrayal of the clear-cut human binary recognisable in the early short stories and some of his earlier full-length novels, here we see depiction of a character who is at once both sinful and yet redeemed, condemned and yet saved. Just as the binary division between the strong and the weak has been shattered by Endō's challenge to the conventional view of the act of apostasy as born of weakness, Endō here brings together a series of 'oppositions', only to focus on the symbiotic relationship that brings the two poles together. The result is a portrayal of faith – and of the inevitable concomitant doubt – that as the Japanese critic, Makoto Fujimura, has noted in his recent study of Endō's artistic world, represents "an honest admission of our true condition".[8] Endō would surely have concurred with Fujimura. The depiction does, after all, resonate with the following portrayal by Endō of humankind in a post-Auschwitz world:

> Man is a splendid and beautiful being and, at the same time, man is a terrible being as we recognised in Auschwitz. God knows well this monstrous dual quality of man.[9]

Crucifixion scene during the shooting of the film *Silence*, by Martin Scorsese.

1. Fujimura, Makoto, *Silence and Beauty: Hidden Faith Born of Suffering*, p 33.
2. Some of these have recently been translated and discussed in Kasza, J., *Hermeneutics of Evil in the Works of Endō Shūsaku* (Peter Lang, 2016).
3. *Endō Shūsaku bungaku zenshū* (The Complete Works of Endō Shūsaku), vol 12, p 300.
4. Ibid., p 24.
5. Significantly, unlike the English translation, this section is not presented as an appendix in Endō 's original: Endō was often at pains to emphasise that he viewed this concluding section, despite the more classical form of language deployed here, as a core part of the novel.
6. "*The Poetics of Conversion and the Problem of Translation in Endō Shūsaku's Silence*", in Dennis Washburn & Kevin Reinhart, eds *Converting Cultures: Religion, Ideology and Transformations of Modernity* (Brill, 2007), p 346.
7. In an interesting acknowledgement of this scenario, Martin Scorsese has chosen to end his recent film version of the novel with a shot of the protagonist lying in his coffin with a crucifix clasped to his chest.
8. Fujimura, Makoto, *Silence and Beauty: Hidden Faith Born of Suffering*, 85.
9. Interview with Endō, in Chesterton Review 14:3 (1988:8): 499.

REFERENCES

Endō Shūsaku bungaku zenshū [The Complete Works of Endō Shūsaku] (Shōgakukan, 2000).

Fujimura, Makoto, *Silence and Beauty: Hidden Faith Born of Suffering* (InterVarsity Press, 2016).

Hughes, Mark, "Review: Silence Is an Oscar Contender with Provocative Religious Message", in *Forbes online journal* (January 3, 2017).

Washburn, Dennis, "The Poetics of Conversion and the Problem of Translation in Endō Shūsaku's *Silence*", in Dennis Washburn & Kevin Reinhart, eds *Converting Cultures: Religion, Ideology and Transformations of Modernity* (Brill, 2007).

Williams, Mark, *Endō Shūsaku: A Literature of Reconciliation* (Routledge, 1999).

THE MAKING OF SAMURAI IN TOKUGAWA JAPAN

Samurai of the Satsuma clan
during the Boshin War.

THE TRIALS OF THE TOKUGAWA AND THE PASSING OF THE SAMURAI

Stephen Turnbull

The Tokugawa Period, and with it the age of the samurai, came to an end with the Meiji Restoration of 1868 and the so-called Boshin War that brought it about. In this essay I will show how the coming of hostilities suddenly and violently re-awakened the ancient but long-dormant tradition of the samurai. This painful process whereby the descendants of warriors became warriors themselves will be demonstrated in particular through its effects on four individual samurai, whose lives hitherto had been luxurious, bureaucratic and peaceful – until the late summer of 1868 when war burst into their tranquil domains for the first time in two-and-a-half centuries. This turn of events forced from them a reaction that was initially amateurish, sometimes heroic, often tragic and occasionally comical, as the shock of the new provided by the arrival of modern warfare took its toll on the cherished ideals they had inherited from their ancestors.

The Boshin War ['The War of the Year of the Dragon'] was fought between the new imperial army of the restored Meiji emperor and an alliance of domains in the Tōhoku region led by the Sendai domain. The coalition began in May 1868 and became known as the *Ōuetsu Reppan Dōmei*, a title loosely but meaningfully translated as the 'Northern Alliance'. The alliance's headquarters was Shiroishi castle (in modern Shiroishi City, Miyagi prefecture), and its armed strength consisted of about 50,000 troops. Their argument was that the emperor was being misled by "evil advisers" from the distant and distrusted southern domains of Satsuma and Chōshū. They also stressed that the northern domains were no less loyal to the emperor than these "selfish and self-seeking" opportunists who sought to dominate the court.

The Northern Alliance never acted as a single cohesive unit. After some early defections its members came and went according to personal considerations determined by individual lords, regarding matters that differed from domain to domain. For a few, their chosen allegiance harked back as far as the land transfer policy of the first Tokugawa shogun, Ieyasu (1542–1616). At that time the *tozama* [outer lords], who had either opposed the Tokugawa or been tardy in acknowledging their triumph, had been relocated to distant areas of Japan. Here, their activities could be monitored by domains related to the Tokugawa family or those ruled by the *fudai*, who were either hereditary retainers of the Tokugawa or very close allies. When political dissatisfaction grew during the 19th century, the main focus of opposition to the Tokugawa emerged within the historic *tozama* ranks, notably the domains of Satsuma (modern Kagoshima prefecture) and Chōshū (Yamaguchi). Having taken up the imperial cause, their soldiers took part in the battles of Toba-Fushimi and Ueno under the newly-created chrysanthemum banner, a public relations coup that proclaimed a legitimacy to which any supporters of the ousted Tokugawa Shogun, who were now labelled as rebels against the throne, could not possibly aspire.

The part of the Boshin War which I shall examine here is the Akita-Shōnai campaign that arose within the situation created by the advance northwards from Edo by imperial forces against the Northern Alliance. One of the few *daimyō* in the north with imperial sympathies was Satake Yoshitaka (1825–84) who held the domain of Akita and was based at the castle of Kubota (the alternative title for the domain) that now lies within modern Akita City. The Satake clan had become *tozama* when their first lord, Satake Yoshinobu, was slow in his support of the Tokugawa in 1600.

In 1868, after finally rejecting overtures from the pro-Tokugawa domains, Satake Yoshitaka's Akita domain decided to stand by its own impeccable pro-imperial credentials, the foundations of which had been laid by the *kokugaku* [national learning] scholar Hirata Atsutane (1776–1843), who was a man of Akita. Long before the Boshin War began, the leaders of Akita had imbibed the ideas that Buddhism and Confucianism were alien traditions, and that Japan was the land of the gods; concepts that had been embraced by the imperialist cause. With Akita as their focus, the overall direction of the imperialist effort in Tōhoku was placed in the hands of the former court noble Kujō Michitaka (1839–1906) – one example of faith unwisely vested in several men like him who had little or no training in military matters, but who were regarded as suitable for command because of their social position and expertise in the Confucian classics.

Considerable military pressure was brought against the area because the harbours of Akita could provide the means for a rear attack against the Northern Alliance. The brunt of this effort throughout the ensuing campaign was to be taken by Akita's near neighbour to the south: the pro-Tokugawa domain of Shōnai, based around Tsurugaoka castle (modern Tsuruoka City, Yamagata prefecture). This was the territory of the senior branch of the Sakai family who had resided in Tsuruoka since 1622 and were descended from the *fudai* Sakai Tadatsugu (1527–96) and his son Ietsugu (1564–1619), two of Tokugawa Ieyasu's closest associates.

Satake Yoshitaka's isolated imperialist enclave of Akita enjoyed a strong defensible position. On its western edge lay the Sea of Japan. High mountains crossed by difficult passes lay to the east, but the most important defensive feature was the great Omonogawa River, a formidable natural moat if the domain's southern outposts were lost to an enemy. When the Shōnai began hostile moves along the simplest approach of the coast road in early June a defensive stance for the Akita domain may well have been advisable. But Satake Yoshitaka decided otherwise and ordered his army to stop the advance in the narrow Misaki Pass, the border between modern Akita and Yamagata Prefectures.

The brief action of the June 8, 1868 was in the hands of Akita's Shibue Naizen, who had an impeccable samurai pedigree, being descended from a retainer of the same name who had served Satake Yoshinobu in 1615 as *karō* [senior retainer] and was killed at Imafuku. The Shibue family had supplied seven *karō* over the centuries and had been active in the encouragement and training of the Akita samurai in the traditional martial arts, but the amateurish attack that followed demonstrated dramatically how the domain had failed to keep up to date in military matters. This deficiency included the supply of arms and equipment, and nothing better illustrates the prevailing ignorance of modern warfare within the Akita than their appearance. Unlike the Shōnai troops, the men of Akita were dressed in full samurai armour at least 300 years old, complete with *jinbaori* [surcoats] and *hata sashimono* [flags worn on the back] brought out from numerous family storerooms. Their firearms were matchlock muskets, and some even carried bows.

The quaint appearance of the Akita army was paralleled by their leader's equally inexpert and anachronistic behaviour. Shibue Daizen's vanguard was led by Arakawa Kyūtarō Hidetane and his 'surprise attack corps', but the Shōnai men, who had been shadowing their movements, were not going to allow themselves to be surprised. Little suspecting that the Shōnai army was waiting for him in the Misaki Pass, Arakawa

Kyūtarō confidently headed south with his army. As they passed through the village of Kisakata he stopped to pay homage at the local Kumano Shrine, where he cut off his pigtail like a samurai general of old, and presented it as an offering for victory. When the forces put on their brilliantly lacquered breastplates and helmets bearing the golden fan-in-a-circle *mon* [crest] of the Satake family they shone in the dawn sunlight, making them the perfect target for the waiting rifles of the Shōnai force. There was such confusion that the Akita men began attacking each other by mistake, and their disastrous first attempt at warfare for two-and-a-half centuries came to an abrupt end.

★

Certain neighbouring domains that, up to that point, had wavered over where their allegiance lay took the opportunity to make a formal declaration of support for the imperialist cause. They included Akita's immediate neighbours to the south: the smaller domains of Kameda, Honjō and Yashima. Shōnai resumed the offensive against Akita on August 23 with an attack on the mountainous domain of Yashima. Yashima lay under the control of Ikoma Chikayuki who was nineteen years old. The Shōnai army advanced against him during the month of September, a time that provided a brief window of opportunity for a daring assault over the summit of Mount Chōkai. So, on September 13 the mountain's southern face was scaled. The army spent the night in the Ōmonoimi Shrine just below the summit, and as dawn broke they descended by rough paths of scree and old snow down the northern side. At the Kizakai Shrine, the assault force divided, and coordinated their movements with perfect timing for a three-pronged assault on Yashima. Ikoma Chikayuki was taken completely by surprise, and as temples, houses and his own mansion burned around him, he fled to the safety of the Akita domain.

A few days later, a second young Akita *daimyō* was to experience an attack by the Shōnai army. This was Rokugō Masaakira, then twenty years old, who ruled the domain of Honjō from his castle in modern Ugo-Honjō City. Samurai ancestry was all that the young Rokugō Masaakira possessed in abundance, but he prepared as best he could for an assault. Unfortunately, his overall commanders decided that Honjō was to be abandoned, and the army had to withdraw north of the Omonogawa, where reinforcements were steadily arriving. When Rokugō Masaakira

The Boshin War.

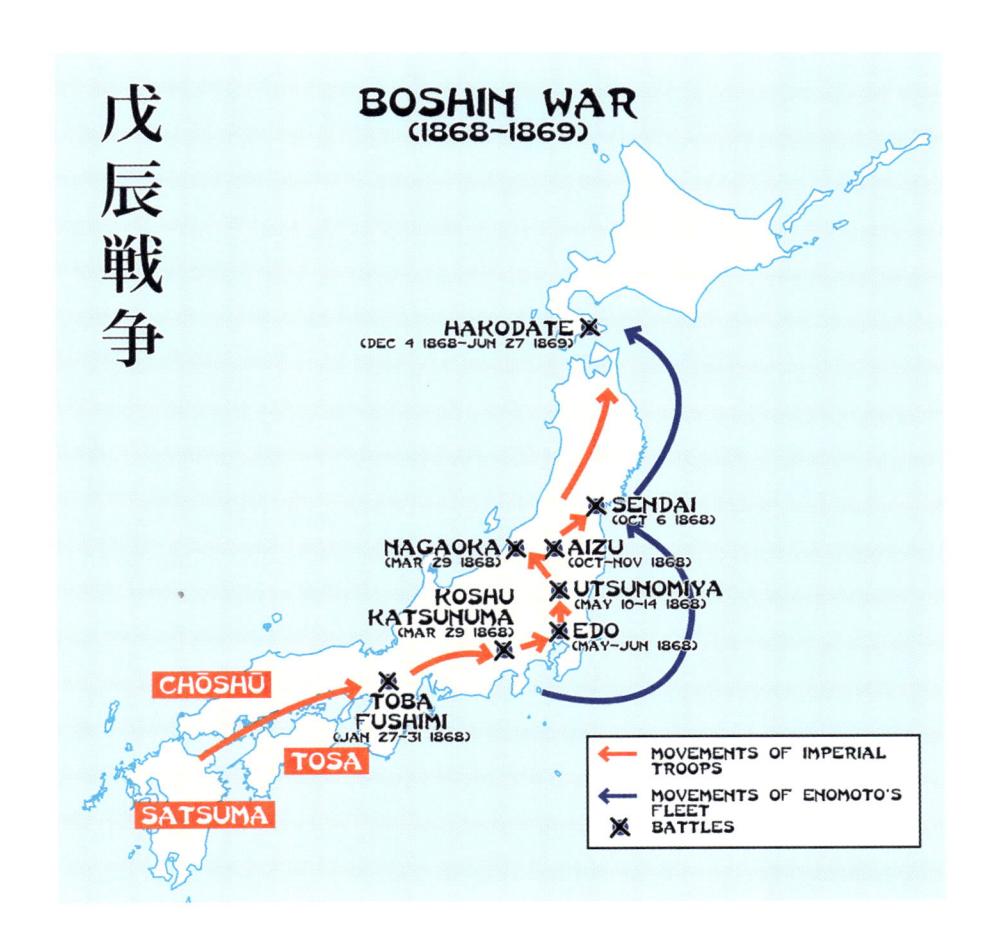

bravely requested permission to launch a surprise attack on the advancing Shōnai army he was ordered to withdraw in compliance with the new strategy. He left Honjō on September 21, and was horrified to see his magnificent castle (an extensive edifice with many houses, barracks and a harbour for cargo ships) being burned down by the retreating imperial forces so it would not fall into the hands of their enemies.

★

At about the same time, another Shōnai army concentrated on the castle of Yokote, the strongest point in the southern part of Akita. It had been the headquarters of the domain of the Onodera whom the Satake had displaced in 1603, but had been burned down at that time. When Yokote was rebuilt, Sadanobu installed as its keeper the grandson of one of his most loyal retainers, Tomura Yoshikuni. Responsibility for Yokote had stayed within the Tomura family over the next two centuries, so that when the Shōnai advanced on Yokote in 1868, a nineteen-year-old descendant of Yoshikuni, Tomura Daigaku, was waiting for them. The main Akita army, however, had abandoned Yokote to make a stand fifteen kilometres to the north at Kakumagawa. Tomura Daigaku was ordered to follow them, but the proud commander of Yokote castle refused to obey orders. Unlike Rokugō and Ikoma, Tomura Daigaku was not a *daimyō*, but the retainer of a *daimyō* to whom he had pledged loyalty and who had entrusted him with the defence of Yokote castle. With a garrison of only 280 men, Tomura Daigaku decided to withstand the entire Shōnai army of 3,000 men on his own.

Tomura's brave gesture was explained to the two officers who brought him the order to withdraw. His words, which may have been recorded at the time, or related by him at a later date, appear with some variation in two separate accounts. In both, he states that the orders may well have come from the second-in-command to Kujō Michitaka, but they were not in accordance with the orders of his master, Satake Yoshitaka. Tomura Daigaku's family had been the keepers of Yokote since the time of his ancestors. To abandon that solemn responsibility and flee would dishonour their spirits. How could he ever show his face in the presence of his lord again? Instead he stated, "I shall fight until my strength runs out, and then die in action with the castle as my pillow". The Akita forces may by then have embraced modernity in their costume and weapons, but

Tomura Daigaku would demonstrate that he was the equal of his illustrious ancestor Tomura Yoshikuni, whose lacquered wooden statue with glaring glass eyes still sits defiantly within the funerary chapel of the Ryōshō-In, the Tomura family temple just below Yokote castle. Yet even though Daigaku's samurai spirit was vibrant, he had little in the way of food supplies, and his armaments demonstrated the overall imperialist strategy of not wasting modern weapons in the defence of an expendable position. Of hand-held firearms, there were only two modern Minie rifles, but thirty-eight old matchlock muskets, together with thirty and 100 shot respectively for twelve small and medium cannons, which were probably just large-calibre matchlocks. Besides these he had bows and spears. Apart from that he had bravery, determination, and a great respect for the traditions of his ancestors.

A similarly nostalgic respect for ancient martial traditions was also revealed among the attacking army at the same time, because as the Shōnai force approached Yokote, twelve cranes appeared in the sky and fluttered around the castle roof. The word for crane appeared in the name of the domain's capital, so it was regarded as a good omen. When the advance began the Shōnai army crossed the river below Yokote castle, giving fire and burning buildings. Artillery was also used against the castle itself, destroying much of the superstructure, and the sound of the cannon added to the noise from the war drums. The climax of the battle for Yokote came on the afternoon of September 26 with two hours of fierce hand-to-hand fighting, during which Tomura Daigaku killed two men with his own sword. Seeing the cause was now hopeless, he prepared himself for suicide, but was urged against it by one of his officers. Instead, Daigaku led a fighting retreat out of the castle to the north, leaving behind the burning building and twenty-one dead from the garrison. Tomura Daigaku survived the Boshin War and went on to become the Mayor of Yokote.

★

Only one domain now lay between the Shōnai army and the Omonogawa. This was Kameda, a fief ruled by Iwaki Takakuni, who had close family links to the Satake. Iwaki Takakuni lived in lavish style in a castle called Amasaki. His army had been fully involved in the fighting ever since joining Akita in the imperial fold, but their leader now expressed horror at the reports reaching him. Would his own beautiful castle suffer the fate

Bakufu troops near Mount Fuji in 1867.

of those domains abandoned to the enemy? He called a meeting of his family and senior retainers within Amasaki castle on September 18 to discuss the crisis. Three days later came the news that Honjō castle had been destroyed by its own allies as part of a scorched earth policy, so to safeguard his ancestral property Iwaki decided not to flee. Instead he made a unique and fateful decision, and on the same day that Honjō was burned to the ground, he changed sides.

Iwaki's treachery was of genuine benefit to the Northern Alliance. The crossing of the natural moat of the Omonogawa was always going to be a major exercise in the campaign, and to have as an ally the man whose domain straddled the river was a great asset. Iwaki's troops knew their area, so (somewhat cynically, one assumes) the Shōnai commanders placed them in the vanguard of their army in the operation to secure the crossing places. Iwaki Takakuni could also provide a useful supply of subservient civilian labour for the northern cause, and it was this factor that was to result in the most acute suffering among any civilian population during the whole of the Akita-Shōnai campaign. With a contempt for the lower orders that was itself part of the samurai tradition, Iwaki Takakuni placed his domain and its inhabitants at the service of his new allies. A document preserved by Ōuchi town records the items that were supplied to the army on an almost daily basis such as straw sandals, bedding, *daikon* radishes and lumber, but these requisitions were not carried out in an atmosphere of safety. Villagers elsewhere may have seen their homes destroyed and their crops looted, but they had usually been able to flee. The farmers who lived near the Omonogawa were trapped by the river on one side and a hungry advancing army – once an enemy but now apparently their friends – on the other.

To make matters worse, imperialist troops – once their friends, but now enemies that included soldiers from distant Kyūshū – were still stationed in the villages that guarded crossing points, while others came across the river on scouting missions. Over a period of a month, local people were literally caught in the crossfire as the Shōnai army attacked these positions and rifle fire was exchanged between the river's banks. Many civilians from the southern bank tried to escape across the river, but unable to do so, fled instead to the hills and marshes, building shelters where women, children, elders and household goods could be hidden. Meanwhile, menfolk were pressed into the Kameda domain army or made to forage, a cruel and painful exercise for which we have a unique written account to set beside the reports of generals and the diaries of soldiers. It is found in the diary of Ōtomo Sadanosuke, who held the position of *kimoiri* [overseer] for the village of Takao. Hostilities were limited to the exchange of rifle fire across the river until October 23, an important day in Japanese history, because on that day the era name was changed and what had been the Fourth Year of Keiō now became the First Year of Meiji. But that momentous event in distant Tokyo escaped the attention of Sadanosuke, who wrote in his diary about the culmination that night of the suffering of the local villagers who were sent in search of food and boats:

> Very great was the suffering of the labourers made to go foraging from the villages in the dead of the night of 23 October. They walked carrying on their backs provisions from unfamiliar mountains and fields, not even carrying pine torches and without any guides. Heads, bodies and limbs collapsed on to the ground here and there amidst the cold wind and the thunder. They were unable to distinguish friend from foe, and to make matters worse the untold suffering experienced during the crossing of the swollen Omonogawa as the wind blew is a thing of such desolation that I will never forget it to the end of my days. It is impossible to express it with my brush.[1]

That same night the Shōnai army crossed the river for what they hoped would be the final assault on Kubota castle. Sadanosuke describes it as 'the battle for the Akita domain'. By this time, however, their ranks had been swollen by soldiers from other divisions who had fought their way along the course of the Omonogawa from the south. The crossing of the Omonogawa took place at 08.00. While artillery shelled Shibue Daizen's position across the river, the Shōnai army crossed using seven boats. There they engaged a major concentration of imperialist forces within a fortified position on high ground at Fukubera on a small peninsula where the river makes a dramatic tongue-shaped curve. Fukubera was defended by local forces including the redoubtable Tomura Daigaku, as ready to make a stand at Fukubera as he had been at Yokote.

★

The imperialist army was soon in full retreat and heading for the only place where a stand could be made outside Kubota castle itself. This was a prominent ridge on which stood Tsubakidai castle. The castle town of Akita, a mere 16 kilometres away, was now in a state of panic, and little Tsubakidai castle was all that stood between it and the advancing Shōnai army. Fully appreciating this point, Kujō Michitaka and Sasaki Yoshitaka gave orders that Tsubakidai would not be abandoned like Honjō and Yokote. Instead, it should be held at all costs.

The battle of Tsubakidai took place in front of the field defences on the plateau and within the valley of the Anjōji River, and the fighting was intense. The Shōnai Army launched their first attack on October 25, but the imperialist line held. The following day the imperialists went on to the attack, supported by cannon fire from forward positions, and drove the Shōnai army back, inflicting casualties on them of 100 dead and eighty wounded, the greatest single loss by the Shōnai army since the campaign had begun. Captain Ishihara Kakuemon of Shōnai wrote of the first day of the battle: "Before dawn that night the enemy had built fortified breastworks at various places and the enemy attacks increased still further". The attacks "destroyed the wooden palisades set up by our side ... As we pulled back III Corps came up in support under Miyoshi Shinbei with a view to a second day of hard fighting".[2] Realising that their advance had been halted, and with no support on their flanks, the Shōnai army began to withdraw as evening came. They pulled back across the Omonogawa at the point where they had crossed it in such triumph only two days earlier. According to the words on the memorial in Anjōji, thirty per cent of the houses in the area were burned down, and many local villagers, who were pressed into service by both sides to make up for the deficit in numbers, lost their lives.

The decisive Battle of Tsubakidai was the turning point in the Akita-Shōnai campaign, but there was one more battle left to fight. Some of the Shōnai army had retreated along the old road north of the river to Kariwano, and combined there to make a last stand. By all accounts this final battle of the campaign was a fierce and desperate one. Captain Mizuno Kyōemon describes his men using the ridges between rice fields at Kariwano as makeshift trenches for protection 'with their heads lowered and their bodies partly concealed'.[3] At dawn on October 31, with their bullets almost used up and their bodies exhausted, the Shōnai army finished their long campaign against Akita in a consummate illustration of the samurai tradition by making a final desperate charge against the Akita positions with their samurai swords. As they pursued the retreating Shōnai army the Akita force took terrible revenge on the traitor Iwaki Takakuni by burning down the castle that he had tried to save by defecting.

★

The samurai tradition had always consisted of two elements: the code of conduct that valued hierarchical Confucian ideals of loyalty above all other things, and the courageous military skills through which that code could be both expressed and defended. Isolated in Tōhoku during the peaceful Edo period, the young leaders of Akita had maintained the former as an ideological concept but had lost the latter through a failure to modernise, a paradoxical situation for samurai that had been satisfactorily rationalised by the progressive (in military terms at least) domains of Shōnai, Satsuma and Chōshū. When war broke through into the cosy domains of Akita these young men began a steep learning curve whereby both the ideological and the practical aspects of the samurai tradition were violently re-awakened, and their subsequent experiences represented a microcosm of the military situation in Japan as a whole. Here was a nation with the two faces of Janus: one looking back to its samurai past, the other one looking forward to what we now call Meiji Japan where, as future events were to show, the desire for glory, the feeling of superiority, the exercise of courage and loyalty and the acceptance of death that were so characteristic of the samurai tradition lived on to find expression during the wars against China and Russia.

There was, however, a fundamental difference in the way these ideals were to be expressed a decade later from the way they were demonstrated in 1868, and this came about as a direct result of the imperialist victory described above. The desire of the Meiji government to establish itself as the equal of the supposedly hostile western powers required the mobilisation of the nation in a common patriotic purpose. The result was the introduction of several measures designed to create an emperor-centred nationalism. The reforms were constitutional, educational and militaristic, and included the introduction of universal conscription in 1872, when old myths and ancient traditions were mobilised along with the soldiers to support the new regime. When conscription was enforced in 1873, the monopoly of the right to bear arms enjoyed by the samurai class ended forever, and, as the sociologist Tsurumi Kazuko has it: "the feudal samurai ethic of dying honourably for the sake of one's lord was transformed

Illustration of the Samurai tradition.

into a universal ethic for the entire population of Japan, through the requirement of honourable death for the sake of the Emperor".[4] As the *Gunjin Kunkai* [Admonition to Soldiers] of 1878 stressed, the ethos of the new army was derived from the ideals of the samurai and passed on to the conscripts:

> Today's soldiers are undoubtedly *bushi, [i.e samurai]* even if their status is not hereditary. It is therefore beyond question that they should exhibit loyalty and courage as their prime virtues, according to the best tradition of the *bushi* of bygone days.

It was a process of socialisation that covered a wider field than just the army, and in its early stages at least, it was welcomed by common people who had envied the samurai's position in society and who now rushed to imitate their lifestyle. It was only later when the effects of conscription were felt by farming families deprived of workers that resentment grew towards this revolutionary measure.

But in 1868, all this lay in the future, and (apart from some use of pressed soldiers from the domains) the Boshin War was a civil war fought between the members of the samurai class, opponents who subscribed to common values and shared the same concept of self-identification. The myths of the samurai tradition that were to be re-awakened were at that time more powerful than the developing imperial myth. It would, however, be many years before any Japanese soldier felt obliged to fight to the death because of the debt he owed to the emperor merely by being born as his subject. Instead, they followed the samurai tradition in its simplest form, a code that embraced "honorific individualism", as Ikegami terms it in *The Taming of the Samurai: Honorific Individualism and the Making of Modern Japan*, and crossed the divide between the rival factions:

> Having become deeply embedded in their self-definition, this synthesis of honor and dignity provided a common source of passion for individual samurai in different ideological camps, whose social and political patterns of behaviour otherwise varied wildly. In an essay entitled 'Plots and Motives in Japan's Meiji Restoration', G.W. Wilson puts it slightly differently when he writes of "a variety of motives that nonetheless coalesce into a situationally transcendent impulse. Some samurai turned old grudges into the stuff of new power relations.

Some sought simple self-gratification". Both these points are illustrated by the behaviour of combatants during the Akita-Shōnai campaign, where respect for the samurai tradition runs through many of the decisions that were made. Striking by their absence, however, are any references to the emperor as a focus of samurai loyalty on the imperial side, so we look in vain in accounts of Tomura Daigaku's defence of Yokote for any allusion to dying for the emperor or any exploration of the abstract *kokugaku* ideas of Hirata Atsutane.

Noticeably absent, too, is any reference to the principles of *bushidō* [the way of the samurai] as a guide for the warrior. Instead, Daigaku simply believes that loyalty to Satake Yoshitaka coupled with personal honour and respect for the spirits of his ancestors compels him to disobey orders. In the Akita-Shōnai campaign we see myths and traditions in operation in Japan for the last time in the service of anyone other than the emperor. The old samurai tradition, where the focus of loyalty is vested in the *daimyō*, had been re-awakened for its final expression.

---

1. Akita Bunka Shuppan Kabushiki-gaisha *Boshin Sensō 130 Shūnen Kinen Shi* (Akita, 1999) p 108; usefully summarised in modern Japanese in the simple local history book by Iwami Seifu *Yuwa Machi no rekishi* (Akita, 1992) p 103.
2. Yoshitake, Kōri, *Akita Shōnai Boshin Sensō* (Akita, 2001) p 201.
3. Yoshitake, Kōri, *Akita Shōnai Boshin Sensō* (Akita, 2001) p 186.
4. Kazuko, Tsurumi, *Social Change and the Individual: Japan before and after defeat in World War II* (Princeton University Press, 1970) p 82.

Ishi-jo, wife of Oboshi Yoshio, 1848.

SAMURAI WOMEN IN EARLY MODERN JAPAN
Anne Walthall

When Hirata Orise followed her husband into exile in 1841, she discovered just how constrained the life of a samurai woman could be. Born the daughter of a tofu maker in a provincial town, she had moved to Edo (now Tokyo) in 1818 to marry Hirata Atsutane, then an up-and-coming scholar and teacher of Japan studies. She enjoyed life in Edo where she participated in drinking bouts with relatives and friends or took Atsutane's grandchildren on excursions to temples and to view the cherry blossoms. When the couple moved to Atsutane's hometown of Akita in the remote northeast, they lived with his samurai relatives while waiting for the domain to give him an appointment with samurai rank and status. As Orise complained in a letter to her stepdaughter, Atsutane's sister warned her that she was not to go out of the family's compound unnecessarily. She had a servant; he was to do the shopping even though he seldom got what she wanted. Even after she and Atsutane moved into quarters of their own, she still had to remain discreetly indoors.

The change in Orise's circumstances points to a major difference between women born or inducted into samurai households and commoner women. There were other differences, of course, and in order to learn about samurai women's lives, it is important to place them in the context of women's lives during Japan's early modern period more generally. It is also important to evaluate their contributions to maintaining the samurai class that dominated this society. Even the staunchest, most heroic warrior had a mother, a wife, and perhaps even daughters. Without women, the samurai as a social status would have ceased to exist. Without a wife, no individual samurai could constitute himself as a full-fledged member of his retainer band. Furthermore, when talking about samurai women, it is worth emphasising that they participated in the ethos of what it meant to be samurai. That is to say, they were expected to live by a code for conduct analogous to that of their menfolk.

Orise went into exile in Akita not for anything she had done, but because her husband Atsutane had for unspecified reasons incurred the shogun's displeasure. Rather than send him off by himself, with no one to cook his food, tend to his clothes, write letters on his behalf, or share his hardships and triumphs, Orise accompanied him because in this society, men and women were interdependent, as I will explain below. The letters that she wrote to the rest of the family left in Edo provide important insights into her activities and thus help illustrate some of the similarities and differences between samurai and commoner women. I also want to focus on the importance of succession to samurai households and women's roles in maintaining it.

Orise died in 1846, twenty-two years before the fall of the Tokugawa shogunate that ended Japan's early modern period. During the brief civil war of 1868, samurai women and men found themselves in combat for the first time since the early 17th century. Much had changed in the intervening 250 years, and one way to illuminate those changes is to explore what women did.

★

Whether at the highest ranks of premodern society or the lowest, men needed women and women needed men. There are exceptions, of course, primarily in religious establishments, but in such cases, same-sex groups replaced heterosexual couples. It is my understanding, however, that even in the mountain top monasteries of Kōya-san, the monks relied on women living at the bottom of the mountain to wash and make their clothes. Other examples of same-sex groups include blind entertainers, either female [*goze*] or male [*zatō*].

For commoner husbands and wives, the social ideal was to live together in a symbiotic relationship, working in concert like two wheels to a cart, to use a common expression of the time. In the case of farm households, women performed crucial roles. Only their fingers were delicate enough to handle tender little seedlings when rice was transplanted, so men carried the seedlings to the rice paddies and offered encouragement by beating drums while women performed the back-breaking work of sticking the plants in the mud. While the plants were growing, women and men did the weeding. Women raised silkworms and spun silk thread, they carded cotton and spun cotton thread, and they picked tea leaves.

Spinning silk from silkworm cocoons.

Spinner.

At harvest time they helped thresh the grain, and when at the new year men pounded rice into cakes (*mochi*), women ducked and darted, thrusting their hands into the mortar to turn the cake between each blow of the mallet. In fishing villages they dived for shellfish. In merchants' houses as well, women ran the back of the house, especially the kitchen, while their husbands managed the front. Without both a man and a woman in the house, it would not survive.

The situation was different for the samurai, at least in theory. Men performed their duties not at home but at the lord's castle or some other institutional venue. They received a stipend based on hereditary status as a warrior that had nothing to do with women. The women born into samurai households needed men for income and protection, if nothing else. But aside from procreation, did samurai men need women? For the poorest samurai, it was said that if they had a servant, they could not afford a wife, and vice versa, suggesting that to a certain extent, women were replaceable. So why bother with women beyond their role as what was dismissively defined as 'borrowed wombs'?

There are two ways to answer this question, one based on the reality of samurai lives, the other based on the organisation of the samurai household. Employment opportunities for samurai men hardly kept most of them busy, leaving them with plenty of time to participate in childcare, educate their sons, even cook and clean or do repairs around the house. Many samurai relied on side-employments, making cricket cages, for example, to supplement their meagre stipends, and women too contributed to the family's income by making paper hair ties, taking in sewing, or doing other odd jobs. Samurai women in the Mito domain did spinning and weaving, for their family and for hire. Atsutane, for example, did much of his work at home, writing treatises, trying to get his books published, or lecturing to his students. He also visited important *daimyō* compounds in Edo hoping for recognition as a scholar and a samurai. While he was out, and before he adopted a son-in-law to marry his daughter, Orise had to stay home to guard the house and entertain any visitors who might show up. In addition, she was expected to keep the family diary that recorded Atsutane's activities and visitors, a duty that she continued to perform in Akita.

The organisation of the samurai household made women necessary. The genealogies kept by the domains listed each member of the retainer band as the head of a household. Although these households were patrilineal, the constitution of a household required that the wife be listed as well, usually in terms of whose daughter she was. The presence of women in these genealogies thus suggests that women played a crucial role in building alliances between households. Samurai of all ranks had to get permission to marry in order to ensure the cohesion of the retainer band, to guard against collusion, and to guarantee that the betrothed couple came from households of more or less equal status. Samurai were supposed to marry other samurai. If a man wanted to marry a non-samurai woman, she had to be adopted into another samurai family, preferably one from the same domain, before the marriage could take place. When Atsutane married Orise, he was only the fourth son of a samurai and had no official rank and status. Even so, before he married her, he had her adopted by his patron, a wealthy and prominent village official, lest her status as the daughter of a mere tofu maker reflect badly on his position and prospects.

Being the head of a household and marriage went together. If any man, samurai or commoner, did not have his own household or the possibility of succeeding to one, he could not get married. In a society that practised primogeniture, this was a particular problem for younger sons. One reason Atsutane had fled Akita at the age of nineteen was because he had little prospect of being anything more than a burden to his family without getting married. If a man did head a household, having a wife gave him stature in his community as a man with adult responsibilities. If we remember the case of the poor samurai with a servant and no wife, he lacked the kind of access to a woman that would have brought him respect. Or to put it another way, the ranking of men in this society pivoted on their access to women and the differential distribution of their access to women. Men at the top, the shogun, the *daimyō*, and their highest-ranking samurai retainers, had not only wives but also female attendants and concubines. Men at the bottom had a hard time even getting a wife.

★

Despite their differences in status, non-samurai women and samurai women performed many of the same activities. In addition to the contributions to subsistence mentioned above, women did the sewing for the household. In order to wash a kimono, for example, it had to be taken apart, the pieces washed, stretched on boards to dry, and then stitched

Lady-in-waiting playing cards,
from a 1893 triptych.

A Lady from a Samurai Household
with Three Attendants, ca 1820.

back together. Clothes also had to be made and mended; another woman's chore. When Orise went to Akita, she consulted with Atsutane's sister regarding appropriate garb for his ceremonial appearances at the castle and then fashioned suitable items herself or asked her stepdaughter in Edo to procure them. Women prepared food, or at least supervised its preparation. Even when the relatives in Akita sent gifts of food, Orise cooked for Atsutane because he preferred the way she seasoned his dishes. Women were responsible for kin work – for keeping in touch with family members. Orise corresponded with the family left behind in Edo; she spent hours with Atsutane's relatives in Akita.

While all women participated in similar activities to keep their families going, appearance and training distinguished samurai woman from commoners. In 1854, the woodblock artist Utagawa Yoshitora created an illustration that shows an idealised representation of women of various status, from farmwomen to a samurai woman. On the left, he depicts two women carrying a bucket of water. They have round faces with prominent features. Their legs and arms are bare. The woman in the centre is more decorously attired with an elaborate hairstyle, and you can barely see one foot, clad in a sock, poking out below her robe. The woman to the right discreetly covers her mouth, and you can see neither her hands nor her feet. This image also speaks to their relative visibility. Farmwomen lived and worked outdoors. Townswomen worked inside but went shopping and went on excursions. Samurai women were expected to remain indoors, and the higher in rank, the less visible they were.

On the rare occasions when samurai women left their house, they never went out alone. Even samurai men always appeared in public with a retainer; for anyone to be by himself invited suspicion. If the woman was of high enough rank, she rode in a palanquin with at least one attendant following along behind. Suitable destinations included twice yearly visits to a woman's natal parents, pilgrimages to local shrines, temples, and graves, plus attendance at the weddings and funerals of relatives. Samurai women were discouraged from going to the theatre or any other place of entertainment and, as we saw in Orise's case, they were not to go shopping.

Even though they rarely appeared in public, samurai women were expected to practise self-cultivation. Women in provincial castle towns, especially in northeastern Japan, had little opportunity to learn more than sewing, household management, etiquette and deportment, a side-employment or two, and the oral traditions of their domain. Many of them had no access to books. One request that Orise made of her stepdaughter was to send textbooks suitable for girls because none were available in Akita. Women who lived in western Japan or closer to urban centres had more options. In addition to the skills listed above, they might learn how to write poetry, how to distinguish different kinds of incense, how to play the *koto* or some other instrument, or how to deploy the *naginata* – a spear with a curved blade, designed especially for women to use in protecting their house and defending their honour. In theory, every samurai woman learned how to use *naginata* and daggers for self-defence; in practice I am not at all certain that such was the case. A woman from Mito stated that by the early 19th century, few women in her domain studied the martial arts. Women were more likely to own a *naginata* than have the ability to use it. Aizu, a northern domain, is one of the few places where it is evident that at least some women trained with this weapon.

Despite their seclusion, samurai women played an important role in building the retainer band's social cohesion. Twice each year, families exchanged gifts with relatives and patrons. Women kept track of these exchanges and prepared the gifts, either wrapping them in paper or leaves or finding a suitable object on which they could be displayed. In addition, close relatives frequently exchanged items on a more informal basis. In her letters to her stepdaughter, Orise always asked for clothing, books, and food that she could then distribute to Atsutane's Akita relatives, and she often reported how pleased the recipients had been.

In addition to managing gift exchanges, samurai women had other social obligations. In an era before telephones, people often dropped by unexpectedly, whenever their schedule permitted without regard for host's convenience. As the person left in charge of the household while her husband was at work, a samurai wife had to entertain his friends when they came to visit by setting out food and making conversation. Bored and lonely as she was in Akita without her family around her, Orise greatly appreciated these opportunities to socialise.

All women in Tokugawa society were expected to conform to the dictates of filial piety, but this had special meaning for a samurai wife. In a samurai household, the husband might spend years away from home in attendance on his lord on the biannual trips to Edo. (Every *daimyō* was required to spend half of his time in Edo in service to the shogun and half of his time in his domain overseeing its administration.) The wife stayed back in the domain to raise any children the couple might have and also

A high-ranking samurai woman entering a palanquin accompanied by an attendant, from a 1893 triptych.

Honda Heihachiro and Senhime, ca 1600.

to take care of her mother-in-law and father-in-law – for women, filial piety meant that they were expected to cherish their husband's parents. When the noted writer Tadano Makuzu married a man from Sendai, she had to move there to stay with his mother even though he visited his home town only rarely. Having lived in Edo all of her life, she hated what she saw as a provincial backwater.

As an extension of filial piety, a wife, particularly a samurai wife, had responsibility for performing rituals to her husband's ancestors. In the shogun's castle in Edo, the Buddhist altar containing ancestral tablets was located in a room right next to the quarters for the shogun's wife, putting it under her protection. Every morning the shogun and his wife prayed before it together. Wives performed similar rituals on a smaller scale in ordinary samurai households. Since only the wife had the authority to perform these rituals and protect the tablets, this was one activity that affirmed her position above the concubines.

Because she had responsibility for her husband's household, a wife had the right to speak in her husband's name when he was absent, and a widow had the right to speak for her deceased spouse. In 1190, Hōjō Masako used her status as the widow of Minamoto no Yoritomo, the lord of Kamakura and the founder of Japan's first military regime, to advance Hōjō interests, even going so far as to acquiesce in the murder of her sons when they threatened Hōjō rule. In the Tokugawa period, the eighth shogun Yoshimune remained profoundly grateful to the sixth shogun's widow for supporting his candidacy to be adopted as the next shogun despite not being from the main Tokugawa line. In ordinary samurai households, women might well play a major role in finding and getting approval for their husband's heir, as I explain at greater length below.

★

Despite the elaborate preparations and ceremonies that attended a samurai wedding, plus the common assumption that a woman should no more have two husbands than a man should serve two lords, samurai women might divorce and remarry, or remarry after their husband's death. Senhime, the first Tokugawa shogun's eldest granddaughter, found herself married twice for political reasons. And in her autobiography, Etsu Inagaki Sugimoto describes how a bride came to marry her brother, only to discover on her wedding day that he had been disowned for refusing to accept her instead of the woman he loved. The bride remained in the Inagaki household until Etsu's mother arranged a good marriage for her. This practice stands in stark contrast to China and Korea where respectable women, even those who had merely been engaged, refused to consider remarriage.

When a samurai man married, his wife and his mother would likely not be the only women in his household. In addition there would be servants. In many households, the line between servant and concubine fluctuated, with a servant who bore the master's child possibly being upgraded to concubine to keep around, possibly being sent home to marry someone else when her term of service was up. In the Hirata family, Atsutane's grandson Nobutane married a woman who proved incapable of bearing a healthy child. Because she suited the family in every other way, he took a concubine and fathered a daughter by her. Later, after he had moved to the new capital of Tokyo while his parents, his wife, his concubine, and her child remained in Kyoto, his students urged him to hire a servant. In one letter to his mother, he mentioned that the servant was not pregnant, leaving it unstated that she might well have been. The child of his previous concubine stayed with his family, and was raised as his wife's child.

During the early modern period, most samurai households practised primogeniture, succession by eldest son. However, if a concubine had borne a man's eldest son and a wife later bore another one, then the wife's son would become the first in line to succeed his father.

Often enough a samurai couple would end up with no sons. This is what happened with Nobutane and his wife. Rather than let the family line die out, with no one to care for the ancestral graves or perform memorial services, let alone inherit the family's status and stipend, the family would turn to adoption. If there were a daughter, then a son-in-law would be adopted to marry her. This is what the Hirata family did, though not for many years after Nobutane died. If the family had no children, then both a daughter and a son would be adopted, usually at an age old enough for the parents to know what sort of people they were getting. As with marriage, samurai adoptions had to be approved by the domain's authorities before they could become official, and both partners had to come from samurai stock. Wives played a crucial role in finding suitable adoptees, scouring their relatives' families, negotiating with go-betweens, and if their husband was already deceased, deciding in his name on a suitable candidate or candidates, sometimes repeatedly if the adoptee died without issue. In the interval between the husband's death and the conclusion of a successful adoption, the wife's presence provided essential continuity.

★

The civil war of 1868, in particular the conflict that erupted in Aizu, provides a clear picture of the tension between what samurai women perceived as honourable and what their menfolk perceived as honourable. In this war, the domain's samurai women had four options. Some fled with their children either to a nearby domain or isolated mountain shacks. Some went into the castle with their menfolk to withstand the siege from there. Some tried to fight in defence of the domain outside the castle. Many committed suicide. Here we will examine those who went into the castle, fought outside, or committed suicide.

Seeking shelter in the castle was by no means an obvious choice. When a castle is under siege, every grain of rice can be precious. Women thus had to justify their presence. In the case of Aizu, the domain lord's sister, Teruhime, moved into the castle to demonstrate her determination to die with the defenders. At a time when the domain's survival was on the line, she showed that women could not stand idly by. The women inside the castle made cartridges, cooked whatever food was available, tended to the wounded, and tried to put out cannon balls before they started a fire, at considerable risk to themselves. A number of women were killed by explosives or by enemy gunfire.

One woman who entered the castle was Yamamoto Yae. She was the daughter of a gunnery instructor, and she had trained in the use of the Spencer carbine. Her brother had died in an earlier battle, so when she went into the castle, she wore some of his clothing and carried as many weapons as she could. Feeling that she had become him and must kill his enemies, she had resolved to fight so long as she had life for the sake of her lord and for the sake of her younger brother. Other women too carried weapons into the castle, hoping to be killed honourably while striking the enemy. However, they were never allowed to fight because to put women into battle would have reflected badly on their lord's name. Yae later married Niijima Jō, a Christian and the founder of Dōshisha University in Kyoto.

Another group of armed women arrived at the castle gates after they had shut. These women went instead to a bridge on the city's outskirts where Aizu samurai were trying to hold off a detachment from the imperial army. There they tried to join the fight with their *naginata*. As one woman recalled: 'From the beginning men had opposed sending our women's brigade to the front because it would be shameful for it to appear that Aizu was in such trouble that it had to rely on women.' One of the women, Nakano Takeko, was killed by an enemy bullet, and her sister risked death to retrieve her head, lest it fall into enemy hands. Today there is a statue of Takeko near the bridge erected in 1982.

Almost 200 women died fighting for Aizu; even more committed suicide. They had two reasons for the latter. First, they did not want their menfolk to worry about them when they should be focused on fighting for the domain. Second, they did not want to risk falling into enemy hands and being dishonoured by rape. For the sake of their family's honour, and their own, they felt that they had no choice but to commit suicide. In the case of Shiba Gorō's family, this meant that all of the men in his family who had entered the castle to fight survived; all of the women perished. The imperial army forbade proper burials for Aizu dead because they were seen as traitors to the throne, and that included the women. The house elder, Saigō Tanamo, erected a simple stone hidden under a wooden shed to commemorate the 21 members of his household who died in this fashion, from his mother down to his youngest daughter, age two. In 1928, local custodians of Aizu history erected a monument to the women who had died by their own hand.

★

Compared to China or Europe, Japan's history contains few accounts of women warriors. In the 12th-century battles between the Taira and the Minamoto immortalised in the epic *The Tale of the Heike*, Tomoe Gozen fights alongside her lover, the defeated Minamoto no Yoshinaka, and tries to hold off the enemy forces while he seeks a place to commit suicide. She is depicted as beautiful, brave, skilled, and strong, but historians doubt whether she ever existed. During the century of civil war between 1467 and 1592, women occasionally appear in the historical record as camp followers. In his history of Japan, the Portuguese missionary Luis Frois recounts how women fought in the 1589 siege of Hondō castle, a Christian stronghold near Kumamoto in Kyushu. Having realised that the defence of the castle had exhausted their menfolk and enemy troops

Samurai Women, 1700.

were preparing to breach the castle walls, the women cut their hair, put on helmets and armour, armed themselves with swords and spears, and attacked the enemy. Despite the ferocity of their assault, the castle eventually fell, leaving few survivors, male or female.

A century of desperate fighting marked by high casualties had battle hardened both the men and women who defended Hondō castle and its attackers, leaving little room for any rules of war or the niceties of honour. In contrast, the short civil war of 1868 followed 250 years of peace during which samurai had plenty of time to refine notions of duty, loyalty, filial piety, and what it meant to be a man or a woman. The actions taken by the women of Aizu and the response of Aizu men show just how different battlefield codes of conduct had become and how the character of battle had changed. In particular, they demonstrate a new tension surrounding notions of honour. The women who tried to fight saw the domain as an extension of the household. Duty-bound to defend their house, they were therefore duty-bound to defend the domain. Male samurai accepted the notion that women had an obligation to defend the household, but in this instance, at least, they did not see the domain as the household writ large. In comparison to the men in Hondō castle, Aizu samurai believed that only men should fight to defend the domain or the castle; for women to fight dishonoured men. In their eyes, and in the eyes of many women, for a samurai woman to defend her honour meant suicide.

REFERENCES

Gramlich-Oka, Bettina, *Thinking Like a Man: Tadano Makuzu (1763–1825)* (Brill, 2006).

Inagaki Sugimoto, Etsu, *A Daughter of the Samurai* (Doubleday, Doran & Company Inc, 1934).

McClellan, Edwin, *Woman in the Crested Kimono: The Life of Shibue Io and Her Family drawn from Mori Ōgai's 'Shibue Chūsai'* (Yale University Press, 1985).

Shiba Gorō, *Remembering Aizu: The Testament of Shiba Gorō* translated by Teruko Craig, (University of Hawai'i Press, 1999).

Yamakawa Kikue, *Women of the Mito Domain: Recollections of Samurai Family Life* translated with an introduction by Kate Wildman (Nakai, 2001).

Yonemoto, Marcia, *The Problem of Women in Early Modern Japan* (University of California Press, 2016).

Ashikaga Tadayoshi. Commonly attributed to be the shogun Minamoto Yoritomo.

THE RISE OF WARRIORS DURING THE WARRING STATES PERIOD

Thomas D. Conlan

Japan has been portrayed as having been "governed" by warriors for centuries. George Sansom, writing in 1958, for example, described how warriors gained "control over the whole country" of Japan as a "ruling class". According to his view, these warriors translated their control over Japanese economic resources and territory into political power, which endured for seven centuries (1185–1868). This sentiment is durable and appears in books published as recently as 2005.

Scholars such as Jeffrey Mass have argued, to the contrary, that this notion of unbroken warrior rule from the 12th century onward is mistaken, in that warriors did not amass considerable fiscal, institutional, and military authority until the 14th century. Mass is correct in that warriors possessed considerable political and military authority in the 14th century. Nevertheless, these warriors clamoured for court ranks and titles, and readily intermarried with courtiers, which suggests that these newly risen warriors remained beholden to the institutions of the court to exercise their newly found hegemony. Analysis of patterns of warrior behaviour and politics reveals that, contrary to common assumptions, warriors governed through the institutions of court until 1551, and did not achieve social or political autonomy from the court until 1615.

★

Warriors were drawn from the ranks of provincial officials who served governors, and were responsible for collecting taxes from each of Japan's provinces. These men, known as *zaichō kanjin*, or provincial office holders, helped these governors to enforce decrees and to collect taxes. These local officials were prosperous, and raised and trained their horses, owned their armour, and trained for war. During a civil war that was known to posterity as the Genpei War (1180–85), a commander named

Minamoto Yoritomo (1147–99) gave his supporters, drawn primarily from the *zaichō kanjin* cohort, the office of *jitō*, or land manager. Some early historians perceived this post of *jitō* as being the lynchpin of a new system of feudalism, whereby a fief, the *jitō* office, was granted to vassals in exchange for their loyal service. The noted Japanese historian Asakawa Kan'ichi considered the *jitō* fief as the cornerstone of feudal Japan, and suggested that this office was granted in exchange for service.

Although Yoritomo rewarded his followers with this *jitō* post, Asakawa's understanding is wrong, because *jitō* posts, once given, would not be confiscated save for instances of legal infractions. To the contrary, the post of *jitō* was hereditarily transmitted, and holders of the post could give it to whomever they saw fit. Instead of being a benefice, the post came to be seen by appointed individuals as an inalienable right. Thus, when Yoritomo's successors punished its *jitō* and confiscated their lands, they earned the enmity of the *jitō*. Rather than serving as the lynchpin for loyal service, the office of *jitō* and their constituent lands became the basis for the identity, and autonomy of these warriors.

Provincial figures, particularly those without the office of *jitō*, favoured the term *gokenin* as a social marker. This means honorable houseman, and became the aspired status for descendants of those who had been known as *zaichō kanjin*. Unlike the clearly defined holders of *jitō* offices, a select group whose holdings were invariably formalised by the possession of documents of investiture or wills from previous *jitō* holders, *gokenin* were determined on an ad hoc basis by protectors [*shugo*], who were responsible for policing the provinces and maintaining order. These protectors created a list of all prominent locals in a province, and those on the list became *gokenin*. With this designation came responsibilities, for those so named had to perform guard duty, or repair dykes, arrest criminals, or otherwise help to keep a province at peace. Not all locals saw the advantages of being on the *gokenin* list, and some turned down the designation, but in the late 13th century *gokenin* were given some more tangible benefits, and the designation became a desirable one. Hence warriors tried to claim that they were *gokenin* even when they were not named on rosters, and thereupon each warrior preserved all investitures, orders, and other edicts so as to "prove" their *gokenin* status.

The *gokenin* was head of the house and exercised authority over all who resided there. The dependent followers of these *gokenin* were generally known as *samurai*, who served their *gokenin* lord. If these figures attempted to act with autonomy, they would quite possibly be killed by their social superiors for their treachery. Thus, the term *samurai*, which came to describe all warriors after 1590, only referred to a subset of warriors, and dependent ones at that, in the 13th and the 14th centuries.

These *jitō* and *gokenin* warriors have been largely misunderstood by later historians. They fought primarily on horseback. The horses that they rode were small, sturdy, spirited beasts capable of traversing broken terrain. The dominant weapon was the bow, and these warriors referred to themselves as practitioners of the bow. To be able to ride a horse and shoot a bow required training from a very young age; accordingly, members of a warrior house had this ability.

Gender mattered less than being of a *gokenin* house. This meant that *gokenin* men and women were rather equal. Women fought in battle, usually on horseback, and their participation did not merit any censure or stigma. Examples exist of warrior armour tailored to female anatomy, and archaeologists have found skeletons of a man and a woman, both with battle wounds, buried together in 1333. Likewise, women are documented as serving on guard duty.

The Japanese long bows were formidable weapons. They could pierce armour at a short range, and modern practitioners have been able to pierce Teflon pans with these arrows. Although "long distance arrows" could be fired for several hundreds of metres, they could only penetrate armour at tens of metres. But archery was the mainstay of battle, as most fought primarily with projectiles rather than attempting to engage in hand-to-hand combat. Warriors had swords, but they were more weapons of self-protection, rather than a dominant battlefield weapon.

Japanese armour was designed to provide protection for horse riders from bows. The early suits of armour did not protect legs, which were not so vulnerable, but rather had steel reinforcement of the breast plate. For the mounted warrior, sleeves [*sode*] served to protect the upper arms from stray arrows, and thus functioned like portable shields. The face and neck were the most vulnerable areas, as arrows plunging into these regions could be lethal, or severely debilitating. Once warfare became common and long-lasting in the 14th century, warrior armour was improved to better protect the face and neck, thereby revealing its functional nature.

Rather than die for a lord, warriors hoped to gain compensation for their service in battle, and so all damages, and verifiable noteworthy acts, were rigorously inspected. Those that desired the greatest rewards strove to stand out on the battlefield, and wore red capes or carried flags, with the expectation that they would receive recognition for their outstanding service. *Gokenin* expected their lords to adequately compensate them so that they could protect, and expand, their lands. Obligations did not exist for *gokenin* to serve their lords, but rather for lords to adequately compensate their followers.

Warriors were proficient writers, and *gokenin* men and women could write wills, letters and petitions. Often *gokenin* referred to masters of "the way of the bow and brush", or *bun* and *bu*; they took this quite literally, with some keeping a brush in their quiver. Perhaps understandably, they exhibited great deference to members of the court, particularly chamberlains [*kurōdo*], who were skilled writers in a cursive style of the most prestigious documents. When confronted with a chamberlain reading an edict, for example, warriors would dismount and listen with respect, and some of these chamberlains parlayed their prestige into military positions, as one, a certain Chigusa Tadaaki (?-1336), commanded an army in 1333.

★

The seat of governance of Japan, since the formation of the state in the 6th century, was the court. Japan was ruled by an emperor, who transmitted messages through courtiers. Courtiers were hereditary officials governed on behalf of the emperor. Some resided in the capital of Kyoto while others were appointed governors, who extracted revenue from the provinces. Early warriors were subservient to these governors, and the court in general, although the Genpei Wars are best conceived as a provincial revolt against their arbitrary authority; the creation of the *jitō* posts constrained the authority of these governors.

Nevertheless, even successful warriors, such as Minamoto Yoritomo, could attain relatively junior court offices. Yoritomo's governing successors, the Hōjō, lacked the rank of even Yoritomo, and did not possess the ability to navigate court circles, or even to have audiences with officials. Instead, they had to rely on a courtier family, the Saionji, to serve as the mouthpiece of the court, but they became liable to manipulation by the Saionji, who, for example, had a rival poet arrested on trumped up charges of treason. Perhaps unsurprisingly, when an emperor and his courtier allies decided to destroy the city of Kamakura, the political centre, they plotted for years before being discovered. When, in 1333 they

The residence of a warrior (gokenin),
from a 14th century painting.

launched an attack on Japan's first warrior government, nearly all its *gokenin* abandoned it, leading to its violent extermination by members of the court.

In the aftermath of the destruction of Kamakura, the norms of warrior behaviour became increasingly contested, with some court leaders like Kitabatake Chikafusa (1293–1354) criticising warriors for their demands of compensation. But the Kitabatake, who held warriors to a higher standard, faltered. Ironically, the ideal of devoted loyal service first arose among courtiers and monks, who emphasised their service to the Ashikaga at a time when most warriors were more devoted to preserving their lands. Thus, even fundamental warrior values such as the concept of unflinching devotion, expected of the *gokenin's* landless followers, achieved new prominence at the 14th-century court, as nobles and monks, more than *gokenin*, became the most trusted supporters of the Ashikaga.

During the time of the short-lived regime (1333–36) of Emperor Go-Daigo (1288–1339, and its rival successor, the Ashikaga shogunate (1336–1573), warrior and court society fused. The Ashikaga occupied key positions at court, and their official portraits invariably depict them in court robes. Epitomising their combined warrior and courtier identity, Ashikaga leaders from the late 14th century onward adopted two signatures, one of "warrior" style, and the other of "courtier" style, and it is telling that the latter is far more common than the former in surviving documents. Not content to wear court robes, or sign their documents in the style of courtiers, the Ashikaga and their collaterals intermarried with courtiers, a practice that would remain common for centuries. The Ashikaga governed through the court, and behaved as members of the court, and became successfully socially and institutionally fused with the court as well.

The need to prosecute the wars of the 14th century led to the development of a new tax, called the *hanzei*, or half tax, which allowed half of a province's revenue to be used for military provisions. This caused a devolution of fiscal powers from the court to the provinces, as half of all provincial income remained with generals, who became incipient provincial magnates, or *daimyō*. Over the next two centuries, these lords eroded the autonomy of *gokenin* and subsumed most, if not all *gokenin*, into *daimyō* regional organisation.

New fiscal powers allowed *daimyō* to conscript and provision a standing army. The soldiers in these armies could be trained to use weapons in formation. Soldiers were equipped with pikes, and devised phalanx formations that were capable of defeating cavalry on the open battlefield. This change happened in the 1450s, and the ensuing wars witnessed the preeminence of defensive tactics, much like those used in Europe during the First World War. Units of pike men dug trenches and occupied central Japan during the decade long Ōnin War (1467–77), and two armies fought a savage war of attrition lasting a decade.

These changes in tactics witnessed shifts in armour, as the *sode* or shoulder boards became decorative, or were omitted altogether, while armour was strengthened to protect the legs, face and body. Not all combatants wore such elaborate protection; some pike men relied on simplified armour. Some *daimyō*, such as the Hōjō, started mobilising armies of such a magnitude that they armed their warriors in lacquered paper armour.

The wars of the 15th century resulted in an enervation of Ashikaga authority. This did not mean, however, that the court ceased to be a vehicle for politics. To the contrary, the most powerful *daimyō* continued to rely on court ranks and rituals. After the Ashikaga regime imploded in the early 16th century, the powerful warrior Ōuchi Yoshioki (1477–1528), led a large army to occupy Kyoto from 1508 until 1518. He governed in the name of the Ashikaga, but most critically, exercised authority through court offices. Yoshioki shared authority with Hosokawa Takakuni, and both cooperated. Yoshioki had the rank of Left City Commissioner [*sakyō daibu*] and Takakuni that of Right City Commissioner [*ukyō daibu*]. These two offices were responsible for population registration, security, tax collection and legal appeals in the capital, and this title remained a symbol of governing authority in Kyoto, showing that major *daimyō* continued to govern through the institutions and the offices of the court.

The Ōuchi, the most powerful *daimyō* of western Japan, continued to govern through the institutions and offices of the court, even when, after 1518, they abandoned Kyoto itself. Instead, they attracted nobles and monks to Yamaguchi, their capital, where they performed most important rites of state. Still, the court became increasingly beleaguered because of the rise of a new group of warriors, the Miyoshi, who no longer held the court in esteem.

Miyoshi Nagayoshi (1522–64) was a radical figure. He did not rely on the court, and rather than focusing on protocols of state, he saw violence

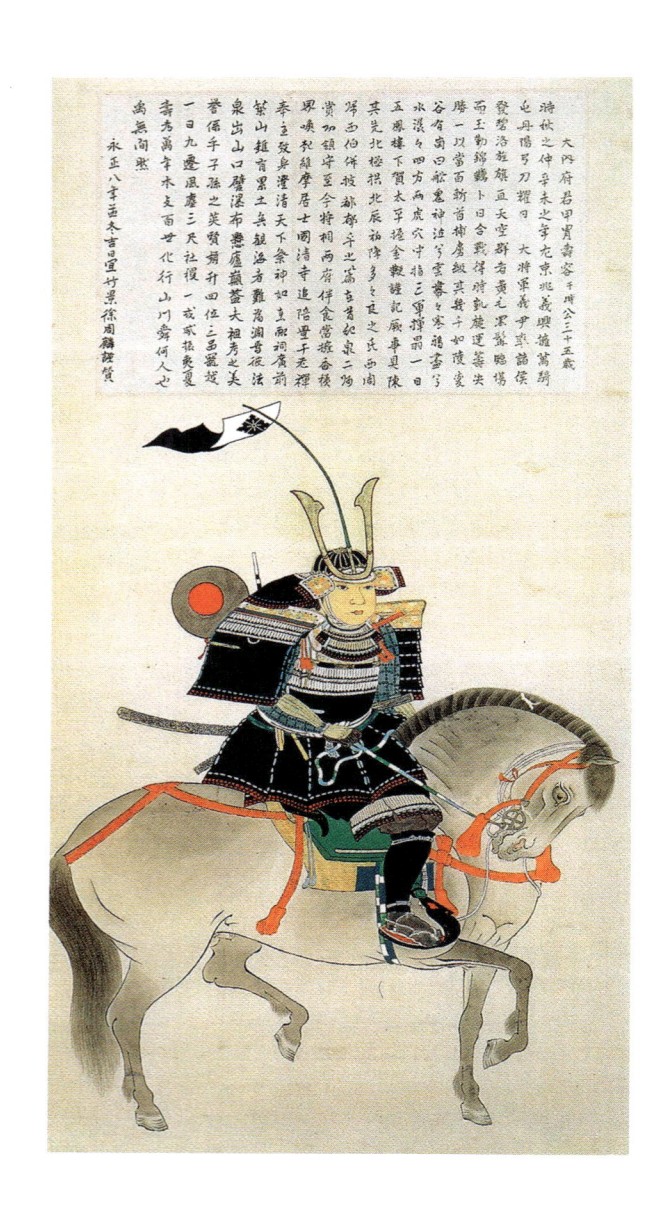

大内府若甲冑壽容千時八三十五歲
游狄之仲早未之年亢京兆義興頓薦騎
毛丹揚弓刀躍日
大將軍義伊禀諸侯
發警浩拔雄匝天空郡黃元黑鬢贈鴙
而王勒錦鸚卜日合戰捍時氣旋築失
勝一以當面新首捕虜級其擬寒搖蹇
谷省南田船伯兮雲書与寥箙罪一日
水漲々四方而虎穴中指三軍擇罪一
五凰楼下質太平揭金轂鞁鹹摩俊
其先北櫻拱北辰拯像多吝若之民西岡
掃西伯併枝都部卒上篤等至艺戎二肉
賞加鎮岸至今持銅雨府伴食當據香橒
男岐紀錄摩居七岡清寺追陸豊千老禪
奉主發臭澄清天下余卻如立船祠廣前
紫山赳貢黑土兵艇海方難高潤音夜法
泉出山口辟溪布惠蘆巌薔大祖考之美
普偏手子悟打四位之丕籠域
一日九龜風慶三天社復一戎威振奥夏
壽為萬年木支面世化行山門奔何人乎
為無間然
永正八辛五冬吉日宣竹景徐周繭證覽

Ouchi Yoshioki (1477–1529).

as the ultimate ritual. Nagayoshi was descended from a warrior family who gained prominence in an uprising in a district in Awa province in Shikoku, and then became retainers of the Hosokawa. Nagayoshi's great-grandfather Miyoshi Korenaga (?-1520), who raised his family's fortunes, had a reputation for being "strong in battle", but also a "source of great evil".

Nagayoshi proved a worthy heir to Korenaga. On July 21, 1547 Miyoshi Nagayoshi defeated Hosokawa Harumoto (1514–63), his nominal lord, with a formidable force of 900 pike men, inflicting hundreds of casualties in the process. In 1549, Nagayoshi defeated the shogun Ashikaga Yoshiharu (1511–50), and expelled him from the capital. Nagayoshi scorned accepted titles as sources of legitimacy and preferred instead to base his authority upon military prowess.

Nagayoshi's relationship with the court was deeply antagonistic. He seized imperial lands and constricted the flow of revenue to the court, making it difficult for rites to be performed in Kyoto. Reliant on force to achieve his political objectives, he gave primacy to military expediency over other considerations and made no effort to obtain imperial sanction or support. Archaeological evidence reveals that he used an ancient tomb as a castle. These tombs had often been plundered, but their incorporation into a castle's structure appears to have been new. Miyoshi Nagayoshi occupied Kyoto on the eighth day of the third lunar month in 1551, and he was so reviled in some quarters that assassins struck five days later, stabbing him twice at a banquet. He escaped with minor injuries.

This turmoil of early 1551 caused Emperor Go-Nara (1495–1557) to make Ōuchi Yoshitaka (1507–51), a rival of Miyoshi Nagayoshi, the 'provisional governor of Yamashiro'. With this title came the responsibility to protect the court. Yoshitaka took these duties seriously, and attempted to move the emperor to his city of Yamaguchi, in western Japan, where many courtiers of varying ranks already resided. Nevertheless, while immersed in these preparations, some of his followers staged a coup, which led to the destruction of the Ōuchi, and the death of all the prominent warriors and courtiers in Yamaguchi. In short, the plotters killed Yoshitaka and his son, slaughtered the courtiers in Yamaguchi, from the youngest, aged 16, to the oldest, in their sixties, and from the highest rank to the very lowest. From then on, violence lasted for two decades.

The autumn of 1551 represents a rupture. After this time, the court remained only as an impoverished and cowed entity, its courtiers fearful of its new masters, the Miyoshi. The differing governing styles of Yoshitaka, the greatest upholder of the court, and Miyoshi Nagayoshi, and their divergent fates, marks an important break; after 1551, warriors did not govern through the court, but merely relied on its surviving shell to confer legitimacy.

Miyoshi Nagayoshi never consolidated control before his death in 1564. Epitomising his disdain for the court, he did not pay for the funeral of the emperor, Go-Nara. Go-Nara remained unburied for over seventy days in 1557, his decomposing body highlighting the decline and degradation of the court. Basing his authority on violence, Nagayoshi, his heirs, and his close supporters resorted to increasingly desperate measures to maintain their authority, murdering the shogun Ashikaga Yoshiteru (1536–65) in 1565 and burning Tōdaiji, the largest wooden building in the world, in 1567. Nevertheless, their reliance on military force alone made them vulnerable to the next powerful warlord capable of supplanting them, a figure named Oda Nobunaga (1534–82).

Nobunaga entered the capital in 1568, and displaced the Miyoshi. He did so with the aim of installing an Ashikaga as shogun, but within a few short years, he turned on the last Ashikaga leader, Yoshiaki (1537–97), because Yoshiaki did not adequately take care of the court. Nobunaga proved as willing as the Miyoshi to rely on untrammelled military force and constituted a worthy heir, but he was more conciliatory and received higher ranks and offices from the court, although late in life he resigned from them. Nobunaga also chose not to live in Kyoto, and founded a castle town at Azuchi. Symbolising his authority, Nobunaga famously used a seal which stated *tenka fubu*, meaning "uniting the realm by force".

★

The Miyoshi paroxysm of violence unleashed a new, more distinct warrior identity that was not beholden to the court. This did not mean that warriors would not govern using its institutions. Toyotomi Hideyoshi (1537–98), the successor to Nobunaga, who was assassinated in 1582, achieved high court rank, governing as if he were a regent, or courtier, relying on the institutions and offices of the court. A generous patron of the court, Hideyoshi even served tea to the emperor in a golden teahouse. Hideyoshi received a new surname, Toyotomi, which meant "the bountiful minister" for his generosity.

Miyoshi Nagayoshi (1522–1564).

Nevertheless, Hideyoshi caused an epochal transformation. He forced all landholders to choose to either accept warrior status, adopt two swords, and be guaranteed revenue from their land, or remain an individual with unfettered control over their land, but become a peasant. Those who decided to become warriors had to abandon their lands and concomitant autonomy, for their position became contingent upon the favour of their *daimyō* lord. They became known as *samurai*. Likewise, those with the land, the so-called peasants, were in principle not allowed to have weapons, although many surreptitiously kept them. Swords had a new significance as a marker of social status, and from Hideyoshi's time onward, would be invested with much meaning by these *samurai*. Accordingly, only from the 1590s can one speak of a sword-wielding *samurai* order as existing. Hideyoshi formalised a sense of warrior identity, and a warrior status, but he still governed through the institutions of the court.

The final transformation occurred after Toyotomi Hideyoshi died in 1598. One of his appointed regents, Tokugawa Ieyasu (1543–1616), instead of upholding Toyotomi rule, undermined it. First, he attacked 'disloyal advisers' to the Toyotomi, and then, after a short, but bloody battle in 1600, he radically redistributed rights of income to strengthen his loyal supporters and undermine Toyotomi partisans. Hideyoshi's heir, Hideyori (1593–1615), continued to have close ties to the court, and high court rank and office. Ieyasu had greater ambitions, but he had to wait until he came up with a suitable pretext. He twice attacked and finally destroyed the Toyotomi regime in 1615.

Ieyasu famously regulated warrior behavior in 1615, but an overlooked, yet arguably more significant edict was issued to the court in that same year. Called the *kuge shohatto*, it limited the ability of courtiers to intermarry with warriors without Tokugawa permission, and stipulated that they were not to engage in politics. The court received funds, but could only engage in cultural activities. Governance was expressed by the shogun, who ruled over a *samurai* order from a massive castle in the new town of Edo (present day Tokyo). The idea that the court was only a realm of culture, rather than politics, became normative, and earlier patterns of governance and society became all but inconceivable.

The violent birth of warrior independence from the court began in 1551, with the actions of Miyoshi Nagayoshi. Thereupon warriors became an independent social order during the time of Hideyoshi, who radically transformed the political and social matrix of Japan in the late 16th century. The court's role as the vehicle for politics, however, was severed through the Tokugawa regulations of 1615, which would remain in force while the Tokugawa regime maintained power. These laws allowed the Tokugawa to create warrior institutions, ideals, monuments and methods of rule that demarcated 260 years of their hegemony. The idea of their court as the vehicle for governance remained, however. Tellingly, when Tokugawa authority weakened, warriors once again relied on the vehicle of the court, and their ties with courtiers, to bring down the Tokugawa in 1868 and usher in a new era, that made the court, albeit briefly, the centre of governance once again.

REFERENCES

Ashikaga kiseiki, in *Kaitei shiseki shūran* vol 13 no 116, 132-264 (Kondō shuppanbu, 1900).

Jōetsu shishi sōsho 6, *Uesugi-ke gosho shūsei* vol 1 (Jōetsu shi, 2001).

Kugyō bunin, 5 vols (Yoshikawa kōbunkan, 1964-66).

Rōmōki (Nakarai Yasufusa), In Takeuchi Rizō, ed *Zoku shiryō taisei* vol 18 (Kyoto: Rinsen shoten, 1967) pp 97-134.

Ōmagaki. In *Zoku gunsho ruijū Kuji bu,* vol 10.2, 3rd revised edition (Zoku gunsho ruijū kanseikai, 1981).

Oyudono no ue no nikki, 11 vols 3rd revised edition (Zoku gunsho ruijū kanseikai, 1995).

Tokitsugu kyōki, 7 vols (Zoku gunsho ruijū kanseikai, 1998).

Yuigahama minami iseki hōkokusho, comp., Kamakura shi Kanagawa-ken. 4 vols (Kamakura, 2001-02).

Asakawa Kan'ichi, "The Origin of the Feudal Land Tenure" *America Historical Review* 20. No. 1 October 1914, 1-28.

"The Founding of the Shogunate by Minamoto Yoritomo", *Land and Society in Medieval Japan,* ed Committee for the Publication of Dr K. Asakawa's Works, 269-89 Japan Society for the Promotion of Science, 1965.

Butler, Lee, *Emperor and Aristocracy in Japan 1467-1680* (Harvard University Asia Center, 2002).

Conlan, Thomas D. *State of War: The Violent Order of Fourteenth-Century Japan* (University of Michigan, Center for Japanese Studies, 2003).

Weapons and the Fighting Techniques of the Samurai Warrior, 1200-1877 (Amber Press, August 2008).

From Sovereign to Symbol: An Age of Ritual Determinism in Fourteenth-Century Japan (Oxford University Press, October 2011).

The Two Paths of Writing and Warring in Medieval Japan. *Taiwan Journal of East Asian Studies* 8.1. June 2011, 85-127.

The Failed Attempt to Move the Emperor to Yamaguchi and the Fall of the Ōuchi, *Japanese Studies* 35.2. September 2015, 1-19.

Ebara Masaharu, *Muromachi bakufu to chihō no shakai.* (Iwanami shinsho, 2016).

Endō Keisuke, "Kofun no jōkaku riyō ni kan suru ichi kōsatsu." *Jōkan shiryō gaku* 3. Jōkan shiryō gakkai, July 2005, 1-22.

Huey, Robert. *Kyōgoku Tamekane: Poetry and Politics in Late Kamakura Japan.* (Stanford University Press, 1989).

Imatani Akira et al, eds, *Miyoshi Nagayoshi* (Miyaobi shoten, 2013).

Sengoku jidai no kizoku: Tokitsugu kyōki ga egaku Kyoto (Kōdansha gakujutsu bunko, 2002).

Sengoku daimyō to tennō (Kōdansha gakujutsu bunko, 2001).

Mass, Jeffrey P. "Bakufu Justice: A Case Study", In Jeffrey Mass, ed *The Development of Kamakura Rule*, (Stanford University Press, 1979), pp 270-76.

Antiquity and Anachronism in Japanese History, Stanford University Press, 1992.

The Origins of Japan's Medieval World: Courtiers, Clerics, Warriors, Peasants in the Fourteenth Century, (Stanford University Press, 1994).
Yoritomo and the Founding of the First Bakufu: The Origins of Dual Government in Japan (Stanford University Press, 1999).
Middleton, John, *World Monarchies and Dynasties* (Routledge, 2005).
Nagae Shōichi, *Miyoshi Nagayoshi* (Yoshikawa kōbunkan, 1968).
Sansom, George, *History of Japan*, vol 1 (Stanford University Press, 1958).
Watanabe, Daimon, *Sengoku no binbō tennō* (Kashiwa shobō, 2012).

Practicing Kendo.

MARTIAL WAYS, WHYS AND WHENS
Karl Friday

Among the most celebrated, and enduring, developments within samurai culture was the organisation of martial training into systems or styles, called *ryūha*. Often prosaically translated as 'school', *ryūha* can be more literally and evocatively rendered as 'branch of the current'. Here, the current represents the onward flow of teaching and learning – and of a stream of thought – through time, while the branches point to the partitioning of that thought, the splitting off and the new growth that occurs as insights are passed from master to student over generations. Dozens of centuries-old samurai training organisations (known as *koryū*, literally, "old schools") remain active today, both in and out of Japan, and their modern cognates, such as *kendō*, *jūdō*, *aikido*, and *kyūdō*, instruct tens of thousands of students all over the world.

The popularity – the relevance for 21st-century men, women and children – of devoting hundreds of hours a year to training in the use of arcane medieval weapons seems puzzling at first sight. And indeed, that such schools have survived, let alone thrived, into the modern age reflects not the efficacy of these arts in combat, but the appeal of another key development within samurai martial culture: the embrace of martial training as a vehicle for completing and fulfilling one's human potential, and toward the realisation of universal truths.

This is a distinctly, and very nearly uniquely, Japanese concept. Certainly, cultures all over the world – and as diverse as the Romans, the Vikings, the Aztecs, the Bedouins, and the Zulu – have exalted warriors and martial training, but nowhere else has the cult of the fighting arts reached the level of refinement and sophistication that it has in Japan. Only in Japan did martial training appropriate the status – as well as the forms, the vocabulary, the teaching tools, and even the ultimate goals – of the fine arts. And only in Japan did study of martial art come to be viewed as a parallel, coequal endeavour to that of calligraphy, music, drama, painting, and other high cultural pursuits – indeed, even of religious practice.

Scholars and practitioners of Japanese martial art have long highlighted a contrast between *bujutsu* ('martial art', training for proficiency in combat) and *budō* ('the martial path', a process by which such training becomes a means to broader self-development and self-realisation). This is a useful distinction to make, but it is important not to forget that it is analytical and modern, not traditional. It traces back only to the Meiji era (1868–1912), when a handful of progressive educators like Kanō Jigorō began to replace the suffix *-jutsu* with *-dō* in the names of their systems, in order to emphasise broader (and in most cases, more modern) physical and ethical education goals and purposes. Accordingly, *kenjutsu* [the art of swordsmanship] became *kendō* [the way of the sword], *jūjutsu* [the art of flexibility, a generic term for unarmed grappling] became *jūdō* ['the flexible way'], and *bujutsu* and *budō* began to take on their modern connotations distinguishing the purely technical applications of martial training from more sublime ones.

Anachronously projecting the *bujutsu-budō* dichotomy backward into Tokugawa times – as much of the literature on Japanese martial art does – has seriously distorted the perceptions of both historians and aficionados. Thus conventional wisdom tends to cast *bujutsu* and *budō* as divergent categories, opposing goals, or sequential achievements in martial training. And this perception has significant implications for conceptualisations of what *bugei ryūha* are and how they function. Ironically, popular notions concerning the relationship of *bujutsu* to *budō* stem largely from a fundamental misunderstanding of the historical development of organised martial training [*ryūha bugei*].

★

Military training and the profession of arms in Japan stretches back to the dawn of history and beyond. Until well into the medieval era, however, warrior training centred on individual families. Some house traditions, like that of the Hidesato-*ryū* Fujiwara, had become famous and well-respected by the 11th century; and one finds scattered references in 13th and 14th-century sources to teachers of mounted archery. In the early 15th century, moreover, Ogasawara Mochinaga and at least two generations of his descendants served as hereditary archery instructors to the

Ashikaga shōguns. Nevertheless, the first true martial art *ryūha* appeared around the turn of the 16th century.¹

By the end of the 17th century, the curriculums and goals of these schools had evolved into educational corpuses intended to guide both the physical and the moral activities of those who practised them. Early modern texts on swordsmanship and other martial art, such as Issai Chozan's 18th-century parable, *Neko no myōjutsu* [The Cat's Eerie Skill], outline extraordinarily complex phenomena in which various physical, technical, psychological, and philosophical factors intertwine and interact. In these texts, expertise in combat and spiritual illumination are not contending, or even sequential, achievements, but interdependent developments – inseparable aspects of the whole – to be experienced simultaneously.²

The conventional wisdom also ties the evolution of Japanese martial art [*ryūha bugei*] closely to the history of warfare, asserting – or rather, assuming – that systems and schools of martial art originally developed as tools for passing on workaday battlefield skills. According to this account, martial art schools and systems took shape in response to intensified demand for skilled fighting men spawned by the onset of the Sengoku [Country at War] age in the late 15th century. Warriors hoping to survive and prosper in the turbulent world of late medieval times began to seek instruction from talented veterans, who in turn began to codify their knowledge and systematise its study. Thus *bugei ryūha* emerged more or less directly from the exigencies of medieval warfare. Then, the story continues, the two-and-a-half-century Pax Tokugawa that began in 1600 brought fundamental changes to the practice of martial art. Most significantly, the motives and goals underlying *bugei* practice were recast. Samurai no longer expected to spend time on the battlefield, sought and found a more relevant rationale for studying martial art, approaching it not simply as a means to proficiency in combat, as their ancestors had, but as a means to spiritual cultivation of the self.³

This view of martial art history, reified in works like the late Donn Draeger's classic *Martial Arts and Ways of Japan* trilogy, is central to popular conceptions – including those of advanced practitioners – of the *bugei*, particularly in the West. It shapes not just ideas on martial art history, but notions of what *bugei ryūha* are, and how they should be studied, as well. It is also fundamentally misleading.

For, the conventional wisdom notwithstanding, *bugei ryūha* did not evolve in linear fashion from schools of combative arts [*bujutsu*] to systems

Portrait of Ashikaga Yoshihisa, ninth shogun of the Ashikaga shogunate, who reigned from 1473 to 1489.

of personal development [*budō*]. What modern observers now call *budō* has, in fact, been a definitive element of *ryūha bugei* from its inception.

In point of fact, early modern pundits like Issai were scarcely the first to contend that martial training can and should reach beyond physical skills and technical expertise. Sixteenth-century instructional writings, as well as early 17th-century texts like Miyamoto Musashi's famous *Gorin no sho* or Yagyū Munenori's *Hyōhō kadensho*, suggest that this notion was already well-established during the late medieval era.[4] Careful consideration of the circumstances under which *ryūha bugei* first appeared, moreover, strongly suggest that these arts were never meant to be straightforward tools of war – that, rather, visions of martial art as a vehicle to broad personal education shaped and characterised this phenomenon from its beginnings.

★

Circumstantial evidence makes it clear, first of all, that the early *ryūha* could not have accounted for more than a tiny portion of 16th-century military training. Estimates based on surviving documentation from the period suggest that there were at most a few dozen *ryūha* around during this period.[5] Armies of that era, however, regularly mobilised tens of thousands of men. The fourth battle of Kawanakajima, in 1561, for example, involved 33,000 troops on both sides; Mikatagahara, in 1572, involved 45,000; Sekigahara, in 1600, involved more than 154,000; and Toyotomi Hideyoshi's invasion force in his first Korean campaign numbered some 158,700 men, with a reserve force of more than 100,000.[6] The relative numbers, therefore, indicate that *ryūha bugei* must have been a specialised activity, pursued by only a tiny percentage of late medieval warriors.

Nor did the skills on which late medieval *bugeisha* (martial artists) concentrated have a great deal of direct applicability to 16th-century warfare. In fact, even the earliest *bugei ryūha* were, at best, anachronistic in this regard.

From the 8th through the late 14th centuries, Japanese tactical thinking was shaped by the arts of bow and horse, which, by the 10th century, had become the exclusive preserve of professional warriors, defined by skills they cultivated on their own, using personal (and family) resources.[7] Early medieval armies were patchwork conglomerations, assembled for specific campaigns and demobilised immediately thereafter. Commanders, therefore, had few, if any, opportunities to drill with their troops in large-scale group tactics, and could not field integrated, well-articulated armies. Accordingly, such forces carried on with little or no direction from their commanders, once the enemy had been engaged. Even senior officers usually fought in the ranks themselves, and were seldom able to exercise much control over the contest beyond orchestrating the initial attack or defensive position. Tactical cooperation, therefore, devolved to smaller units and components.[8]

During the 15th century, power continued to devolve steadily and decisively from the capital to the countryside until, in the aftermath of the Ōnin War (1467–77) only the thinnest pretext of local rule drawing its legitimacy from a central governing authority remained. The province-wide jurisdictions of the *shugo-daimyō* (military governors ruling under the authority of the Muromachi Shogunate) broke apart into smaller territories controlled by a new class of local hegemon. These *sengoku daimyō* ruled all but autonomous satrapies whose borders coincided with the area they – and the lesser warriors whose loyalties they commanded – could dominate by force.

One effect of this new political reality was a shift in the purpose of war. For the first time in the history of the samurai the primary strategic objective of warfare became the capture or defence of territory. At the same time, the armies fielded by the emerging hegemons were increasingly composed of contingents of fighting men bound to their commanders by standing obligations to service, rather than by short-term contractual promises of rewards. These developments transformed samurai from mercenaries to soldiers and refocused their attention on contributing to the success of the group rather than on distinguishing themselves as individuals.

The changing make-up and goals of late medieval armies in turn concomitantly made possible and demanded increasingly disciplined group tactical manoeuvre, and an enhanced role for infantry. Faced with a new strategic imperative to capture or defend specific geographic areas, and armed with a growing ability to drill and discipline troops and therefore to field versatile, articulated armies, Japanese commanders now shaped their tactics around companies of archers – and later gunners – utilised to break enemy formations, which could then be chased from the field by pikemen.

Thus martial art schools, which focused on developing prowess in personal combat, emerged and flourished in almost inverse proportion to the value of skilled individual fighters on the battlefield. Moreover, the weapon that played the most prominent role in this new phenomenon, the sword, played a decidedly minor role in medieval warfare.

★

Films, television programmes, and popular images notwithstanding, swords were never at any time a key armament in Japan. They were, rather, supplementary weapons, analogous to the handguns and trench knives carried by modern soldiers. While literary accounts – such as *Heike monogatari* or *Taiheiki*, which chronicle the Genpei wars of the late 12th century and the Nanbokuchō wars of the 14th century, respectively – do feature swords rather prominently, recent work by military historians has persuasively undermined many long-cherished presumptions about both early and late medieval warfare, demonstrating that battles, throughout the epoch, were actually dominated by missile weapons: arrows, rocks, and later bullets.

All warriors carried long swords, as well as shorter, companion blades, and trained at grappling; but they viewed these weapons as back-ups to their bows and arrows (or in later medieval times, to firearms and spears), never as replacements for them. Hand-to-hand combat with bladed weapons of any sort did not play a pivotal role in either early or late medieval battles, and swords were never the weapon of choice when troops did engage at close quarters. Swords were, in fact, rarely employed except under circumstances in which warriors could not use their principal weapons; they were actually mainly used in street fights, robberies, assassinations and other (off-battlefield) civil disturbances.[9]

Scholars and popular audiences alike have shown a remarkable reluctance to accept this reality, and have tended instead to confound the symbolic importance of the sword to early modern samurai identity with prominence in medieval battles. Historians, while acknowledging that the early samurai were created and defined by the skills of bow and horse, have been both dedicated and creative in their efforts to identify a point at which swords displaced bows as the samurai's weapon of choice. Multiple hypotheses have been advanced. None, however, stands up well to scrutiny.

The most compelling evidence on this point comes from analyses of statistics on wounds, compiled from battle reports. Thomas Conlan, for example, looked at 1,302 such documents, cataloguing 721 identifiable wounds. Of these, arrows caused some 73 per cent, while only 25 per cent were the result of sword strokes, and fewer than 2 per cent involved spears. Suzuki Masaya examined 175 such documents, and found that nearly 87 per cent of the 554 identifiable casualties reported therein came from arrows, 8 per cent were caused by swords or *naginata* [a bladed weapon with a long shaft], just under 3 per cent were the result of troops having been struck by rocks, and 1 per cent were caused by spears. Shakadō Mitsuhiro's less extensive survey of some 30 battle reports indicates that 82 per cent of the wounds were caused by arrows.[10]

Similarly, Suzuki found that of the 620 battle wounds recorded in the documents he examined for the period of 1501 to 1560, arrows inflicted 380, spears 133, stones (thrown by hand or by sling) caused 100, and only twenty-one were caused by swords. For the period of 1563 to 1600 – after the introduction of the gun – 584 reported casualties break down to 263 gunshot victims, 126 men wounded by arrows, ninety-nine wounded by spears, forty victims of sword wounds or 'cutting injuries' (*kiri kizu*), thirty men struck by rocks, and twenty-six troops injured by combinations of the foregoing weapons – including one unfortunate who was shot by both bullets and arrows *and* stabbed with a spear! Similarly, Thomas Conlan's analysis of 1,291 casualty reports from the 15th and 16th centuries reveals 179 deaths – for which no cause was reported – 439 arrow wounds, 343 gunshot wounds, 192 spear wounds, seventy-nine injuries caused by stones, and fifty sword cuts. In other words, both studies roughly agree that missile weapons (bullets, arrows and rocks) accounted for 75 per cent of the casualties reported during the pre-firearm era and 73 per cent of the casualties occurring after the popularisation of guns. Sword wounds, by contrast, amounted to just 5 per cent of the casualties for both periods.[11]

★

It would seem, then, that current scholarship on late medieval military history raises several thorny questions about the goals and purposes of 16th-century martial art *ryūha*: Why did these organisations, and the arts they promulgated, emerge when they did – at a time when generalship, the ability to organise and direct large forces, was rapidly coming to overshadow personal martial skills as the decisive element in battle, and the key to a successful military career? Why were there so few *ryūha* around

Musicians from the Muromachi period (1538).

during the late medieval era, and why did they proliferate so rapidly during the early Tokugawa period, after the age of wars had passed? And why did swordsmanship, an art that was, at best, of tertiary value to warriors in battle, play so prominent a role in even the earliest martial art *ryūha*?

All these questions become much easier to answer if one sets aside the premise that *bugei ryūha* originated as instruments for teaching the workaday techniques of the battlefield. And indeed, there is little basis for that hoary assumption, beyond the fact that war was endemic in Japan when the first martial art schools appeared. The received wisdom rests, in other words, on what amounts to a *post hoc ergo propter hoc* fallacy.

A growing body of evidence, on the other hand, points to the conclusion that martial art schools and the pedagogical devices associated with them aimed from the start at fostering more abstract ideals of self-development and enlightenment. That is, there was no fundamental shift of purpose in martial art education between the late 16th and mid-17th centuries. Tokugawa era *budō* represented not a mutation of late medieval martial art, but its maturation. That is, late medieval *ryūha bugei* itself constituted a new phenomenon – a derivative, not a linear improvement, of earlier, more prosaic military training.

As noted above, the first true *bugei ryūha* appeared around the late 15th century. This timing is significant, for it marks the emergence of martial art schools as part of a broader trend toward systemisation of knowledge and instruction in various artistic pursuits.

During the Muromachi period, virtuosos of calligraphy, flower arranging, music, drama, painting and the like began to think of their approaches to their arts as packages of information that could be transmitted to students in organised patterns, and to certify students' mastery of the teachings with licences and diplomas.[12]

The nascent martial art schools appropriated the forms, teaching methods, and vocabulary of these other applied arts. More importantly, however, the martial and other arts also shared a sense of ultimate – true – purpose, defined in the medieval Japanese concept of *michi,* or path.

This construct, born of implications drawn from a worldview common to Buddhism, Taoism and Confucianism, saw expertise in activities of all sorts, from games and sports to fine arts, from practical endeavours to religious practice, as possessing a universality deriving from its relationship to a common, ultimate goal. It held concentrated specialisation in any activity to be an equally valid route to attainment of universal truth, asserting that all true paths must lead eventually to the same place, and that therefore complete mastery of even the most trivial of pursuits must yield the same rewards as can be found through the most profound. *Ryūha bugei*, emerging within this cultural and philosophical milieu, took its place alongside poetry composition, incense judging, *Nō* drama, the tea ceremony, and numerous other medieval *michi*.[13]

Considered in this context, it becomes apparent that Iizasa Chōisai, Sōma Sadakuni, Aisu Ikōsai, Tsukahara Bokuden, Kamiizumi Ise-no-kami, and other pioneers of *ryūha bugei* were seeking and developing something related to, but not synonymous with, military training per se. That this new form of martial education was never meant to become boot camp, or even advanced schooling, for the rank and file of medieval armies is clear from the relative numbers involved. And the involvement of men of low social status, like the famous Miyamoto Musashi, demonstrates that it could not simply have been instruction for officers or other elites, either.

In their quest for perfection of skill in the arts of individual combat, Chōisai, Sadakuni, Bokuden, Musashi and their fellow martial artists were military anachronisms, out of step with the changing face of warfare in their times. And in their pursuit of this quest through training pilgrimages [*musha shūgyō*] and other ascetic regimens – their devotion to their arts over conventional military careers and service – they were self-indulgent and quixotic.

None of this, however, detracted from the value or the appeal of what they were doing, for *ryūha bugei* was an abstraction of military science, not merely an application of it. It fostered character traits and tactical acumen that made those who practised it better warriors, but its goals and ideals were more akin to those of liberal education than vocational training. That is, *bugeisha*, even during the medieval era, had more in common with Olympic marksmanship competitors – training with specialised weapons to develop esoteric levels of skill under particularised conditions – than with military riflemen. They also had as much, perhaps more, in common with Tokugawa era and modern martial artists than with the ordinary warriors of their own day.[14]

Viewed in this light, the prominent role of the sword in medieval *ryūha bugei* is much easier to understand. Their secondary role in battlefield combat notwithstanding, swords enjoyed a singular status as heirlooms and symbols of power, war, military skill and warrior identity. The elegantly curved, two-handed *Nihontō* was born about the same time as the warrior order itself, and during the early modern era came to be identified as 'the soul of the samurai'. Swords, as emblems of power, appear in the earliest Japanese mythology, and were regularly presented by medieval warrior leaders as gifts or rewards to their followers. By the Muromachi period, expressions like "clash of swords" [*tachi uchi, katana uchi*, or *uchi tachi*], or "wield a sword" [*tachi tsukamatsurare*] were recognised as generic appellations for combat, irrespective of the actual weapons employed.

Thus swordsmanship represented a symbolic *sine qua non* of personal combat: the favoured weapon for off-battlefield duelling, and a kind of *michi* within a *michi* for martial artists, then as now. This representational function is reflected in the popularisation of the term *hyōhō* (or *heihō*), which, until late medieval times, designated military science or martial art in the broad sense as a synonym for *kenjutsu*.

The special place and nature of *ryūha bugei* as abstract personal education, rather than workaday military drill, was precisely the reason it was able to evolve so rapidly during the early decades of the Tokugawa period.

The most conspicuous developments – the specialisation in weaponry, the formalisation of training, the lengthening of apprenticeships, the expansion of the *budō* ideal, the exponential proliferation of new *ryūha*, the increasingly cabalistic dedication to principles [*ryūgi*] that uniquely defined each school, and the like – did not involve abandonment or betrayal of earlier warrior legacies. They merely represented logical evolutions within one particular legacy. Specialisation, formalisation, and idealisation of *ryūha bugei* were not inherently harmful to military preparedness, because this form of martial training had never been about readying troops for war. Military science writ large continued in new schools of strategy and tactics, called *gungaku*, while *hyōhō* continued to focus on personal development.[15]

Nevertheless, the cumulative effect of decade after decade of peace took an inevitable, and well-studied, toll on samurai battle worth. By the 18th century, it was having a concomitant effect on contemporary perceptions of martial art as well. Samurai, who had not made or even trained seriously for war in generations, had lost sight of any separation between martial art and military training. Indeed, *ryūha bugei* had long since overshadowed other kinds of soldierly drill. For most samurai of the mid-Tokugawa period and later, there was but one form of sophisticated

The Tokugawa era ended with Emperor Meiji. Japan went from being an isolated, feudal society to a more Western-oriented country.

combative training: the individual-centred, self-development-oriented arts of the various *ryūha*.

This evolution in perspective was, no doubt, exacerbated by government exhortations and policies that encouraged samurai to believe that only minor differences of circumstance distinguished them from their medieval forebears. One important result was the conviction that the swordsmanship and other martial arts of the day descended directly from instruments of war, and that *bugei ryūha* originated as vehicles to train warriors for battle.

Pundits and scholars ever since have evaluated Tokugawa (and later) martial art in this light. In consequence, they have directed a great deal of what is ultimately unreasonable, even irrelevant, criticism at late Tokugawa period *bugei*, lamenting their inapplicability to the conditions of medieval battlefields, without realising that the arts from which they grew were never directly appropriate to battle.

Appraising *ryūha bugei* in terms of its utility to warfare and military science is, however, not merely unfair, it is counter-productive to understanding what really happened during the Tokugawa period, and what these arts and schools really were, and are today. By recognizing that *ryūha bugei* began as an activity that was both more and less than mundane military training, it becomes apparent that the modifications and innovations of the early modern era represented progress and sophistication, rather than deviation from or degeneration of the original goals and purpose. The proliferation of these arts, and the extent to which Tokugawa samurai substituted them for other forms of military training, were little more than ancillary phenomena to the broader, underlying changes sweeping through warrior society. The evolution of what scholars today term *budō* was a consequence or a symptom, not a cause, of declining war-readiness among the *bushi*.

Ironically, the martial arts today are closer in role and character, particularly in their perceived role and character, to their remote medieval progenitors than to their late Tokugawa period parents. By rendering the weaponry of the traditional martial arts all but worthless on the battlefield, the modern transformation of warfare has restored, and dramatically magnified, the boundaries that originally separated martial art from military drill. Because they can no longer harbour any illusions that they are training for war, modern martial art students need no longer be troubled by many of the doubts and criticisms that plagued their

Tokugawa era counterparts. They can freely and unapologetically embrace the objectives that drove their medieval forebears: the quest for perfection of skill in personal combat, and through this, the physical and spiritual cultivation of the self.

1. For background on the Hidesato-ryū Fujiwara, see Friday, Karl, *Hired Swords: The Rise of Private Warrior Power in Early Japan* (Stanford University Press, 1992), pp 88–91.
2. See Friday, Karl, "The Cat's Eerie Skill: a Translation of Issai Chozan's *Neko no Myōjustu*", in *Keiko Shokon*, ed Diane Skoss (Koryu Books, 2002), pp 17–34; and Friday, Karl, "Beyond Valor & Bloodshed: the Arts of War as a Path to Serenity", in *Knight and Samurai: Actions and Images of Elite Warriors in Europe and East Asia*, ed Harald Kleinschmidt and Rose Marie Diest (Kümmerle Verlag Göppingen, 2003), pp 1–14.
3. See, for example, the treatments of *bugei* history in Draeger, Donn F., *The Martial Arts and Ways of Japan*, vol 1, *Classical Bujutsu* and vol 2, *Classical Budo* (Weatherhill, 1973); or Hurst III, G. Cameron, *Armed Martial Arts of Japan: Swordsmanship & Archery* (Yale University Press, 1998).
4. For examples of 16th-century *bugei* instructional texts, see Tsukahara Bokuden's *Ikunsho* (also called *Bokuden hyakushu*), reproduced in Imamura Yoshio, et al, eds, *Nihon budō taikei* (Dōshōsha, 1982) vol. 3: pp 58–66. Fuller discussions of martial art texts can be found in Friday, *Legacies*, pp 137–51. For examples of other early texts, see Watanabe Ichirō, *Budō no meicho* (Tōkyō kopii shuppanbu, 1979) and Imamura Yoshio, et al, ed, *Nihon budō taikei* (Dōshōsha, 1982).
5. Imamura Yoshio, "Budōshi gaisetsu", pp 12–15, identifies 39 core *hyōgaku, kyujutsu, bujutsu, kenjutsu, sōjutsu, hōjutsu*, and *jūjutsu ryūha* which evolved, by late Tokugawa times, into some 1,189 distinct schools.
6. Suzuki Susumu, *Nihon kassenshi hyakubanashi* (Tokyo: Tatsukaze shobō, 1982), p 150, p 166; Takayanagi Mitsutoshi and Suzuki Tōrou, *Nihon kassenshi* (Tokyo: Gakugei shorin, 1968), p 260; Mary Elizabeth Berry, *Hideyoshi* (Cambridge, Mass: Harvard University Press, 1982), p 209.
7. For more on the origins and early development of the warrior class, see Karl Friday, *Hired Swords: The Rise of Private Warrior Power in Early Japan*, (Stanford University Press, 1992).
8. See Friday, Karl, *Samurai, Warfare and the State in Early Medieval Japan,* (Routledge, 2004), pp 102–5.
9. See Conlan, Thomas D., "Instruments of Change: Organizational Technology and the Consolidation of Regional Power in Japan, 1333–1600", in *War and State Building in Medieval Japan*, ed John A. Ferejohn and Frances McCall Rosenbluth, (Stanford University Press, 2010); Conlan, *State of War: The Violent Order of Fourteenth Century Japan*, Michigan Monograph Series in Japanese Studies, (University of Michigan Center for Japanese Studies, 2003); or Friday, *Samurai, Warfare, and the State.*
10. Conlan, *State of War*; Masaya, Suzuki, *Katana to kubi-tori: sengoku kassen isetsu* (Heibonsha shinsho, 2000); Mitsuhiro, Shakadō, "Nanbokuchō ki kassen ni okeru senshō", *Nairanshi kenkyū* 13, 1992, pp 27–39, 37–38.

11. Suzuki Masaya, Teppō to Nihonjin: *'teppō shinwa' ga kakushite kita koto* (Yōsensha, 1997); Conlan, "Instruments of Change".
12. Nakabayashi Shinji, "Kendō shi" 42-44; Friday, Karl, *Legacies of the Sword: the Kashima-Shinryū & Samurai Martial Culture* (University of Hawaii Press, 1997), pp 14–15.
13. Konishi Jin'ichi, *Nihon koten*, vol 3, *Michi: chūsei no rinen,,* (Kodansha gendai shinso, 1975); Ueda Makoto, *Literary and Art Theories in Japan,* (Western Reserve University Press, 1967); Eno, Robert, *The Confucian Creation of Heaven: Philosophy and the Defense of Ritual Mastery,* (State University of New York Press, 1990), pp 64–66; Friday, *Legacies*, pp 16–17.
14. This was not the first time that *bushi* had embraced ritualised or symbolic forms of military exercises. The *yabusame* mounted archery demonstrations and competitions of the early medieval period also followed formats that put a premium on skills only abstractly related to the demands of Kamakura era battlefields.
15. Hyōdō Nisohachi, *Gungaku kō*, (Chūō kōron shinsha, 2000), offers an excellent introduction to the subject of *gungaku*.

Armour presented to King James I
by Shogun Tokugawa Hidetada in 1613.

ARMOUR FOR AN AGE OF PEACE
Natasha Bennett

In 1613, the ship of Captain John Saris of the Honourable East India Company returned to England after a long voyage to the mysterious country of Japan. Part of its cargo included a gift of two Japanese suits of armour, which were delivered to King James I according to instruction. The armours had been sent as a gift from the Shogun, Tokugawa Hidetada (son of Tokugawa Ieyasu), to mark the establishment of the first diplomatic and trade interactions between Japan and England. One of the armours was put on display at the Tower of London, where it must have seemed like something from another world to the eyes of 17th century visitors. As part of the collection of the Royal Armouries, it can still be seen on show at the Tower to this day.[1]

One complete heraldic crest [*kamon*] survives on the armour, picked out in gold lacquer. Identification of this *kamon* has shown that the armour was probably originally owned by a member of the powerful Takeda family. The Takeda domains were finally conquered by Tokugawa Ieyasu and his forces during 1582; it seems likely that this armour was a war booty prize, refurbished for presentation. It is a high quality set of equipment. The *dōmaru* structure (meaning that the cuirass – the breastplate and backplate – extended all around the body and overlapped to be secured under the right arm), the lamellar construction (rows of hundreds of overlapping individual scales which were then laced together to form the main sections of armour), the dense silk lacing over the surface of the armour, and the sizeable shoulder guards were all typical features of traditional styles of armour which had reached this developed form by the 14th century. They remained popular after this time with the highest-ranking samurai, who could afford the labour-intensive production they required. However, when this particular suit of armour left the shores of Japan in the early 17th century, it may well have been regarded as somewhat archaic in nature, at least in comparison to a lot of contemporary equipment that was being produced for use in battle.

Before the rule of the Tokugawa shogunate brought a period of enforced peace to Japan, the landowning class or *daimyō* had fought between themselves across the length and breadth of the country for over 150 years. This protracted period of civil war was known as *Sengoku Jidai,* or Age of the Country at War. Battlefield tactics evolved, fighting forces expanded, new weapons like the matchlock musket were adopted on a large scale, and more and more individuals experienced fighting as a way of life. To keep pace with these changes, Japanese armour was developed to a pinnacle of practicality and efficiency.

The Royal Armouries holds a precious surviving example of a practical fighting armour which was probably made and worn in the mid-16th century. This dating comes from tracing the armour's initial arrival in Europe; it was probably one of the numerous gift armours brought over by the Tenshō Mission,[2] a group of Japanese Christians who embarked on a voyage to the Spanish court, funded by three prominent *daimyō* who wanted to improve their diplomatic links with Europe. The armour seems to have been presented to King Philip II of Spain, as the first clear documentary evidence for it is found in a 1603 list which describes the armour, and details its proposed removal from the Treasure House to the Spanish Royal Armoury.[3] Despite the contrast in appearance with the more flamboyantly laced gift armour given to James I, this more muted armour would also have been made for a warrior of high rank; it is of superior quality and marked with a *kamon* associated with the Shimazu clan of Satsuma.[4] It provides an excellent example of some of the ways in which Japanese armour had evolved during the *Sengoku Jidai* era.

Whereas previously mounted archers using the longbow had predominated on the battlefield, now infantry equipped with spears and matchlock guns had become the main threat. The larger solid plates in the body armour and the sleek, compact helmet provided better protection against musket fire than the finely laced rows of separate lamellar scales of medieval armours, which tended to shatter into tiny fragments. Larger iron and rawhide plates also meant that far less lacing was required for a secure construction. This reduced the weight and the potential for water saturation, lice infestations and damage during inclement weather and long periods of siege warfare. The thigh defences were split into more sections which allowed greater freedom of movement because more fighting was now performed on foot. This armour was clearly intended for use as a field armour for effective protection in battle, as evidenced by the damage probably left

Mid-16th century field armour used during the Sengoku Jidai period.

十八番弓

An illustration of a traditional medieval ō-yoroi ('great armour') from the book Yoroi Chakuyo Shidai (Order of Putting on Armour), early 19th century.

by a sword blade which can still be seen on one of the sleeves. It was still recognisably Japanese in appearance, still lacquered and laced, but it had advanced significantly from the box-like ō-yoroi or 'great armours' which had been so popular between the Heian and Nanbokuchō periods. Put simply, it aspired to do the job expected, in the circumstances for which it was made. As the Japanese historian of armour Sakakibara Kōzan wrote in the late 18th century: "Armour is a means of protecting a warrior's person from bow or gunshot wounds and at the same time should permit of easy and valorous action whether in the van or the rear of the fight".[5]

If we now jump from the time when this austere armour was created to the middle and later years of the Tokugawa era in the 18th and 19th centuries and compare production, we can see that the armour industry was certainly still active. Indeed, much of the Japanese armour that survives in museum and private collections across the world today dates to the later Edo period.

However, by the 18th and 19th centuries, the armourers were producing much more visually striking commissions. Such armours were often of superb artistic quality, costly to produce, and on first glance, far more impressive to look at than the less glamourous, more reserved armour of two centuries before. Yet in several respects they would probably offer inferior protection to that provided by the 16th-century armours, should they ever have to be worn in battle. In a preface written for Sakakibara Kōzan's work on armour, Hayakawa Kiūkei mused: "The taste of the passing day rules the making of armour. The proper forging of an iron plate yields in importance to the decorative appearance of the work. Armour is looked upon as a mere plaything of a peaceful age. What chance has it against the power of modern gunfire?"[6]

Members of the military class *buke* still retained their martial identity and high rank in society. If anything, their duties and responsibilities and the expectations placed upon them were increasingly codified; both through the instructions of the Tokugawa government and the growth in fascination with *bushidō* or "the way of the warrior". If samurai were still theoretically required to defend their society and their honour at a moment's notice, why then did armour apparently halt in its practical advancement, frequently demonstrating a diminished capacity to provide effective protection as the Edo period progressed?

The Tokugawa regime came to power at the end of a prolonged and bloody era of civil strife. One of their main concerns was to consolidate

'Fuji Seen In The Distance from Senju Pleasure Quarter' by Katsushika Hokusai, Edo, 1830–33. *Daimyō* retainers bear guns in the foreground.

their position of strength and command, and extinguish all sources of revolt. In a country where a large section of the population was used to no other life but war, and weapons and military equipment abounded, rigorous controls were put in place to discourage unrest. Domains were carefully distributed between *daimyō* so that those nobles who were loyal supporters of the Tokugawa family could maintain a close watch on less trustworthy individuals. External influence was reduced significantly, thanks to the policy of isolation or *sakoku*, which effectively banished foreigners and their products from Japan, with the exception of small trading enclaves maintained by the Dutch and the Chinese. The Japanese people were themselves prohibited from leaving or re-entering the country. The production and use of weapons was formally regulated, and gun production had to be licensed. The majority of gunsmiths were compelled to operate in Sakai or Nagahama in central Japan, and had to journey to Edo (present-day Tokyo) to be issued with a permit every time they received an order. This made the production and acquisition of muskets so prolonged and cumbersome that the development of firearms stalled. Rather than being intended for any significant practical use in fighting, guns often become symbols of prestige and status to be carried in procession for those who could afford to equip their retainers with such weapons. Edicts were enforced that forbade any but samurai to carry a long sword or more than one sword. The sword was an incredibly potent symbol, immediately redolent of the power and authority of the samurai, and much emphasis was placed on proper swordsmanship. Thus, with the circulation and availability of firearms heavily curtailed, and the attention of the military elite redirected to the individual skill and privilege required to wield a sword, finding the opportunity and inclination to equip large forces for rebellion became more difficult.

In particular, the demands exerted by the *sankin kōtai* or "alternate attendance" policy ensured that landed nobles had little time or scope to foment unrest. This diktat decreed that all *daimyō* had to split their time between their provincial domains and their mansions in Edo, although their wives and families had to remain in the Edo residences all the time as security to guarantee the lords' good behaviour. Travel between the court at Edo and homes in the provinces was accomplished on a grand scale with the *daimyō gyōretsu,* the procession of a lord accompanied by large numbers of retainers in full pomp and splendour. These travelling parades provided excellent opportunities for *daimyō* and their ranks of samurai followers to prove their wealth, status and prestige by displaying impressive armour, weapons and equipment as part of this approved exhibition of power.[7] At the same time, these marches placed enormous demands on the time and resources of those involved, which meant that they were less able to devote themselves to more covert and dangerous activities, such as challenging the established regime.

Against this background, the lifestyle and outlook of the *buke* began to adjust. In principle, adherence to high-minded warrior ideals was an intrinsic part of samurai culture. They were still expected to be able to take up arms on behalf of their master if called, and great emphasis was placed on virtue, loyalty and honour. Martial skills were revered and increasingly formalised and refined. But in practical terms, the likelihood of becoming immersed in perpetual warfare and embroiled in actual battles diminished as the Edo period wore on and the Tokugawa regime of peace became more entrenched.

This becalmed and closed environment provided the context against which the role of armour began to change. Much of the armour now being produced was primarily for ceremonial wear rather than for personal protection during fighting. The aesthetics of artistic workmanship and the importance of outward appearance began to overtake concerns for functionality. As a result, there was a burgeoning interest in the ancient, visually evocative styles of armour which had been popular until the 14th and 15th centuries, before the expanded use of infantry and the introduction of the gun on the battlefield demanded more utilitarian qualities. By the 18th century, samurai were generations removed from direct involvement in the violence of the Age of Battles – but they could still capture the feats and glory of an illustrious legacy by looking to historic armours to inspire a contemporary image for themselves.

A large number of ancient armours had been preserved for centuries in shrines and temples throughout Japan. These provided the focus for the ninth volume or 'Armour Book' element of the *Honchō-Gunkikō*, a work compiled in the early decades of the 18th century by the historian and court tutor Arai Hakuseki. This was the first widely available written account of Japanese arms and armour; it drew an avid audience in the warrior class, and was quickly followed by numerous similar guides, which also concentrated on antique medieval armours.[8] This flurry of scholarship helped to prompt a large-scale revival of these old forms for

Illustrations from a book entitled *Yoroi Chakuyo Shidai* (Order of Putting on Armour), early 19th century. The warrior dons an ō-yoroi or 'great armour'.

newly-commissioned sets of equipment, and enthusiasm for archaic styles of armour grew apace.

At first, individual features reverted to older types. For instance, during the *Sengoku Jidai*, compact helmets referred to as *zunari kabuto* [head-shaped helmets] with close-fitting neck guards had become popular. These were made from a few large plates, rendering the wearer less vulnerable to the effects of spear-thrusts and musket fire, and were quick to produce. Yet as traditional tastes reappeared, a fashion materialised for incorporating antique helmet bowls (or modern productions manufactured in an antique style) as part of new sets of armour. These helmets, or *kabuto*, reverted to a construction which used multiple plates, which were often studded with prominent rivets. Neck guards started to spread outwards once again. Big, broad shoulder guards, developed to provide medieval warriors with hands-free shields while engaging in archery combat on horseback, had been reduced in size or dispensed with altogether for a lot of the armour produced during the civil wars of the 15th and 16th centuries. Like the medieval helmet styles, they made a comeback and assumed large, imposing proportions again, despite the fact that this made them more of a hindrance than a help for effective fighting on foot with swords or staff weapons. Stencilled leather was frequently used as ornamentation. Dense, richly coloured lacing [*kebiki odoshi*] returned to cover the surface of cuirasses and neck guards. The construction of body armour was also adapted to suit demand for an old-fashioned appearance; large plates were frequently built up with lacquer to resemble rows of individual scales in imitation of the old lamellar structures, and sometimes actual scales [*sane*] returned in a true, painstaking renewal of past techniques.

The combination of features spanning different eras often led to anomalies and problems, which perhaps provides as good an indication as any that these armours were not primarily utilitarian. For instance, enlarged shoulder guards encouraged the return of the large ornamental bow, or *agemaki*, historically required as a fastening to secure the shoulder guards and prevent them from dropping forwards during action. However, this was often attached alongside a more modern fitting used to hold the staff of a heraldic banner or *sashimono*, which warriors slotted down their backs for identification on the battlefield during the civil wars. If used together, the *sashimono* holder and the *agemaki* could very quickly become entangled and hamper ease of movement, and this problem was often further compounded by the inclusion of a widespread neck guard. By the end of the 18th century though, wealthy samurai were commissioning armours which were near perfect copies of the classical forms, including *dōmaru* and *haramaki* and even full scale *ō-yoroi*, from the times when archers on horseback had dominated the battlefield. *ō-yoroi* were the elaborate lamellar armours specifically designed to defend mounted warriors from arrows. The large shoulder guards [*ō-sode*] and pronounced turnbacks [*fukigayeshi*] at the front of the helmet all helped to deflect arrows during combat, while the front of the cuirass was often covered by a sheet of stencilled leather to prevent the bowstring of the Japanese longbow [*yumi*] from snagging on the rows of lacquered lamellar scales when drawn. *Dōmaru* ['around the body'] and *haramaki* ['belly wrapper'] armours were simpler and lighter in construction. They were originally developed for use by retainers who had started to conduct more fighting on foot, because they allowed greater ease of movement.

Civilian clothing for the military class tended to be austere in appearance, reflecting the sober demeanour and respectability that samurai were expected to epitomise in their daily activities. Armour therefore provided an outlet for a warrior to identify with his individual rank and prestige, and his cultural heritage and ideals. The peace and settled power of the Tokugawa period meant that there was more time and resources to devote to the cultivation of the arts, beauty, and meaning. Many armours commissioned around this time embodied these elevated interests, projecting poetic visions such as cherry blossoms in spring through lacing in pale green, pink and white, for example. Armourers were able to capitalise on this enthusiasm. The stability of the period meant that craftsmen were able to develop and perfect their artistry. Their creativity and output escalated to meet the growing demand for skilled ornamentation for armour and weapons, which were ever increasing in symbolic importance for those who wore or displayed them. One school, the Myōchin armourers, became particularly well known for their intricate embossed armours and reproductions of medieval styles of helmets. Embossed armour had to be produced from comparatively soft iron, and therefore its defensive capabilities were negligible. Yet the Myōchin were meeting a demand; there would have been little point in manufacturing modern, functional armours when nobody was commissioning them. Those who could afford to have armours made for them were no longer required to don them for battle. But by acquiring elaborate, impressive armour made

Helmet forged in the shape of an aubergine, late 17th century, attributed to the armourer Myochin Ryoei.

in old or flamboyant styles, they could display the admired qualities of their class in a very visual manner, and continue to reinforce the concept that the physical prowess, martial skill and honour of the samurai assured their power and control over the rest of the population.

By the turn of the 19th century, some interested commentators had started to express anxiety about the tendency to prioritise appearance and superficial characteristics of armour. In his work *Chūkokatchū Seisakuben* [The Manufacture of Armour and Helmets in Sixteenth-Century Japan] which was published in Edo in 1800, Sakakibara Kōzan lamented what he regarded as a serious decline in the quality of the armour manufactured since the rigorous fighting of the *Sengoku Jidai* had faded into the mists of time. He blamed writings such as the *Honchō Gunkikō* for encouraging an adherence to outdated models which were no longer relevant for modern requirements. He pointed out that the pastiches of medieval armour would be of little or no use in practical warfare of the type that had been endemic in Japan before the 17th century and could potentially happen again:

> The spirit of the Armourer in the Age of Battles was quite different from that animating his brother in the Age of Peace. [...] Your modern armourer, living in an age of peace, forgets that armour is made for use in war. Think of the disgrace which will fall on the memory of the maker of today should his work be pierced by arrows or gunshot a hundred years hence and the wearer fall a victim in consequence [...]
>
> Nor should the soldier himself be lulled by the peacefulness of the age into carelessness as to the quality of the materials and the work put into the armour worn by him. No less disgrace must attach to the ancestor whose descendant, wearing an armour handed down from him, perishes in battle owing to its shortcomings. If we must pass our armour on to our posterity, let it at least be as perfect as we can make it.[9]

Despite the prevailing regime of stability, some observers were clearly far from comfortable with the outlook. There was evidently anxiety that peace could not be permanent and that the incumbent, untested *buke* would be unfit to combat any return of real violence should it occur. This was apparently mixed with a wistful nostalgia for the demands of continuous warfare. These had, after all, spurred the demonstrations of courage and honour that continued to define the prevailing popular conception of what a samurai should represent. Physical danger had encouraged progress and development for armour and weapons; the return to outdated models was seen as a risk by some, indicating a softening or weakening of soldierly capability. Interestingly, the warnings of Sakakibara Kōzan do seem to have had an effect in the early decades of the 19th century: more armours were produced which reused or recalled the practical features of 16th-century models, reverting to solid plates, reduced shoulder guards, sparser lacing and more compact helmets. This process accelerated as Japan's isolation from the outside world was increasingly challenged by pressure from foreign powers to open the country up for trade, brought to a head by the forceful arrival of American warships under the command of Commodore Perry in 1853. An invasion was regarded as imminent, and it must have seemed sensible for those samurai who could afford it to commission a functional field armour in readiness, in addition to their gorgeously arrayed, pseudo-traditional armour for display and parade.

Despite this partial return to utilitarian models, however, all the armour of the samurai could not stand against the ultimate threat: the end of an isolated feudal culture which had promoted its continued use. The massed ranks of armoured warriors could not hold back the forced diplomacy of the outside world; against the industrialised West with its mechanised armed forces, pretty much all armour was archaic and obsolete. Within a few decades, Japan had modernised and adopted a national army, and the elite status of the samurai was terminated. With neither a practical function nor an enduring ideal to uphold, armour was rendered more or less useless for both makers and users in the domestic market. Many armours old and new were sold off to interested new collectors in the West who were suddenly able to engage with a country which had previously been off-limits, and who were swept up by an explosion of enthusiasm for traditional Japanese art and culture.

Perhaps this is one reason why the Edo period armours imitating antique styles, with their beautiful vivid silk lacing, flamboyant ornamentation, and dramatic helmets and shoulder guards, have found and maintained such popularity and longevity in institutional and private collections. Despite the frequent discrepancy between their apparent impracticality and the demands of warfare, the armours can still be

Gold lacquered armour from the late Edo period. The helmet crest is a *shishi*, a mythical creature lion and dog hybrid.

appreciated as signifiers of the image and prestige of samurai across the ages, and they continue to transport audiences back to the days of legendary warriors. It seems reasonable to assume that they played a similar role when first produced for parade and ceremonial wear during the time of Tokugawa rule. The ancient armours they emulated were synonymous with the values, duties and historic achievements which had inspired the establishment of the warrior class centuries before. Whether or not this rejuvenation of old armour forms was an effective way for samurai to promote such ideals as a continuing and relevant part of their identity and authority as they navigated a new environment of prevailing peace needs to be considered in more depth. Yet by reiterating the connection between the *buke* and the glorious associations of a distant military past in a way that was visual and explicit, it certainly seems likely that armour helped to secure and validate an institution which continued to exist until after the Meiji Restoration, even though it was ultimately doomed to redundancy. The samurai may not have required their armour to shield them from physical damage for most of the Edo period, but it continued to protect them in different ways during the Age of Peace experienced by Tokugawa Japan.

---

1. The other suit of armour now forms part of the Royal Collection (accession number RCIN 71611).
2. See Ian Bottomley 'Japanese diplomatic gifts of arms and armour to Europe of the 16th and 17th centuries' in *East meets West: Diplomatic gifts of arms and armour between Europe and Asia*, ed T. Richardson (Royal Armouries, 2014).
3. Ibid., pp 10–11.
4. The armour was reassembled and re-laced with green braid in the mid-19th century. Fragments of the original black lacing have been found during scientific analysis and conservation.
5. Sakakibara Kōzan, *Chūkokatchū Seisakuben* or *The Manufacture of Armour and Helmets in 16th Century Japan* (Edo, 1800), translated by T. Wakameda, revised by A.J. Koop and Inada Hogitarō (1912), revised and edited by H. Russell Robinson (The Holland Press, 1963), p 15.
6. Ibid, p 13.
7. See Constantine N. Vaporis's essay in this volume, p 369.
8. One example of these is a block book entitled *Yoroi Chakuyo Shidai* [*Order of Putting on Armour*], produced during the early 19th century. A copy is held in the archives at the Royal Armouries, Leeds.
9. Sakakibara, pp 23-24.

REFERENCES

Arai Hakuseki, *The Armour Book in Honchō-Gunkikō*, translated by Y. Ōtsuka, edited by H. Russell Robinson (The Holland Press Ltd, 1964).

Bottomley, I., 'Japanese diplomatic gifts of arms and armour to Europe of the 16th and 17th centuries' in *East meets West: Diplomatic gifts of arms and armour between Europe and Asia*, edited by T. Richardson (Royal Armouries, 2014), pp 1–39.

Bottomley, I., 'Yukinoshita Dō', Nihon-No-Katchū Samurai Armour Forum, [Accessed June 14, 2017]

Bottomley, I., *An Introduction to Japanese Armour* (Royal Armouries, 2002).

Bottomley, I., *Japanese Arms and Armour* (Royal Armouries, 2017).

Dunn, C.J., *Everyday Life in Traditional Japan* (1st edition 1972, this edition, Tuttle Publishing, 2008).

Hayakawa Kiūkei, 'Preface', in Sakakibara Kōzan, *Chūkokatchū Seisakuben* or *The manufacture of armour and helmets in 16th century Japan* (Edo, 1800), translated by T. Wakameda, revised by A.J. Koop and Inada Hogitarō (1912), revised and edited by H. Russell Robinson (The Holland Press, 1963), pp 13–14.

Irvine, G., 'Japanese arms and armour after 1600', in *Art of Armour: Samurai armour from the Ann and Gabriel Barbier-Mueller Collection* (Ann and Gabriel Barbier-Mueller Museum, in association with Yale University Press, 2011), pp 109–117.

Perrin, N., *Giving up the Gun* (David R. Godine, 1979).

Richardson, T., 'Arms and armour from the Kofun Period to the introduction of firearms', in *Art of Armour: Samurai armour from the Ann and Gabriel Barbier-Mueller Collection* (Ann and Gabriel Barbier-Mueller Museum, in association with Yale University Press, 2011), pp 91–97.

Robinson, H.R., *Japanese Arms and Armour* (Arms and Armour Press, 1969).

Sakakibara Kōzan, *Chūkokatchū Seisakuben* or *The Manufacture of Armour and Helmets in 16th century Japan* (Edo, 1800), translated by T. Wakameda, revised by A.J. Koop and Inada Hogitarō (1912), revised and edited by H. Russell Robinson (The Holland Press, 1963).

Vaporis, C.N., *Tour of Duty: Samurai, Military Service in Edo, and the Culture of Early Modern Japan* (University of Hawai'i Press, 2008).

Samurai on horseback.

PERFORMANCE, DISPLAY, AND THE SPECTACULAR

Constantine N. Vaporis

Let me begin with a short quotation that provides a point of entry to make a critique of the way that Tokugawa society in general, and the nature of samurai and samurai culture in particular, have been viewed. In this quotation the eighth shogun Tokugawa Yoshimune (1684–1751) is responding to an adviser's comments lamenting the consequences of the peace:

> All the struggle and pain Lord Ieyasu endured was to bring peace to all Japan. Therefore, it is worthy of celebration that bows and arrows are kept in bags and swords in wooden cases. That the shogun's men keep their armor in merchants' storehouses means that Japan is now enjoying unprecedented peace. The ultimate wish of Tôshôgû [the deified Ieyasu] has been realized. You should not be sorrowful that swords and bows rot in pawnshops.

Reflecting the adviser's comments, the Tokugawa period (1603–1868), referred to by contemporary Japanese as a time of the 'realm at great peace,' is often viewed negatively for the perceived ill-effects produced by an absence of war. It has been viewed as creating political stasis, international isolation, cultural stagnation, and bringing about a marked decline in the martial character of the samurai.

However, from a 21st-century perspective, what I find remarkable is that cultural production in Tokugawa did not stagnate or simply replicate itself. Nor were all elements of colour and flamboyance extinguished from samurai culture. In fact, samurai culture, particularly in terms of what the anthropologist Clifford Geertz refers to as the 'public performance of signs and symbolic acts,' continued to develop and to assume new forms during the Tokugawa period.

Moreover, to view samurai culture and the samurai themselves as a story of decline is to read history backwards – and to miss the more

Daimyō procession at Kasumigaseki in Edo.

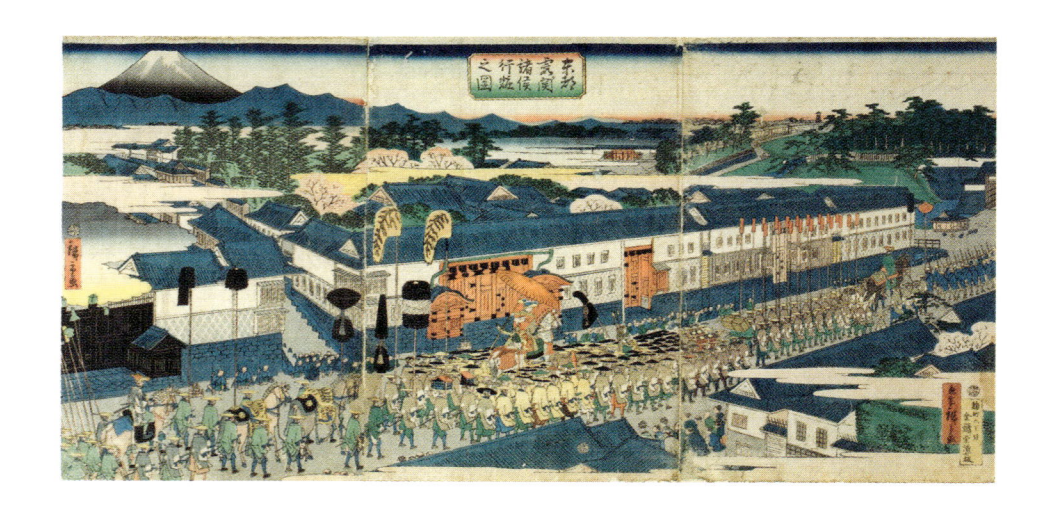

important story of their development into cultured and cultural elites.

In this essay, I will examine several elements of cultural production in Tokugawa Japan in which colour and flamboyance in samurai culture remained visible and vibrant: in horse-riding ceremonies; in *daimyō* processions; and in the helmets or *kabuto* that were a part of a full set of armour, and which were sometimes utilised in both of the abovementioned events. In so doing, I aim to draw some conclusions about the nature of samurai rule and identity during the Tokugawa years.

★

Horse riding had been an essential skill for samurai retainers of substantial rank since the 11th or 12th centuries. With the onset of the Tokugawa peace after 1615, however, there were fewer occasions to exercise those skills. Moreover, with the increasing financial difficulties that most samurai faced from the early 18th century onwards, particularly in the face of *daimyō* [lord] efforts to economise by reducing samurai stipends, it became more difficult for samurai to even own horses.

In Tosa domain, the main source for this part of the essay, and also in many other domains, retainers with stipends of 200 *koku* (one *koku* = five bushels of rice) or more were required to maintain one horse as part of their preparedness for wartime service to the *daimyō*. Over time, as the economic foundations of the samurai eroded, fewer were able to maintain horses. Consequently, we find that horses were shared, or that higher-ranking retainers with more than one horse lent them to others. It was also possible to ride one of the animals maintained by the domain government, either in the castle town (the domain headquarters) or in the capital city of the Tokugawa shogunate, Edo (present-day Tokyo). Despite these difficulties, horse riding remained an important – if underappreciated – part of samurai life throughout the Tokugawa period.

There were further, perhaps better-known, practices involving riding other than the ceremony on which I will focus in this part of the essay: for example, *inuomono,* which involved samurai on horseback moving in a circle trying to hit dogs with non-lethal arrows. This seems not to have been practised much during the Edo period, possibly as a result of the fifth shogun Tsunayoshi's edicts of the late 17th century aimed at reducing violence in society, including towards animals. The other practice was *yabusame,* a type of horseback archery [*kyûba*]. While it had a resurgence under the eighth shogun, Tokugawa Yoshimune, in the early 18th century, *yabusame* was mainly performed in conjunction with religious festivals at Shinto shrines.

Given the above, the fact that annual horse riding rituals, referred to in Tosa domain as *onorizome* ['the first horse riding ceremony'], and as *baba hajime* [with the same meaning] elsewhere in Japan, are not better known or appreciated for their impact on samurai culture is quite surprising.

In Tosa, a large domain that comprised the southern half of the island of Shikoku, and in many other domains across Japan, exhibiting horse riding skills in a public forum became an important demonstration of a samurai's ability to serve the lord. *Onorizome* (the honorific 'o' indicates that it was an official domain event) in Tosa took place on the 11th day of the new year, part of a roughly two-week long period of official festivities. It was the largest of these events, signalling its importance, and one of several activities that combined elements of religious meaning with an exercise in martial readiness: for example, it was followed several days later by *funanorizome* ['the first boat riding ceremony'], an exercise in maritime preparedness.

This horse-riding ceremony was held every year in Tosa during the entire Edo period and beyond, until 1871, three years after the demise of the Tokugawa shogunate. It was an annual ritual in which the domain's retainers demonstrated their horse-riding skills on an 870-metre (half a mile) course down a major road near the main gate of Kōchi castle, where the main trolley line of the Toden Densha Company runs today.

Participation in *onorizome* was at first limited to those with full samurai status – those who were included in the domain's official registry of retainers [*bugenchô*]. In 1662, this meant 1,296 participants. At the end of the 17th century, the event involved close to a thousand riders; later in the period there was a general drop in numbers, with only 500 to 600 men participating in 1758 and in 1826, the two years for which there are statistics. However, during the year of a new lord's first visit to Tosa, the entire retainer core – meaning both upper and lower samurai – were required to participate, and that typically involved over 2,000 men. Additionally, each retainer was accompanied to the ceremony by the requisite number of attendants as befitted his status, minimally one or two persons, so there were several thousands of people involved.

It is not clear whether similar conditions existed in other domains, but in Tosa, the ceremony became even more inclusive during the middle of

Daimyō procession crossing trestle bridge.

Norizome ceremony.

the 17th century when participation was broadened to include a larger portion of the overall retainer corps, not just full samurai. From early on, in 1649, Tosa's rural samurai, known as *gôshi*, petitioned to be included. Their formal request was a cause for considerable tension in the retainer corps, since *gôshi* were not considered full samurai, and in a time of peace, samurai were very protective of their status privileges. But in Tosa, *gôshi* had much higher status than in most domains: they occupied the highest rank among the lower samurai. A decision to include them was made in 1649, and in the one year for which there are statistics (1758) they comprised roughly 18 per cent of the total, or 107 out of 598 men.

Before the ceremony even began, prayers were recited for three days and two nights by Shinto priests at Shinmei shrine, near Kōchi castle, and at the Hachiman shrine, located within the castle grounds. Hachiman is the *kami* [Shinto deity] of war and archery. All along the course, purifying sand was scattered in preparation for the event, a custom that was also carried out prior to the passage of *daimyō* processions through castle towns.

The *onorizome* ceremony itself took place over the better part of a day, from early morning until evening. At about 6am the lord exited the castle in his palanquin, passing by his top seventy or eighty retainers on their knees at the main gate as he traversed a short distance to the residence of one of the senior councillors. There, the lord occupied the seat of honour in a specially constructed two-storey viewing tower. After partaking of a special new year's meal and receiving formal greetings from high-ranking retainers, the lord began the day's festivities by riding a short distance to the east and west on a steed. In this way he exhibited his own riding skills, although in a limited and conservative fashion. He then returned to his position in the tower and, before the activities proceeded, he was handed a ledger listing the names of the participants, as well as the type of horse being ridden by each, compiled in the order in which they were scheduled to ride.

Participants, for their part, dressed for the event at their homes in the samurai residential district of the castle town. Before departing, they drank a celebratory cup full of sake known as *kadode no shukuhai* ['the celebratory cup prior to departure'], an act associated with ritual purification, also carried out prior to setting out for battle in a previous age.

The ceremony proceeded as follows: the formal opening was marked by the sound of a conch shell blown from the observation tower. The riders, organised according to their military unit (usually ten), assembled one unit at a time in the rectangular-shaped open area known as *masugata* that lay before the beginning of the course.

Previous to this, riders warmed up before proceeding on horseback to the starting point [*noridashi*], where one-by-one they waited for the signal to start: their name called plus a combination of drumbeat and the wave of a military fan [*gunbai*] by an official. The samurai rode down the course, one-by-one, from the starting point to the end [*horizume*], a distance of over 870 metres, at full speed. Officials were present along the course to monitor the event, and a vet stood by in readiness, if needed, to care for injured animals. The process of riding one-by-one continued until every samurai had had their turn, which usually required a full day.

The ride was complicated by the customary bow to the lord required of all participants. It was expected that the rider bow his head in respect as he passed the spot about midway on the course where the lord sat, a tacit acknowledgment of the reason for the ceremony: the performance of service. According to a contemporary image that captures this moment for an unnamed rider, the lord's position is marked simply by a flag bearing the Chinese character *mu* [nothingness], which had Daoist overtones connoting rulership through "inaction". The motion of bowing, however, created some tension on the part of the rider: the fear that even a momentary break of concentration might cause him to stumble and fall.

A mis-step or tumble at any part of the course would bring the rider more than a momentary feeling of shame. It could in fact have significant long-term consequences, as the names of riders who had fallen were publicised. This indicates that the possibility of falling or being thrown from the horse was taken quite seriously. After the ceremony the shamed rider was also subject to an interview with an inspector [*metsuke*]. There was a clear connection between this and Tosa domain's military law [*gunpō shohatto*, 1649], which stated that if a mounted samurai was thrown from his horse in battle he would be demoted and fined. Whether in war or peace time, a samurai was expected to train his horse, if he owned one, or at least to have a sufficiently firm command of riding skills should he be called upon to exercise them in battle. Pleading illness on the day of the ceremony would not save a samurai either, as Shibuya Dennai found out in 1722. His repeated yearly absence due to "illness" led to an official investigation, a demotion in status, and the confiscation of his fief of 250 *koku*. Not coincidentally, the year he was punished he was reportedly seen at the event, sight-seeing.

The demonstration of riding skills in the *onorizome* ceremony put the samurai in full public view, as even commoners were allowed to watch from the south-facing side of the course. The house flags and banners [*hata, sashimono, horo*] attached to the back of the rider and/or to the horse clearly marked his identity. A good performance in the *onorizome* ceremony would bolster a samurai's reputation, but the potential for public humiliation made it an event that could not be taken lightly.

Participation also provided an opportunity for the samurai to display the family armour or prized attire. In principle, retainers were supposed to ride in full armour, but gradually the requirement was relaxed (likely for economic reasons), and they were allowed to wear other types of outerwear, for example, *jinbaori* [formal battle overcoats], leather overcoats in various colours or in a "Chinese style", or in the style of a warrior monk [*yamabushi*]. A private, non-official, account from the 18th century records a list of what the riders were wearing, including what type of armour or overcoat, giving some indication of its importance in marking identity and status.

Given the potential costs of non-performance – or failure to perform adequately in the *onorizome* – successful completion of the event was a cause for celebration. After the last rider had concluded his run, participants would partake in a celebratory meal, drawing to an end a ceremony that began with the cup of sake drunk that morning.

With no battles to wage, a samurai could demonstrate his loyalty by following the so-called "twin ways of the civil and military arts", *bunbu ryôdô*. The civil, or literary, arts ranged from basic literacy to classical, largely Chinese, learning. The latter could be put to good use in bureaucratic service to the lord, if one was fortunate enough to have a job in the domain government; many samurai were unemployed or underemployed, but they were still retainers on stipends. The military arts ranged from archery, swordsmanship and fighting with a spear, to swimming, military science and tactics. To be sure, maintaining one's skills in the martial arts was a struggle in a time of peace, as there were periodic calls for military reform. But in Tosa, and in other domains that held similar ceremonies, the ability to perform on horseback remained an essential part of service to the lord. The writing brush, figuratively speaking, may have increased in importance in samurai life during the 17th century onwards, but horse-riding and other martial arts could not be easily ignored. This tension between the civil and military arts – often referred to as the two wheels of a cart or the two wings of a bird – remained a constant throughout the Tokugawa period and played a major role in defining samurai identity.

★

The Tokugawa established their dominance on the battlefield at Sekigahara in 1600, and after the Siege of Osaka in 1615 the armies of the *daimyō* no longer needed to move to defend domain borders or wage aggressive war. Nevertheless, military exercises did not simply cease; rather, they were transformed, in frequency and from an irregular to a regular, cyclical pattern, as the more than 250 *daimyō* were required by regulation issued by the Tokugawa government to travel to Edo to wait upon the shogun every other year. As military exercises, the *daimyō* processions were also transformed substantively: they assumed new incarnations, developed new forms of cultural expression, and became clearly pegged to social status in a variety of ways. In general, although they remained essentially a type of military exercise, the *daimyō* processions came to mimic rather than to replicate the military movements of the 16th and early 17th centuries. They assumed notable theatrical elements and became a type of cultural performance. The road, if you will, became the stage; the members of the retinue, particularly the infamous *yakko* footmen, the players; the implements carried, the props; and the people lining the road, the audience.

Still, the march that the men in the processions made was a type of military manoeuvre, with forced progress of upwards of twenty-five miles a day, and the composition of the retinue replicated the form of a military force setting out for battle, but with some important modifications. In wartime, the vanguard or attack unit was the largest part of the military force, led by a senior vassal of the lord and containing large numbers of mounted warriors. In peacetime, however, the advance group tended to be abbreviated, although it retained some of its former significance in that the men carried three principal types of weapons: guns, bows and spears. The group's symbolic function was to clear the way for the main body of the procession, where the lord was located, and which in Tokugawa times assumed greater centrality; it became the largest part of the procession.

Symbolism was thus emphasised in this type of display that characterised the modified procession of the Tokugawa period. Similarly, the much

Kabuto or samurai helmet,
18th century.

reduced number of horses in the processions of the era was also indicative of the changed character of these in a time of peace.

Processions can be thought of as theatres of power, forms of dramatic representation and performance. They used a system of signs and emblems for several purposes: to distinguish one political power (*daimyō*) from another; to awe the spectator with the military might and authority of the lord; and lastly, the implements and emblems the *daimyō* used in the procession clearly translated the principles upheld by the lord. These included the notion that his authority was based on military force – but in some cases it also suggested a religious basis to that authority.

There were many elements to the theatrical or dramatic character of the processions, and these heightened their political impact. First, there was the element of size – that is, the sheer number of men and horses that moved together, generally in a stately manner. The scope of the processions was pegged to the status of the *daimyō*, according to Tokugawa regulation, and the largest of them had impressive retinues of 1,000–3,000 men. A second element to the spectacle of the processions was attire, which was usually coordinated and colourful. The uniformity of costume heightened the image of order created by concerted movement. The third element was the military gear and the other implements carried. All of these elements constituted a demonstration of military power that was meant to awe, and display the lord's status and authority – a reminder that the Tokugawa order was built upon military control and the implicit threat of violence. The implements – guns, lances, bows – had a military function or another utilitarian purpose, but all served as status markers. The type and the number of many of these objects were regulated by the status of the *daimyō*.

There were, however, other objects carried seen to have had both religious and theatrical elements. In a scroll of the Sendai domain depicting a procession dating from 1842 we see this from the very beginning of the ceremony, which was marked by four sets of porters carrying long containers, each covered in red cloth and topped with a purifying Shinto wand and masks. The masks are representations of Ebisu, the *kami* of good fortune; Okame, a folk symbol of fertility; and the humorous *hyottoko* mask. These various religious and folk objects, which were often used in the local festivals of commoners, presented the *daimyō's* arrival as a festive occurrence, one that would bring happiness and good fortune and drive away evil. In this specific case, the scroll marks the lord's first appearance in the domain as ruler, and as such the symbols conveyed an ideological message that his rule would not be harsh, but rather would bring prosperity to all.

Of particular interest is the rather exotic object appearing towards the middle of the same Sendai procession, in line with the lord's horses, which looks a lot like the chairs used by head monks in Buddhist monasteries. Perhaps this was merely another unusual artefact used to signify the lord's high status, but the association with a wise, benevolent Buddhist leader was probably intentional.

Two other elements of the theatrical performance involved movement, that is, the way the men in the retinue made their progress and the sounds that accompanied it. The German physician Englebert Kaempfer, who witnessed *daimyō* processions during his two stays in Japan in the late 17th century, noted that the men in the procession of Kii domain marched in strict formation so that "they somehow seemed to be crouching together and march[ing] in total silence". These *daimyō* processions exhibited a degree of restraint that was a striking contrast with royal retinues in contemporary Europe.

Just before entering a population centre, members of the procession were ordered to "fix the line" – to align the queue, adjust helmets, synchronise steps, raises lances from a resting position, and mount their horses. This reveals the *daimyō* as a conscious political actor who wanted his procession, his performance, to impress. In some cases, observers noted that when passing through, the men in the procession looked sideways at the spectators in an intimidating fashion. Dance-like movements also added to the theatre that was the *daimyō* procession. With their free hand held straight out, the footmen, or *yakko,* seem to be, in Kaempfer's words, "swimming in air", a movement that was eerily similar to one used in the *kabuki* theatre.

The regulation of regalia in this discussion brings to mind the notion of the Tokugawa as a "flamboyant" state, whose leaders employed displays of the nominal authority to service important symbolic functions. All the pomp that the term implies was utilised by the Tokugawa leaders not only in their political use of *Noh* drama, monumental castle architecture, and tea ceremonies, but also in the *daimyō* processions that paraded on the highways leading from all corners of the country to Edo and back. During those migrations, the shogunate was, in effect, parading *daimyō* past other *daimyō* – and past the commoners who may have lined the roads – in a type of showy performance that expressed the supreme position of its authority, since everyone knew the purpose of these biennial mass movements to Edo and back was service to the Tokugawa shogun.

★

The third example of flamboyance in samurai culture that I will briefly examine are *kawari kabuto*, which we might translate as "spectacular" or "fantastic" helmets. These were made by transforming the entire shape of the helmet, rather than simply adding a variety of attachments, *kuwagata*, to the front of it, such as horns or rabbit ears.

These extreme designs were created by using lighter materials – wood, bamboo, paper, leather, fabric, lacquer – that were carved or shaped to represent the desired subject. Additions were affixed with leather ties to the metal helmet bowl, which thereby served as a base for the sculptural design. The entire design was then consolidated with a filler made of chopped hemp and lacquer (known as *harikake*). As a final step, the entire form was lacquered, often in black or some other colour. This resulted in sculptural forms that might totally obscure the original helmet.

The historian John Hall argued that the fantastic helmets "were definitely out of phase with the mood of the 'Great Peace'". But I would argue they were very much a reflection of their time. Peace only increased the need for personal identification, and for clarifying status distinctions, and *kawari kabuto* continued to be constructed long after the last battles of the Tokugawa period had ended. On a basic level, the helmet protected the head, but it also often served to transform the wearer in the manner that a mask does. It added a performative element to the samurai's attire, and could bring about a transformation by calling on a religious force like a Buddhist deity, such as Aizen Myô-ô, King of Passion, or natural, animalistic, forces such as conch shells or crabs. Other helmets simply displayed an aura of ferocity, exoticism or even whimsy, such as a pumpkin-shaped helmet, which goes against the rather staid reputation of samurai.

Some of the themes displayed in the *kawari kabuto* are perhaps even more surprising, as they diverge wildly from typical images of samurai helmets one might see in films. Aubergines, dragonflies, rabbit ears, and the Japanese god Jurôjin were frequent shapes. This leads us to ponder: why would a samurai want to wear such helmets? Is there some connection between aubergines, rabbits, dragonflies and samurai? The meaning of the dragonfly is perhaps the most uncomplicated: dragonflies can only fly straight forward, a course of action that any samurai could identify with – charge towards an enemy, never retreat. But what then of the rabbit and the aubergine? The latter is an auspicious sign, a symbol of good fortune and prosperity. And according to Japanese folklore there is a mythical association between rabbits and longevity, for the Japanese are said to see in the moon an image of a hare pounding the elixir of life. The rabbit, then, has the same association as Jurôjin, the *kami* of longevity. This element is particularly remarkable as a theme for a helmet made by a samurai, given their image as death-obsessed. The *kawari kabuto* lead us to question our preconceived notions, and furthermore to ask, how does the apparent embrace of these themes impact our accepted notions of samurai masculinity?

In conclusion, by examining several aspects of samurai culture – horse-riding ceremonies, *daimyō* processions, and extraordinary helmets – we can see that during the Tokugawa years samurai culture assumed a greater performative quality. Samurai performed for the lord, for each other, and to some extent for a wider non-samurai public. This performative element assumed greater significance – in fact one might argue that it became a defining characteristic of samurai culture – during the peacetime of the Tokugawa period. With peace, the Tokugawa state, the *daimyō* rulers, and the samurai more generally, relied on flamboyance as a means to demonstrate their authority to rule. With peace, and the erosion of the economic position of the samurai, it became increasingly important to define and to maintain status – boundaries between the samurai and commoners – in order to preserve samurai leadership.

The element of flamboyance, as witnessed in *onorizome*, in *daimyō* processions, and in the spectacular helmets, could have a light, whimsical or exotic element to it. This aesthetic quality is often overlooked – or consciously neglected – in considerations of samurai culture, particularly from the Meiji period onwards (1868–1912), when an invented tradition known as *bushidō* was created. This, it appears, was part of the construction or refashioning of samurai identity for political purposes, as the Meiji leaders sought to unify the country in the face of foreign threat and to create a nation in which everyone was a samurai. In this way, only a portion of samurai culture was appropriated in the creation of a new national identity.

Miniature model of Mount Fuji,
Katsushika Hokusai (1760–1849).

Finally, looking at the horse-riding ceremony, we can say that samurai did more than pay lip-service to their martial traditions, as they are often accused of doing. Many strove to strike a balance between *bun-bu*, the civil and the martial arts. It was most likely middle and upper-ranking samurai, with both the time and the financial resources, who were best able to balance the two. For example, Asahi Monzaemon Shigeaki (1674–1718), a retainer from Nagoya domain with a stipend of 100 *koku*, regularly practised several military arts, including sword-fighting, sword-drawing (*iai*), archery, and spearmanship (*sōjutsu*). On the literary side, he engaged in scholarship and wrote poetry, in both Chinese and Japanese. Mori Kanzaemon Yoshiki (1768–1807), a retainer of 200 *koku* from Tosa domain, similarly engaged in a number of military pursuits, including horsemanship, gunnery, horseback archery, and military tactics; in the cultural realm, he practised the way of tea (*sadō*), the way of incense (*kōdō*), and stone tray arrangement (*bonseki*). He also wrote poetry in Japanese, engaged in scholarship, and studied ancient rites and comportment (*kojitsu*). While the samurai in general may have experienced a relative decline in martial skills, given the long years of peace, they remained formidable warriors – as evidenced by the accounts of Westerners who encountered them in the mid to late-19th century and the violent political history of the closing decades of the period after Western gunships appeared in Japanese waters.

REFERENCES

Geertz, Cliffford, "Thick Description: Toward an Interpretive Theory of Culture", in *The Interpretation of Cultures: Selected Essays by Clifford Geertz* (Basic Books, 1973).

Hall, John Whitney, "A Personal Image of Power: The Rise of the Daimyo Warlord", in Alexandra Munroe, ed, *Spectacular Helmets of Japan, 16th–19th Century* (Kodansha International, 1985).

Hirao Michio, Yamamoto Dai, et al, ed *Kaizanshû*, vol 4: *rekishi (3) hen* (Kôchi kenritsu toshokan, 1976).

Kaempfer, Englebert, *Tokugawa Culture Observed*, translated by Beatrice Bodart-Bailey (University of Hawai'i Press, 1999.)

Ôno Mitsuhiko, *Jôka no fûkei. Ry*ôma no ikita Tosa (Kôchi shimbun, 2010).

Tokugawa Tsunenari, *The Edo Inheritance*, translated by Tokugawa Iehiro (International House of Japan, 2009).

Vaporis, Constantine N, *Tour of Duty. Samurai, Military Service and Culture in Early Modern Japan* (University of Hawai'i Press, 2007).

"Staff drills" in Hokusai Manga.

THE INVENTION OF THE SAMURAI IN EARLY MODERN JAPAN

Michael Wert

In 1800, a new book published in Kyoto claimed to impart the secrets of swordsmanship [*kenjutsu*] to its readers. Its author, using the pseudonym Sen'en, explained his reason for writing *The Secret Transmission of Solo-Training in Swordsmanship*: "I have written this book for those who are busy working and do not have time to practice, for those who live out in the sticks and can't find a teacher or don't have any friends, and for those who are motivated to learn, but because they are poor, cannot afford to study under a teacher". He advocated enlisting the help of one's siblings or neighbourhood children – simply give them some basic equipment and use them as dummies for attack and defence. This hardly seems like the popular depiction of swordsmanship and samurai, indeed, Sen'en's book was not intended for a samurai readership. He wrote for the growing number of non-samurai participating in swordsmanship since the mid-18th century, and his book is but one example of how commoners participated in the invention of the samurai.

I claim, perhaps controversially, that the samurai, or at the very least samurai culture, were invented during the Tokugawa period (1603–1868). This preceded the modern invention of the samurai image, especially the infamous *bushidō* code that began in the late 19th century as the Japanese increasingly interacted with Westerners, and contained earlier forms of warrior culture. It was only in the Tokugawa period that samurai became "objects" for consumption by all status groups. In earlier times, nobles and clergy wrote about warriors, and commoners might have been familiar with war tales retold orally, but in the Tokugawa period commoners too began to produce knowledge about samurai, reading and publishing in increasing numbers. Military books were used as primers for elite commoner children and, like samurai, tales of historical warriors served as models for leadership and ethics among educated village elites. Warrior symbols, values, history, martial culture, and even sexual practice, were imitated, celebrated, parodied, and criticised in a variety of genres including literature, theatre, art, and physical culture. Thus, rather than see the relationship between samurai and those of other social status in terms of difference – for example, the legal distinctions between samurai and non-samurai, or the markers of status like the wearing of two swords that distinguished warriors from commoners – we should consider similarities: moments of convergence rather than divergence. Warriors and non-warriors shared a fascination with an idealised set of warrior histories, practices, and values: ideals unattainable by actual samurai.

★

The centre of warrior authority, the Tokugawa shogunate, was located in Edo (now Tokyo). What started as a small fishing village quickly became one of the early modern world's largest urban centres as over 260 warlords [*daimyō*] were required to maintain walled compounds in the city. *Daimyō* travelled back and forth every other year from their home domains scattered across Japan, bringing with them hundreds to thousands of warrior retainers and servants. *Daimyō* wives and heirs lived permanently in Edo, virtual hostages, acting as a check against any warlord who might consider rebelling against the Tokugawa shogun who controlled the regime.

Commoners lived on the outside of the warrior residential area at the centre of the city, serving the ever-increasing population. This number of warriors from diverse geographical and cultural backgrounds had never lived in such proximity before, except in Kyoto during the 15th and 16th centuries, although to a much lesser degree. The warlord Hideyoshi Toyotomi was the first conqueror who tried to separate warriors and commoners into distinct status groups, but his reign did not last long enough to see this become a well-established nationwide policy, and the process of differentiating the two continued well into the 17th century. Only after the establishment of Edo was there a need to differentiate people based on occupation and obligations to warrior regime. The emergence of this status system helped foster a shared samurai identity.

The earliest example of "creating" the samurai arose from solving a practical problem: how to keep track of all the samurai in Edo. The best-selling books in early modern Japan were rosters known as "warrior mirrors" [*bukan*]. They listed the names, addresses, family members, clan crests and lineages, and job positions of every *daimyō* and samurai working in any significant position within the Tokugawa shogunate. *Bukan* were sold in unabridged and pocket-sized editions, and could be updated at bookstores several times throughout the year as warrior positions changed. Commoners, not samurai, produced, distributed, and bought these books, primarily for practical reasons. For example, a merchant would have to know where to deliver goods or identify samurai who came into a shop. Merchants also read military etiquette manuals to better interact with samurai customers, for example, to learn how to examine a sword properly. While the shogunate distributed shorter memos that provided only basic lists of warrior bureaucrats, commoner-produced *bukan* contained information not required for commercial use. *Bukan* often listed the types of gifts given to, and received from, the shogun, distances from *daimyō* compounds to the shogun's castle, and other minor details not directly applicable to simple trade relations.

Each detail in the *bukan* reflected what warriors themselves gradually believed to be important to their identity as a social group. As warfare subsided and Japan entered several centuries of peace, samurai commentators had to define what it meant to be a warrior in times of peace. Even the most mundane aspects of warrior life had changed. For example, the production of arms and armour declined after the last major battle during the Tokugawa period, the Shimabara Rebellion (1637–38). More bureaucrats than fighters, samurai looked back to pre-Tokugawa warriors for models of action and behaviour. Even lower-ranking warriors began to create and publish family lineages, a practice that only influential warrior families would have engaged in before the Tokugawa period. And publishing the exchange of gifts among warriors indicated shifts in prestige among *daimyō* families. In fact, teaching warrior families how to create and preserve their identity became a source of employment for some wandering samurai who were left without a warlord after the end of the Warring States period. Many were hired as samurai tutors and could help a family plan and participate in warrior ceremonies that increasingly became part of warrior social life, especially in Edo. Others published military histories or military science books, such as the famous 17th-century text *Military Mirror of Kai* [*kōyō gunkan*] whose author, Obata Kagenori, became a sought-after teacher of military science.

The leading researcher of *bukan*, Fujizane Kumiko has argued that they also functioned as a source of entertainment in the same way as baseball rosters, for example, do today: possessing and updating them was fun.

On the one hand, *bukan* are an example of how warrior authority was constructed through commoner recognition of the samurai role in Tokugawa Japan. In buying these *bukan*, commoners acknowledged the samurai as a social group in which even seemingly minor details were important. As the philosopher Slavoj Zizek put it, "a King is King because his subjects loyally think and act as if he is King". On the other hand, however, danger to that authority could originate from how commoners appropriated warrior values for unintended purposes.

★

Kabuki theatre is probably the most well-known performance art that originated in the early modern period. Its importance extended beyond theatre, influencing woodblock art, fashion, poetry, and popular literature. Although *kabuki* is typically associated with urban commoner culture, often featuring a dandy fighting for his love, recent research has pointed to its solidly warrior origins.

During the 17th-century, when *kabuki* originated, most plays were held in warlords' residences; public theatre was not yet in vogue. Given the largely warrior audience, playwrights drew upon warrior history and values. While pre-Tokugawa performances centred on the heroic actions of nobles, 17th-century *kabuki* celebrated warrior achievements. After *kabuki* moved to publicly assessable licensed districts, plays retained the warrior notions of loyalty, self-sacrifice, and martial machismo even when they featured commoner protagonists.

The most frequently performed *kabuki* play was called *The Treasury of Loyal Retainers*, also known as the Akō incident or the story of the forty-seven ronin (recently fictionalised in the 2013 Keanu Reeves film *47 Ronin*). It first appeared as a puppet play [*jōruri*] based on a historical event in the early 18th century, when a *daimyō* named Asano attacked a senior *daimyō* named Kira during a ceremony within the shogun's castle. The cause of the attack may never be known but it is thought to have arisen from some insult by Kira against Asano. Since drawing a sword in the shogun's castle was against the law, Asano was immediately arrested, put to death, and his Akō domain dissolved, forcing his retainers to become "masterless warriors" [*rōnin*]. After over a year of planning to avenge their lord's death, forty-seven (some say only forty-six) of the *rōnin* attacked and killed Kira. It is believed that the *rōnin* hoped to avoid harsh punishment because their actions reflected loyalty to their lord. Many samurai believed that a samurai should not let an enemy's offence go unanswered, especially an attack against one's master. Ultimately, however, the *rōnin* were forced to commit *seppuku*, ritual suicide by disembowelment. Why? Asano died because the shogunate executed him for disobeying the shogun's law, he was not murdered by a rival. Thus the *rōnin's* actions were deemed unjustified.

Although the incident itself passed with little comment when it first occurred, audiences loved the dramatised versions retold through popular culture. First, the attack and mass ritualised suicide made for dramatic scenes. Second, these were lowly samurai acting in unison against the authorities, sacrificing themselves as a group, a theme that might have appealed to urban commoners who often interacted with low-ranking warriors. *Seppuku* as a part of samurai identity was an invention of the early modern period. It had occurred before the Tokugawa period, but it was fully institutionalised as capital punishment only in the Tokugawa period, and was meant to evoke a very martial, masculine form of punishment. Some dramatisations focused on individual *rōnin* themselves and their romantic relationships, mixing the celebration of warrior values with stories popular among city dwellers.

Kabuki was not limited to cities. Rural plays featuring martial valour with large casts that involved youth associations, where everyone could be involved, were also popular in the countryside because they broke the monotony of everyday life.

★

Rural *kabuki* was not the only instance of commoner engagement with warrior culture. From rural elites who donned warrior identity, to martial art techniques used in village festivals, rural Japan became a site for appropriating and creating warrior culture. During the final decades of the Tokugawa period, some authorities looked to the countryside to rekindle samurai martial identity.

As civil war throughout Japan gradually settled, Hideyoshi and the early Tokugawa shoguns forced warriors into a choice: renounce their claims to warrior status and settle down as commoners in the countryside or keep their warrior status and relocate to a local castle town. Many former warriors who forfeited their warrior status still served as rural elites,

忠臣蔵夜討之図

Utagawa Kuniyoshi (1797–1861) Treasury of the
Loyal Retainers, Night Attack, 1851.

becoming village headmen for example, and were called "rural samurai" [*gōshi*]. Some kept their weapons and passed them on to their descendants, but these were the exceptions rather than the rule; rural Japan was largely disarmed and urban samurai monopolised the means of violence.

Long after warfare had subsided and the division between warriors and commoners had settled in the countryside, rural entrepreneurs sought to translate their economic successes into cultural prestige by petitioning local *daimyō* for permission to wear swords, a right typically reserved for warriors, and receive official recognition as "rural samurai" regardless of their lineage. *Daimyō* might award these privileges to entrepreneurs who reclaimed new lands or developed local industry that contributed to the domain's tax income. By carrying swords and earning titles, they argued, other peasants would respect them, making their service to the *daimyō* more efficient. Wearing the two swords was not enough for many would-be rural samurai; rural elites who wanted to connect to a warrior legacy, fictional or not, studied swordsmanship to embody the warrior past. As the French sociologist Pierre Bourdieu noted, "The body believes in what it plays at: it weeps if it mimes grief. It does not represent what it performs, it does not memorize the past, it enacts the past, bringing it back to life. What is 'learned by the body' is not something that one has, like knowledge that can be brandished, but something that one is". As with other arts, the realm of martial practice provided a space where a teacher's social status mattered little when interacting with students. Networks across status lines increased during the latter half of the era when newly acquired wealth among rural elites fostered the pursuit of cultural activities such as writing poetry, studying nativism, or sponsoring local theatre. The social benefits accrued by forming connections through one activity could transfer to another. In one example of how social networks could lead to endless connections among commoners and warriors, a village headman from the Kantō region outside Edo studied nativism, through which he encountered a Confucian scholar, which led to an introduction to a gunnery instructor where he met other rural commoners who were also studying gunnery, and finally added spearmanship to his hobbies. Moreover, rural commoners did not passively receive these teachings as students, but taught swordsmanship to each other and to warriors. In fact, elite commoners and low-ranking warriors introduced fencing, a new trend in swordsmanship that began during the 18th century. While swordsmanship using wooden swords in two-person

Scroll from Nen-ryū style of swordsmanship, 1854.
Read from right to left, it imparts teachings and lists
lineage of teachers.

choreographed drills had existed since the 17th century, freestyle fencing with bamboo swords and protective armour was new.

Some warrior leaders within the Tokugawa shogunate looked to those rural swordsmen when reforming the overwhelmingly un-martial warrior status group. The Higuchi family, which still teaches *Nen-ryū* swordsmanship today, was famous for educating a wide range of students including *daimyō*, samurai, and fellow commoner elite men (and occasional women) in Edo and the surrounding countryside. Matsudaira Sadanobu, a prominent samurai official, was impressed with the headmaster of *Nen-ryū*, Higuchi Sadataka, who had demonstrated *Nen-ryū* in the shogun's castle. Sadanobu gave him a scroll with the Chinese characters reading "phoenix", which is still in the possession of the Higuchi family. The choice was significant. In Chinese folklore, the phoenix was said to appear with the rise of virtuous rule in society. In praising Sadataka, Sadanobu not only saw someone who had perfected himself through martial training, but held him up as an exemplar of moral superiority that could be possessed even by rural elites. Sadanobu threw himself into martial art training which influenced his political reforms, much like his grandfather Tokugawa Yoshimune who had also been a diligent martial arts practitioner. Sadanobu sought to reinvigorate samurai identity through the practice of martial arts, swordsmanship in particular, because they were, after all, warriors in name if not necessarily in deed. He even forced military exercises on his retainers, conducting hikes through the countryside. Swordsmanship, whether useful or not, compelled the samurai to embody their warrior heritage.

Some rural commoners studied martial arts to use in village cultural activities. There are examples of peasants who hired low ranking warriors to teach them weaponry to use specifically in rural festivals. In some villages, peasants performed stylised two-person drills to predict the weather, or engaged in choreographed matches to predict the future. Villagers organised their teachings into formalised styles [*ryūha*] complete with scrolls that imparted 'secret teachings' or designated rank and mastery. In Shizuoka prefecture, peasants practised the *Heki-ryū Insai-ha* style of archery for use in competitions and religious ceremonies. Archery teachers complained that some commoners studied the otherwise dignified warrior art of archery for rural gambling. In the second month of 1741, for example, villagers held a five-day archery contest to bring good crops and ward off harm. One samurai lamented in 1835 that commoners received rank in *Heki-ryū*, even though they were just meeting to bet on competitions. He felt that this would hurt the reputation of *Heki-ryū*, and respectable people would stop sending their children to study the art.

Rural swordsmen, unlike their urban counterparts, trained in martial arts not only for social inclusion or entertainment, but also for collective self-defence. Roaming samurai, gangs, and peasant uprisings increased throughout the 19th century. Typically, peasant uprisings are described as having rarely targeted individuals, their rage focusing, instead, on property. However, the nature of protests changed in the 19th century. Young men no longer followed the accepted forms of peasant protest in which harm against individuals and arson had been avoided. Groups of young men referred to as "evil bands" began carrying weapons, stealing, committing arson, and attacking other peasants.

Violence was extended beyond the confines of protest, as the theme of revenge, present in much Tokugawa period popular culture, became reality among commoners. In the 19th century, the number of commoners who registered for revenge killings exceeded registrations by samurai. Murder, not surprisingly, was a crime in Tokugawa Japan, but under exceptional circumstances, namely, avenging the murder of one's own father, could be considered a 'legal' act if the proper paperwork was submitted and accepted. These officially approved and registered "revenge killings" became a reason to study swordsmanship. A peasant sent a letter to the headmaster of the *Nen-ryū* telling him of his long-cherished desire to study swordsmanship. He explained that ever since his father's accidental death ten years earlier, he had been weak and timid and wanted to improve himself. The young peasant's true intention was to kill his father's murderer, a goal he accomplished after years of training in *Nen-ryū*.

★

Not all commoner participation in warrior identity creation was celebratory or flattering. The fantasy image of past heroic warriors found in art and theatre, and the masculine ideals embodied in sword practice hardly represented warrior reality. Like Sadanobu, other samurai and ex-samurai writers complained about samurai degeneration. For example, Buyō Inshi in his 1816 book *Matters of the World: An Account of What I Have Seen and Heard*, wrote that *daimyō* had no compassion for commoners suffering in their domains, and made no effort to keep people from falling into poverty. Middle-ranking samurai, meanwhile, did nothing to constrain their lavish spending and fell into debt, heaping even more suffering upon commoners from whom they demanded more loans. Comparing the samurai of his day to those of the past, Buyō wrote: "In past ages, it was common for warriors to mock those who pursue elegance as 'courtiers'. Now, though, it is the better warriors who behave like courtiers; the majority have become like women".

Hiraga Gennai, a true renaissance man who was a teacher, writer, and inventor, mocked samurai in his 1771 satirical essay titled *On Farting*. The essay tells of a performer who excels at farting, and in so doing, critiques the artistic and intellectual trends of his day. One character, a country bumpkin samurai named Crankshaw Stonington, Esquire, admonishes the "fartist" and the crowd that gathers to hear the performance. The shogunate, he argued, only allowed public performances in order to teach the public about fealty and loyalty, citing the *Treasury of Loyalty Retainers* as an example. "Flatulence", he added, "is, after all, a personal matter and should not be aired in public. Any proper samurai would be mortified to the point of suicide if he were inadvertently to let, uh, fly in polite company".

Gennai's work demonstrates that *kabuki* was a vehicle for spreading samurai values. Yet Crankshaw plays the part of the straight man in this comedy; Gennai uses him to make fun of a popular *kabuki* play meant to promote samurai-approved moral lessons. He also directly attacks the notion of samurai honour – even a harmless fart could push a samurai to commit suicide rather than risk public shame.

Artists also criticised samurai ideals. Katsushika Hokusai, famous in the West for his woodblock print often known as the *Great Wave*, created a book of prints that depicted everyday life, especially the various positions of the body, including the practice of martial arts.

Inside the book is a print titled *Privy*, which shows a mid or high-ranking samurai using the toilet while his warrior retainers stand dutifully close by. Despite the obvious stench, the retainers refuse to back off. The image highlights the limitations of loyalty and obligation in samurai reality.[1]

"Toilet" in Hokusai Manga, published in
the 19th century.

What was the official reaction to these iterations of warrior culture by commoners? Nobody could talk directly about current events using names of warriors, but censors probably overlooked *kabuki* plays and woodblock prints that used the pre-Tokugawa past to comment on the present. There were edicts forbidding commoners from practising any form of martial art. Yet samurai shogunate representatives in the countryside began to depend upon rural elite commoners who used swordsmanship practice as a network to build local militias. When the shogunate advised *daimyō* to reform their militias in response to the increased Western presence in East Asian seas, some hired commoner sword teachers who specialised in fencing, believing that this was more practical for military training than the older forms of swordsmanship dominated by samurai.

Criticism of warriors, their ideals, and the shogunate itself, such as those found in Hokusai's *Privy* or Gennai's *On Farting*, did not threaten warrior society. In fact, I would argue the opposite: the real threat to warrior domination could be found in the commoner celebration of samurai values. Over-identification with samurai ideals by those who had the most to gain and the least to lose, namely, disaffected low-ranking samurai and the occasionally inspired elite commoner, represented the true threat – it exposed the antagonism, the gap, between the idealised, fantasy image of the samurai, and the day-to-day reality. Those young men led the movement to overthrow the Tokugawa shogunate in the name of loyalty to the Meiji emperor, thus ending the Tokugawa Period. The final *bukan* ever published stated it simply: "This is the last one".

1. For a fuller discussion of samurai critique in both Gennai and Hokusai's respective works, see Hirano Katsuya, *The Politics of Dialogic Imagination: Power and Popular Culture in Early Modern Japan* (University of Chicago Press, 2014).

Battle before Kumamoto Castle
by Tsukioka Yoshitoshi
(1839–1892).

CONSTRUCTING THE SAMURAI, CONSTRUCTING THE NATION

Oleg Benesch

Bushidō is one of the most popular concepts associated with the samurai, martial arts, and Japanese society in general. It is usually translated as the "way of the samurai" or the "way of the warrior". *Bushi* means warrior, and is often translated into other languages (as well as modern Japanese) as samurai, while *dō* means way. *Bushidō* is often portrayed as the driving force behind Japan's modern development, an intrinsic part of the Japanese national character, and even as the very soul of Japan. The content of *bushidō* varies depending on the specific interpreter, but typical lists of supposed *bushidō* virtues include loyalty, honour, self-sacrifice, frugality, righteousness, courage, respect, and duty. Between the late 19th century and the present day, thousands of books and articles have been written on *bushidō* in many different languages, reflecting a continued fascination with the samurai and their legacy. The vast majority of these works portray *bushidō* as a traditional warrior ethic that developed along with the samurai many centuries ago.

The popular view is misleading, however, as the term *bushidō* only came into widespread use in the early 20th century. As the other contributions to this volume indicate, there is a discrepancy between the historical samurai and what is popularly viewed as *bushidō* today.

As early as 1912, the renowned Japanologist Basil Hall Chamberlain observed:

> As for *bushidō*, so modern a thing is it that neither Kaempfer, Siebold, Satow, nor Rein–all men knowing their Japan by heart–ever once allude to it in their voluminous writings. The cause of their silence is not far to seek: *bushidō* was unknown until a decade or two ago! THE VERY WORD APPEARS IN NO DICTIONARY, NATIVE OR FOREIGN, BEFORE THE YEAR 1900. Chivalrous individuals of course existed in Japan, as in all countries at every period; but *bushidō*, as an institution or a code of rules, has never existed. [Original emphasis retained].

This essay discusses the development of *bushidō* in the late Meiji period (1868–1912), when a new samurai ethic was invented as part of a search for a Japanese national identity. In this process, the earliest promoters of *bushidō* relied heavily on European models, especially the Victorian notion of the gentleman that was popular at the time.

By the mid-19th century, the issue of the purpose and future of the samurai class was one of the most hotly debated topics in Japan. Although ostensibly Japan's ruling elite, many samurai were underemployed or unemployed, and the quality and character of the samurai class were being widely questioned. Some commentators even argued that it would be militarily more effective to arm and train commoners, and that the samurai should pursue other vocations.

Although there was disagreement on the specific measures that should be taken, the desire for reform of the prevailing order was generally accepted. This was only heightened following the collapse of the Tokugawa shogunate in the Meiji Restoration of 1868, as the new government promoted greater equality and an abolition of traditional class structures. One of the Meiji government's first priorities was to establish a modern army, which relied on commoner conscripts rather than samurai, and the military responsibilities of the latter were gradually phased out. These and other reforms brought major changes to the samurai, many of whom struggled to adapt to the new order. Based on his experiences in Japan in the early 1870s, the missionary William Elliot Griffis wrote in his 1876 *The Mikado's Empire*: " ... the majority [of samurai] spent their life in eating, smoking, and lounging in brothels and teahouses, or led a wild life of crime in one of the great cities. When too deeply in debt, or having committed a crime, they left their homes and the service of their masters, and roamed at large". Griffis' description of the samurai as violent loafers and a burden on society may have overstated their transgressions, but it reflected widely held negative views of the samurai in Japan at the time.

The violence of the 1877 Satsuma Rebellion, which involved thousands of disgruntled former samurai gathered around the restoration hero Saigō Takamori (1828–77), further demonstrated the gap that had developed between mainstream society and the former samurai who had been left behind. Popular sentiments towards former samurai in the early 1880s were conflicted and often negative. At the top, there was widespread

Samurai Receiving a Letter from a Courtesan in the Pleasure Quarters by Masanobu Okumura (1686–1764).

Yukio Ozaki, politician and journalist (1858–1954).

resentment of the ruling oligarchy dominated by former samurai from the domains of Satsuma and Chōshū, while at the other end of the spectrum there were calls for sympathy for the poor samurai who had failed to adapt to the new order. The critical state of poverty-stricken former samurai is attested to by a number of works calling for compassion and support for them for their "past accomplishments" on behalf of the country.

Throughout the 1880s, many writers criticised the samurai and their ethics, dismissing these as relics of a bygone age. Even in the 1890s, negative assessments of the samurai continued to hold sway, as reflected in David Murray's 1894 book *The Story of Japan*:

> [The samurai] were left penniless and helpless. The traditions under which they had been trained led them to look down upon labor and trade with disdain, and rendered them unfit to enter successfully on the careers of modern life. In many cases worry and disappointment, and in others poverty and want, have been the sequels which followed the poor and obsolete samurai.

Throughout the 1880s and even beyond, the idea that a "way of the samurai" – even if such an ethic had existed before – could benefit the new Japan would certainly have seemed anachronistic at best, and *bushidō* was by no means a natural candidate for a national ethic.

In this situation, it is perhaps not surprising that the impetus for a positive assessment of *bushidō* came from overseas, albeit through a Japanese traveller by the name of Ozaki Yukio (1858–1954). Ozaki is often called the "god of constitutional government in Japan" by his admirers, serving in the Imperial Diet and then the National Diet for over sixty years, as well as in several high government offices including mayor of Tokyo. In the context of *bushidō*, however, his early life as a journalist and political activist is most significant.

Ozaki had studied at Keio Gijuku, now Keio University, where the famed journalist and educator Fukuzawa Yukichi (1835–1901) became his mentor. Like many Meiji Japanese, Ozaki's education exposed him to many foreign ideas, and he devoured many Victorian moralistic texts, such as *The Boyhood of Great Men* and *John Halifax, Gentleman*. It has been argued that Samuel Smiles' seminal 1859 book, *Self-Help*, was the most popular and influential book in Meiji Japan, and Ozaki's highly idealistic views of England were common at the time. Ozaki greatly desired to visit the UK for himself, and was pushed to do so in 1888, when he was arrested along with other advocates of representative government and exiled from Tokyo for three years. Ozaki first took a ship to the United States, but his impressions were mixed and he was happy to set sail from New York and head to Europe.

Upon his arrival in Liverpool, Ozaki claimed to have been immediately impressed with the politeness and character of the people, and decided to spend a considerable amount of time in England. He was not wealthy and did not have any real contacts, so he took a room in a simple boarding house in London. Ozaki observed that the standard of living was much lower than he had experienced during his time in the United States, but he considered England far superior on account of what he believed to be its national character. He claimed to witness this moral excellence on a regular basis through his interactions in the UK, and he spent a considerable amount of his time exploring the country. Ozaki's views in this regard are exemplified by an incident that he recorded at the time and also recounted on many occasions throughout his later life (although some of the details would vary). One day in London, Ozaki decided to go for a boat ride on the Thames, which was teeming with activity. He approached the captain of one ship, who agreed to take him on. But before he could board, the owner of another boat came up and tried to lure Ozaki to his own vessel. The first captain was angry at this attempt to poach his fare, and the two began to argue before ultimately squaring up to fight. Ozaki watched them swing at one another until the first captain landed a blow on the nose of the second, felling him in what Ozaki described as a rain of blood. To Ozaki's amazement, the first captain then helped his fallen adversary up, and the two squared up again. The result was the same, with the second captain going down in a bloody heap. On this occasion, the second captain declined the offer of another round, and the first captain helped him to the edge of the water so he could rinse the blood off of his face and clothes. Having looked after his defeated adversary, the first captain returned to Ozaki, apologised for the delay, and they boarded the ship.

This incident was very important to Ozaki, as is evidenced by his frequent retelling of it (in one later version the boatmen fight with oars). Ozaki felt that this event encapsulated the essence of English "gentlemanship". First, Ozaki was impressed that these were not ruffians fighting, but ship captains, who placed so much importance on their honour that they would risk their health and safety to defend it. In Japan, Ozaki surmised, people would have quietly abided something as minor as someone poaching a fare in this way, and Ozaki criticised this as evidence of excessive passivity. In contrast, the English willingness to engage in physical fights struck Ozaki as evidence of a powerful and vigorous civilisation. Ozaki was also greatly impressed by the spirit of fair play that he saw in the fight, when the first captain repeatedly helped his adversary up after knocking him down. In Japan, Ozaki felt, when a person had been knocked down they would be kicked and beaten even more savagely than before, and certainly not given a chance to get back up.

Ozaki used his experiences in England to confirm his high opinion of English gentlemen and gentlemanliness developed through avid reading of Victorian moral tomes in his youth. During his journeys, Ozaki regularly transmitted his views of England back to Japan in dispatches published in the *Chōya shinbun*, one of the nation's largest newspapers. It was in one of these dispatches, in 1888, that Ozaki first discussed *bushidō*. In this article, titled *Shinshi* [Gentleman], Ozaki extolled the virtues of English gentlemen, comparing them with the men who called themselves gentlemen in Japan: "A Japanese gentleman is generally taken to be someone with a lot of money and luxurious lifestyle. Gold watches, top hats, black carriages are the necessary requirements of Japanese gentlemen, as are buying geisha and playing cards. The qualifications of being a Japanese gentleman are 21 evil pastimes". According to Ozaki, Japanese gentlemen were "worlds apart" from the English concept of the gentleman. He continued, "How does a person come to be called a gentleman in England? Not by his fortune, but by his deeds and actions. Not by his appearance, but by his heart and intentions. If these are gentle and pure and good, then one will be called gentleman even if one is poor". According to Ozaki, gentlemen were the key to the strength of the British Empire, and Japan needed gentlemanship in order to succeed and even survive in the evolutionary struggle of nations.

Ozaki argued that the best translation for "gentleman" might be *bushi*. Ozaki cited the widespread Victorian view that traced gentlemanship back to medieval chivalry. Throughout Europe, interest in chivalry has remained strong as the centuries since the medieval period have passed. The longing for past ideals is common to many societies, and romanticisation of chivalric codes is one manifestation of this. The popular appeal of knightly tales in 17th-century Spain inspired Cervantes to satirise them in *Don Quixote*, while Mark Twain later mocked similar inclinations in the United States in *A Yankee in King Arthur's Court*. The latter was first published in 1889, reflecting the international spread of these ideals in the years when Ozaki was abroad. The continued influence of the chivalric ideal in Europe can be seen in the traditional awarding of knighthoods to honour exceptional individuals, and reflects the popular view of chivalry as an ethic of exemplary behaviour, even if its specific prescriptions were not always clear or widely practised.

Arguably, the greatest revival of idealised knightly virtues in the modern world occurred in Georgian and Victorian England, where re-interpretations of chivalry influenced education, architecture, literature, and art, as well as providing a rapidly industrialising society with moral guidelines supposedly rooted in ancient and noble tradition. The ideal of the English gentleman that came to define the national character in the 19th century was typically traced back to medieval knighthood, and the term "chivalrous" today retains its positive connotations.

The promulgation of the Meiji Constitution in 1889 was accompanied by a general amnesty for political exiles, and Ozaki returned home. The mood in Japan had changed perceptibly during his absence, with nationalistic currents becoming stronger due to pride in the new constitution and frustration with foreign reluctance to revise the unequal treaties. In this environment, Ozaki wrote a second article on *bushidō* in 1891, which was much more assertive than the first:

> If Japan desires to create a civilizational heaven and to trade with all the nations in the world, we should not discard *bushidō* even for a day. … in England they are called gentlemen, here they are called *bushi*. Although the terms are different, they are ultimately the same. … In English, gentlemanly and ungentlemanly are two words that determine the failure or success of a man. In our country, being labeled with the word *bushi* should also have the same force.

While still holding the English gentleman up as the best role model, in this article Ozaki argued that Japanese *bushi* were in no way inferior. Unfortunately, their ethics had been neglected and almost lost, but through a concerted effort of revival, Japan could be successful. According to Ozaki, like England, Japan also had a 'feudal knighthood', and this could serve as a reference for a native gentlemanship, or *bushidō*.

THE SEVEN VIRTUES OF BUSHIDO

GI	REI	YU	MEIYO	JIN	MAKOTO	CHU
Integrity	Respect	Heroic Courage	Honor	Compassion	Honesty and Sincerity	Duty and Loyalty

GI — Integrity
Be acutely honest throughout your dealings with all people. Believe in justice, not from other people, but from yourself. To the true warrior, all points of view are deeply considered regarding honesty, justice and integrity.

Warriors make a full commitment to their decisions.

REI — Respect
True warriors have no reason to be cruel. They do not need to prove their strength. Warriors are courteous even to their enemies. Warriors are not only respected for their strength in battle, but also by their dealings with others.

The true strength of a warrior becomes apparent during difficult times.

YU — Heroic Courage
Hiding like a turtle in a shell is not living at all. A true warrior must have heroic courage. It is absolutely risky. It is living life completely, fully, and wonderfully.

Heroic courage is not blind. It is intelligent and strong.

MEIYO — Honor
Warriors have only one judge of honor and character, and this is themselves. Decisions they make and how these decisions are carried out is a reflection of whom they truly are.

You cannot hide from yourself.

JIN — Compassion
Through intense training and hard work the true warrior becomes quick and strong. They are not as most people. They develop a power that must be used for good. They have compassion. They help their fellow man at every opportunity.

If an opportunity does not arise, they go out of their way to find one.

MAKOTO — Honesty and Sincerity
When warriors say that they will perform an action, it is as good as done. Nothing will stop them from completing what they say they will do. They do not have to "give their word." They do not have to "promise."

Speaking and doing are the same action.

CHU — Duty and Loyalty
Warriors are responsible for everything that they have done and everything that they have said, and all of the consequences that follow. They are immensely loyal to all of those in their care.

To everyone that they are responsible for, they remain fiercely true.

Some idealized virtues ascribed to the samurai by *bushidō* theorists in the modern period.

Ozaki's articles provoked a number of responses from other writers before the Sino-Japanese War began in 1894, with Ozaki's former mentor Fukuzawa Yukichi the most prominent commentator. In 1891, Fukuzawa discussed *bushidō* as a manifestation of what he considered to be an all-important ethic of "dignified and unyielding resistance', which he credited with enabling small nations such as Holland and Belgium to survive amid so many larger states. According to Fukuzawa, Japan had itself possessed this spirit in the past, but it had been lost in the 1860s with the Tokugawa surrender. Ozaki's *bushidō* was also taken up by the Protestant minister Uemura Masahisa (1858–1925), who saw possibilities in comparisons between *bushidō* and chivalry, and believed that this might be a vehicle for spreading Christianity in Japan. As other Japanese Christians would later phrase it, *bushidō* was the best stock upon which to graft the gospel. Uemura himself wrote: "*Bushidō* might save Japan, but *bushidō* combined with Christianity has the power to save the world".

Other respondents to Ozaki included the ultra-nationalistic journalist, mercenary, and politician Suzuki Chikara (1867–1926), who took *bushidō* in a new imperialistic and chauvinistic direction. Writing in 1893, he insisted on a new "true spirit of the nation". Suzuki saw both Meiji former samurai and earlier Tokugawa samurai as decrepit, and sought the roots of Japan in the Warring States period. Suzuki argued that Japan's martial culture was superior to those of other nations and should be promoted at home and abroad, by force if necessary. According to Suzuki, the "natural spirit" of medieval Japanese pirates should be revived, and Japan should advance into China and Taiwan in a similar aggressive manner to the western powers. Suzuki's views foreshadowed the more militaristic *bushidō* that would come to dominate in the first half of the 20th century.

Significantly, Ozaki and the other writers on *bushidō* had spent considerable time abroad, and were proficient in at least one western language. The presence of a foreign other, or others, was an essential element in the development of modern *bushidō* as a national ethic, and the development of *bushidō* was equally, or more, influenced by current events beyond Japan's borders than by the historical samurai class. The 1890s saw an increased interest in a number of nationalistic concepts, with *bushidō* given a boost by the rehabilitation of the samurai image. The passage of time had dulled memories of the actual samurai, and especially the rebellions of the 1870s. At the same time, contemporary European discourse on chivalry and gentlemanship acted to legitimise the search for comparable sources of morality. This development had a reciprocal influence on trends in historiography that sought to redefine the Japanese past in terms of European models, with concepts such as "feudalism" and "medieval" gaining broad acceptance. Within a decade, Westerners and Japanese would come to see Japanese society as the heir of medieval knighthood and as a potential model for other nations to channel the strength of their own 'feudal' past.

Victory in the Sino-Japanese War in 1895 resulted in a "*bushidō* boom" that lasted for almost two decades. Buoyed by the success of the war, many currents of Japanese thought became increasingly nationalistic, and it was natural that a "native" ethic such as *bushidō* would gain currency during this period. Whereas some of the *bushidō* theories before this time could be considered more internationalist than nationalistic, the tone of discourse changed considerably after 1895. The newly confident, and often chauvinistic, *bushidō* that marked the boom of late Meiji built on the earlier foundations but quickly superseded them. The legitimacy bestowed on *bushidō* by its alleged relationship with the historical samurai, combined with a lack of concrete historical roots that could be used to define or refute it, meant that *bushidō* was an ideal vehicle for nationalist sentiments of the type that came to the fore in the years around 1900. Furthermore, *bushidō* combined easily with Shinto and Buddhism, especially Zen, to create new ideologies.

Comparisons with European chivalry became less common in Japan, and people began to look back at earlier Japanese history and texts to find "true" *bushidō*. By examining history with a samurai ethic in mind, it was possible to carefully select texts and events that would support certain *bushidō* interpretations, resulting in a new *bushidō* focused on loyalty, frugality, and self-sacrifice; all virtues considered useful in strengthening the nation and, later, for preparing for conflict on several fronts. The first major work on *bushidō* in this period was a monthly journal published by the Great Japan Martial Arts Lecture Society in 1898, titled *Bushidō*. The journal only ran for four issues, but the list of contributors was staggering and reads like a who's who of Meiji intellectual society. The contributions to the journal were eclectic, to say the least, including articles by Ozaki and Uemura, but also from military officers and martial arts promoters with highly nationalistic agendas.

The profile of *bushidō* was raised even further by publication of Nitobe Inazo's (1862–1933) *Bushidō: The Soul of Japan* in English in 1900, even if

Nitobe's specific theories were largely dismissed within Japan. Nitobe's version of *bushidō* became very popular in the West, especially after the Russo-Japanese War of 1904–05. Echoing Ozaki's interpretations, Nitobe's *bushidō* incorporated significant aspects of contemporary English notions of gentlemanship, such as an emphasis on fair play, compassion for the weak, and an independent spirit. It was natural that these more Western interpretations of *bushidō* resonated among Western readers, and became the most popular interpretations outside of Japan.

Within Japan, the role of one of Nitobe's greatest critics was more significant. Inoue Tetsujirō (1856–1944) referred to himself as "the greatest philosopher East of Suez", and as professor of philosophy at Tokyo Imperial University, he had tremendous influence, and was the most dominant figure in *bushidō* discourse from 1901 until 1945. He first discussed *bushidō* in a lecture at the Officers' Training School in 1901, and initiated a pattern of cooperation between military and civilian education institutions that would last through to the end of the Second World War. Inoue's writings on *bushidō* were significant not only because of their wide dissemination, but also because of several elements he introduced. One of these was a focus on loyalty to the emperor, which became the core tenet of the "imperial *bushidō*" that became a dominant ideology from the Russo-Japanese War onward. Inoue also carefully selected Edo-period texts to support his theories, giving *bushidō* an apparent historical legitimacy. In addition, Inoue and his collaborators attacked what they considered to be "unorthodox" *bushidō* interpretations, thereby ensuring that 'imperial *bushidō*' became the dominant interpretation. This also contributed to the fact that most earlier writings on *bushidō*, such as those of Ozaki, Uemura, and Fukuzawa, were ignored or forgotten by the first decade of the 20th century.

During the second half of the *bushidō* boom, from 1905 until 1914, *bushidō* became a widely popularised subject both in Japan and abroad. Through government support and legitimisation by Inoue and other official figures, the imperial *bushidō* ideology became firmly established in military and civilian education, especially with the growth of spiritual education programmes used to indoctrinate troops with the desired virtues of loyalty and self-sacrifice. The popularity and unquestioned patriotic credentials of *bushidō* led to its frequent mentions by writers of both literature and pulp fiction, while academics wrote many volumes on the subject. Members of religious orders and promoters of various types of sport, both native and foreign, called upon *bushidō* to popularise their causes and give them the patriotic legitimacy that was deemed so important at the time. Foreign interpreters of Japan also showed great interest in *bushidō*, further raising its profile. By the end of the Meiji period, Japanese public life was saturated with *bushidō*, and there were few Japanese or foreigners interested in Japan who had not heard of *bushidō* and did not have a general idea of its meaning.

By the 1930s, *bushidō* was firmly established in the education system and was widely believed to be an ancient ethic that originated with the historical samurai. In the 1930s, *bushidō* rapidly became a key component of the legitimising ideology of the imperial state, and *bushidō* can be found in almost all important propaganda texts from the time. Nationalistic and militaristic texts such as Hiraizumi Kiyoshi's *Revival of Bushidō,* written by the Tokyo Imperial University history professor in 1933, went through millions of printings, while specially edited versions of death-focused samurai writings were distributed to troops heading to war. The pervasiveness of "imperial *bushidō*" in the military has been one of the more sensationalised aspects of *bushidō*, and most books on wartime Japan address the subject.

Bushidō also served to orientalise Japan from the perspective of its enemies, and the notion that Japanese were *bushidō*-driven automatons guided much of Allied strategy. This included the idea that Japanese troops and civilians would never surrender; and the possibility that all Japanese would have to be killed to end the war was seriously considered at the highest levels of the US government and military.

While *bushidō* was used for propaganda on all sides of the conflict, this obscures the fact that *bushidō* discourse remained highly diverse even during the wartime period. Critics from both the left and right disagreed with the government's interpretation of *bushidō*. The poet Hagiwara Sakuratō, for example, claimed that *bushidō* was mistaken, as the Japanese were the least warlike of peoples. This, he argued, was because Japanese warfare had always been domestic, and therefore more tragic than in other countries where wars tended to involve foreign enemies. On the other side, the ultra-nationalistic writer and "war god" Sugimoto Gorō criticised *bushidō* for having been merely a class-based ethic that did not promote sufficient worship of the imperial house. It was also during this period, in 1938, that the Christian Yanaihara Tadao completed his translation into Japanese of Nitobe Inazo's *Bushidō: The Soul of Japan,* which continues to be the most widely read version.

After 1945, *bushidō* was immediately rejected, along with the imperial state and other wartime ideologies. Unlike its ideological brethren, however, *bushidō* was soon rediscovered and reinterpreted for the new postwar order. By the 1960s, historical research on *bushidō* had increased considerably, although scholars did not generally question the origins or historical legitimacy of *bushidō*, having grown up with it in the prewar education system. Instead, scholars portrayed "imperial *bushidō*" as a corruption of tradition, and instead tried to find "true" *bushidō* by studying premodern warriors. This resulted in an enduring tendency for writers on *bushidō* to examine samurai writings and behaviour using frameworks created largely in the early 20th century. This is problematic, as when one approaches pre-Meiji Japanese history with a samurai ethic in mind, sources are often read in ways that support that contention. Much of the popular *bushidō* canon was carefully selected, compiled, and interpreted by prewar scholars, and this continues to influence scholarship today.

Beyond academic history, the diversity and flexibility of *bushidō* have allowed it to be revived in many different cultural spheres. In the late 1960s, a minor revival of a more nationalistic *bushidō* occurred, with the playwright Mishima Yukio (1925–70) as its figurehead. This revival was fairly short-lived, however, as Mishima's dramatic suicide by *seppuku* in 1970 shocked mainstream society, presenting *bushidō* as an anachronistic and potentially extreme ideology. In the 1980s, *bushidō* experienced another, more lasting popular revival, this time centred around the writings of Nitobe Inazō. Although Nitobe's *bushidō* theories were largely ignored within Japan during his lifetime, the universal nature of his *bushidō* made it well-suited as a potential vehicle for cross-cultural understanding in the more peaceful and internationalist atmosphere of the 1980s. Japan's tremendous economic success led both Japanese and foreigners to seek cultural explanations for this miracle, and *bushidō* was held up as a possible model. Theories drawing similarities between modern companies and traditional warrior houses, or modern workers and samurai, abounded, and books on samurai business strategies became international bestsellers.

At the same time, *bushidō* began to appear more and more frequently in popular culture, sports, and politics, as the negative associations with the wartime had been largely forgotten within Japan. In recent years, there has been a great upsurge of interest in *bushidō* in various quarters, including among the increasingly prominent right-wing groups in Japan.

Problematic texts from the prewar and wartime periods are being republished in their original form, while certain military figures have been increasingly advocating the implementation of *bushidō*-based spiritual education for the troops of the Japan Self Defence Forces. It is important not to exaggerate the importance of these movements, or to compare them directly with the imperial period, but the internet gives them great possibilities for disseminating their views.

As the past century has shown, *bushidō* is very open to interpretation for a wide variety of ends. It originated largely during a specific historical moment: the search for national identity in Meiji Japan, which was in turn inspired and influenced by international cultural trends, especially a widespread interest in an idealised medieval history. The foreign aspects of these origins were soon forgotten as *bushidō* became an important ideological pillar of imperial nationalism; a supposedly historical ethic with no concrete roots or accepted doctrine. This flexibility has given it great resilience, as the lack of firm historical roots means that there is nothing solid at its base that could be definitively refuted. For this reason, we can expect to continue to see cycles of *bushidō* growth and decline in the future, both in Japan and other countries. In this context, the content of a specific *bushidō* interpretation will often reveal a great deal more about the personal motivations of the author, as well as the social and historical context in which it was written, than it will about the samurai or traditional culture.

JAPAN'S PAST AND PRESENT

Dragon.

THE FACES OF MEIJI
James L. Huffman

The question 'what was Meiji?' can be answered, at the superficial level, in three statements. First, Meiji was the reign name of Mutsuhito, the teenager who came to Japan's throne in 1867. Second, it was the label applied to an 1868 coup – the Meiji Restoration – in which the Tokugawa family was overthrown after 268 years in power. Third, it denotes the era (1868–1912) over which Meiji reigned, a time that began with leaders saying "everywhere there is confusion" and ended with a Beijing newspaper praising the emperor as a "hero of a generation" who had changed the Japanese "dragonfly" into a "dragon or tiger".[1]

At the core of each of these statements was a single characteristic – transformation, meaning that "Meiji" may be characterised quite simply and accurately as the era, presided over by the Emperor Meiji, when Japan changed so rapidly that, in the words of the expatriate Basil Hall Chamberlain, "to have lived through the transition stage of modern Japan makes a man feel preternaturally old".[2]

None of these characterisations is, however, as simple as it sounds. Meiji the man was simultaneously phlegmatic and forceful, assertive and passive. Meiji the "restoration" may have been a simple *coup d'état* or it may have been the start of a revolution; historians still have not reached agreement. And while everyone agrees that Meiji the era involved dramatic change, the nature and meaning of that change varied from day to day and place to place. Sometimes it brought progress; sometimes its effects were cruel; sometimes it made life better, sometimes worse; sometimes the path tended toward democracy, often toward autocracy. If the aim of this essay is to seek as clear an understanding of the nature of Meiji as possible, the best approach may be to examine the ways it affected four major actors of the late 19th-century world: the domestic elites, for whom everything was about national power; the Western imperialists, for whom Meiji Japan posed unprecedented challenges; the nations of Asia, who found both inspiration and threat in the Meiji evolution; and Japanese commoners – a massive group usually overlooked by scholars – for whom the era was all about jobs, income, and a changing sense of self.

If change was the coin of Meiji, the educated elites were the ones who consciously guided and propelled that change, with a goal of keeping their land secure from Western intrusion by making it strong and rich. One of the era's most striking characteristics was the leaders' insistence that all their work was done, not for individuals, but "for the sake of the country" [*kuni no tame*]. In the political sphere, conservatives like education minister Inoue Kowashi maintained that national prosperity required an authoritative state, while popular rights activists like Nakae Chōmin said it demanded radical democracy. Said Inoue: "*Kokutai* [the national polity] based on the imperial line unbroken for ages eternal [must be] the first principle of our education ... if the Japanese people are not imbued with patriotic spirit, the nation cannot be strong". Countered Nakae: "Absolute monarchy is stupid ... democracy, though, is open and frank, without a speck of impurity". Both, however, put the nation at the centre of their arguments.[3] Even the late-Meiji anarchist Kanno Suga employed similar language, recounting in her diary two days before she was hanged for treason that a dream about the sun and moon coming together portended "a great calamity ... about to befall the nation".[4]

Such rhetoric may not be surprising for political activists, but nation-centredness characterised the worldview of the elites in every other line of work too. In the fledgling press of the early 1870s, the brash young samurai Fukuchi Gen'ichirō called the reporter the "uncrowned king" of a modern nation; boasted that his paper was a *goyō shinbun* [government patronage paper]; and said that the key to writing, whether in journalism or in his later field of drama, was: "Know Japan! Know Japan!" Two decades later the mass-oriented editor Kuroiwa Shūroku demanded that even slum dwellers take to the streets to change national policies. When General Nogi Maresuke committed ritual suicide to honour the Meiji emperor on his death in 1912, Kuroiwa pronounced that this medieval style of self-sacrifice "will inspire us to the end of time".[5]

Everything, for the popular journalists as well as the establishment editors, was about the nation. In the world of literature too writers focused on nation-centred transformation. When a naturalist literary movement began to grow in the late Meiji years, an essayist in the intellectual journal *Taiyō* criticised it in terms of what it meant for the nation, saying overly realistic literature was "driving the youthful blood to moral recklessness"

Map of Tokyo. Woodblock print, 1880.

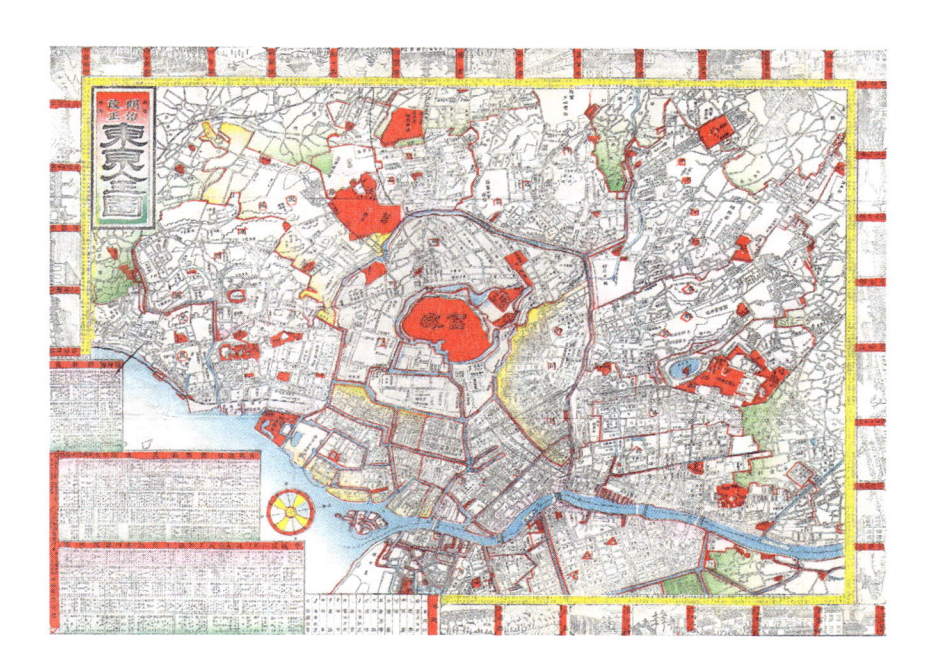

and "undermining the national strength". "Do they know why Japan ... got to the position of a first-class power?" he asked. "It was due to the rigorous discipline and militant spirit of the nation".[6]

No field displayed this nation-centred rhetoric more tellingly than business, the sphere that had been denigrated (though far from ignored) in the pre-Meiji, Confucian world. Freed in the mid-1800s to engage in international trade, yet restricted by unequal treaties that gave great advantage to European and American industries, Japan's entrepreneurs proved nothing if not innovative and aggressive in the Meiji years. Men like the young bureaucrat Shibusawa Eiichi, declaring "I would rather be in the business world, where I have better hopes for the future", imported Western technology and management skills (including a capitalist's commitment to profit over everything else) and turned Japan into a major world trading partner, first in silk, then in cotton and woollens.[7] Other entrepreneurs built 2,000 miles of railway tracks and launched a massive shipping industry in the first twenty Meiji years, even as they linked the country by telegraph lines. Perhaps no one typified the Japanese aggressiveness better than Shimizu Makoto, who went to France in his early twenties to study Western technology, then came back to start a match factory in 1875. Four years later, he went to Sweden to study the match business further. By the 1890s, his industry was producing three billion matches a year in some 200 factories, and by the end of Meiji, matches were bringing in a whopping 33 million yen a year in foreign sales.[8] The important point here is that, like their peers in other fields, Shimizu and his fellow entrepreneurs spoke the language of national progress and welfare, even as they profited personally. Shibusawa put it most explicitly, arguing continuously that the purpose of strong business was "building a strong country". That was why, he said, business success required that "I began studying and practising the teachings of the *Analects of Confucius*", which provided "the ultimate in practical ethics for all us to follow in our daily living".[9] Whether in politics, journalism, literature, or industry, the elites defined Meiji as a national programme intended to make Japan strong.

For the Western imperialist powers, by contrast, Meiji represented primarily a challenge, not only to their military and economic might, but to the philosophies and theologies that shaped their worldview. That was true from the start of Meiji in the world of diplomacy, where the Japanese negotiated with an unexpected skill. When, for example, a

Chinese detainee jumped overboard from the Peruvian barque Maria Luz in Yokoyama harbour in 1872, to protest the slave-like conditions in which 230 workers were being transported to the mines and plantations of South America, Japanese officials did the unexpected. They released all the "coolies", announcing Japan's decision "that no labourers ... shall be taken beyond its jurisdiction against their free and voluntary consent".[10] Asked to arbitrate when Peru protested, Western diplomats supported Japan's action, although they expressed alarm privately, worried that an Asian nation had so quickly mastered the details and rhetoric of international law. They were right to be concerned, because the forceful action was a foretaste of the challenge Japanese diplomats would pose in the coming decades – in their bitter debates over treaty revision and trade disagreements. In 1897, the Tokyo-based journalist Edward H. House wrote an impassioned letter to the American diplomat John Hay, urging that the United States send more capable ambassadors to Tokyo lest it be outflanked by Japan's statesmen who were "so adroit, so tactful, so resolute and courageous that they could beat most of their European adversaries at any game of wit". He warned that if America did not send better representatives, "there will be a season of disagreement and altercation more than likely to end in a prolonged estrangement". Japanese diplomacy had become more than a mere threat; it was besting the Americans.[11]

Nothing dramatised the threat more clearly than Japan's own turn down the imperialist path in the 1890s. By the 1880s, opinion leaders had begun talking about the need for Japan to be more assertive, and in 1891 the young essayist Miyake Setsurei set out on an unsuccessful, six-month trip around the Pacific to find an "unclaimed" island because "we felt Japan had to acquire territory".[12] When Japan defeated China in 1895 in the Sino-Japanese War, it took its first colony, Taiwan. By the time Meiji died in 1912, it had established additional colonies in Korea and Sakhalin, and had begun expansion into northeastern China. The audience likely was charmed when the young bureaucrat Itō Hirobumi said in San Francisco in 1872 that "the red disc in the centre of our national flag shall no longer appear like a wafer over a sealed empire, but henceforth be in fact what it is designed to be, the noble emblem of the rising sun, moving onward and upward amid the enlightened nations of the world".[13] Had he made that same comment in 1900, the response would have been more complex, because Japan had become a rival in the empire game. Indeed,

The poet and revolutionary Qiu Jin,
who studied in Tokyo.
The statue is in Hanzhou, China.

when US President Theodore Roosevelt decided to send America's sixteen-battleship Great White Fleet around the world in 1907, one aim was to demonstrate American strength to Japan, which had recently beaten Russia in war. "The Japanese are a formidable military power", he wrote to one friend; to another he wrote that "the best information is that we shall have a war with Japan and that we shall be beaten".[14] Even as the Meiji successes in developing a modern army impressed the world, they threatened the imperialist status quo.

An important element in that status quo was the assumption of innate Caucasian superiority. It is hardly surprising that early Western visitors to Meiji Japan exhibited what Edward Said later called orientalism. Steeped in beliefs about the superiority of Christianity and Euro-American culture, even enlightened visitors and expatriates frequently painted the Japanese as strange and backward. The traveller Isabella Bird, for example, described the people she saw on landing as: "small, ugly, kindly-looking, shrivelled, bandy-legged, round-shouldered, concave-chested, poor-looking beings in the streets". Moving to the countryside, she said 'the houses were all poor, and the people dirty both in their clothing and persons ... soap is not used.'[15] The businessman and traveller Percival Lowell said the country was "topsy-turvy", a place where they "speak backwards, write backwards, read backwards".[16] Even those who loved the country emphasised the exotic and the bizarre.

By era's end, however, the imperialists were struggling to explain how such an "exotic" country could have become a world power. The Japanese were neither Christian nor Anglo-Saxon; yet they had been able in 1904–05 to defeat the Western giant Russia militarily. 'Many saw Japan as an intellectual and a strategic challenge,' said the historian Joseph Henning. "How could they reconcile Japan's allegedly inferior racial and religious characteristics with its emergence as a modern power?" One of the most contorted, yet widespread, responses to this question was to turn the Japanese into quasi-Westerners, into people who operated by Christian principles and might even have Caucasian blood. One writer proclaimed in 1904 that Japanese diplomacy was "two centuries more Christian" than Russia's was. The influential minister and scholar William Elliot Griffis advertised his 1907 book, *The Japanese Nation in Evolution*, as a groundbreaking work that would show "the white blood in the Japanese", arguing that the original Japanese were Ainu with Western ancestors. It was easier to redefine the Japanese and twist facts than to give up on ideas of racial and religious superiority.[17] That did not make Meiji less of an economic or military threat, but it carved out a space in which racism and religious exclusivity could persist despite the threat.

Meiji's face for a third group – the peoples of continental Asia – was Janus-like, both ferocious and inspirational. Timing was the key here. For two millenniums China had dominated Asia. Both its Chinese and Japanese names – *Zhongguo* and *Chūgoku*–meant "middle country", a word with philosophical as well as geographical connotations. From the early 1800s, however, China's ruling Qing dynasty had been in decline, and by the last third of the century it was reeling from attacks by foreign armies and domestic rebels, even as Japan was marching forward. In 1885, the educator and journalist Fukuzawa Yukichi published an influential essay saying the Chinese were "deep in their hocus pocus of non-scientific behaviour" and calling for Japan "to leave the ranks of Asian nations and cast our lot with civilised nations of the West".[18] When Japan defeated China in war a decade later, then began taking its own Asian colonies, most of the continent felt under threat. China's most prominent diplomat, Li Hongzhang, articulated the fear when he said to Prime Minister Itō Hirobumi, Japan's representative at the war-ending negotiations: "Surely you cannot expect to exterminate my nation!"[19] A decade later, Korea's Confucian scholar Ch'oe Ikhyŏn captured the anger and apprehension of his fellow countrymen as they watched Japan taking control of the peninsula. Declaring that no people 'deserved to be destroyed,' he said defiantly: "To die defending the king and the nation is preferable to living the life of a slave".[20]

Fear and resentment was, however, only half of the Meiji story in Asia. For every person who hated the Japanese, there was one who found inspiration, even hope, in their modernising model. When, for example, the Meiji Constitution was promulgated in 1889, editorialists across the continent praised Japan for demonstrating that Asian nations were capable of creating modern governmental structures, and when Japan defeated Russia in war, as the historian Jonathan Spence puts it: "the admiration of these Chinese students was unbounded".[21] The Meiji modernity project provided evidence, first, that Asian-based cultures could hold their own against Western ideas and, second, that crusty old regimes could be reformed or replaced. India's poet scholar Rabindranath Tagore was inspired by what he saw as an Asian alternative to European materialism. Speaking in Tokyo four years after Meiji died, he described Japan as the

There were more than
40,000 rickshaw drivers in Tokyo.

most human of modern countries: "Never in my travels did I feel the presence of the human so distinctly as in this land ... In Japan ... you see everywhere emblems of love and admiration, and not mostly of ambition and greed". Not all would have agreed with him, certainly not many of those in Japan's colonies. But he was convinced that spirituality grounded Japan's material advancement in a way that it did not in Western countries.[22]

For most Chinese, it was the second image – the model for reform – that was most enticing. The reform advocate Kang Youwei wrote a book for the Chinese emperor in the mid-1890s outlining the changes that had propelled Japan to greatness, and suggesting that the same was possible at home. In the next few years, Chinese students flocked to Japan by the thousands to study reform, prompting the Marxist scholar Kuo Mo-jo's observation that "modern Chinese literature has for the most part been created by Chinese students returned from Japan".[23] Among them was the young revolutionary Qiu Jin who in 1904 sold her jewellery, deserted her husband and two children, and headed for study in Tokyo, writing in a poem:

> Cut off from my family I leave my native land ...
> Alas, this delicate kerchief here
> Is half stained with blood, and half with tears.

And it was in Japan that revolutionary groups such as Sun Yatsen's Revolutionary Alliance were born, counting hot blooded students like Qiu among their members. "Look at Japan", wrote Sun. "She opened her country for Western trade later than we did, and her imitation of the West also came later. Yet only in a short period her success in strengthening itself has been enormously impressive".[24] Lu Xun too, generally considered the greatest fiction writer of early 20th-century China, gained his revolutionary fervour while studying in Japan. That did not mean he loved Japan. Like most Asians, he found Meiji complex: a source of oppression and a cause for anger, yet a model of modern transformation to be emulated by other Asians.

A fourth group, the poor commoners of Japan itself, also found complexity in the Meiji visage, but in a more practical, less theoretical way. Commoners, of course, made up the vast majority of the Meiji population: the farmers and fishermen, the school teachers and petty officials, the Hokkaido miners, and even tens of thousands of workers on Hawaii's sugar plantations. Here, I will focus on a specific commoner group: the very poor city dwellers, or *hinmin*, who made up between ten and wenty per cent of the urban population in the late Meiji years, a group that drew special attention from journalists and reformers after the 1890s as part of the cities' exploding *shakai mondai* [social problem].

The first thing Meiji meant to this group was displacement and economic hardship. When the reporter Hita Ikaru looked at sprawling neighbourhoods of *hinmin* houses in 1898, each dwelling with "walls crumbling, a decaying threshold whose doors will not shut, and a worn roof that does not keep out the rain and dew ... a place like a pigsty",[25] he was seeing the abodes of people who had moved from rural villages to urban slums as a direct result of official Meiji policies. The national government's deflationary programs in the 1880s caused massive depression in the countryside, where hundreds of thousands of farmers lost their land and bankruptcies soared. As a result, the decade gave birth to a huge migration of job seekers to the cities that challenged city planners and prompted the rise of "poor people's caverns" [*hinminkutsu*] or slums.

Asked what 'Meiji' meant, slum dwellers likely would have had three answers: new jobs, impoverishment, and fresh ideas about 'public' life. One of the most important aspects of Meiji modernity – indeed, a key reason for the great migration – was a mushrooming of jobs required for the country to become rich and modern. Factories were producing textiles and cigarettes for export. Inventions such as trains and telephones required thousands of workers. As populations grew, new eating places required young women to serve and clean. Because everyone had to get around, the Japanese invented a new form of transportation – the rickshaw, which in 1890s Tokyo provided work for more than 40,000 pullers [*shafu*], men who were notorious for their colourful behaviour as well as for the foul-smelling food they ate on the run. An official index late in the 1890s listed 358 different job categories, including people who made saw teeth and those who wove fabrics.[26] The fundamental fact of Meiji for most poor urbanites was simple: if modern life required it, poor people would do it.

The second fundamental fact was that they would be poorly paid. Few stories are less adequately told in the standard accounts of Meiji than the heavy toll exacted on *hinmin* for the construction and operation of a modern country. Every worker group one looks at screams hardship. Surveys of wages show repeatedly that the typical household head's income rarely amounted to more than half of what was needed to put a barebones,

The Japanese flag.

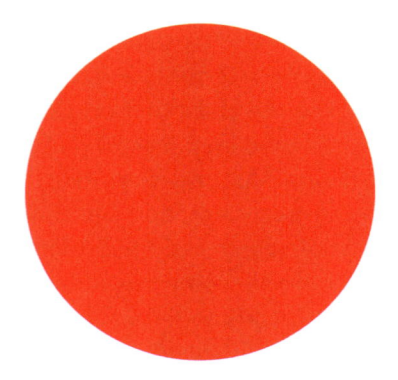

non-nutritious meal on the table – which meant that wives and children had to work too. Many families lived in tiny rowhouse apartments along dirty alleys where their laundry was soiled by factory smoke. Rents frequently were paid by the day, because there was no money for bi-weekly or monthly payments. One survey showed that at Meiji's end, nearly three-quarters of families (with as many as five or six people) in Tokyo's Sumida River slum regions lived in one-room apartments of about a hundred square feet.[27] If illness or crisis came, there were no margins to pay for treatment or aid. Indeed, it was common for poor neighbourhoods to be quarantined when an infectious disease hit, so outsiders would not be infected.

Nothing spoke more clearly to the poverty of the *hinmin* than child labour, which made it impossible for children to get the education that modern life required. Three out of every five match and matchbox makers in one Osaka survey were under the age of sixteen; factories hired girls under ten. This was not because parents did not value education. They simply had no choice: children brought in an income or the family did not eat. Although national laws made education compulsory, Meiji cities exempted *hinmin* children, colluding with industrialists determined to maintain a cheap labour supply. As one journalist wrote in 1902: "the poor as a whole never have an education [because] they never have any leeway in matters of food and clothing".[28] When the journalist Matsubara Iwagorō called charity a "cloak for former robbery", he was referring to the crime of not paying living wages for *hinmin* labour. When he wrote that the poor "lay themselves down at night, some to sleep and some to die",[29] he was talking about the poverty that made life itself uncertain for many.

Fortunately, Meiji's meaning did not stop with economic despair for most *hinmin*. Asked to describe the period, they likely would have talked about *kindaika* or "modernisation", an idea that encapsulated something most had not known back in the village: a feeling of connectedness to the broader public arena. It is hardly surprising that commoners participated in the chaotic street life that surrounded their slums: the markets on major bridges, the temple festivals with cheap food, the cherry blossom celebrations. What is more surprising is that they also took part in politics. In part, this was because they read newspapers. Kuroiwa's ambition of publishing a paper that was accessible to the "common average [*futsū ippan*] person" was realised beyond what he surely expected. An 1898 survey showed that a third of his 105,000 subscribers lived in the regions of the poor, and when newspapers began soliciting reader correspondence near the turn of the century, a "chief characteristic", says the press historian Yamamoto Taketoshi, "was the fact that this correspondence came from the lower classes".[30] Of equal importance, when protesters took to the streets by the thousands in the late Meiji years to demand lower prices and criticise government corruption, *hinmin* were at the forefront. When, for example, Tokyo was rocked in 1905 by three days of demonstrations and violence over Japan's supposedly inadequate settlement at the end of the Russo-Japanese War, as many as seventy per cent of those arrested had *hinmin* occupations such as factory workers and rickshaw pullers.[31] And the *hinmin* demonstrators framed their demands with shouts that "the constitutional system belongs rightfully to us".[32] They may have lived in subhuman conditions; they may have felt powerless in the workplace; but along with hardship, urban modernity had given them a belief that the governmental system owed them something. Even as the Meiji era impoverished them, it also made them citizens.

Every era in every place changes the world, but few have done so as rapidly or as radically as Meiji did. In the mid-Meiji words of Chamberlain: "Feudalism has gone, isolation has gone, beliefs have been shattered, new idols have been set up, new and pressing needs have risen ... Japan is transported ten thousand miles away from her former moorings". Nothing gives more striking proof of the impact of the era than the varied yet equally fundamental effects it had on each of the actors I have examined here. For the much studied elites, the word Meiji signified a national transformation that catapulted their land to the ranks of world power. For what Chamberlain called the "hugely ignorant foreign public", the word connoted challenge; the rise as early as the 1890s of the term "yellow peril" and growing doubts about Anglo-Saxon superiority.[33] Asians looked at Meiji Japan with fear, sometimes with loathing, but just as often they were inspired by the remarkable progress of a non-Western people, particularly when Japan stopped the encroachment of Russia into eastern Asia. And for the vast majority of ordinary Japanese, Meiji meant primarily a change in daily life: new jobs that paid too little, alongside a growing sense that they belonged to an entity bigger than their own families, a nation state called Japan. Near or far, small or large, powerful or weak, every part of the turn-of-the-century world found itself changed by the Meiji advance, but always in highly diverse ways.

1. 'Confusion': Kaishū, Katsu in Walthall, Anne and Steele, M. William *Politics and Society in Japan's Meiji Restoration* (Boston: Bedford/St. Martin's, 2017), p.131. 'Hero': in Keene, Donald *Emperor of Japan: Meiji and His World, 1852–1912* (New York: Columbia University Press, 2002), p.708.
2. Chamberlain, Basil Hall *Japanese Things* (Rutland, VT: Tuttle, 1974; originally published as *Things Japanese*, 1890), p.1.
3. Pittau, Joseph 'Inoue Kowashi and the Meiji Educational System,' in Shiner, Irwin *Modern Japan: An Interpretive Anthology* (New York: Macmillan Publishing, 1974), pp.178–79; Chōmin, Nakae *A Discourse by Three Drunkards on Government* (New York: Weatherhill, 1984), p.50.
4. Hane, Mikiso ed. and trans., *Reflections on the Way to the Gallows: Voices of Japanese Rebel Women* (New York: Pantheon Books, 1988), p.72.
5. Fukuchi: Fukuchi Gen'ichirō, *Shinbun jitsureki* [My newspaper career], in Izumi, Yanagida ed., *Fukuchi Ōchi shū* [Collected works of Fukuchi Ōchi], vol.11 of *Meiji bungaku zenshū* (Tokyo: Chikuma Shobō, 1966), p.328 (king); Izumi, Yanagita *Fukuchi Ōchi* (Tokyo: Nihon Rekishi Gakkai, 1967), p.317 ('Know Japan'). Kuroiwa: in Ono Hideo, 'Kuroiwa Shūroku,' Sandai genronjin shū (Anthology of three generations of journalists) vol. 6 (Tokyo: Jiji Tsūshinsha, 1962), p.68.
6. In *Sun Trade Journal, Taiyō* (1 October, 1908), 4, in Rubin, Jay *Injurious to Public Morals: Writers and the Meiji State* (Seattle: University of Washington Press, 1984), p.67.
7. Eiichi, Shibusawa *The Autobiography of Shibusawa Eiichi*, trans. Teruko Craig (Tokyo: University of Tokyo Press, 1994), pp.139–40.
8. Data from Yutani, Eiji "Nihon no Kaso Shakai' of Gennosuke Yokoyama,' Ph.D. dissertation (University of California, Berkeley, 1985), pp.302–04; *Brisbane Courier*, March 6, 1924: http://trove.nla.gov.au/ndp/del/article/20683707.
9. Eiichi, Shibusawa *Ginkō o sodatete* [Building Banks], in Lu, David J. ed., *Japan: a Documentary History* (Armonk, N.Y.: M.E. Sharpe, 1997), p.356.
10. Statement of Kanagawa governor Ōe Taku, 'Case of the Peruvian Barque *Maria Luz*', with Appendix, Tokyo: Foreign Department, Japanese Government, 1872.
11. Letter, 6 February, 1897, the Edward House Collection, University of Virginia.
12. Setsurei, Miyake cited in Pyle, Kenneth B. *The New Generation in Meiji Japan* (Stanford, CA: Stanford University Press, 1969), p.159.
13. In Walthall and Steele, p.151.
14. Letters from Roosevelt to Speck von Sternberg (16 July, 1907) and Elihu Root (23 July, 1907), in Esthus, Raymond A. *Theodore Roosevelt and Japan* (Seattle: University of Washington Press, 1967), p.191.
15. Bird, Isabella L. *Unbeaten Tracks in Japan* (New York: ICG Muse, 2000; originally 1885), pp. 4, 83.
16. Quoted in Benfey, Christopher *The Great Wave: Gilded Age Misfits, Japanese Eccentrics, and the Opening of Old Japan* (New York: Random House, 2004), p.181.

17. Henning, Joseph M. *Outposts of Civilization: Race, Religion, and the Formative Years of American-Japanese Relations* (New York: New York University Press, 2000): pp.138–39 ('strategic challenge'), p.145 ('more Christian' by Erickson, Hugo), p.160 (William Griffis).
18. 'Datsu-a ron', in Lu, pp.352–53.
19. Cheng, Pei-kai and Lestz, Michael with Spence, Jonathan D. eds., *The Search for Modern China: A Documentary Collection* (New York: W. W. Norton and Company, 1999), p.175.
20. Ch'oe, Yŏng-ho Lee, Peter H. and de Bary, Wm. Theodore *Sources of Korean Tradition II: From the Sixteenth to the Twentieth Centuries* (New York: Columbia University Press, 2000), p.293.
21. Spence, Jonathan D. *The Gate of Heavenly Peace: The Chinese and their Revolution 1895–1980* (New York: Penguin Books, 1982), p.85.
22. Tagore, Rabindranath 'The Spirit of Japan,' The Literature Network: http://www.online-literature.com/tagore-rabindranath/4393/.
23. Tse-tsung, Chow *The May Fourth Movement: Intellectual Revolution in Modern China* (Stanford, CA: Stanford University Press, 1960), p.32.
24. Spence, *Heavenly Peace*, p.85 (Qiu). Chang and Lestz, *Search for Modern China*, p.171 (Sun).
25. Hita Ikaru, 'Hinminkutsu' (Slums), *Fūzoku Gahō* (10 November, 1898), pp.9–10.
26. *Tokyo fu tōkeisho* (Tokyo city statistics, 1901), pp.384–90.
27. Nakagawa Kiyoshi, 'Senzen ni okeru toshi kasō no tenkai, jō' [Evolution of the urban lower classes in prewar Japan, part one], *Mita Gakkai Zasshi* 71, no. 3 (June 1978), pp.85–86.
28. Tōfū, Harada *Hinminkutsu* (Slums) (Tokyo: Daigakukan, 1902), p.103.
29. Matsubara, Iwagoro *Sketches of Humble Life in the Capital of Japan* (Yokohama: The 'Eastern World' Newspaper, Publishing and Printing Office, 1897): p.40 (charity), p.5 (to die).
30. Kuroiwa: *Yorozu Chōhō*, 1 November, 1892. Correspondence: Yamamoto Taketoshi, *Kindai Nihon no shinbun dokusha sō* (Structure of newspaper readership in modern Japan) (Tokyo: Hōsei Daigaku Shuppankyoku, 1981), pp.129, 359.
31. See chart, Gordon, Andrew *Labor and Imperial Democracy in Prewar Japan* (Berkeley: University of California Press, 1991), p.37.
32. *Yorozu Chōhō*, 8 July, 1911, in Yoshimi, Uchikawa and Eiichi, Matsushima eds., *Meiji nyūsu jiten* [Encyclopedia of Meiji news], vol. 8 (Tokyo: Mainichi Komiyunikēshiyon Shuppanbu, 1983–1986), p.566.
33. Chamberlain, *Japanese Things*, pp.6, 7, 9.

Folding map of Japan, 1878.

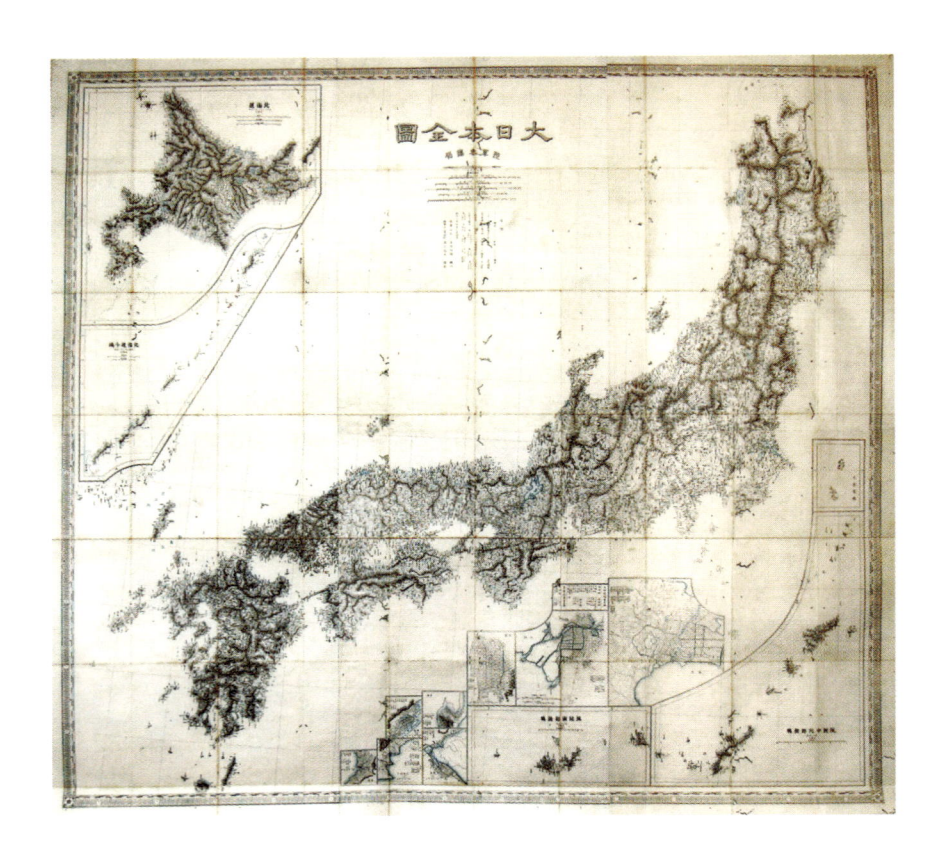

FROM AN OUTWARD-LOOKING SOCIETY TO AN INWARD-LOOKING ONE

Naoki Sakai

I recall that the Japanese mass media celebrated the centenary of the Meiji Restoration in a big way fifty years ago, when I had just started university in Tokyo. All the major newspapers devoted much space to articles by historians and technocrats and interviews with elder statesmen and industrial leaders. They discussed the significance of this hundredth anniversary of the modern state of Japan. The centennial was regarded as marking the greatest accomplishment in Asia, and virtually every adult in Japan was expected to be proud of it. In 1968, there was almost unanimous agreement among the Japanese public that the Meiji Restoration denoted the beginning of a hundred years of exceptional achievement, which had opened up the country to the world, and eventually brought modern civilisation to the inhabitants of the Japanese archipelago. Moreover, it gave rise to what was applauded by American proponents of modernisation theory as "the only genuinely modern society in the entirety of Asia".

Of course, some contested this exceedingly self-congratulatory evaluation. Some historians highlighted the brutal exploitation and miserable living conditions the rural peasantry had to undergo, without which modern industrial capitalism would never have accomplished the primitive accumulation of capital in Japan; others did not hesitate to remind the public of the environmental pollution from which millions of Japanese were suffering in their everyday lives in big cities and agrarian communities all across the country.

A half-century later, the lack of public interest in the Meiji Restoration and the subsequent rejuvenation is striking. One wonders why the nation has ceased so drastically to be interested in Japan's modernisation. What happened between 1968 and 2018?

The Meiji Restoration has often been described as an event that opened Japan to the modern world. Prior to it, from the early 17th century, the general agenda regulating diplomatic policies of the feudal confederation of the *baku-han* system, an assembly of semi-autonomous states, has been portrayed as that of *sakoku*, meaning "the closed country". Thus, it has been understood that the country was only opened to the rest of the world when the Tokugawa shogunate collapsed and the new centralised sovereign state was established in 1868. Yet, what was meant by "the country" [*koku* of the compound s*akoku*] is far from self-evident. First of all, the *baku-han* system was by no means comparable to a nation state, the basic unit of the modern international world. In the terminology of modern international politics, the inhabitants of the Japanese archipelago neither constituted themselves collectively as a unified population subjugated to a sovereign state, nor were they individually subject to any central authority. In this respect, until the Meiji Restoration, there had been no nation in the Japanese archipelago. Strictly speaking, Japan was neither open nor closed to the world; it was not a political entity with a defined territory; it was almost impossible to tell geographically where the inside of Japan ended and its outside began.[1]

What was supposed to have happened in 1868 was, first of all, an inauguration in which Japan declared itself to be the sole juridical authority headed by the sovereign, the Meiji emperor, governor of the entire land surface of the Japanese territory. In other words, the new Japanese state claimed that it was a territorial sovereignty comparable to modern states like the United Kingdom and France.

The Meiji Restoration was an event of exceptional significance not only in the context of Japan's domestic politics, but throughout East Asia. For the first time, Japan joined the modern international world as a territorial sovereign state, and announced it would conduct diplomatic policies, not according to the protocols of a Sinocentric tributary, but following a Eurocentric system of international law – *Jus Publicum Europeaum*. On the western shores of the Pacific, Japan was the only state whose bureaucrats comprehended international law, and what it meant both economically and culturally as well as the political significance of a Eurocentric system of interstate rules. Japan's neighbouring countries, the Qing dynasty in China and the Yi dynasty in Korea, refused to recognise these rules of the modern international world. It was for this reason that Japan was one of the very few countries in East Asia to escape colonisation by Euro-American powers.

Let me return to 1968, the year of the hundredth anniversary of the Meiji Restoration. By the end of the 1960s, the vast majority of the

Shiba Ryôtarô (1923–1996),
author of *Clouds Above The Hill*.

Japanese conceded that Japan's subsequent modernisation was something positive, and they were proud of themselves for this extraordinary accomplishment. Underlying this affirmative attitude toward Japan's past (despite Japan's colonialism and its defeat in the Asia-Pacific War) was a sense of a collective superiority as a nation. The Japanese public were convinced that in East Asia, only Japan had succeeded in creating a modern political system and a governing bureaucracy. This they saw in terms of appropriating the spirit of modern scientific and technological rationality, of competing with Euro-American nations in industrial capitalism, and of establishing an exceptionally high standard of living and education that set it apart from the rest of Asia. South Korea and Taiwan were still very poor countries with a per capita income of less than a tenth of Japan's. Even though Japan was defeated in the Second World War, losing sovereignty over Korea and Taiwan, it could still enjoy the status of an empire, at least in economic terms. The gap in the standard of living between Japan and its former colonies was tangible.

This sense of self-congratulatory hubris is best captured by Shiba Ryôtarô's historical novel *Saka no Ue no Kumo* [Clouds Above the Hill].[2] It is set in the Meiji period and focuses on three male characters who grow up in Matsuyama in Shikoku; they embody the Japanese resolve for modernisation and illustrate personal struggles in the achievement of modernity. The novel invokes not only the Japanese collective memory of glorious success in becoming a first-class international power through two victories, the first Sino-Japanese War (1894–95) and the Russo-Japanese War (1904–05), but also the national euphoria of the 1960s when Japan was recognised internationally as the symbol of successful modernisation in Asia.

The title of the novel summarises the positive viewpoint of the Japanese regarding the international world at that time. *Clouds Above the Hill* outlines the very attitude of people in the process of constituting themselves as a national community during the Meiji period (1868–1912): they look up above them at vague and abstract ideals as they struggle to continue on their steep, ascending path. At the summit are some goals that, like distant clouds, are only given in abstract and illusory forms. The road is sheer, but no matter how difficult it may be to reach the top, there is no going back once the journey has begun. These clouds are above their heads, but not within their country; rather they hang over a distant land called 'the West', a remote place where only foreigners live. In order to reach them, they must look outward and venture into the outside world. Of course, this is one of the most typical symbolic representations of modernisation.

One cannot imagine a better metaphor than the ascending road, *saka*, to represent a typically modern sense of historical time; in *Clouds Above the Hill*, history is apprehended as a continuous linear progress in which everyone is destined to move forward. It is a historical vision particular to the logic of the capitalist market in which you are either ahead or behind somebody else, a history that is always set in the form of evolution and competition. Shiba Ryôtarô does not allow for a different form of historical time; neither did Japanese readers want to entertain different ways of imagining its passage. In this respect, they were no different from the American ideologues of modernisation theory. They simply could not find any reason to reject the idea that unmodernised societies must be less advanced than modernised ones; they believed the entire world was governed by the law of progress or endless advancement.

It is this scheme of historical time that the Japanese public firmly believed in; it is thanks to this belief that, just as Shiba Ryôtarô portrayed, the Japanese during the Meiji period were optimistic and outward-looking; curious not only about their future but about foreign lands, other civilisations, and the world in general. This is why, from the Meiji period until the 1960s and beyond, youth in Japan symbolised a burning intellectual curiosity about the outside world; a desire to experience the foreign and the unknown – a belief that bestowed on young people a certain prestige. Hence, Shiba Ryôtarô's representation of the mythic image of young Japanese. In 1968, this myth was fully alive.

Of course, this pattern could not be discussed independently of the modern international world; it was a world structured by what Stuart Hall called "the discourse of the West-and-the-Rest",[3] the world in which Western Europe established itself as the centre, with the rest of the globe viewed as potential virgin land for colonial conquest by European states. During the Meiji period, Japan joined this hierarchically-ordered world, and *Clouds Above the Hill* was nothing but a success story for the Japanese. Through victories in the first Sino-Japanese War and the Russo-Japanese War, Japan obtained colonial territories in Taiwan and the Korean peninsula and joined the ranks of internationally recognised superpowers.

In stark contrast, fifty years later, this evolutionary narrative of Japan's modernisation can no longer invoke the sort of enthusiasm that it once

Next pages: Sino-Japanese War. The Japanese Navy Victorious Off Takushan.

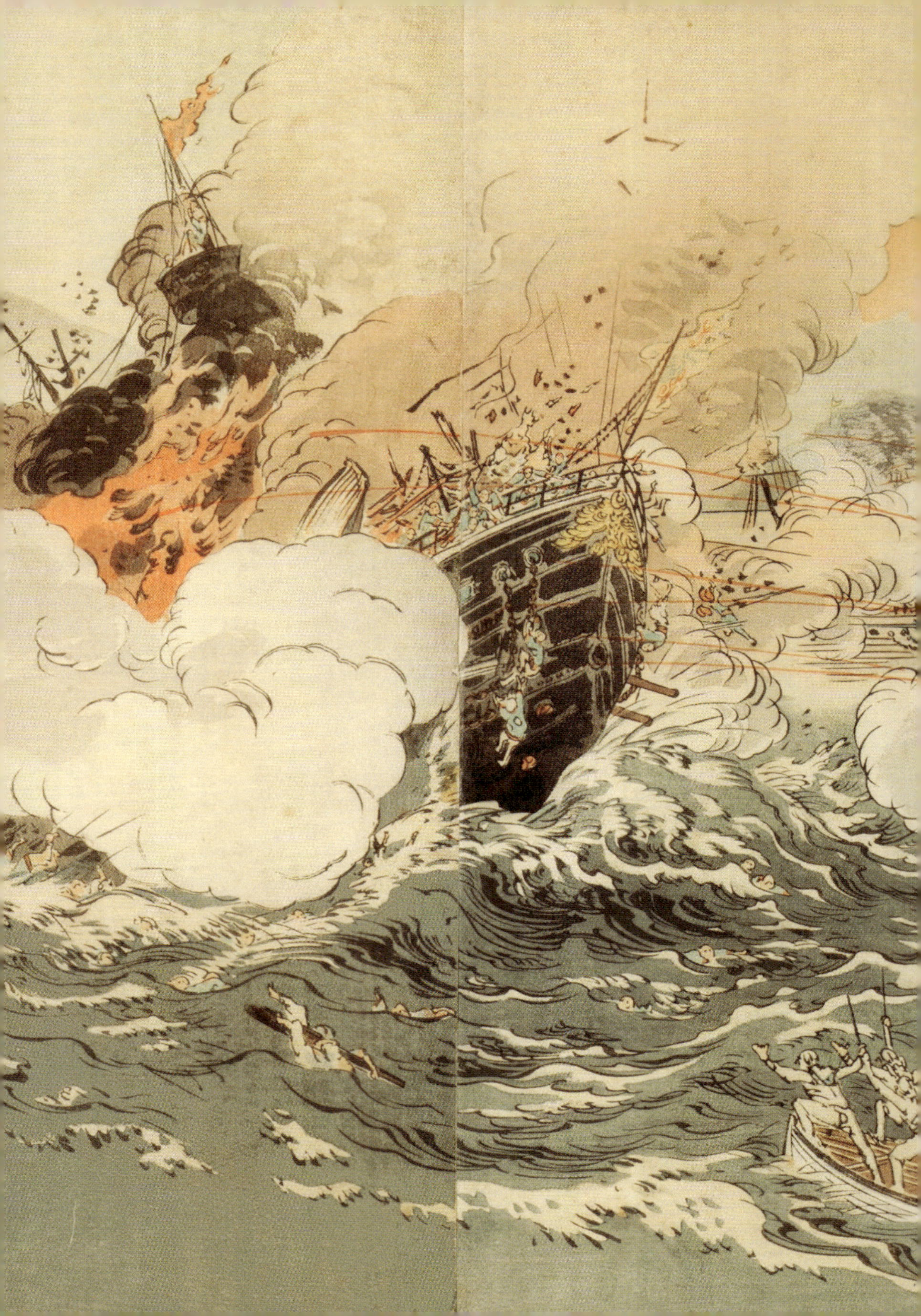

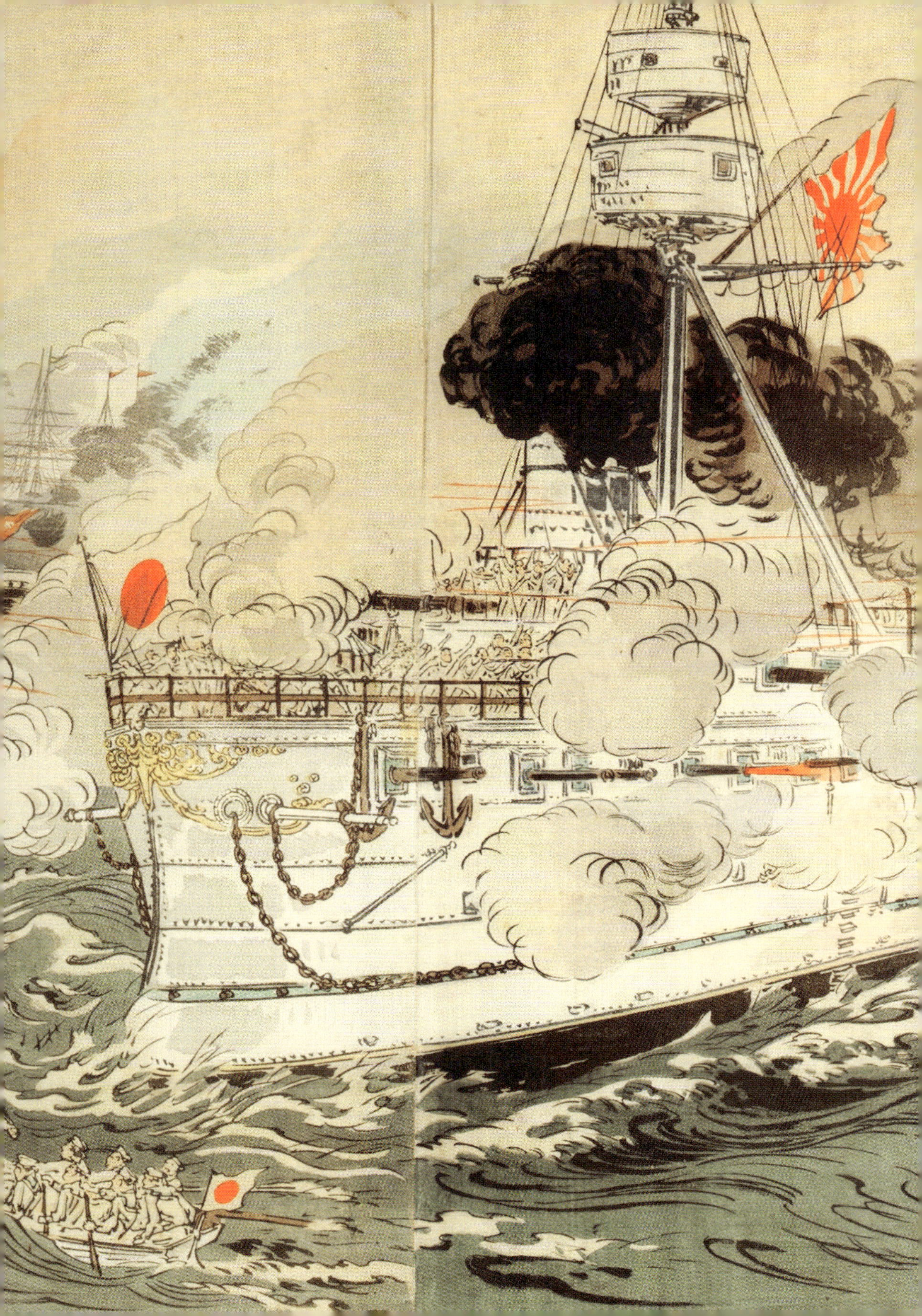

did. Today, one finds oneself exposed to relatively little publicity about the 150th anniversary of the Meiji Restoration. And it is no longer fashionable to imagine the nation's history according to the trope of an ascending linear passage to the top of a hill.

In the last five decades, some reconfiguration of international politics must have occurred on the western shores of the Pacific, as well as in Japanese national self-esteem.

When I examined the drastic changes undergone by societies in this region, I could not evade the issue of the myth of Japan's successful modernisation, a myth that used to give its people a sense of colonial self-esteem.

In the 1990s, I was compelled for the first time to reflect critically on this myth, partly because I witnessed the advent of a social phenomenon called *hikikomori* [reclusive withdrawal]. The term, used by some social workers, sociologists and mental health experts, refers to young people (it is said to be mostly men, but some women; recent government reports also include some older people in their forties and fifties who refuse to emerge from their bedrooms or their parents' houses, thereby alienating themselves from social life. Besides this, *hikikomori* also designates the societal phenomenon of this type of extreme alienation.

Although hesitant, I began to use the idiom "nationalism of *hikikomori*" to roughly group an assembly of socio-political issues in some way related to emerging reactionary, discriminatory and exclusionary political trends observable in Japan during what is generally called "the two lost decades" [*ushinawareta nijûnen*] from the 1990s through to the 2010s. It is necessary here to clarify my use of *hikikomori* in the idiom "nationalism of *hikikomori*": this does not refer to *hikikomori* people; instead it designates a parallel socio-political tendency witnessed in many post-industrial societies, sometimes labelled "inward-looking society". By using this phrase, therefore, I designate a social and political constellation based upon the fantasy of a nation as an enclosed space of security, almost an equivalent of the enclosed space of a bedroom for the *hikikomori* people. Adherents of this type of nationalism fear their national space is vulnerable to the intrusion of aliens, and so advocate building a metaphorical or physical wall to stop them.

Of course, Donald Trump is a case in point. He repetitively fabricates and falsifies issues about immigration without articulating what constitutes immigration problems. In doing so, he advocates the fantastic politics of what Tongchai Winichakul called "the geo-body of a nation", according to which, supposedly, the integrity of a national community is constantly threatened by potential intruders.[4] No doubt Trump's rhetorical tactics are entirely fantastic, but, regardless of how derisive they may sound, they have successfully convinced a certain portion of the population in the United States. Similar rhetoric has proven effective in some countries in Europe as well. It must be acknowledged that Trump's fantastic politics is somewhat inherent in the very constitution of the modern national community: the nation form cannot be entirely cleansed of this type of anti-immigrant racism.

However, let me emphasize that, in their political orientation and conduct, the *hikikomori* people have little in common with these anti-immigrant racists who speak loudly for the nationalism of *hikikomori* or whose behaviour is largely inspired by this type of nationalism.

During the 1980s and 1990s a number of significant political reforms were implemented in Taiwan and South Korea, thanks to which parliamentary democracy seems to have taken root in these former Japanese colonies. Furthermore, these political changes were accomplished against the backdrop of rapid economic growth.

The following statistics amply show trends in the per capita GDP in five countries: the United States, China, Japan, South Korea and Taiwan in the last four decades. (Figures are in per capita GDP purchasing power parity values).[5]

1982: US$14,410;   China $327;   Japan $10,615;   South Korea $3,040;   Taiwan $4,466.
1992: US$25,467;   China $1,028;   Japan $21,057;   South Korea $9,443;   Taiwan $11,901.
2002: US$38,123;   China $2,884;   Japan $26,749;   South Korea $18,878;   Taiwan $21,613.
2012: US$51,704;   China $9,055;   Japan $35,856;   South Korea $31,950;   Taiwan $38,357.

In current US$, IMF estimates.

In the early 1980s, per capita GPD in Taiwan and South Korea was about 45 per cent and 30 per cent that of Japan's respectively; ten years later the figures were 56 per cent and 44 per cent And by the early 2000s they were 81 per cent and 71 per cent. In the same period, China's per capita GDP increased from 3 per cent to 5 per cent to 11 per cent by 2002, and then 25 per cent by 2012, while Japan's remained almost the same in relation to the United States of America's.[6] What is worth noting is that during the decade 2002–12, Taiwan's per capita GDP exceeded that of Japan (at 107 per cent). And in 2017, Taiwan's per capita GDP (ppp value) exceeded that of both the United Kingdom and France.

Hikikomori: "pulling inward". Estimates suggest that half a million Japanese youths have become social recluses.

Of course, this is one of many indicators, and one cannot draw conclusions from statistics in isolation. However, they help us to understand how drastic the social changes have been in the last four decades in this region. It also means that Japan's position relative to other countries in East Asia has been redefined throughout the late 20th and early 21st centuries. As "an empire under subcontract",[7] Japan used to enjoy prestigious status under the American Policy of Containment and benefited greatly from the special treatment it received from the United States. During the political climate of the Cold War, and thanks to the global conditions set by *Pax Americana*, the Japanese people were allowed to behave as if they continued to be part of a nation of colonial suzerainty, even though Japan had lost its overseas colonies. As a result, many Japanese people have failed to shed the old habit of looking down on their Asian neighbours.

But since the 1980s, with the global hegemony of the United States gradually eroding, a new configuration of interstate politics has finally emerged in East Asia. Not being able to liberate itself from its reliance on *Pax Americana*, the Japanese public finds it increasingly difficult to view the position of Japan with its Asian neighbours through the lens of *Clouds Above the Hill*. Finally, the Japanese nation had to face what has been described as "the loss of empire" in British cultural studies. As a telling indicator of the Japanese attitude toward the outside world, let me mention other signs of the loss of empire.

In the 1980s, many Japanese students were visible on university campuses throughout the United States. Their presence was understood as a manifestation of the worldwide trend toward globalisation, just as compact Japanese automobiles began to dominate the American market. As time passed, the number of Japanese students was surpassed by that of Korean students, and the globalisation of higher education in the United States became indisputable. In the last two decades, a larger number of students have begun to arrive at American universities from India and China. Even at Cornell, where I have taught for the last thirty years, this trend has been irrefutable.

Since the 1990s, the composition of the American university student body has undergone a drastic change. In 2016 the total number of international students (including both undergraduate and graduate) studying at American universities exceeded one million, of which 320,000 were from China, 170,000 from India, and 80,000 from South Korea.[8] In spite of this increase in international students from Asia, however, the number of

Japanese students in the United States has gone down in the last three decades. As of 2016, the total number of students from Japan at American universities is less than those from Taiwan – even though the population of Taiwan is less than one fifth that of Japan.

It is not merely the number of Japanese students at American universities that has dwindled; the level of intellectual curiosity about the outside world among young people in Japan has drastically declined.

Recently a friend of mine who works in political science in Japan gave me a thought-provoking datum: only 5 per cent of Japanese people in their 20s have ever applied for passports. In the last five years, this percentage has fluctuated between 5 per cent and 6 per cent. Fifteen years ago, the figure was about 9 per cent, so it is obvious fewer young people are interested in going abroad. Since about 24 per cent of the total population of Japan own passports, this is an astonishingly low figure.[9] While one must not overlook the economic adversity experienced by an increasing number of young Japanese in the last few decades, there are more statistics that paint a picture of changing attitudes.

According to a 2015 survey conducted about Japanese corporations, 63.7 per cent of new employees responded negatively to the question "are you willing to work abroad?", while 36.3 per cent responded affirmatively (9.1 per cent said they would work in any country; 27.2 per cent would not work in certain countries). In 2001, only 29.2 per cent answered the same question negatively, while 70.7 per cent answered affirmatively (17.3 per cent would work in any country; 53.1 per cent would not work in certain countries). Evidently, a drastic change in attitudes toward overseas experiences has taken place.

These findings seem to confirm the trends that I have observed about Japanese society in the last three decades. I am now convinced that it is on the mark to portray today's Japan as an "inward-looking society".

In his brilliant study of the imaginary formation of nationhood in today's Thailand, the historian Thongchai Winichakul coined the concept "the geo-body of a nation" and explored how modern cartography contributed to the process in which the kingdom of Siam was transformed into the modern Thai nation, and how the technology of modern mapping gave rise to a collective imagining that allowed people to imagine themselves as members of a new collectivity called 'a nation'. A nation is a particular form of modern community whose imaginary constitution is closely tied with geographic enclosure; it is embodied in a national territory, a geographic space bound by national borders. Therefore, a nation is not only a collectivity of people connected to one another through what John Stuart Mill called "sympathy".[10] In this respect, a nation is not only an imagined community but also a community of patriots bound together by the fantastic bonds of sympathy. Sympathy that binds a nation together is regulated by the image of a "geo-body"; it also signifies a collectivity of people who are geographically bound, distinguished from the rest of humanity by the fact of their residence in a determinate territory. It follows that their membership in this community – exclusive membership is indeed called "nationality" – is marked by a national border, and that all the individuals living outside this border must be regarded as aliens, excluded from nationality or from sympathy. In other words, for a nation to exist, it is essential that fraternity, a bond of national camaraderie, must never be shared with foreigners.

By now it will be evident why I have adopted the term *hikikomori* in describing a certain nationalism that has characterised Japanese society in recent decades.

Confinement to one's bedroom is one thing, while metaphorical confinement to the geo-body of a nation is quite another. *Hikikomori* people are afraid of the social space outside their homes, but are not necessarily afraid of a possible intrusion from the world outside their nation. On the other hand, the nationalism of *hikikomori* suffers from a phantasmic fear of intrusion from outside the national territory. This is why the nationalism of *hikikomori* is insistent upon the building of a wall, in fantasy or actuality, to prevent alien intruders from entering the national interior.[11] It is important to note that this is not unique to Japan, while *hikikomori* as a sociological phenomenon may, at least statistically, appear particular to Japan; it is universal in the sense that the nation state cannot be built without this mechanism of exclusion based upon the geo-body of a nation. Every formation of a modern community called a nation potentially includes *hikikomori*.

Hikikomori nationalism shares many features of an "inward-looking society", including anti-immigrant racism, that have been observed in many post-industrial countries. And in Japan, the "inward-looking society" seems to manifest itself in the public's changed attitude toward the Meiji Restoration, which is no longer depicted as an event symbolised by the outward-looking attitude of youth. Instead of being curious about foreigners, an increasing portion of the Japanese people are afraid to encounter them, and wish to distance and insulate themselves from them.

What historical conditions have compelled so many people in post-industrial societies to withdraw into the confined fantasy space of a nation? Could the nationalism of *hikikomori* be a repetition of what the world witnessed in the 1920s and 1930s – a repetition of what is loosely called fascism?

1. The absence of clearly bounded territory later gave rise to a number of problems. For instance, the northern territory of Hokkaido except for the southern tip was not integrated into the *Baku-Han* System. After 1868, it had to be colonised and its inhabitants brutally subjugated.
2. 『坂の上の雲』(Tokyo: Bungei Shinju, 1999) was serialised in the *Sankei Shimbun*, a right-wing tabloid from 1968 through 1972. It was translated into English as *Clouds Above the Hill* by Juliet Winters Carpenter, Andrew Cobbing, and Paul McCarthy (New York: Routledge, 2015).
3. Hall, Stuart, 'The West and the Rest: Discourse and Power' in *Modernity – An Introduction to Modern Societies*, edited by Hall, David, Held, Don, Hubert, Stuart and Thompson, Kenneth (London: Blackwell, 1996), pp.184-227.
4. Winichakul, Tongchai *Siam Mapped: A History of the Geo-Body of a Nation*. (Honolulu: University of Hawaii Press, 1994.)
5. Per capita gross domestic product purchasing power parity value is gross domestic product converted to international dollars using purchasing power parity rates and divided by total population.
6. 74% in 1982, 83% in 1992, 70% in 2002, and 69% in 2012.
7. For 'an empire under subcontract' please refer to my recent publication *The Nationalism of Hikikomori* (『ひきこもりの国民主義』, Tokyo: Iwanami Shoten, 2017) An English version is forthcoming from Duke University Press.
8. *Time*, 14 November, 2016.
9. This figure may also appear low, but it was 8-9% in the 1990s. http://www.mlit.go.jp/common/001083168pdf. Information provided by the tourism strategy division, Japan Tourism Agency in the Ministry of Land, Infrastructure, Transport and Tourism.
10. John Stuart Mill defined the nation as 'the society of sympathy'. See: 'Considerations of Representative Government', in *John Stuart Mill*, edited by Acton, H.B. (London: Everyman's Library, 1972; first published 1861), pp.187-428.
11. Japan is surrounded by the sea, so there is no social movement calling for the building of a wall at the national border. Due to policies adopted since the collapse of the Japanese Empire in 1945, the number of immigrants in Japan is very small. Yet, the last few decades have seen the rise of an anti-immigrant racist movement called *Zainichi tokken o yurusainai shimin no kai* (Association of Citizens against the Special Privileges of the Zainichi), openly targeting resident Koreans and Taiwanese Chinese.

Emperor Meiji by Takahashi Yuichi.

SEEKING KNOWLEDGE THROUGHOUT THE WORLD

Peter Nosco

A little over 150 years ago in January 1868, a coalition of Japanese *daimyō*, some from domains with long histories of hatred for the feudal Tokugawa military government, and others inspired by more patriotic concerns, led a *coup d'état* that culminated in the last Tokugawa shogun 'returning' power and authority to the sixteen-year old monarch Mutsuhito who would be known to posterity as Meiji. It is an interesting footnote in Japan's diplomatic history that this new government's very first treaty opened formal relations with the kingdom of Sweden.

In April 1868, on the occasion of Meiji's enthronement, a five-article Charter Oath [五箇条の御誓文 *Gokajō no Goseimon*] was promulgated in Meiji's name, heralding the anticipated themes of the new government: establishing deliberative assemblies; uniting the classes behind the new administration while allowing for individual self-determination; embracing the laws of nature; and seeking knowledge throughout the world in order to strengthen the new monarchy. This last proposition is generally regarded as the most radical of these because of its contrast with the world within walls of Tokugawa Japan: a world to which Europeans had no access for two centuries before the 1850s, other than through the Dutch East India Company on the artificial islet Deshima in Nagasaki Bay.

Writing in 1872, just four years after the "restoration" of monarchical rule, Fukuzawa Yukichi (福沢諭吉, 1835–1901), a paragon of and spokesman for Meiji civilisation and enlightenment [*bunmei kaika* 文明開化],[1] set the tone for this perspective as follows:

> In the time of the Tokugawa Shogunate, the distinction between samurai and common people was sharply drawn. The military families recklessly brandished their prestige. They treated the peasants and townsfolk as despicable criminals. They enacted such notorious laws as that which gave a samurai the right to cut down a

commoner [*kirisute gomen* 切捨御免]. According to these laws the lives of the commoners were not truly their own, but merely borrowed things [*karimono* 借物] ... [The Shogunate and the 300 daimyō] treated the peasants and townsfolk despotically. They sometimes seemed compassionate to them, but they did not really recognise their inherent human rights [*mochimae no kenri tsūgi* 持前の権利通義]. [2]

Fukuzawa's influence and importance in the Japan of the 1860s and 1870s was such that textbooks used in Japanese secondary schools in the early years of the 21st century continue to emphasise a contrast depicting the Edo (or Tokugawa) period as a dark time of oppressed and overly taxed peasants, famines, economic and social inequality, a general hostility toward science, and a general backwardness relative to the "brighter" [*akarui* 明るい] civilisations of Europe and North America. [3]

In Japan this view has been supported by two main tropes with quite different interests. On the one hand we find the Meiji oligarchs, who sought to represent the new state in ways that they hoped would encourage the revision of unequal treaties and Japan's entry into the first rank of the world's nations. On the other hand, we find Marxist historians for whom representing the new state as the culmination of revolutionary forces conformed more closely to their desired model of history. [4] These two combined to form a view of a "good Meiji, bad Tokugawa", which has by no means disappeared, especially when the topic of scientific knowledge arises.

This perspective, however, requires ignoring the activities, observations and significance of an 18th-century Swedish scientist named Carl Peter Thunberg (1743–1828), an interesting figure who remains little known outside Sweden.[5] Thunberg was a botanist and physician who lived in Japan for fifteen months during the years 1775-06. After his return to Europe in 1779, he published in Uppsala a record of his travels in four volumes, over several years beginning in 1788.[6] Within a few years this chronicle was translated and published in German (1792, 1794), English (1793–1795), and French (1794, 1796). In the process, and in the words of his Swedish biographer and recently retired professor of literature at Uppsala University, Marie-Christine Skuncke, Thunberg became "the only European scientist who visited and published his observations of Tokugawa Japan in the 18th century". [7] His writings on Japan became mandatory reading for those who would later attempt to penetrate this island's "world within walls", and I used them extensively in a recently published study of individuality in early modern Japan.[8] At the same time, one senses that Thunberg may have been telling us indirectly a great deal about the Sweden of his own age, a land to which he was holding up Japan as, in many ways, an unflattering mirror.

★

The 1770s were a fascinating time in Europe and in Japan. Europeans were asserting their mastery over the physical world in any variety of ways, including introducing taxonomies or ways of categorising. In the world of botany there arose a frenzy for collecting exotic living and dried plants, not just among scientific botanists but also among those with sufficient surplus wealth to satisfy their curiosity. In this world, the Uppsala professor Carl Linneaus (1707–78) was a kind of god, especially to his students whom he actually styled his "apostles": emissaries on a kind of divine mission to discover, describe, name, collect and categorise plants from around the world.

Carl Peter Thunberg was one of Linneaus' students, and in 1771 Nicolaas Burman, the son of Linneaus' friend Johannes Burman, wrote to Thunberg offering to send him to Japan on the condition that he make "a sacred promise to send all seeds and natural history specimens that [he could] acquire in Japan or in the whole of the Indies to our Botanical Garden [in Amsterdam]".[9] It is important to understand how foreign Japan in all respects would have been in the 1770s to any European, but especially in terms of scientific taxonomy. Japan was virtually *terra incognita* to European botanists, whose knowledge would have been limited to Engelbert Kaempfer's *Amoenitatum exoticarum*, published in 1712. The chance to travel there was a once-in-a-lifetime opportunity for the twenty-eight-year-old Thunberg.

To reach Japan, Thunberg first had to make his way to Batavia (present-day Jakarta) from where he departed for Japan on 20 June, 1775. He arrived in the Bay of Nagasaki nearly two months later on 13 August, but his world for all but three of his fifteen months in Japan was the narrow confines – some 215 metres by sixty-five metres – of Deshima in Nagasaki Bay.

This was the tightly monitored outpost of the Dutch East India Company or VOC, the Dutch being the only Europeans allowed to live in and

Gingko biloba. From Flora Japonica by the botanist Carl Peter Thunberg.

trade with Japan at the time, and Thunberg (a Swede), like Kaempfer (a German), had to pretend to be Dutch in order to reside there.

Like all of his fellow Deshima residents, Thunberg was a kind of prisoner consigned to viewing Japan from afar for most of his stay. For a botanist and one of Linnaeus' apostles, this must have been agony, and in a letter written to his patron Bergius some two months after his arrival, Thunberg lamented that, "it grieves me in my heart to see these rare and beautiful hills, cultivated by the industrious Japanese in patches up to the very top, without having the liberty to go there".[10] At the same time, Thunberg was the company's physician, an exalted position in Japan because of the intense Japanese interest in European science, especially anatomy, surgery and medicine, which gave him a narrow opportunity for access to the materials he sought. Prior to 1720, books in Western languages were forbidden in Japan owing to the strict prohibition on Christianity, but that year the enlightened shogun Tokugawa Yoshimune relaxed this ban, opening the way to Western scientific knowledge. Nagasaki was the principal window to this world of Western learning, which was known in Japanese as *Rangaku* (Dutch learning) as an acknowledgement of the role of Holland [*Jpn Oranda*] in this enterprise.

Japanese scientific knowledge was typically several decades behind the most recent European discoveries, but knowledge of Europe generally and European science in particular was more readily available in mid-to-late Tokugawa Japan than one would believe from reading Fukuzawa Yukichi. For example, in March 1771, the same month in which Thunberg received his invitation to visit the country, an autopsy was performed in Japan using, not the traditional charts derived from Chinese medicine, but rather the anatomical charts contained in Johann Kulmus' 1725 *Anatomische Tabellen*. The Rangaku scholars who supervised the autopsy were so impressed by the superior accuracy of the European charts that they immediately undertook to translate Kulmus' tome into Japanese and published it under the title *Kaitai Shinsho* [解体新書] in 1774. Though the reception of this knowledge was inevitably delayed en route to Japan, it can thus be said that after 1720 Japan was increasingly prepared to seek scientific knowledge throughout the world so long as that knowledge did not directly contain knowledge of, or reference to, Christianity.

In this respect, Thunberg was the proverbial bridge between East and West. He never learned Japanese and was thus dependent on his team of Nagasaki interpreters, whose assignment was to learn as much as possible about Europe and European science while at the same time disclosing nothing about Japan to the visitors. Thunberg lamented in another letter that "the interpreters, themselves watched by other watchers, hardly dare to communicate anything to us".[11] Nonetheless, during his time on Deshima, Thunberg learned how to barter with his interpreters: in exchange for his European medical knowledge, they were prepared to provide specimens of fresh plants as well as collections from the Japanese pharmacopeia and minerals. In this respect, Thunberg was a successor to Engelbert Kaempfer, and a predecessor of his own better-known successor on Deshima, the German physician and botanist Philipp Franz Balthasar von Siebold (1796–1866), who lived in Japan in 1823-26 and was the father of the first Japanese female doctor, Kusumoto Ine.

But it is Thunberg's role as a transmitter of knowledge about Japan to Europe that I wish to concentrate on in the remainder of this essay. European intellectuals in the late 18th century were engaged in their own search for knowledge throughout the world and had an insatiable appetite for exotic knowledge. This was the highpoint of the age of sail, with maritime networks linking Europe with North and South America to the west, and with Asia to the east. Through trade, a variety of "others" – from Arabia to India to China to Indonesia – fuelled the imaginations of European men of letters, providing them with the idea of a binary opposition between the lands of heathen but nonetheless noble savages on the one hand, and the luxurious realms of grandees and potentates on the other.

As noted, Thunberg's opportunities to directly observe the Japan outside Deshima's walls were severely constrained, the principal exception being the three months when he accompanied the head of the VOC on the annual embassy to Edo and the Shogun's court. Thunberg left Nagasaki in March 1776 and arrived in Edo on 27 April. He stayed there for four weeks, living as these embassies always did within the Nagasaki-ya, in a residential inn set up for precisely this purpose.

During his stay at Nagasaki-ya, Thunberg was allowed to receive visitors, but not to go out, and the highlight of this stay was his audience on 18 May with Tokugawa Ieharu (1737-86), the reigning shogun, who would have been twenty-nine at the time. A week after this audience, Thunberg departed Edo, returning to Nagasaki and Deshima in June. Five months later, Thunberg left Japan, returning to Uppsala in 1779 as its professor of botany, the legendary Professor Linneaus having died in early 1778.

CARL. PET. THUNBERG.

*M. Dr. Prof. ord. der Botan. zu
Upsala u. d. Wasa Ord. Ritter.
Geb. zu Joenkoeping d. 11 Nov. 1743.*

Carl Peter Thunberg. Engraving by C. Westermayr.

Thunberg worked assiduously on the chronicle of his travels, and in his preface to part one wrote: "I have endeavoured to delineate this nation such as it really is, without on the one hand too highly extolling its advantages, or on the other too severely censuring its defects. I put down daily upon paper whatever came to my knowledge". He then organised his notes around such topics as internal economy, language, government, public worship, and so on.[12]

Is it the case that the grass always appears greener elsewhere, or were there areas where Thunberg's Sweden could genuinely learn from Thunberg's Japan? Thunberg is consistent in his praise of Japan and its people, with the single exception of scientific knowledge, "by whose brighter rays it has not as yet had the good fortune to be illumined".[13] Regarding the Japanese, he wrote that they "are in general intelligent and provident, free and unconstrained, obedient and courteous, curious and inquisitive, industrious and ingenious, frugal and sober, cleanly, good-natured and friendly, upright and just, trusty and honest, mistrustful, superstitious, proud and unforgiving, brave and invincible".[14] Even allowing that those with whom Thunberg would have come into contact would likely not have been commoners in any literal sense, as Thunberg seems to acknowledge by his qualifier "in general", his admiration is nonetheless unmistakable, though at times conflicted – for example, "trusty" yet "mistrustful".

Thunberg repeatedly comments admiringly on Japanese frugality and freedom from wasteful ostentation at all levels of the society:

> That idle vanity, so common amongst other Asiatic as well as many African nations, who adorn themselves with shells, beads and glittering pieces of metal, is never to be observed here, nor are these unnecessary European trappings of gold and silver lace, jewels and the like, which serve merely to catch the eye, here prized at all.[15]

Though it is likely that Thunberg would have not been able to develop a truly discerning eye regarding the subtler qualities of Japanese finery, what he observes instead is a people content "with decent clothing, palatable food and excellent weapons"; a country in which there is an abundance, "even to superfluity, of all the necessaries of life".[16] Thunberg goes so far as to assert that "dearth and famine are strangers to this country, and that in the whole extent of this populous empire scarcely a needy person or beggar is to be found".[17] To be sure, the residents of Deshima lived in a gilded cage in which their physical needs and wants could always be met for a price, and it is certain that the roads were swept of beggars and other unfortunates during Thunberg's travels to and from Edo. Nonetheless, if Thunberg had visited Japan a decade later, he would have arrived toward the end of the horrific Tenmei famine when as many as a million perished and countless more suffered.

Thunberg is equally admiring of the government, which in his words "has existed without change or revolution for ages, [with] strict and unviolated laws, the most excellent institutions and regulations in the towns, the villages and upon the roads; a dress, coiffure and customs that, for several centuries have undergone no alteration; [and] innumerable inhabitants without parties, strife or discord, without discontent, distress or emigrations".[18]

High praise indeed, but we can also discern where Thunberg simply gets it wrong. While one could argue that in the divided monarchy of *tennō* and Shogun, one can observe structural continuities stretching back for centuries, the forms of government were continuously evolving according to the needs of the times and the persons involved, neither conspicuously more nor less than in Sweden. Though court costume remained unchanged, whether in town or country, the most popular fashions never stopped changing during the Tokugawa period. And as for discontent or distress, there were well over a dozen peasant rebellions in Japan just during Thunberg's fifteen months there, which was average during the decade of the 1770s.[19] One of his observations regarding the Japanese polity seems particularly arguable. Thunberg wrote that "Japan is in many respects a singular country when compared with the different states of Europe".[20] Relative to Europe this is probably true, but at the same time there existed such diversity among the sixty-six *kuni* [国] or 'countries'[or 260 plus domains that comprised Japan that the historian Luke Roberts has persuasively likened Tokugawa Japan to an international order. That Thunberg might not have observed this is altogether understandable, but it is unlikely to have escaped the notice of generations of his predecessors as chief physician to the VOC.

Thunberg echoed numerous other observers, both foreign and domestic, when he comments on the honesty of Japanese people generally, but at other times his observations are decidedly surprising, as when he remarks that "liberty is the soul of the Japanese".[21] Thunberg distinguished this liberty from licentiousness or riotous excess, regarding it instead as a

Carl Linnaeus in Sami costume.
Painting by Hendrik Hollander, 1853.

liberty that is exercised under strict subjection to the laws. Elsewhere I have argued that a remarkably high degree of individuality – understood as the acceptance of individual difference – emerged in 18th-century Japan, and one way to understand Thunberg's observation is to think of his understanding of liberty as the freedom or liberty to be oneself within the law.

Equally remarkable is Thunberg's high praise for Japanese jurisprudence. He writes that "the rights and liberties of the higher and lower class of people are equally protected by the laws" and comments that "justice is held sacred all over the country". He claims that at their tribunals, "causes are adjudged without delay and without intrigues or partiality".[22] Yet Thunberg seems blithely unaware of the fact that to be imprisoned for even a few weeks while awaiting trial was tantamount to a death sentence for the majority of those so detained – less a matter of torture than of sheer squalor.

Marie-Christine Skuncke has suggested that "'Japan was [for Thunberg] what Sweden [in the 1770s and 1780s] was not: a land of plenty, where order, discipline and thrift went hand in hand with a free economy". Perhaps we can take Skuncke's general principle here a bit further: could it be that in Thunberg's extolling of Japanese liberty, stable government, material abundance, and equality before the law, he was reflecting what an improved Swedish society of the 1780s might resemble? Was Thunberg in this respect a kind of Jonathan Swift, whose 1726 *Gulliver's Travels* used a fictional chronicle of wanderlust to satirise his own times? I wish I knew enough about the Sweden of some 230 years ago to comment, but for now I must settle for simply raising these questions. What is certain is that Thunberg valued an orderly and disciplined society that disdained extravagance and tolerated difference.

To be sure, Thunberg's observations were uneven in quality, and it is curious how he, at times, made sweeping generalisations that are factually wrong, with perhaps the most obvious being his claim that Japan had never had territorial ambitions. In Thunberg's words:

> The monarch never injures any of his neighbours, and no instance is to be found in history, ancient or modern, of his having shown an ambition to extend his territories by conquest. The history of Japan affords numberless instances of the heroism of these people in the defence of their country against foreign invasions or internal

insurrections, but not one of their encroachments upon the lands or properties of others. The Japanese have never given way to the weakness of conquering other kingdoms, or suffering any part of their own to be taken from them.[23]

It is remarkable that the ill-advised invasion of Korea during the 1590s could have been so thoroughly concealed from Thunberg. And although Thunberg cannot be faulted for being unable to foresee the future, it is curious that a century later, late-Tokugawa and early-Meiji concessions calculated to keep alien imperial powers at bay were part of a broader strategy intended to protect Japanese territory and sovereignty.

Björn Wittrock (b. 1945), the well-known Swedish historiographer, has written of Thunberg that "it is tempting ... to speculate that [he] ... was [sufficiently] free from the emerging sense of European superiority to allow for a description of Japanese botany and society that was characterised by openness and respect".[24] There is no disputing the fact that Thunberg was a brilliant observer, immensely skilled at extrapolating insights from mere scraps of information and occasional glimpses of the world beyond Deshima's confines. Further, all of us who have lived abroad know what it is to return to our homes with eyes that see the once familiar in changed ways. In our minds, we create intensely personal imaginary realms that incorporate the best of the worlds we've visited while surgically excising the undesirable. Perhaps all of this figured kaleidoscopically in Thunberg's observations of Japan acquired over his 15 months there in the 1770s.

In conclusion, and returning to the questions with which we began this essay, in 2018, we celebrated what could be regarded as the 150th anniversary of the ongoing Japanese search for knowledge throughout the world as expressed in the Charter Oath, and Japan's partnership with Sweden in this quest. In this essay I have attempted to historicise Japan's quest for knowledge by locating roots that extend to the 1720s; and if we are curious about how Sweden might have figured in this, then we have also observed how the quest was well underway even before Thunberg arrived in Nagasaki Bay in 1775. The largely forgotten moment over two centuries ago when Thunberg encountered Japan, and vice versa, was when Japan and Sweden first learned much of mutual benefit from each other. The medium was the remarkable Carl Peter Thunberg, and the message was the importance of seeking knowledge of the world throughout the world.

1. On Fukuzawa, the definitive work in any western language remains Carmen Blacker's *The Japanese Enlightenment: A Study of the Writings of Fukuzawa Yukichi* (1964).
2. Dilworth and Nishikawa 2012: p.14.
3. Nishio 2007: pp.10-26; Brown 2009: pp.73-75.
4. Dower 1975.
5. This paper is profoundly indebted to Marie-Christina Skuncke's *Carl Peter Thunberg: Botanist and Physician* (Uppsala: Swedish Collegium for Advanced Study, 2014), and Timon Screech's translated and annotated *Japan Extolled and Decried: Carl Peter Thunberg and the Shogun's Realm, 1775–1796* [sic] (New York and London: Routledge, 2005).
6. *Resa uti Europa, Africa, Asia förättad Åren 1770–1779* [Travels in Europe, Africa and Asia between the years 1770–1779].
7. Skuncke: p.15.
8. Nosco, Peter *Individuality in Early Modern Japan: Thinking for Oneself* (New York and London: Routledge 2018), pp.54, 58, 85, 125-8, 134n8.
9. Skuncke p.39.
10. Skuncke p.103.
11. Skuncke, p.105.
12. Screech, p.158.
13. Ibid. p.159.
14. Ibid. There is an echo here of St Francis Xavier's initial report of the Japanese in 1549 two centuries earlier that they are 'the best people yet discovered … [and] who esteem honour more than anything.'
15. Ibid.
16. Ibid.
17. Ibid. p.161.
18. Ibid. p.173.
19. On a personal level, I would note that it took me a very long time indeed to recognise that much of what I had been told in Japan about Japan both past and present simply was not so.
20. Ibid. p.173.
21. Ibid. p.159.
22. Ibid. pp.160-61.
23. Ibid. p.160.
24. Skuncke, p.9.

REFERENCES

Blacker, Carmen *The Japanese Enlightenment: A Study of the Writings of Fukuzawa Yukichi*, (University of Cambridge Oriental Publications, no. 10. Cambridge: Cambridge University Press, 1964).

Dilworth, David A. trans., and Shunsaku Nishikawa intro., *The Thought of Fukuzawa 2: Fukuzawa Yukichi – An Encouragement of Learning*, (Keio University Press,).

Dower, John 'E.H. Norman, Japan and the Uses of History' in *Origins of the Modern Japanese State: Selected Writings of E.H. Norman*, edited by Dower, John (New York: Pantheon Books, 1975).

Kanji, Nishio 西尾幹二, *Edo no dainamizumu*『江戸のダイナミズム』. Bungei Shunju 文藝春秋, (2007).

Nosco, Peter *Individuality in Early Modern Japan: Thinking for Oneself* (New York and London: Routledge, 2018).

Roberts, Luke *Mercantilism in a Japanese Domain: The Merchant Origins of Economic Nationalism in 18th-Century Tosa*, (Cambridge: Cambridge University Press, 1998).

Screech, Timon translated and annotated, *Japan Extolled and Decried: Carl Peter Thunberg and the Shogun's Realm, 1775-1796* [sic], (New York and London: Routledge, 2005).

Skuncke, Marie-Christine *Carl Peter Thunberg: Botanist and Physician* (Uppsala: Swedish Collegium for Advanced Study, 2014).

Caricature from the magazine Marumaru chinbun
relating to the closure of the
Historiographical Institute in 1893.

CHINESE LEARNING [KANGAKU] BETWEEN CLASSICAL AND NATIONAL SCHOLARSHIP

Margaret Mehl

On 22 April, 1893, the satirical magazine *Marumaru chinbun* published an intriguing caricature that occupied a double page spread. Three men are pushing and pulling a cart laden with document boxes labelled *shishi* [historical materials] and *hensan* [compilation], as well as a pile of traditionally bound volumes. The man pushing the cart has a calligraphy brush for a head; the two pulling it an ink block and an ink stone. One is pointing at a sign advising vehicles to stop, in front of a fence barring the way. The caption reads:

"Damn! If only we had known that we would be stopped so suddenly, we would have taken a byway, how annoying! Now nothing can be done, oh, one mistake and everything ends up like this. We tried a fresh start, but then the thought/Chinese learning [*a somewhat clumsy pun with kangae, thought, and kangaku, Chinese learning*] – oh what a hateful business!"[1]

Whoever came up with this image clearly perceived *kangaku*, or Chinese learning, to have hit some kind of a dead end. *Kangaku* means mainly Confucian studies, but includes Chinese history and culture in a broader sense, as well as *kanbun* (classical Chinese and Sino-Japanese language and the literature written in it) and *kanshi* (poetry written in the Chinese style). *Kangaku* dominated education before the Meiji Restoration of 1868 and continued to be regarded as the hallmark of a good education for most of the Meiji period, while *kanbun*, or at least a heavily sinicised writing style, remained the language of scholarship, official documents and 'serious' writing in general.[2]

So, had *kangaku* really hit a dead end in 1893? And if so, in what way? And why at this particular point in time?

On a superficial level the question is easy to answer. The caricature appeared only days after the minister of education, Inoue Kowashi (1843–95), had ordered the closure of the *Shishi Hensan Kakari*, or Department for Historical and Topographical Compilation, the predecessor of the present Historiographical Institute at the University of Tokyo, on 10 April, 1893.³

Inoue gave two reasons for his decision to close the department. First, in the twenty years of its existence it had not produced the expected results – that is an official history of Japan. Second, the history was being written in Sino-Japanese [*kanbun*], although this language was no longer used in administration and education. Another reason, not stated in the official proposal, was that Inoue objected to some of the interpretations produced by scholars at the department. Indeed, the closure came only a year after the "Kume affair", when the historian Kume Kunitake was dismissed following the outrage caused by his article "Shinto is an Outdated Custom of Heaven Worship" [*Shintō wa saiten no kozoku*].⁴

None of the reasons, however, was stated publicly, so the press could only speculate.⁵ On the other hand, Inoue was not the first to criticise the slow progress and the choice of *kanbun* as the language of the official history. But the caricature's implication appears to be that it was not just the language, but *kangaku*, the tradition of scholarship the language stood for, was the problem. This is interesting because it seems to point to something beyond the work being carried out at the Historiographical Institute.

Of course, the very project of compiling an official history of Japan originated from a worldview that was still steeped in Confucian thought and the notion of "China" as a universal normative reference.⁶ It began with the Imperial Rescript on Historiography, issued in April 1869, which ordered the compilation of a government-sponsored history of Japan modelled on the *Rikkokushi*, that is, the official histories compiled in the 8th century, which in turn were modelled on Chinese dynastic histories:

> Historiography is a forever immortal state ritual (*taiten*大典) and a wonderful act of our ancestors. But after the Six National Histories it was interrupted and no longer continued. Is this not a great lack! Now the evil of misrule by the warriors since the Kamakura period has been overcome and imperial government has been restored. Therefore, we wish that an office of historiography [*shikyoku*史局] be established, that the good custom of our ancestors be resumed and that knowledge and education be spread throughout the land, and so we appoint a president. Let us set right the relations between monarch and subject, distinguish clearly between the alien and the proper [*ka'i naigai*華夷内外] and implant virtue throughout our land.⁷

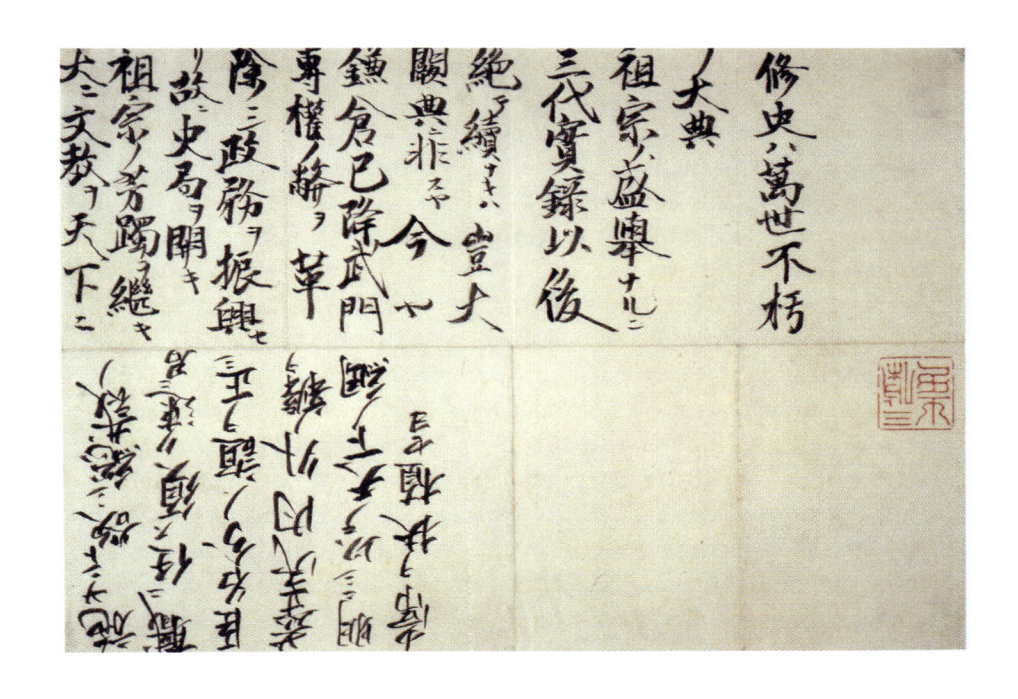

Imperial Rescript on Historiography, 1869.

In accordance with the Rescript on Historiography, a succession of offices in the government engaged in the compilation of history in various forms, although the compilation of the actual history of Japan in accordance with the rescript was not formally begun until early 1882.[8] Already in the weeks before the proclamation of the rescript of 1869, an Office for the Collection of Historical Materials and Compilation of a National History [*Shiryô Henshû Kokushi Kôsei Kyoku*] was established. It was, however, short-lived. In the following year centralisation of government was achieved with the abolition of the feudal domains, which were replaced by prefectures with centrally appointed-governors. In 1872 a Department of History [*Rekishika*] was set up within the central government. Its main task appears to have been the collection of information, contemporary as well as historical, as a basis for administration. At this stage, recording current affairs and writing history were not clearly distinguished in the office.

A major step towards the compilation of a national history [*kokushi*] was taken in 1875 when the Department of History was replaced by the Office of Historiography [*Shûshikyoku*] and its work completely reorganised. This followed a major political crisis which threatened the unity of the government. A compromise between the opposing political leaders was reached at a conference in February 1875, which included an agreement to work towards a constitutional government with an elected parliament. An imperial edict issued on 14 April sanctioned this resolution. The Office of Historiography was established on the same day, suggesting that the compilation of a national history was perceived as a significant project in preparation for a constitution. Financial difficulties, however, which became particularly acute during the war against the former feudal domain of Satsuma (Kagoshima prefecture) in 1877, hampered the work. That year, the central government was reorganised yet again, and the office was replaced by the College of Historiography [*Shûshikan*] with a much reduced budget.

A further major political crisis, in 1881, gave the quest for a constitutional government a renewed urgency, and on 12 October an imperial edict set a deadline by announcing the opening of an elected parliament in 1890. In the following years, drawing up the new constitution and reorganising government institutions in preparation for the future parliamentary system dominated domestic politics. The reorganisation of the College of Historiography in December 1881, although partly in response to internal problems, was also motivated by the October edict; the envisaged history was to be completed by 1890. The main task of the college was for the first time clearly defined as "compilation of a chronological history", titled *Chronological History of Great Japan* [*Dai Nihon hennenshi*], which was to take precedence over other work. The fact that it was to be completed by 1890 was underlined when the Council of State was abolished and replaced by a cabinet system in 1885: the College of Historiography became the Temporary Office of Historiography [*Rinji Shûshikyoku*]. Three years later, in 1888, it was moved to the Imperial University (today the University of Tokyo) and renamed the Temporary Department for the Compilation of a Chronological History [*Rinji Hennenshi Hensan Kakari*] later renamed Shishi Hensan Kakari, or Department for Historical and Topographical Compilation, in 1891.

The Chronological History of Great Japan was planned (as its name suggests) as a strictly chronological history structured around the reigns of the emperors. It was to cover the period from the beginning of the 14th century to the Meiji Restoration. That means it was now conceived not as a continuation of the Six National Histories, but of the History of Great Japan [*Dainihonshi*] compiled during the Tokugawa period in Mito domain. Incidentally, work on this continued into the Meiji period, and the final version was not completed until 1906. *The History of Great Japan*, the only Japanese work that faithfully followed the format of the Chinese dynastic histories, was thus accorded the status of an official history or *seishi*. By 1882, most of the members in the Office of Historiography were scholars of Chinese learning and the *Dainihon hennenshi* was written in *kanbun*, the obvious choice for them.[9]

In the 1880s, however, the decision to write in *kanbun* was also a controversial choice. Historical periodisation is always difficult, especially when complex, long-term processes are involved, but we might single out the year 1879. It saw several events that we could describe as markers in the transformation of *kangaku* in Meiji Japan, because they illustrate some of the trends that became increasingly evident in the 1880s.[10]

In June 1879, Shigeno Yasutsugu, one of the leading members of the College of Historiography, in a lecture at the Tokyo Academy of Science (established the same year), called for the study of the contemporary Chinese language and for sending students to China in order to train experts who could usefully serve the nation. That autumn, Katsura Tarô (1848–1913), who was later to become war minister and then prime minister, embarked on an exploratory mission to northern China together with several other military officials in order to collect information on military and strategic matters. Although at first sight unconnected, these events were part of a trend to treat China not as a universal reference, but as a contemporary nation, separate from Japan, and a potential rival.[11]

The Sinocentric world order was challenged by the incorporation of the Ryukyu Islands into Japan as Okinawa Prefecture in April 1879. In the early modern period, the Ryukyu kingdom was largely independent, while at the same time, a tributary state of the Chinese empire. It had been invaded by the Satsuma domain in 1609, and Satsuma claimed political supervision. The Meiji government from the beginning aimed to put an end to the ambiguous status of the island kingdom and integrate it into the Japanese state, and finally achieved this by a combination of negotiation with China and unilateral, forceful action.[12]

Nakamura Masanao's English-Chinese-Japanese dictionary, published in 1879 likewise illustrates the trend to "sinicise" what was previously perceived as universal. And in December 1879, the president of Tokyo University proposed the establishment of a special programme to train students in the Japanese and Chinese classics. The study of these texts was thus to be treated as a philological discipline that met the practical needs of the Meiji government; another illustration of the move away from the perceived universal to the particular, in this case also the particularisation of Chinese learning into separate academic disciplines and the separation of moral education from academic training. Not all elements of Chinese learning fitted easily into modern Western categorisations like "science" [*Wissenschaft*] and "religion"; Confucianism with its emphasis on moral conduct as well as book learning is a case in point. In order to address this dilemma, the scholar Nishimura Shigeki (1828–1902) proposed to the Tokyo Academy of Science in 1879 a Confucian "science of the sacred" as the Japanese answer to the Western discipline of theology.

More significant for securing a place for Confucian morals in the transformed educational landscape was the "Imperial Will on Education" [*Kyōgaku seishi*], written by Confucian scholar Motoda Nagazane (or Eifu, 1818–91), senior adviser and personal tutor to the emperor, and issued in September 1879. The emperor's statement on education called for the integration of what the emperor perceived as traditional morals into the modern education system, which was largely based on Western models. The moral concepts named: benevolence, justice, loyalty, and filial piety, were essentially Confucian and the "Imperial Will" thus represents part of the trend to Japanise them.[13]

Confucianism never did attain the status of a religion. Instead, it was skilfully amalgamated with state Shinto notions of the unbroken line of emperors since the Age of the Gods in the "Imperial Rescript of Education" [*Kyôiku chokugo*] in 1890, which also incorporated concepts of modern Western constitutionalism and civic values. Its principal architects included both Motoda Nagazane and Inoue Kowashi who has already been mentioned as the education minister responsible for the temporary closure of the Department for Historical and Topographical Compilation in 1893.[14]

The Imperial Rescript, which schoolchildren were expected to memorise until the end of the Second World War, was written in a highly sinicised style that remained typical of government documents; but already new writing styles, closer to the spoken language, were gaining currency. In 1881, *kanbun* was explicitly named as a school subject for the first time, suggesting that it had begun to be regarded as separate from the national Japanese language.[15] The development of a national language went hand-in-hand with the emerging nationalism that stressed the particular, and the individualism of each country.

The years around 1890 can be regarded as a watershed.[16] With the promulgation of the constitution of 1889 and the opening of the first parliament in 1890, Japan's political framework was determined. The educational reforms of the 1880s created the system that prevailed until 1945, while the Imperial Rescript of 1890 codified the ideological concepts that governed it. In the following years the most pressing foreign policy challenge, the revision of the unequal treaties Japan had been forced to sign in the wake of its enforced opening in the 1850s, were revised; Japan defeated China in the war of 1894-95 and embarked on a course of imperial expansion that made it the only non-Western colonial power in the world. By the time the Meiji era ended in 1912, Japan was a very different country from the one it had been at the time of the Meiji Restoration in 1868.

Thus, even as scholars in the College of Historiography began in earnest to compile the official history, the project was already an anachronism. Dynastic history with a moral agenda was out of step with both modern nationalism and the emerging modern academic disciplines, including national history as distinct from both Western and Chinese history. As the concept of a national language gained ground in the 1880s, *kanbun* was widely perceived as the wrong choice for a history of the nation as well as becoming obsolete as a language to write in. At the same time the place of *kangaku* was under discussion and often subject to criticism as the new disciplines formed. The caricature in *Marumaru chinbun* appeared in this context.

So, had *kangaku* reached a dead end in 1893?[17]

Yes and no. Yes, in the sense that "China" as a normative reference was well on the way out, as was *kangaku* in the sense of a "universal" culture of knowledge. Confucian scholarship, Confucian morals and *kanshi* poetry were no longer one integral whole. The study of China was split into the modern scientific disciplines of Chinese philosophy, Chinese literature and Chinese history.[18] China and Japan were increasingly perceived as distinct nations which, while they had much in common, were separate and in competition with each other. The school system envisaged in the law of 1872, which privileged Western knowledge, became a reality in the course of the 1880s. Meanwhile, the private academies or *juku* that had filled the gap in state provision and often continued to specialise in *kangaku*, dwindled.[19] With the development of a national language the need for advanced *kanbun* skills declined.

Ultimately, however, the answer is no. One might say the men who pulled the cart did find a way around the obstacle. By 1893 *kangaku* was well on its way to being transformed. Chinese texts were still studied, but within the modern academic disciplines. *Kanbun* was no longer written, but it was, and still is, taught in schools, together with the practice of *kundoku* that consisted in decoding a foreign-language text without actually translating it. Chinese characters [*kanji*] were never abolished, despite proposals to do just that. In fact, both Chinese characters and the compounds that could be formed with them, as well as the special *kundoku* practice, played an important role in the acquisition and assimilation of Western knowledge, something contemporaries were well aware of.

Unlike Confucian historians, scholars of the modern discipline of history are not supposed to apportion "praise and blame". The classic British spoof history textbook, *1066 and All That* ridicules the didactic approach to writing history by labelling historical events as a "Good Thing" or "Bad Thing".[20] Nevertheless, and perhaps inevitably, historians, do often evaluate, albeit less crudely. In conclusion, therefore, I will permit myself to be a little provocative. After all, the modern nation state has its critics, as does the practice of taking the nation state as a given that characterised

A Chinese-style garden, part of the 'Kangaku no sato' (Home Village of Chinese Learning) museum in Shitada, Niigata prefecture.

the modern scientific discipline of history and other academic disciplines as they emerged in the 19th century (social scientists speak of "methodological nationalism").

On the plus side was liberation. In a process not dissimilar to that in Europe, what the academic Rens Bod calls "the classical yoke", was gradually discarded,[21] making it possible to accord the history of Japan the same importance as that of ancient China, as well as the study of contemporary China. Both fields benefited from this. In the new fields of Japanese history and literature, for example, enormous amounts of sources were collected, subjected to textual criticism and published in annotated editions with extensive commentaries, which still benefit researchers today.[22]

On the minus side, the breakdown of the unity of the "universal" China and the particularisation of knowledge meant that those elements of *kangaku* that did not fit into modern categories have been neglected. Liberation from the classical yoke by embracing nationalism resulted in a new yoke, which all too soon proved equally limiting.[23] The idea of the nation state is, after all, a Western construction of fairly recent origin.[24] The nationalist yoke has virtually cut Japan off from an important part of its cultural heritage, particularly Japanese literary production in *kanbun*. Nationalism (methodological and otherwise) on both the Japanese and the Chinese side, not only hinders research into *kangaku*, but also the enhanced mutual understanding that a shared appreciation of a heritage not conceived of in national terms might bring.[25]

1. Quoted from Meiji Hennenshi Hensankai, ed. *Shinbun shûsei Meiji hennenshi*, 15 vols., vol. 8 (Zaisei Keizai Gakukai, 1936), p.406.
2. The standard work on education in Tokugawa Japan is still R. P. Dore, *Education in Tokugawa Japan* (The Athlone Press, 1984). See also Peter Nosco, ed. *Confucianism and Tokugawa Culture*, Second (revised) ed. (Honolulu: University of Hawaii Press, 1996). For the history of Confucianism and Chinese learning in Meiji Japan, see Warren Smith, *Confucianism in Modern Japan: A Study of Conservatism in Japanese Intellectual History* (Tokyo1959); Margaret Mehl, 'Chinese Learning (*kangaku*) in Meiji Japan,' *History* 85. (2000): 48-66.
3. For the history of this institution, see Margaret Mehl, *History and the State in Nineteenth-Century Japan: The World, the Nation and the Search for a Modern Past (Second edition with new preface)* (Copenhagen: The Sound Book Press, 2017; 1998).
4. See Margaret Mehl, 'Scholarship and Ideology in Conflict: The Kume Affair, 1892,' *Monumenta Nipponica* vol. 48.3 (1993): 337-57.
5. See also Margaret Mehl, 'The mid-Meiji 'history boom': professionalisation of historical scholarship and growing pains of an emerging academic discipline,' *Japan Forum* vol. 10.1 (1998): 67-83, 73-74.
6. David Mervart, 'Meiji Japan's China Solution to Tokugawa Japan's China Problem,' *Japan Forum* vol. 27.4 (2015): 544-58.
7. Imperial Rescript on Historiography, 4 April, 1869 (*Meiji Tennô shinkan gosatasho, Meiji ninen shigatsu yokka,* Historiographical Institute at the University of Tokyo, S0471–4).
8. The following is a brief summary of Mehl, *History and the State in Nineteenth-Century Japan: The World, the Nation and the Search for a Modern Past (Second edition with new preface)*, pp.19-39.
9. In the early years, the government office had also included scholars of National learning (*kokugaku*), and their opposing views had been a source of conflict. See ibid., pp.20-22, 138–141.
10. See Facius, Michael, *China übersetzen: Globalisierung und Chinesisches Wissen im Japan im 19. Jahrhundert* (Frankfurt/M.: Campus Verlag, 2017), pp.194-250, for most of the following (although his emphasis is different).
11. Katsura's mission was followed by others in the 1880s and 1890s, increasingly in anticipation of an eventual military conflict.
12. China at this time was in no position to resist, but it formally acknowledged Japanese sovereignty over the Ryukyu only after its defeat in the Sino-Japanese war of 1894-95. See McCormack, Gavan and Satoko Oka Norimatsu, 'Ryukyu/Okinawa, From Disposal to Resistance', *The Asia-Pacific Journal* vol. 10.38.1 (2012). At the same time, this was the first step towards acquiring China's historical dependencies (soon to be followed by Taiwan and Korea) and a significant milestone in 'Japan's attempt to inherit China.' Ben-Ami Shillony, 'The Meiji Restoration: Japan's Attempt to Inherit China,' in *War, Revolution & Japan*, ed. Ian Neary, (Sandgate, Folkestone, Kent: Japan Library, 1993), p.29. One might argue

that this ambition reflects the old world view of a sinocentric order; and is an example of the complex transitions that characterise Meiji Japan.

13. For the text and a detailed discussion of the 'Imperial Will on Education', see Benjamin Duke, *The History of Modern Japanese Education: Constructing the National School System, 1872–1890* (New Brunswick, NJ: Rutgers University Press, 2009), pp.257-83.
14. For a discussion of the 'Imperial Rescript on Education', see Carol Gluck, *Japan's Modern Myths: Ideology in the Late Meiji Period* (Princeton, NJ: Princeton University Press, 1985), pp.120-28; Duke, *The History of Modern Japanese Education: Constructing the National School System, 1872–1890*, pp.348-69.
15. Facius, *China übersetzen: Globalisierung und Chinesisches Wissen im Japan im 19. Jahrhundert*, pp.238-49.
16. See for example, Gluck's discussion of the period and her characterisation of it as a 'time of settlement': Gluck, *Japan's Modern Myths: Ideology in the Late Meiji Period*, pp.17-26.
17. For contemporary discussions about the place *kangaku* and observations of its alleged decline, see Facius, *China übersetzen: Globalisierung und Chinesisches Wissen im Japan im 19. Jahrhundert*.
18. For history and the reconfiguration of China as 'Japan's Orient', see Stefan Tanaka, *Japan's Orient: Rendering Past into History* (Berkeley: University of California Press, 1993).
19. For the role of *kangaku juku* in education in the Meiji period, see Margaret Mehl, *Private Academies of Chinese Learning in Meijji Japan: the Decline and Transformation of the Kangaku Juku* (Copenhagen: NIAS Press, 2003).
20. Walter Carruthers Sellar, Robert Julian Yeatman, and John Reynolds, *1066 and All That* (London: Methuen & Co, 1930).
21. Rens Bod, *A New History of the Humanities: The Search for Principles and Patterns from Antiquity to the Present* (Oxford: Oxford University Press, 2015; 2013), p.352.
22. Michael Wachutka, *Kokugaku in Meiji-Period Japan: the Modern Transformation of 'National Learning' and the Formation of Scholarly Societies* (Leiden: Brill, 2014), p.227. The point is equally valid for the contribution of *kangaku* scholars to research in the history of Japan.
23. Bod, *New History*, p.357; ibid.
24. See, for example, Benedict Anderson, *Imagined Communities* (London: Verso, 1991).
25. Here Denecke's comparison with the European discipline of classics is enlightening: Denecke suggests that East Asianists can learn from European classicists, in that classics is a 'catholic, denationalised field' cosmopolitan and egalitarian. See Denecke, Wiebke, *Classical World Literatures: Sino-Japanese and Greco-Roman Comparisons* (Oxford: Oxford University Press, 2014), pp.13–15, 38-39. It has been pointed out that a Japanese sense of their own distinct culture that might be called nationalism can be identified in ancient times, but most scholars appear to agree that even the heightened cultural confidence of the Tokogawa period, of which

the emergence of national learning [*kokugaku*] was a part, cannot be equated with modern nationalism, and that pre-Meiji Japan was not a modern nation state. For a brief, recent discussion, see Peter Francis Kornicki, *Languages, Scripts, and Chinese Texts in East Asia* (Oxford: Oxford University Press, 2018), pp.305–10.

REFERENCES

Anderson, Benedict *Imagined Communities*, (London: Verso, 1991.)

Bod, Rens *A New History of the Humanities: The Search for Principles and Patterns from Antiquity to the Present*, (Oxford: Oxford University Press, 2015, 2013).

Denecke, Wiebke *Classical World Literatures: Sino-Japanese and Greco-Roman Comparisons*, (Oxford: Oxford University Press, 2014.)

Dore, R. P. *Education in Tokugawa Japan*, (The Athlone Press, 1984.)

Duke, Benjamin *The History of Modern Japanese Education: Constructing the National School System, 1872–1890*, (New Brunswick, NJ: Rutgers University Press, 2009.)

Facius, Michael *China übersetzen: Globalisierung und Chinesisches Wissen im Japan im 19 Jahrhundert*, (Frankfurt/M.: Campus Verlag, 2017.)

Gluck, Carol *Japan's Modern Myths: Ideology in the Late Meiji Period*, (Princeton, NJ: Princeton University Press, 1985.)

Kornicki, Peter Francis *Languages, Scripts, and Chinese Texts in East Asia*, (Oxford: Oxford University Press, 2018.)

Mccormack, Gavan and Norimatsu, Satoko Oka 'Ryukyu/Okinawa, From Disposal to Resistance', *The Asia-Pacific Journal* vol.10.38.no.1 (2012).

Mehl, Margaret 'Scholarship and Ideology in Conflict: The Kume Affair, 1892', *Monumenta Nipponica* vol.48.3 (1993) 337-57.

Mehl, Margaret 'The mid-Meiji 'history boom': professionalization of historical scholarship and growing pains of an emerging academic discipline', *Japan Forum* vol.10.1 (1998): 67-83.

Mehl, Margaret 'Chinese Learning (*kangaku*) in Meiji Japan', *History* 85. (2000) 48-66.

Mehl, Margaret *Private Academies of Chinese Learning in Meijji Japan: the Decline and Transformation of the Kangaku Juku*, (Copenhagen: NIAS Press, 2003.)

Mehl, Margaret *History and the State in Nineteenth-Century Japan: The World, the Nation and the Search for a Modern Past*, (Copenhagen: The Sound Book Press, 2nd edition with new preface, 2017; (998).

Meiji Hennenshi Hensankai, ed. *Shinbun shûsei Meiji hennenshi*. 15 vols. vol. 8: Zaisei Keizai Gakukai, (1936).

Mervart, David 'Meiji Japan's China Solution to Tokugawa Japan's China Problem', *Japan Forum* vol. 27.4 (2015) 544-58.

Nosco, Peter ed. *Confucianism and Tokugawa Culture*. (Honolulu: University of Hawaii Press, 2nd 1996.) Sellar, Walter Carruthers, Yeatman, Robert Julian and Reynolds, John *1066 and All That: A Memorable History of England, comprising all the parts you can remember, including 103 Good Things, 5 Bad Kings and 2 Genuine Dates*, (London: Methuen & Co, 1930.)

Shillony, Ben-Ami 'The Meiji Restoration: Japan's Attempt to Inherit China' in *War, Revolution & Japan*, edited by Ian Neary, pp.20-32, (Sandgate, Folkestone, Kent: Japan Library, 1993.)

Smith, Warren *Confucianism in Modern Japan: A Study of Conservatism in Japanese Intellectual History.* (Tokyo: Hokuseido Press, 1959.) Stefan Tanaka, *Japan's Orient: Rendering Past into History.* (Berkeley: University of California Press, 1993.)

Wachutka, Michael *Kokugaku in Meiji-Period Japan: the Modern Transformation of 'National Learning' and the Formation of Scholarly Societies.* (Leiden: Brill, 2014.)

Ise meisho junro no zu
[A Guide to Ise's Famous Sites], 1911.

SHINTO IN MEIJI JAPAN: REFLECTIONS ON ISE

John Breen

Estimates differ, but there were probably in excess of 150,000 "Shinto" shrines across Japan at the time of the Meiji Restoration in 1868. The number includes the great shrines in Ise, the twenty-two shrines of the home provinces, the *ichinomiya* provincial shrines, not to mention the many district and village shrines, some attended by priests but many not. Of these, very few escaped the attentions of the Restoration government. Bureaucrats now sanctioned the stripping from shrines of their sacred Buddhist objects, such as statuary, bells and sutras, the confiscation of shrine land, the excision of shrine priests, the displacement of shrine *kami* [gods], the reconfiguring of shrine rites, and interventions in shrine festivals.[1] Many shrines were destroyed.[2] And the purpose of this bureaucratic endeavour? To prime shrines for their new public role: as carriers of the imperial myth. The modern state tasked shrines and their priests with bearing ritual witness to the truth of the emperor's descent from the sun goddess, Amaterasu Ōmikami. This was the imperial myth in which the new government rooted its legitimacy.

Yet, even in their modern Meiji guise, government bureaucrats hardly privileged shrines or their priests. Bureaucrats blew hot and cold, and, if the truth be known, there were but two shrines in all the realm which they unfailingly favoured: the Ise shrines in south central Japan, and the Yasukuni shrine in Tokyo. Ise was a 7th century shrine-complex that enshrined Amaterasu, the sun goddess, at the Inner Shrine [*naikū*] – one of its two main sanctuaries – and Toyouke, a servant deity, at the Outer [*gekū*]. In the early modern period, at least, the Ise complex was the greatest site of popular pilgrimage in all Japan. The Yasukuni shrine, by contrast, was a 19th-century invention; it was created by the modern state to commemorate, and celebrate, the sacrifice of the 3,500 or so men who died for the imperial cause in the Boshin Civil War of 1868.

As determined by the Meiji government, there quickly emerged two broad categories of shrine: "state shrines" or *kansha* and "miscellaneous shrines" or *shosha*. The former, broadly speaking, were traditionally important shrines sponsored by central and provincial governments. It is true that the Meiji government initially sponsored these sites, their rites and their priests, but in 1887 it drew up plans to set them all adrift and have them fend for themselves. Only Ise and Yasukuni were exempted.

The discussion of Shinto and the state that follows centres on the Ise shrine complex and the dynamics of its Meiji period transformation. Ise may not be typical, but it became the most sacred site in the modern state. No account of Shinto in Meiji can ignore it.

★

In order to gauge the impact of the Meiji Restoration on the Ise shrines, it will be useful first to get a sense of Ise's shrinescape as it was on the eve of the Restoration. Tenaka Toshikage, a pilgrim from Sagami province in east-central Japan, will serve as our guide. Tenaka was one of some 400,000 pilgrims who headed to Ise in 1841. We know of his movements thanks to the diary he kept. Using his diary and the *Ise sangū meisho ichiran* [Ise's Famous Sites: An Overview for Pilgrims], an 1856 pilgrims' guide to famous places, we can explore Ise's topography. Tenaka arrived in Ise in New Year 1841, and crossed the Miyakawa River. Heading east along the pilgrims' road, he passed through Yamada into the Furuichi pleasure quarters, and on to Futami on the coast, where he purified himself in the sea. He backtracked to Yamada to check in at the Kameda Inn, whose owner served him up a feast. The next day he worshipped at the Outer Shrine, and its forty auxiliary shrines, and then climbed Mount Takakura, the site of the Heavenly Rock Cave [*Ama no Iwato*], where he took in the views of Yamada town. He returned to the inn for a performance of *kagura* dance, and more feasting. Tenaka spent a day at the inn waiting for the rains to clear, before setting off again through Furuichi to Uji, where he worshipped at the Inner Shrine and its cluster of eighty auxiliary shrines. He climbed Mount Asama, venerated at the Kongōshōji temple there, and enjoyed the stunning vistas of Ise Bay before returning to Furuichi. And there, in the Bizen'ya, the most famous of Furuichi's many brothels, he spent the night.[3]

We have been in Tenaka's company long enough to grasp the defining features of the Ise shrinescape as it was on the eve of Restoration. First, Ise comprised two centres – the towns of Yamada and Uji, built around two

Ise sangū meisho ichiran [Ise's Famous Sites: An Overview for Pilgrims], 1856.

sacred sites, the Outer and Inner Shrines. Pilgrimage studies lead us to expect a single centre, perhaps, but Ise has two. What is especially noteworthy is that for centuries they have been at each other's throats; the very nature of the sacred in pre-Restoration Ise is contested. And secondly, Ise has at its epicentre the flourishing Furuichi pleasure quarters. Furuichi straddles the pilgrims' path so that Tenaka Toshikage and all Ise pilgrims have no choice but to negotiate it. For a time, it is perhaps the third largest pleasure quarters in all the land. This interconnectivity between the secular and the sacred in pre-Restoration Ise is distinctive.

★

In the modern Meiji period, an erstwhile Ise priest called Matsuki Tokihiko reflected on the importance to pilgrims of the pleasure quarters:

> There was nobody who did not associate Ise pilgrimage with Furuichi. It was famous throughout the land ... Pilgrims came to Ise in their tens of thousands, and of the vast amounts of cash they dispensed with, almost all went into Furuichi. It was never the case that those vigorous young men ... came to Ise to offer thanks to the *kami* with performances of *kagura* dance, or to recite prayers for family wellbeing. Their one and only purpose was to blow all their cash on a night of pleasure in the [Bizenya] brothel.[4]

Matsuki Tokihiko was an influential and respected figure in Meiji period Ise; we should not dismiss his observations lightly. Matsuki is proposing that we regard early modern Ise pilgrimages as "sex tourism". Indeed, pilgrims' diaries, like the diary of Tenaka Toshikage, attest to the validity of his proposal. Matsuki's statement is furthermore an invitation to reflect on the highly gendered nature of the early modern Ise pilgrimage: it was primarily a male undertaking.[5]

Furuichi's origins can be traced back to the late 17th century. By 1700 there were sixty brothels accommodating 162 women, but a century later in 1800, 1,000 women were working in Ise's seventy-four brothels. This was a time when popular culture picked up on Furuichi as never before. In 1796, there was a mass murder in the Aburaya brothel, instigated by one of the patrons, a certain Magofuku Itsuki of the famous Magofuku family of shrine priests, who went berserk. The incident was written up into a famous *kabuki* play, called *Ise ondo koi no netaba* [Ise Dancing: The Dull Sword of Passion] which was performed in theatres in Kyoto, Osaka and the capital, Edo. The following year, Furuichi featured prominently in the *Ise sangū meisho zue* [Ise Pilgrimage: An Illustrated Guide], a new, popular and abundantly illustrated guide for Ise pilgrims. Then in 1802, the writer Jippensha Ikku published a revised edition of his hit comedy novel, *Tōkaidōchū hizakurige* [Shanks' Mare], which has the two protagonists, Yaji and Kita, head to Ise. Their first port of call, and the scene of much merriment, is Furuichi. Note that Furuichi always offered more than sex: there were also three theatres where *kabuki* was performed. In the late 18th century, it was said that an actor who performed well in Furuichi was guaranteed success in Edo, Osaka and Kyoto. There was too, for a while, *noh* drama performed by women, and magic shows besides.

★

Any discussion of the sacred in pre-Restoration Ise must focus on the Outer and Inner Shrines, and the tensions between their priests. What accounts for these tensions? Ise priests were, broadly speaking, of two varieties. Some attended to the shrines, performing there daily and seasonal rites; others, known as *oshi*, were primarily pilgrim-oriented. The former all belonged to one of two hereditary priestly families: the Watarai family served at the Outer shrine in Yamada, while the Arakida family were attached to the Inner shrine in Uji. The *oshi* families were also attached to one or other shrine. There were some 600 families altogether, two thirds of which were Yamada-based Outer Shrine *oshi*. Our pilgrim, Tenaka, stayed at the Kameda Inn, the Kameda being a middle-ranking *oshi*. Some of these *oshi* accumulated fabulous wealth. The Mikkaichi, for example, ran a "parish" that extended from central to northern Japan, comprising a staggering 354,000 households. *Oshi* met parishioners' spiritual needs – *oshi* is an abbreviation of *onkitōshi* or "prayer master"; they dispatched deputies, known as *tedai*, to the provinces yearly to sell amulets and offer prayers. They also arranged pilgrimages, and provided accommodation in their often luxurious inns back in Ise.[6] Parishioner pilgrims, then, were the source of *oshi* livelihoods; the greater their number, the greater the *oshi*'s income. The principal cause of conflict was the *oshi* appropriation of each other's parishioners.

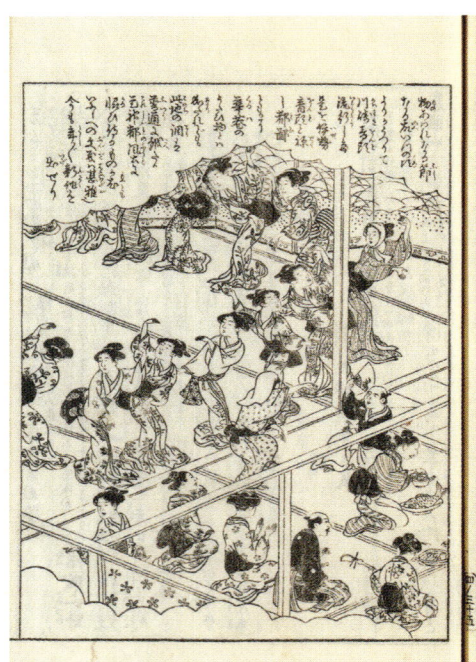

The Furuichi pleasure quarters in Akisato Ritō and Shitomi Kangetsu. *Ise sangū meisho zue* (Ise Pilgrimage: An Illustrated Guide), Tōyōdo, 1944.

But theology was at stake, too. Above all, it concerned the identity of the Outer Shrine and its *kami*, Toyouke Ōkami. Pre-Restoration Outer Shrine theory proposed that Toyouke Ōkami was a mystical manifestation of two *kami*, Kunitokotachi no mikoto and Amenominakanushi no kami. Now, these two *kami* are respectively the first to appear in the *Nihon shoki* and the *Kojiki*, the two 7th-century myth histories; they are primordial *kami* and, in some versions, creator *kami*. This theory had its distant origins in medieval Ise theology; it was then forgotten and rediscovered in the 17th century.[7] There is, incidentally, nothing at all in the myth histories to suggest either Kunitokotachi or Amenominakanushi were in any way connected with the Outer Shrine in pre-medieval times. The theory was important, though, as an assertion that the Outer Shrine trumped the Inner Shrine; their *kami* – as *kami* of origin – was superior to the Inner Shrine *kami*, the *kami* of the sun. In the early 19th century, Motoori Norinaga, the pioneering scholar of the *Kojiki*, struck back, arguing the absurdity of equating Toyouke Ōkami with cosmogony. Norinaga's counter-theory scoffed at Outer Shrine pretensions, and resituated Toyouke as a servant *kami*, subordinate to the sun goddess Amaterasu. Inevitably, Outer Shrine priests returned fire.

It is difficult to know what impact, if any, these theories exerted on the practices of the common pilgrim. Diaries reveal frustratingly little: "Worshipped at the Outer shrine and the forty auxiliary shrines; venerated at the Inner shrine and the eighty auxiliary shrines; climbed Mt Asama".[8] In this typical entry, there is no sense of awe; no sense, either, that the pilgrim has any particular knowledge of the shrines or their *kami*. Scattered sources do suggest, though, that Outer Shrine theory did leave its mark. The protagonists of Jippensha's 1802 novel, for example, knew the *kami* of the Outer Shrine to be Kunitokotachi. In his writings on Japanese society in the 1850s, an Osaka merchant celebrated the Outer Shrine precisely on account of its primordial *kami*. The Outer Shrine, moreover, was always more important to pilgrims, it seems, than the Inner Shrine. This was partly the result of *oshi* propaganda and partly a consequence of easier access. But the point is made with graphic force by Andō Hiroshige in his 1856 print, *Ise sangū ryakuzu* [Ise Pilgrimage: An Abbreviated Guide]. It is the Outer Shrine, its priests and its pilgrims, that dominate the foreground here; the Inner Shrine – and the sun goddess too – are reduced to a mere label in the background.

伊勢參宮略圖

二見浦
内宮正殿
外宮拜殿
玉串御門
朝熊山
古市

By Andō Hiroshige. *Ise sangū ryakuzu* [Ise Pilgrimage: An Abbreviated Guide], 1856.

Before the Restoration, pilgrims numbered between 300,000 and 400,000 a year. They were mostly men, their pilgrimages funded through membership of Ise's countless pious associations, known as *Ise kō*.[9] But, on three occasions, in 1705, 1771 and in 1830, pilgrims came to Ise in their millions. Numbers were swollen by women, children and people of all social classes; precisely those not normally admitted to the pious associations. What generated these extraordinary phenomena, known as *okage mairi* or "thanksgiving" pilgrimages, was the expectation of miracles.[10] The miraculous emerges as a key feature of the sacred in early modern Ise. Miracle stories proliferated in these years, and local men of letters, like Minowa Zairoku, compiled them. The events of 1830, for example, began when an eight-year-old boy from Awa province leapt on a white horse and headed to Ise; he later returned home, dismounted, and turned around to find that the horse had disappeared leaving only a pile of dung; close by lay an Ise amulet. People understood this as a summons to Ise, and responded. Such, at least, was Minowa's understanding. Many stories featured, and were clearly targeted at, women: women, whose husbands suffer paralysis when they refuse wives and children permission to go to Ise; women who recover miraculously from disease en route to Ise; women who lose their children only to find them again due to divine intercession. Other stories featured Buddhists, like a monk in Kawachi province, who swept up Ise amulets that had fallen miraculously from the heavens to burn them. He himself suffered terrible burns when the flames ignited his robes; his parishioners took this as divine punishment, and duly headed off to Ise.[11]

★

It is spring 1869, and the Meiji emperor, en route from Kyoto to the new capital of Tokyo, is poised to enter Ise's Inner Shrine. This is an epoch-making moment, as Meiji is the first emperor in Japanese history ever to set foot here. He proceeds through to the shrine's inner sanctuary, stops at the foot of the wooden steps, and makes an offering to the sun goddess. He reports to her on the formation of the new Restoration government and prays for Japan's fortunes. The emperor's presence here is transformative: it locates Ise anew as a public, imperial site; it identifies the Inner Shrine *kami*, Amaterasu, as the emperor's ancestress and him as her filial descendant. The emperor worships his divine ancestress, and the event is

By Matsuoka Eikyū. "Jingū shin'etsu"
[The Emperor's Ise Audience], 1937.
The Meiji Shrine in Tokyo.

proclaimed as the ultimate act of filial piety. This is the myth upon which the new government built its ideological foundations, and hereafter several things happened in quick succession.

First, government bureaucrats issued a formal declaration of Inner Shrine superiority, and even debated demolishing the Outer Shrine. The primordial *kami* of pre-Restoration Ise theory, Kunitokotachi and Amenominakanushi were banished now for good. Bureaucrats excised the entire Ise priesthood, ending the practice of heredity. The priests of the Watarai and Arakida families who served the Outer and Inner shrines were removed, and replaced by state appointees with links to neither family. The Fujinami and Kawabe families, whose heads had for generations supplied the incumbents of the Ise chief of rituals and the Ise chief priest respectively, were ousted, their place taken by members of the new nobility. Bureaucrats banished all 600 *oshi* priest families, effecting the collapse of their nationwide network of parishioner-pilgrims; pilgrim numbers plummeted. Bureaucrats also sanctioned a devastating purge of Buddhism, removing from Ise and its environs 183 Buddhist temples in all. They also swept aside the cluster of forty auxiliary shrines in Yamada and the eighty shrines in Uji. They reconfigured Ise's annual cycle of shrine rites, abandoning twenty-six traditional rites, creating twenty-one anew, and revising some forty-two others. Ise's modern rites now chimed with the ritual cycle of the modern imperial court.[12]

These reforms were fashioned by ideologues and commissioned by central government. Yet no man had a greater impact on their creation than former Inner Shrine priest Urata Chōmin: the reforms can all be traced back to petitions Urata submitted to central government in the wake of the restoration. Government officials acknowledged his vital contribution, and rewarded him with a posting to Tokyo in 1871. There he worked with other bureaucrats on an extraordinary scheme to remove the sacred mirror from Ise's Inner Shrine, and enshrine it in the Tokyo palace. Urata later distanced himself from the scheme, and returned to Ise in 1872 as assistant chief priest. His influence continued; his work was far from done. He developed a striking new Ise theology that reimagined Amaterasu as creator of heaven and earth. He built a college in Ise – the Jingū kyōin – where the new theology would be taught and studied; and he created a nationwide network of local "churches" [*kyōkai*] based on the old provincial pious associations. These became the foundation for a new religion, Jingūkyō. The influence on Urata of Western Christianity was profound.[13]

There was also a striking physical dimension to the reforms that swept through Ise after the restoration. It is evident in the somewhat later illustration from 1895 on the following pages. Bureaucrats wrapped the Inner Shrine – and the Outer Shrine too – in new head-high, fourfold fencing. The idea was not so much to prevent pilgrims from worshipping at Ise – after all, in 1871, the government allowed Buddhist monks, as well as members of the erstwhile outcaste communities, and foreigners, too, to venerate at Ise for the first time. Rather, it was to prompt awe among pilgrims for a site that bureaucrats increasingly referred to as the emperor's 'ancestral mausoleum' [*daibyō*]. Thus, the Inner and Outer Shrines at Ise were primed for their vital role in the modern Japanese nation state. These major reforms were imposed on Ise from above, as it were; but they were complemented by much endeavour initiated from below.

The single most important figure here was a man called Ōta Kosaburō, the manager of the Bizen'ya, the most successful of Furuichi's many brothels. In the 1880s, he found common cause with the new Ise chief priest, a man called Kashima Norifumi. Both men were profoundly concerned at the drop in pilgrim numbers, and were determined to take action. They joined forces with the Mie prefecture governor, and with Urata Chōmin, who was now governor of Watarai district, and founded a charitable organisation called the Shin'enkai or Sacred Garden Society. Their purpose was to transform the Ise shrinescape, the better to encourage the pilgrims' return. They proposed a two-phase transformation. The first phase involved the demolition and removal of houses, inns and restaurants from the Inner and Outer shrines' immediate vicinity; reimagining and redesigning these formerly cluttered, bustling spaces as 'sacred gardens'. The second phase was altogether more ambitious. It involved the purchase and development of a large swathe of land on Kuratayama, a hill equidistant between the Outer and Inner Shrines. The idea was to create "a vast park space", featuring a history museum, an agricultural museum, a library, an aquarium, a zoo, and a racetrack. The declared aim was to "stimulate the senses of the modern pilgrim with natural and manmade objects from across the world". The final piece of the plan involved constructing a new road to link Kuratayama north to the Outer Shrine and south to the Inner Shrine, thus transforming the entire Ise shrinescape.

All of this required raising stupendous sums of money. Ōta and Kashima set off for Tokyo at the end of 1888 to elicit the support of the

Kōtai jingū kyūchū no zu [Main Sanctuary Inner Shrine: Illustration] in Jingū Shichō, ed. *Shinto meishōshi* [Record of Famous Sites in the Sacred Capital] (vol.4), Jingū Shichō, 1895.

great and the good, to boost their fundraising campaign. Their excursion proved an extraordinary success. Prince Arisugawa no Miya, Ise's Tokyo-resident chief of rituals, agreed to join the Sacred Garden Society as president. The under-secretary of the Imperial Household Ministry became chairman; and among those who filled the vacant positions of trustees were the justice minister and the finance and home affairs minister, and the great entrepreneur, Shibusawa Eiichi. The empress and the empress dowager both made substantial donations to the society. The Sacred Garden Society flourished for the next two decades, before disbanding in 1911 at the very end of the reign of the Meiji emperor. The society left a lasting legacy, which is easiest to grasp visually. The illustration on page 488 is styled the *Ise meisho junro no zu* [A Guide to Ise's Famous Sites], a print of modern Ise produced for pilgrims in the year the society disbanded.

The print is framed by the Inner Shrine compound on the right, and the Outer Shrine compound on the left. It is the expanse between them that draws our gaze. This is Kuratayama, opened to the public in 1909 as a quintessentially modern space. In the end, there was to be no aquarium, zoo, or racetrack, but it is extraordinary nonetheless. The central domed-structure is the Chōkokan, Japan's first ever history museum. It was designed by the architect, Katayama Tōkuma, responsible for the national museums that now stood in the cities of Tokyo, Kyoto and Nara. It was built of stone in the Western style, and boasted a garden inspired by Versailles. Its exhibits were arranged thematically not chronologically. Intriguingly, there were Buddhist objects aplenty here; but no space was set aside to articulate the myth of the emperor's descent from the sun goddess. In front of the Chōkokan, the Nōgyōkan is visible. This building in wood, inspired in its design by the Phoenix Hall at the Byōdōin Buddhist temple in Kyoto, was Japan's first ever municipal natural history museum. The roofed structure to the rear of the Chōkokan is the Gyobutsukan, a gallery displaying Ise shrine treasures.

The print illustrates well the centrality of Kuratayama to modern Ise, a centrality which owed much to the completion of the Imperial Road [*Miyuki dōri*] in 1910. The Sacred Garden Society funded the road from Kuratayama north to Yamada in 1903; in 1910, Mie prefecture funded the final stretch from Kuratayama south to Uji. One outcome of the road's construction was immediately clear: no pilgrim – emperor or commoner – need now travel the narrow steep path from Yamada through the

Furuichi pleasure quarters to Uji. This new road is effectively a Furuichi by-pass. It dislocates the pleasure quarters from Ise's epicentre, dealing a fatal blow to Furuichi's fortunes. Kuratayama takes its place, at least in the imagination of Ōta Kosaburō and the Sacred Garden Society. The irony here is inescapable: Ōta, after all, was Furuichi's wealthiest brothel keeper.

The print also shows the new gardens of the Inner and Outer Shrines. The Inner Shrine garden is visible just to the left of the shrine compound. Standing erect in the centre is a cannon barrel, a gift from the imperial navy following Japan's victory in the Russo-Japanese war. The new garden itself, based on a design by Ozawa Keijirō, comprises thousands of square metres of lawn, linked by paths packed with white gravel. There are pines, plum, cherry and peach trees, and thousands of shrubs. The consensus was that these gardens more than fulfilled their brief of entertaining and enlightening Ise's modern pilgrims. Contemporary guidebooks are fulsome in their praise for these new spaces, and the pleasures they bring to the modern pilgrim. Finally, note the steam train crossing the Miyakawa Bridge into Yamada Station. The advent of the train – as much as anything – brought pilgrims back to Ise in something like pre-Meiji numbers. There are streetcars, too, running between Yamada and Uji, and out to Futami on the coast. Steam trains and streetcars were not part of the Sacred Garden Society project, but they were as integral to Ōta Kosaburō's vision of modern Ise as museums and gardens. Ōta founded the Pilgrims' Railway Company [*Sangū testudō kabushiki kaisha*] in 1890, the year after his fund-raising trip to Tokyo. The railway reached Yamada in 1897. Ōta also founded the Ise Electric Company [*Ise denki kabushiki kaisha*], which brought street cars to Ise. They were running in Yamada in 1903, and they linked the Outer to Inner shrines via Kuratayama in 1906.

★

To all this endeavour, there was an imaginative legacy. Pre-Restoration pilgrims headed to Ise in expectation of carnal pleasures and miraculous happenings. Notwithstanding former shrine priest Matsuki Tokihiko's assertions about sex and pilgrimage, Ise was also a place where private prayers were offered, and no doubt answered. However, modern pilgrims came to imagine contemporary Ise as something quite other: public not private, sacred yet certainly not religious – religion meant Buddhism and

Christianity – and as quintessentially modern. They knew Ise as the sovereign's ancestral mausoleum; as physical – and so irrefutable – evidence of the sacred nature of Japan's imperial line.

So much then for Ise's dynamic transformation at the hands of central bureaucrats and local entrepreneurs during the Meiji period. What though was the fate in the Meiji period of the realm's 150,000 or so other shrines? By the end of the period, every shrine was now, in name at least, a non-religious site for the performance of state rites, supervised by the Home Ministry's new Shrine Bureau [Jinjakyoku]. Shrine priests across the land were banned from preaching, from selling amulets and from performing funerals; their sole task was the performance of modern rites designed to ensure the imperial myth reverberated across the realm. The Shrine Bureau disbursed funds, but only to the small number of elite national and imperial shrines [*kansha*]; the remainder [*shosha*] struggled to survive on their wits and the goodwill of parishioners. The most significant legacy of the Shrine Bureau? It was perhaps the unleashing of a wave of violence that reconfigured the national shrinescape. At the end of Meiji, the bureau oversaw the obliteration of some 80,000 shrines, deemed unworthy or incapable of performing state rites. In late Meiji, after the Russo-Japanese war, "One Village, One Shrine" was the new slogan; shrines were henceforth to be the official centre for moral regeneration in villages and towns across the land.[14] The history of the Meiji state in its relationship to Shinto is nothing if not complex.

1. For the impact of these policies as they played out on the Hie shrines in Shiga Prefecture in the early Meiji period, see Breen and Teeuwen 2010, pp.108–115.
2. Breen (2000, pp.243–48) documents the early Meiji destruction of shrines in the Tōhoku region.
3. For details of Tenaka's Ise sojourn, see Teeuwen and Breen 2017, pp.140–41.
4. Matsuki 1932, pp.3–4.
5. On sex and the Ise pilgrimage, see Teeuwen and Breen 2017, pp.141–43.
6. The heads of the wealthiest *oshi* families also served as aldermen on the town councils of Yamada and Uji. On *oshi* and their parishioner-pilgrims, see Teeuwen and Breen 2017, pp.147–54.
7. For medieval outer shrine theory, its early modern rediscovery and dissemination, see especially Saitō 2016, pp.152–59.
8. This is cited in Kai 2015, pp.65–166.
9. On the workings of these pious associations, see Teeuwen and Breen 2017, pp.152–54.
10. On Ise pilgrimages in these years, see especially Davis 1992, Nenzi 2006 and Hardacre 2017, pp. 287–95.
11. These and other stories are discussed in Teeuwen and Breen 2017, pp.155–57.
12. For an overview of the early Meiji reforms in Ise, see Teeuwen and Breen 2017, pp.164–72 and Hardacre 2017, pp.371–73.
13. On Urata's endeavour, see Teeuwen and Breen 2017, pp.174–76.
14. On these so-called shrine mergers, see Fridell 1973 passim and Hardacre 2017, pp. 416–18.

REFERENCES

Breen, John 'Ideologues, bureaucrats and priests: on Buddhism and Shintō in early Meiji Japan,' in John Breen and Teeuwen, Mark eds. *Shintō in history: ways of the kami*, (Honolulu: Hawaii University Press, 2000.)

Breen, John and Teeuwen, Mark *A New History of Shinto*, (New Jersey: Wiley-Blackwell, 2010.)

Davis, Winston *Japanese Religion and Society: Paradigms of Structure and Change*, (Albany NY: SUNY Press, 1992.)

Fridell, Wilbur M. *Japanese Shrine Mergers 1906–12: Shinto moves to the grassroots*, (Tokyo: Sophia University, 1973.)

Teeuwen, Mark and Breen, John *A Social History of the Ise Shrines: Divine Capital*, (London: Bloomsbury, 2017.)

Hardacre, Helen *Shinto: History,* (Oxford: Oxford University Press, 2017.)

Kai Motozumi, *Ise sangū nikki o yomu,* (Fukuoka: Kaichōsha, 2015.)

Tokihiko, Matsuki *Shinto hyaku monogatari*, (Furukawa Shoten, 1929.)

Nenzi, Laura 'To Ise at All Costs: Religious and Economic Implications of Early Modern *Nukemairi'*, *Japanese Journal of Religious Studies*, vol. 33:1 (2006), pp.75–114.

Hideki, Saitō 'Yomigaerareta Ise jingū: Deguchi Nobuyoshi, Motoori Norinaga o chūshin ni'. In Breen, John ed., *Hen'yō suru seichi: Ise.* (Kyoto: Shibunkaku, 2016.)

一、廣ク會議ヲ興シ萬機公論ニ決スベシ
一、上下心ヲ一ニシテ盛ニ經綸ヲ行フベシ
一、官武一途庶民ニ至ル迄各其志ヲ遂ゲ人心ヲシテ倦マザラシメン事ヲ要ス
一、舊來ノ陋習ヲ破リ天地ノ公道ニ基クベシ
一、智識ヲ世界ニ求メ大ニ皇基ヲ振起スベシ

我國未曾有ノ變革ヲ爲ントシ朕躬ヲ以テ衆ニ先ンジ天地神明ニ誓ヒ大ニ斯國是ヲ定メ萬民保全ノ道ヲ立ントス衆亦此旨趣ニ基キ協心努力セヨ

Government documents of the Japanese empire: Charter Oath of the Meiji Restoration.

THE BUDDHA IS DEAD, LONG LIVE THE BUDDHA

James E. Ketelaar

A common litany of Meiji era (1868–1912) refigurations of the social order in Japan may read as follows: a divinised and recentralised imperial polity; expanded programmes for education, conscription, and taxation; a vitalised industrial and mercantile economy; the creation of national railway, banking, postal and telegraph systems; Asia's first constitution; the defeat of China and Russia; and the establishment of the Japanese imperial colonial empire. The Meiji era discourse on culture, to which these refigurations are intimately related, revolved around the creation – some would say recovery – of a national identity. This identity was manufactured by means of the staging of ostensibly ancient institutions and symbols and the simultaneous insistence upon the eternal efficacy of the "Japanese" spirit that formed the ground from which these symbols emerged. The "unity of [religious] rite and [political] rule" [祭政一致 *saisei itchi*], it was claimed, was possible (or rather necessary) precisely because of the ontological primacy of the imperial state. "Japan" existed as an always already present consubstantiality of the land, the people and the imperially sanctioned ruling bureaucracy. To be born in this land was to "be" Japanese; clearly, such a strategic ontology was not without profound and far reaching consequences.

In the early years of the Meiji era, when the desire for the holy grail of "civilisation and enlightenment" [文明開化 *bummei kaika*] was swelling to unbearable levels, an eclectic plethora of institutions and practices was perceived as devolutionary anathema, worthy of the most profound censure. The promise of the fourth article of the Meiji state's Charter Oath promulgated in 1868 was that "evil customs of the past shall be broken off and all based upon the just laws of nature". Even as the conception of "nature" here was to slide between positivistic or scientific conceptions of the world and a divinely ordained ontology and epistemology, so too were the interpretations of "ancient evils" to escape a static definition. Most certainly, families, institutions or practices associated with the

Next pages: Buddha in Nirvana.

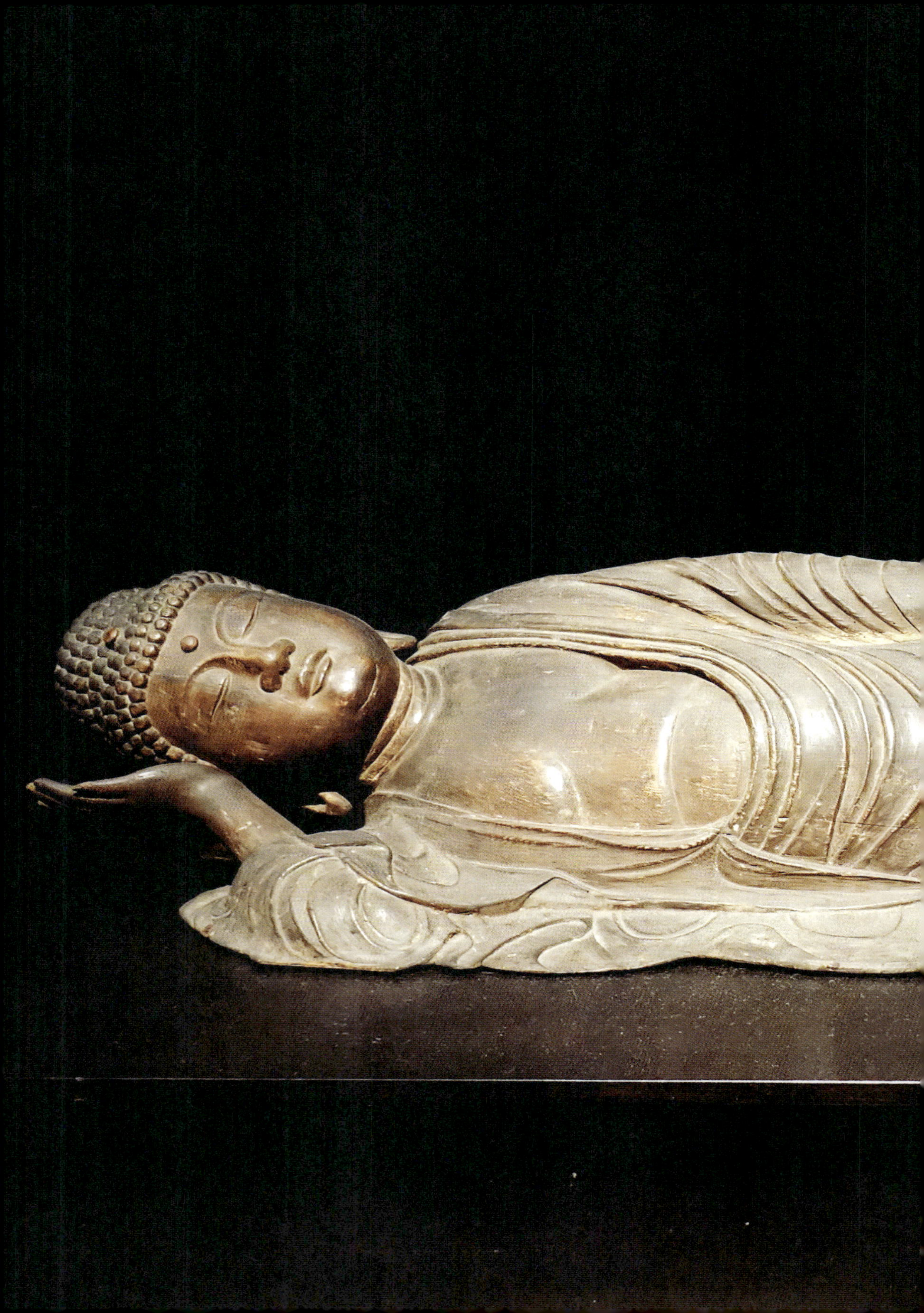

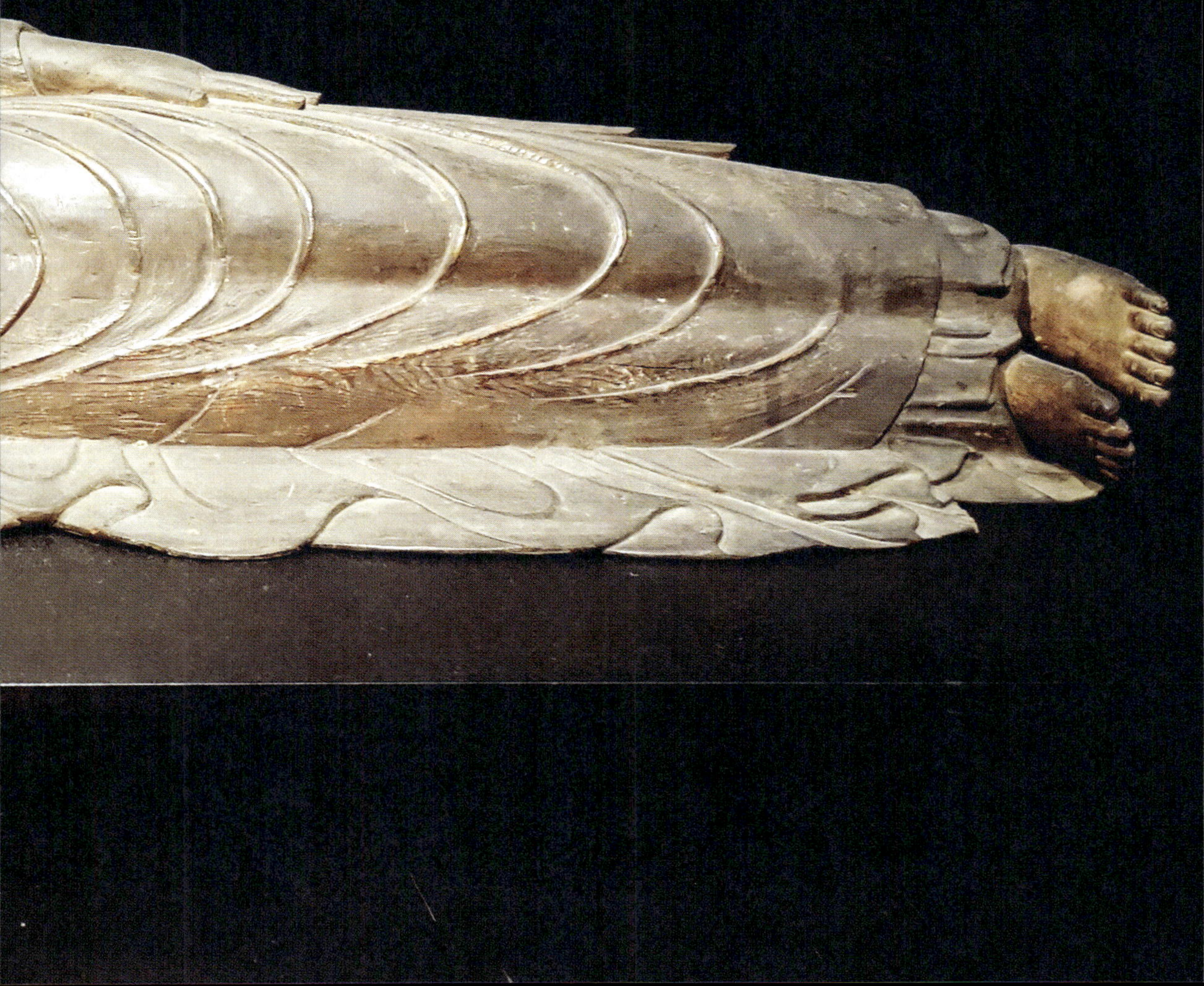

erstwhile ruling Tokugawa clan and its bureaucracy were cast immediately as a persecutable other. Witness, for example, the confiscation of the Tokugawa clan's ancestral Buddhist temple, the *Zôjô-ji*, and its subsequent use as the national headquarters of the fledgling Meiji government's Ministry of Doctrine: an ideological tour de force of overlaying the old with the new. As the conception of "civilisation" gradually took hold, the list of persecutable ancient evils also expanded. Prostitution and concubinage, fixed class and employment status, divination and possession, public nudity and stand-up comics, and numerous other practices counter to the national evolution were variously attacked, outlawed or, through the process of education, otherwise gradually removed from the list of acceptable national customs. Such cultural restructuring was a necessary prerequisite to entering what statesman and diplomat Mori Arinori in 1874 called the "glorious realm of enlightenment". Only after such a cultural enlightenment of the general populace could the nation "construct machines, erect buildings, dig mines, build ships, open seaways, produce carriages, and improve highways". These were the means, that is, by which "the virtues of social intercourse [would] spread through the liberal expansion of commerce, products [would] reach perfection as machines are increasingly refined, and men [could] ultimately appreciate the true value of civilisation".[1]

★

In fact, the brunt of this cultural *auto-da-fé* was initially borne by Buddhism. Identified as "foreign" in origin (thus antithetical to nativist conceptions of ontological purity), economically unproductive (thus a drain on the "national" drive towards a "wealthy nation and a strong military"), and culturally primitive (thus inappropriate in a land dedicated to cosmopolitan enlightenment ideals), Buddhism was attacked from all directions. Ubiquitous, popular and powerful, Buddhism, humbled by this heretical refiguration, sought desperately during the early Meiji era for a strategy capable of withstanding these multifaceted critiques. Institutional Buddhism finally succeeded, I contend, in escaping from this charge of cultural heresy by acknowledging and incorporating the power of "civilisation" and its outriders of utilitarianism, nationalism and positivism. Institutional Buddhism succeeded, that is, in re-reading its 19th-century persecution as a necessary step in the creation of its

A torii or formalised gateway arch that traditionally marks the entrance to a Shinto shrine.

modern subjectivity. Concomitantly, the martyrdom of "traditional" Buddhism, along with the plethora of other "ancient evils", was an essential component of the newly created national identity.[2]

The means by which Buddhist thinkers and activists succeeded in extricating institutional Buddhism from its persecution is a topic much larger than the scope of this short essay. The methods of Buddhist self-redefinition are in fact related to the foundations of "modern Japan" per se and the manifold creations of this volatile era. Similar to the early Meiji ideologues' creation of an "imperial system" [*tennôsei*], ostensibly derived from ancient formulas yet inexorably a child of the modern imagination, the New Buddhism [新仏教 *Shimbukkyô*] and its attendant buddhology [仏教学 *Bukkyôgaku*] and Buddhist historiography [仏教史学 *Bukkyôshigaku*] claimed an ancient and verifiable origin yet could do so only through a radical attack on its own presuppositions. Some Buddhists turned to history to "defend the dharma" [護法 *gohô*] from its ever present and vociferous enemies. Indeed, history could and did serve the strategic function of allowing for the creation of critical positions from which a countering of anti-Buddhist rhetoric and legislation was possible. Charges of anti-imperialism, for example, could be met by appealing to the historical record to enumerate the numerous emperors and members of the imperial family who had taken Buddhist vows, built Buddhist temples, or otherwise supported the promulgation of the Buddhist teachings. The incorporation of historical strategies into an analysis of the Buddhist position in 19th-century Japan was, moreover, based upon the assumption of the possibility of hermeneutic exegesis, the positivistic analysis of necessarily verifiable facts, and a rational clarity of narrative presentation. One result of this marriage of 19th-century historiographical practice and Buddhism was, I contend, the veritable death, if not the murder, of Buddha.

Broadly speaking, Buddhism sought to constitute itself as a social, political, philosophical, and historical religion; it sought to become a modern, cosmopolitan and universal religious organisation. Or, in the words of one prominent Meiji Buddhist priest: Japanese Buddhism must "become a Buddhism for the family, a Buddhism of marriage, a Buddhism for the workplace, a Buddhism for the military, a Buddhism for celebration, a Buddhism for all ages".[3] Accompanying, indeed in support of, this self-definition was the exhaustive researching and writing of the history of Buddhism per se. To bridge the vast expanse of time and place that separated the "origin" of Buddhism from the contemporary world they found it necessary, in the words of Murakami Senshô,[4] one of the first modern Buddhist historians, to discard the "imaginary age" (空想時代 *kûsô jidai*) and ascertain the "actual age" (事実時代 *jijitsu jidai*) of Buddha's life and Buddhism's past. Such an epistemological shift would be possible only through rigorous "logical research" and "historical excavation" which must be presented to both Buddhists and non-Buddhists alike in a "sober-minded", "trustworthy", and "commonsensical" fashion.[5]

In practical terms, Meiji era Buddhists accomplished their escape from persecution in several ways. Obfuscation was very popular (for example going through the motions of carrying out "Shinto" style rituals but continuing with Buddhist practices on the sly); local popular faith was another: in many cases direct and extensive appeals curtailed, and even stopped, the persecutions. Luck and common sense occasionally figured as well (the Kofukuji pagoda, now recognised as an important cultural property, was sold solely for its metal fittings, and escaped being burned to the ground merely due to the fear of the spread of fire).[6]

In addition to these circumstantial incidents, Buddhist leaders and supporters were of course also engaged in more comprehensive and sustained efforts. One relatively unexplored area here, which I have written about elsewhere, is the connection between the massive surveys of Japanese art carried out in the early and mid-Meiji period ostensibly to preserve and protect Japanese art on the international stage. These efforts, by elevating Buddhist icons to the status of "national art treasures", also provided significant respite from local, materially minded persecution exercises.[7] From a different perspective, and, again, as I have written of elsewhere, Meiji Buddhists feared the extinction of the historical existence of the founder of their religion under an avalanche of uncertain chronology, speculative theology and sloppy record keeping. Because of the interdependent nature of the Buddha's enlightenment experience, the Buddha's teaching and thus the very existence of Buddhism per se, there was, moreover, the simultaneous potential erasure, however seemingly unimaginable, of the historical nature of Buddhism itself.[8] To avert such a debacle of a Buddhism without a Buddha, Meiji Buddhologists set out to create (some would say record) the history of Buddhism and the biography of the Buddha. The creation of this history, however, ironically necessitated the death of the Buddha, that is, determining the actual historical death of the Buddha was in fact instrumental to the birth of Buddhist history. In other words, concomitant to the creation of the historical death

Ainu people from the island of Ezo, now Hokkaido, in traditional costume. Print from 1880.

of the Buddha was the historicisation of Buddhism per se. This historicisation was created by Meiji Buddhologists to preserve the possibility of the teaching of the Buddha.[9] The Buddha's method of teaching, described as the simultaneous revelation of the fullness of the Buddha's message in all languages to all peoples at all levels of ability [*upâya*], moreover, was to become the ideal of Buddhology itself. It is this quest for a transcendent, pure *upâya* teaching that was not only consonant with, but also a direct contributor to, the evolution of the human race that drove Meiji Buddhist scholars. Within the discursive field of Meiji scholarship this new teaching was to be found in comparative religion or, from a specifically Buddhist perspective, Buddhology.

Beyond the uses and advantages of historicisation in imagining a world without the modern persecution of Buddhism, there is yet another macrosystemic means by which institutional Buddhism succeeded in reconstructing its social identity in the modern age. The colonisation of the northern territories in Japan was successful in establishing not only Japan's first colonial arena, it was also the field within which modern Buddhism first succeeded in acting both independently and, ironically, simultaneously as a crucial aspect of the newly forming imperial state apparatus.

★

Ouchi Seiran, Sôtô priest, president of Tôyô University, founder of the first Buddhist newspaper [*Meikyô shinshi*] and the first Buddhist journal [*Hôshi sôdan*], in 1891 wrote a series of articles regarding proselytism and Hokkaidô.[10] Ouchi asserts that "proselytisation in Hokkaidô is not a problem for individual sects or their branches. Rather, it is an issue for all offices of Buddhism. It is an issue that concerns all sects equally ... We must consider this the *most urgent priority* for all sects today". Why would a prominent figure such as Ouchi make such a comprehensive call to arms regarding a place as far afield as Hokkaidô? Ouchi, like many others in the mid-Meiji period, saw frontier Hokkaidô as a field both ripe and under-cultivated. There are, Ouchi notes, over 150,000 farmers, fisherman, soldiers and "erstwhile aborigines" [*kyûdojin*, that is the Aynu] registered in Hokkaidô and each of them is in need of Buddhism's assistance. Buddhism, he claims, has an "intimate relation" [*misetsuna kankei*] with those who farm, fish and defend the nation in the far north. In fact, by virtue of their very labours under the extremely harsh conditions found in Hokkaidô, these people are predisposed to the ideals of fortitude, cooperation and experimentation essential to modernity and to modern Buddhist practice. That is, Hokkaidô colonists are not merely concerned with present gratification but also have a clear sense of creation and expansion, a clear sense of the future. For Ouchi, the colonial spirit [*kaitaku seishin*] is *already* engaged in practices central to the new Buddhist opening of the teaching [*Bukkyô kaikyô*].[11]

Part of Ouchi's concern for Hokkaidô is generated by the presence of Christianity. Ouchi is harsh in his criticism of Buddhism's lack of skill and enthusiasm compared to Christianity when it comes to reaching out to new believers in new lands. So vital is the Hokkaidô arena for Buddhism that Ouchi asserts that:

> Hokkaidô is, without question, the place where the strengths of Buddhism and Christianity will be tested. Hokkaidô is where the winner and loser of these two religions in Japan will be determined.[12]

Hokkaidô was thus essential to the formation of modern, post-persecution Buddhism for several reasons. Mid-Meiji Hokkaidô was no longer the *tabula rasa* it had been in the 17th and 18th centuries. Extensive exploration and significant efforts towards developing urban areas, exploitation of natural resources, transportation and agriculture had resulted in significant changes, especially in the southern and central parts of the island. But Hokkaidô still served as the repository of hopes in the modern imagination: vast reserves of natural resources; seemingly limitless agricultural and industrial possibilities; and international trade seen as the harbinger of Japan's participation in a global economy. On the individual level, the possibilities of self-advancement were understood to be limited only by one's abilities and luck. The northern frontier was truly the land of opportunity and promise. The "colonial spirit" [開拓精神 *kaitaku seishin*] was interpreted as the concrete manifestation of the spirit of modernity. The ubiquitous Meiji era ideal of 開化 *kaika* or "enlightenment", when put into the geopolitical frame of Hokkaidô, became 開拓 *kaitaku* "opening the land" or, indeed, "colonisation". The challenge for post-persecution Buddhists then was to link the spirit of these new colonists to the spirit of modern Buddhism: that is *kaitaku* is linked to *kaika* is linked to *kaikyô* (opening of the teaching, new Buddhism). "Aah,

Hokkaidô!" Ouchi writes, " ... we must break new ground, increase our population and expand our hopes there. I believe that the day is not far off when all of Hokkaidô will have been opened [*kaitaku*] and Buddhist immigrants will dwell throughout the land".[13]

Most Meiji Buddhist sects rose to the frontier challenge, and great efforts were directed towards Hokkaidô as a field profoundly suitable for Buddhist contributions to the Meiji state. The Higashi Honganji proved to be the most aggressive in their contributions to state building in Hokkaidô (in fact building much of the needed infrastructure).[14] But other sects also moved to expand their proselytisation efforts in Hokkaidô. For example, the Shingon sect had established a seventeen-point protocol for proselytisation by 1891. Shingon concerns reflected a clear-headed vision of the demands on priests sent to Hokkaidô: they needed to be in robust health, well trained and mature in their practice, committed to extended periods of deprivation and willing to work under extreme conditions with very little institutional support.[15]

In contrast, the Sôtô sect, traditionally prominent in Hokkaidô, expanded its proselytisation efforts there relatively late, and in 1896 it laments that:

> Shingon, Jôdo, Nichiren and both the Nishi and Higashi Honganji have all been working unceasingly; they have created special groups of proselytisers and have invested vast amounts of capital and other resources in Hokkaidô. Especially the Nishi and Higashi Honganji have invested unparalleled sums to carry out their proselytisation efforts.[16]

At this juncture the Sôtô sect made a strategic choice and decided to sustain its limited proselytisation efforts in Hokkaidô, but to also expand them in Taiwan. While maintaining a barely competitive priestly force in Hokkaidô, the sect was proud to assert that "our sect is the first to enter Taiwan" the most recent of Japan's "protectorate" states. The Sôtô sect had two goals in this move: first, to contribute directly to the "imperialisation" [*kôminka*] of the Taiwanese population through the instruction of Japanese language, culture and Sôtô religious practices. Such efforts would result in their "constructing a new configuration of religion" on the island that contributed directly to "our form of government". Second, recognising the increasing competition from other Buddhist sects, they hoped to stake out new, exclusive preaching privileges. The Sôtô sect thus hoped to expand its sectarian influence alongside its contributions to the imperial government's creation of "citizens of the New Dominion" [*shin hanto jimmin*] in Taiwan. In very short order the sect mounted one of the largest Japanese Buddhist foreign proselytisation movements to date: the financial commitment in Taiwan was eight times the size of the Sôtô Hokkaidô mission.[17]

There is a clear relation between Japanese imperial expansionism and modern Buddhism's own evangelical expansion. *Kaikyô* means, in part, to bring the teaching to new areas; this, in turn, resulted in a close coordination between Buddhist institutions and the expanding imperial state. Or, as the Sôtô sect's own history of proselytisation puts it: "promulgation of our sect's teaching abroad was closely aligned to international conditions and the Japanese sphere of influence." Or again, more succinctly and here in reference to preaching efforts in China: "Without question, our efforts began with the outset of war and ended with Japan's defeat".[18] Moreover, the practices initiated in Hokkaidô clearly formed the basis for subsequent sectarian models: organisational structures, costs, and methodologies were all initially set forth in the Hokkaidô colonies. Hokkaidô thus served as the testing ground for many ideas related to modernity and state building, and the possible relations between Buddhism and the modern state was one of those ideas being tested.

★

When I first came across the word *kaikyô* in these many Buddhist documents I assumed it meant simply proselytisation, to bring the Buddhist teaching to people and communities that were not already affiliated with a Buddhist organisation. I was quickly disabused of this by the fact that virtually all the early missions were, in effect, preaching to the converted. During the early and mid-Meiji era *kaikyô* generally meant to promulgate the Buddha dharma in an area it had never been revealed in before; if it happened that new people were ushered into the doctrine, so much the better. Only later, when the Buddhist missionaries were forced to confront an increasingly non-Japanese population in Taiwan and on the continent did the term take on clearer evangelical qualities. In Taiwan the first mission attempts were to reach the already established Buddhist communities on the island and thus segue slowly towards the more

Ainu fishermen, 1906.

general quest for converts. Another example of the transition of the meaning of *kaikyô* can be seen in the Buddhist participation in the Parliament of the World's Religions in Chicago in 1893; there it was clearly opening in both a new arena and before a new, uninitiated audience.[19]

But it was also *not* the case that there were no non-Japanese or non-Buddhists in the Hokkaidô colonies. The native population, Aynu, are continually referenced in Kaitakushi (The Office of Colonisation) reports and also show up in several Buddhist reviews of the period. We know the Aynu were employed on, in fact pressed into, colonial construction projects, many of which were run by Buddhist organisations. Much of the cross-island Honganji Highway follows Aynu foot trails created by generations of local hunters. We know they were resident at every trading post and river head where Buddhist temples were built. Occasionally, the Aynu figure in Buddhist discussions of Hokkaidô. Ouchi Seiran, for example, in his discussion noted above, wrote that the Aynu, with their "natural religiosity" [*shizen no shûkyô shin*] would need only the slightest bit of "indoctrination" [*kyôka*] in order for "their dark superstitions to be exposed and for them to be provided with the illumination of a new light".[20] But when Ouchi concluded his argument for a Hokkaidô Buddhism with a discussion of the vital need for and reception of Buddhist teachings by the residents of the new colonies, intriguingly, he made no mention whatsoever of the Aynu. In fact, it appears that there was virtually no effort by Meiji-era Buddhists to bring the Aynu into the fold. The Aynu were put to work, registered, taxed, regulated and traded with, but the Aynu were not considered as potential Buddhists in the Meiji period.[21]

Be this as it may, I have, however, found two *pre*-Meiji, pre-19th-century, cases wherein the Aynu were indeed considered worthy of Buddhist conversion efforts. One occurs in the years immediately after the formation of the 三官寺 *Sankan-ji* (three administrative temples) by the Tokugawa government in 1804, and the other a decade and more later; both were at the same temple, one of the three administrative temples, the Jôdo sect Zenkôji in Usu on Volcano Bay. The first was led by the priest Ranshû who advocated the practice of chanting the *nembutsu* accompanied by passing a large (several metres in diameter) string of prayer beads among the participants. Ranshû himself had previously engaged in one million continuous repetitions of the *nembutsu* and used this method to bring Aynu closer to the Buddhist teaching. Copious quantities of *sake* and viands also accompanied these prayer sessions. Though the attendance rate does seem to have fluctuated depending upon the refreshments served, Aynu participation in these events reportedly continued for several years.

Ranshû's successor and third abbot of Zenkôji, Benzui, continued the Aynu mission but changed the practice from *nembutsu* recitation to a collective singing of a song accompanied by a group dance. The song, in its entirety, is translated here:

> Gather round people, listen to the teaching.
> Whether sooner or later, we all die some time.
> If you are troubled by death, chant the *nembutsu*.
> Chanting people know that when their time comes
> this borrowed body, even upon death,
> like a cicada's shell, can be easily discarded.
> The moon and sun too, pass into the undying land,
> born again and again, just as they are.
> If your wife and child are dear to you,
> together chant the *nembutsu*, chanting with them is good.
> In this world without fail we endure pain and suffering.
> But in the next world,
> we will be born into the Pure Land,
> on one lotus platform we will dwell.
> Forever, happily, without death.[22]

Benzui went on to be known as the Nembutsu Shonin (master or saint of the Nembutsu); his song was printed in 1832 and again in 1853 and circulated throughout the waning years of the Tokugawa period.[23] And yet there seems to have been little to no other interest in bringing the Aynu into the Buddhist church except here at the Zenkôji.

In conclusion I would like to speculate as to why this might have been so. Given the deep and abiding connections that various Buddhist teachers and institutions were attempting to construct between the new Buddhist idealism and the modernist and expansionist claims of the Meiji imperial state, emphasis was placed entirely upon the construction of a modern Buddhist self. This self was socially active, widely informed, devoted to the Buddhist teachings and loyal to the state. The Aynu were perceived of by the Tokugawa state largely as labourers and as potential threats to the polity should they have cause to revolt (which indeed happened on several occasions, most recently in 1789), or if they were to align themselves with Russia and its trading and territorial interests. The Tokugawa preferred a Buddhist Aynu to a Russian Orthodox one, and thus it is no coincidence that the special administrative temple in the southern district, the Zenkōji, took it upon itself to begin the conversion of the local Aynu populace.

The fact that these conversion efforts had limited effect, coupled with the increased recognition of the limits of Russian powers and the continued displacement and disenfranchisement of the Aynu, gradually removed the Aynu from Buddhist concern. Sectarian attention was gradually shifted to other lands and other peoples more closely aligned with the expanding states' needs. Put in the baldest terms, I think we can argue that for Meiji-era Japanese Buddhist evangelicals, in order for one to be a modern Buddhist one finally needed to be either "modern" or "Japanese": preferably both. Conversion of Koreans, Chinese, Manchurians or even Chicagoans would be possible to the extent that they understood either modernity, Japanese-ness or (again, preferably) both. Unlike these modern peoples or the Japanese colonists, the Aynu were considered beyond the pale, and thereby all but vanished as shadows within the Buddhist contributions to the expanding powers of the Japanese colonial apparatus, and to the modern constructions of Buddhism itself.

1. Mori Arinori, 'First Essay on Enlightenment' in *Meiroku zasshi,* (1874) vol. 3, in William Braisted, trans., *Meiroku zasshi: Journal of the Japanese Enlightenment* (Cambridge: Harvard Univ. Press, 1976), pp.30–31.
2. For a fuller discussion of anti-Buddhist rhetoric and issues related to the early Meiji persecution of Buddhism see my book *Of Heretics and Martyrs in Meiji Japan: Buddhism and Its Persecution* (Princeton: Princeton Univ. Press, 1990).
3. This quote is taken from the Shin priest Yatsubuchi Banryû's reminiscence of his participation in the Parliament of the World's Religions held in Chicago in 1893: 'Daikai no genjô oyobi kansatsu,' *Kokkyô,* no. 31 (3:1894) 34–35.
4. Murakami (1851–1929) in many ways exemplifies the career of the Meiji-era scholar priest (*gakusô*). After beginning his life as a young priest in present-day Aichi prefecture and becoming the head priest of the Nyukaku-ji (1876) he went on to become, in 1889, a lecturer in Indian philosophy at Tokyo Imperial University.
5. Murakami Senshô, '*Bukkyôshi kenkyû no hitsuyo o nobete hakkan no yûrai to nashi awasete honshi no shugi mokuteki o hyohakusu,*' in the inaugural volume of *Bukkyô shirin* (4: 1894) vol.1, no.1: 1–11.
6. For these and many other examples see Tsuji Zennosuke, et al, eds., *Meiji Ishin Shinbutsu bunri shiryô,* five volumes (Tokyo Teikoku Daigaku Shiryô hensanjo, 1926-29): especially. vol 1, pp.1–80 and Tsuji's introductory essay 'Shinbutsu bunri no gaikan'.
7. See my essay 'Putting the 'ism' in 'Buddhism': Objects, Objectification and a (Domestic) Japonisme' in Josef Kreiner, ed., *Japanese Collections in European Museums vol. 5 With Especial Reference to Buddhist Art* (Bobb: Bier'sche Verlagsanstalt, 2016): pp.185–204.
8. It can of course be asserted that the conception of the 'historical' Buddha, Shakyamuni, held differing significance for different sects in Japan. The doctrine of the three Buddha-bodies, for example, suggests a displacement of the physical primacy of the historical Buddha across a vast and transcendent epistemological and ontological field. It is one of my contentions, however, that Meiji-era Buddhism incorporated a profoundly physical conception of Buddhist practice and experience. This may be due in part to the dominant role played by Shin sect theologians in the formation of this new Buddhism. The increasingly significant role of positivistic conceptions of history and sectarian emphases on the sociality and politicality of religion that emerged in the Meiji era should also not be overlooked here.
9. James E. Ketelaar, 'The Non-Modern Confronts the Modern: Dating the Buddha in Japan' in *History and Theory: Studies in the Philosophy of History,* Theme Issue 45: Religion and History, (Wesleyan University, 2006): 62–79.
10. These essays were titled 'Hokkaidô fukkyô ron' and can be found in the *Meikyô shinshi* part 3:1891, nos. 2862–67.
11. Ouchi, 'Hokkaidô fukkyô ron': 'Most urgent priority' comes from part 6, no. 2866, p.4; the comments about Hokkaidô residents is from part 3, no. 2864, p.5.

12. *Meikyô shinshi*, part 3:1891, no. 2866.
13. Ibid., p. 4.
14. In this regard, see also my 'Hokkaido Buddhism and the Early Meiji State' in Helen Hardacre, ed., *New Directions in the Study of Meiji Japan* (Brill, 1997): pp. 531-48; esp. pp. 539-46
15. In the *Meikyô shinshi*, part 3:1891, no. 2868: pp. 6–7.
16. See the Sôtô sect's journal *Shûhô*, vol.12:1896, no. 1: pp.12–13.
17. Ibid. pp.13–17.
18. *Sôtôshû kaigai kaikyô dendôshi* (Sôtô sect: 1980) pp. 6–7.
19. See Ketelaar, *Of Heretics and Martyrs*; chapter 4.
20. *Meikyô shinshi*, part 3:1891, no. 2864 p.5.
21. Though outside the scope of the present essay, it should be noted that there was a very active missionary effort among the Aynu carried out by the British Church Missionary Society, most prominently represented by the Rev. John Batchelor. So successful was Batchelor's sixty-year mission (ending in 1941) that virtually the entire Aynu population around Sapporo and significant numbers throughout the island eventually converted to Christianity.
22. This poem is rather hard to find; the version I have is from a manuscript copy held at the Zenkoji and reprinted in Sudô Ryûsen, 'Nembutsu shonin kohiki uta' ni tsuite' in *Taisho Daigaku gakuho* no. 24 (vol. 3:1965) pp.14–17. It can also be found in a slightly different version in Matsuura Takeshirô's *Higashi Ezo nisshi*. Matsuura's version includes the curious amended line 'Japanese and Aynu will both in the next world be born into the Pure Land' which succeeds in ironically reinforcing the difference between the Aynu and the Japanese even as it claims it does not exist.
23. Both Ranshû, Benzui, as well as the fourth abbot of Zenkoji, Bentei, are discussed in Sudô Ryûsen, *Hokkaidô to shûkyôjin* (Hakodate: Kyôgaku kenkyûkai, 1965) pp. 54–57.

Otome Tōge Martyrs' Shrine, Tsuwano, Shimane prefecture.

THE LAST PERSECUTION OF CHRISTIANITY IN MEIJI JAPAN

M. Antoni J. Ucerler, SJ

The relationship of Meiji Japan to religion was quite complex, and to a significant extent presented a break with the previous Edo period under the Tokugawa regime on account of the reformers' desire to establish a new centre of unity for the nation. One of the defining characteristics of this time was a return to the idea and practice of Shinto as both the native and the national religion. Adherents of the school of National Learning or *kokugaku* 国学 had been key players in bringing about the Meiji Restoration. One of the principle slogans they publicly adopted, *sonnō jōi* 尊皇攘夷 or "respect the emperor and expel the barbarians" represented more than just a political agenda. It also had deep religious overtones.[1]

The promulgation of the idea of "unity of government and religion" 祭政一致 as official policy through a series of decrees between 1868 and 1870 was a conscious and concerted attempt to institutionalise and centralise control over Shinto in a way not previously attempted. One of the government's first acts was to place all shrines and Shinto priests under the authority of the Jingikan 神祇官 or Department of Divinities, re-established to promote unity. The restoration of the emperor to a position of authority required a public form of religious conformity that underlined his divine authority. These declarations unambiguously sought to remind the populace of the indissoluble union between nation and sovereign.[2] In this 19th-century Japanese worldview, "foreign" religions and religious traditions could only be considered a potential threat. One might argue that this was no different from the anti-foreign, or more accurately anti-Western, policies of the previous Edo government, which only allowed limited trade with the Dutch – though this did have an effect even on the Chinese merchants in Nagasaki.

What was new, however, was the open hostility towards Buddhism, a religion that had been practised in Japan for over a thousand years. Beginning in the Middle Ages, the Japanese had found a way to accommodate the beliefs of the two faiths and merge them into a new religious system that incorporated elements from both. This doctrine, known as *shinbutsu shūgō* 神仏集合 [or *shinbutsu konkō* 神仏混淆], took on many different forms, including the unique idea that Buddhist deities left their "native" or "original ground" [*honji* 本地] and manifested themselves in Japan as native gods that still maintained a "trace" [*suijaku* 垂迹] of those origins. With the advent of the new Meiji government, officials promulgated an order issued on 5 April, 1868 to separate Buddhism from Shinto. This was inspired, among others, by the teachings of the prominent scholar of *kokugaku*, Hirata Atsutane (1776–1843), whose disciples became influential at this time. The decree precipitated the violent *haibutsu kishaku* 廃仏棄釈 or "Abolish Buddhism and Destroy Shākyamuni" movement to destroy Buddhism and eliminate its cultural influence. Thus, between 1868 and 1874 tens of thousands of temples were destroyed or seriously damaged, as were works of Buddhist religious art.[3]

This set the scene for the fate that Christians were to suffer during the first years of Meiji. Christianity was another religion that had its own foreign "entanglements". Moreover, most Japanese were certain that it had been definitively suppressed in the mid-17th century. It turned out this was not the case when Christians re-emerged in Nagasaki in the 1860s – something that came as a complete shock to the new government and its officials, who were already disposed to favour anything that did not promote Shinto. To understand how Christians survived into the 1860s, we must briefly go back to the time when Christianity first appeared on the shores of the Japanese archipelago.

The Portuguese were the first Europeans to set foot in Japan in 1543, and they quickly developed a lucrative trading relationship with a number of local feudal lords on the island of Kyushu. In 1549 Francis Xavier, a Jesuit missionary, arrived on a ship from Goa and began to preach the Christian faith in Kagoshima, Yamaguchi, and Hirado. This took place during a century of intense internecine strife, known as the Warring States Period, when the sixty-six kingdoms or domains were vying for advantage and engaged in warfare with each other. A generation later, Toyotomi Hideyoshi, the imperial regent or *kanpaku* 関白, and one of the unifiers of the country, decided to expel the missionaries for what he considered political meddling. In the expulsion decree [*Bateren tsuihōrei* 伴天連追放令] he issued on 25 July, 1587, he declared that Japan was the "land of the gods" [*shinkoku* 神国] and therefore there was no place for a foreign religion like Christianity – which the decree referred to as an "evil law" or "evil teaching" [*jahō* 邪法]. The rationale that foreign religious teachings were incompatible with Japan set a precedent that would continue even into the Meiji Restoration.

Despite this decree, and his execution of twenty-six Christians on Nishizaka Hill in Nagasaki in 1597, Christian communities managed to survive and even to thrive over the next ten years. Things took a decided turn for the worse, however, when the shogun, Tokugawa Ieyasu, ordered the Buddhist monk and trusted political adviser, Konchiin Ishin Sūden 金地院以心崇伝 (1569–1633), to compose a nationwide decree prohibiting preaching and practising Christianity, issued on 28 January, 1614. In the immediate aftermath of this pronouncement, the shogunal authorities launched an intense persecution of Japanese Christians. This was followed by numerous public executions both in Kyushu and Nagasaki. A few mass executions, including one in 1623, took place in Edo itself for the benefit of the populace, not unlike the public spectacles or *autos-da-fé* of the Portuguese and Spanish Inquisitions.

This period would reach its climax with a revolt that broke out among Christian peasants protesting over excessive taxes imposed in Amakusa and Shimabara by local lords, Matsukura Katsuie 松倉勝家 (1598–1638) and Terasawa Katataka 寺沢堅高 (1608-47) respectively. The rebellion began in December 1637 and was suppressed on 15 April, 1638. The rebels held out at Hara Castle on the Shimabara peninsula and were led by a young Christian, Amakusa Shirō 天草四郎 (1621-38). The vehemence of the opposition startled and alarmed the shogunate, which was forced to respond with a massive force of 125,000 samurai. Having finally gained control of the castle, they executed all 37,000 remaining rebels, including peasants, craftsmen, merchants, and lordless samurai or *rōnin*. This was the first time the Tokugawa authorities had faced a military challenge on such a scale since the fateful campaigns that led to the elimination of the Toyotomi clan with the fall of Osaka Castle in 1615 and the death of Hideyoshi's heir, Hideyori 豊臣秀頼 (1593–1615).

In the wake of the Shimabara affair, the shogunate, suspicious of foreign influence and opposition, decreed the expulsion of the Portuguese – which followed the earlier banishment of the Spanish in 1624. This effectively limited regular trade with Europeans to the Dutch, who were confined on the artificial island of Dejima in Nagasaki.

With these turbulent events, the Christian story of Nagasaki had seemingly come to an end. But had it really? To ferret out any remaining Christians, rich rewards of hundreds of pieces of silver were offered for the denunciation of missionaries and/or Japanese Christians. Many believers had gone underground, continuing to worship in secret, and the authorities were adamant about stamping out any traces of the "evil teaching". One way to accomplish this systematically was to enact a temple registration system obliging all inhabitants to be part of a Buddhist temple [*danka seido* 檀家制度].[4] Every new year, beginning in 1626, officials would go street by street, ledgers and brushes in hand, and compel all men, women, and even children in previously Christian areas, to step on a sacred Christian "trampling image" or *fumi-e* 踏絵. This was to confirm publicly their apostasy of the foreign faith.

Compliance with the ritual or lack thereof was recorded, by district and by temple, in carefully compiled "ledgers of religious investigation" [*shūmon aratame-chō* 宗門改帳]. By the beginning of the 18th century, the shogunate was convinced that no more Christians remained in the country. But many, in outlying areas and on remote islands such as Hirado and the Gotō archipelago, had concealed themselves, even to their neighbours, and continued to practise their faith. To mask their worship, they often used Buddhist objects, such as the goddess of mercy or Kannon 観音, whose representation resembled the Virgin Mary and child. At other times they used authentic Christian statues and paintings they had succeeded in hiding or even created by themselves for the same purpose.

As the shogunate entered the 18th century, there seemed little reason to doubt they had finally instilled a sense of ideological and religious conformity. But then came the fateful summer of 1853. The American naval commander, Commodore Matthew Galbraith Perry, arrived in July in Uraga Bay, near Edo, with large gunboats equipped with modern cannon, and demanded that trade negotiations begin forthwith. Thoroughly unprepared for such a foreign intrusion and violation of its sovereignty, Perry's entreaties were unwelcome. Despite declaring that he desired nothing more than the establishment of peaceful trade relations, he was viewed as an imminent threat to the status quo.

To exacerbate the situation, other nations followed on the heels of the Americans; within a year or two "unequal treaties" were signed with the US, Russia, France, England, and the Netherlands. These nations all insisted through their ministers that Japan cease persecuting Christians,

Saint Francis Xavier, 18th century,
attributed to Giovanni Battista Gaulli.

but the authorities firmly resisted these entreaties – until they realised they had little choice but to make concessions. On 29 December, 1857, the practice of requiring Christians to trample on sacred images was finally abolished after more than two centuries. This, however, did not spell the end of their troubles.

The following year on 29 July, 1858, Townsend Harris concluded the Treaty of Amity and Commerce between the United States and Japan. Article eight of this treaty ensured the right of Americans to worship freely in Japan and to erect places of worship for that purpose. In return, Americans would promise not to injure or offer insult to any Japanese temple, shrine, or religious object, and would not interfere in any religious ceremony. The French followed on this agreement and signed – like the Dutch, British, and Russians – their own version of it on 9 October, 1858. The content was basically the same and guaranteed the new foreign residents freedom of religious practice and freedom to erect their own chapels, churches and the like. But article four of the treaty with France added a curious statement not included in the treaty with the United States: "The Japanese Government has already abolished the use of practices injurious to Christianity" – a clear reference to the abolition of the *ebumi* 絵踏 or image trampling.

It was under these circumstances that the French undertook diplomatic and trade relations with Japan. Soon thereafter, Bernard-Thadée Petitjean (1829-84) and his fellow members of the Paris Foreign Missions Society [*Missions étrangères de Paris*] decided to take advantage of this new freedom of worship; he arrived in Nagasaki in 1863, after first spending time in the new international trading port of Yokohama. His main purpose was to take care of the spiritual needs of the French inhabitants. Two years later, he completed the construction of the famed Ōura Tenshudō Church 大浦天主堂 – now a designated Japanese national treasure.

Less than a month after the completion of its construction, the French made a great discovery. On 17 March, 1865, a group of Japanese walked into the church, looked around, and then cautiously asked three questions: where is the statue of the Virgin Mary? Did he [Petitjean] have a wife? And who was the high priest of his religion? Petitjean set out to show them the statue, and explain it was that of the Mother of God; he told them he was not married on account of being a priest, and explained that Catholics looked to the pope, the Bishop of Rome, as their head. Satisfied with the answers he had provided, a fifty-two-year-old woman named

Sugimoto Yuri, whose photograph survives, revealed to Petitjean that they too were of the "same mind and heart". She is said to have used the word *mune* 宗 to refer to the Christian faith, which orally could also have been interpreted as "heart" from the homonym that refers to "chest" 胸, or what one harbours within oneself. This discovery, commemorated on a bas relief in front of Urakami Cathedral in Nagasaki, soon reverberated around the world. Petitjean began to visit nearby villages, where he met with a number of hidden Christian community elders. But these developments did not go unnoticed by the authorities.

Within a short time, other Christians emerged and four chapels were built for their use. As they gained confidence, an incident took place that triggered a crisis. They refused to make a donation to a Buddhist temple in 1866, despite being obliged to do so as registered parishioners. And in 1867 a Christian family refused to have a local Buddhist priest conduct a funeral – another obligation of the *danka* system. This prompted a swift backlash. The Nagasaki Magistrate's Office [*Nagasaki bugyōsho* 長崎奉行所], which had played a key role in extirpating Christianity in the 17th century, conducted an investigation; the first sixty-eight Christian leaders were arrested on 13 June, 1867 and tortured. This prompted an immediate reaction from the French consul and French minister. The latter, Léon Roches (1809–1901), requested an audience with the shogun, Tokugawa Yoshinobu (1837–1913), which took place in Osaka on August 21 of that year. While the ban continued, the shogun declared that in the future, when Japan was ready to enact it, religious freedom would and should be granted to all – a statement that Yoshinobu reiterated in a letter to Napoleon III. An official, Hirayama Shōsai, also informed the French Consul that the shogunate no longer regarded Christianity as an 'evil form of religion'. It is undoubtedly an interesting fact of history that after almost 250 years of official prohibition by the Edo government, it was none other than the last shogun who promised that one day religious tolerance for Christianity would become a reality. A month after he wrote this letter, the shogun resigned; and by January 1868, the restoration of imperial power in the person of Emperor Meiji had begun.

Nationalist and nativist forces soon prevailed; and the principle of the "unity of government and religion", mentioned earlier, was promulgated on 5 April, 1868. This required a renewed effort to stamp out Christianity. Arrests were conducted in Nagasaki beginning in March of the same year, in the nearby village of Urakami; instead of execution, however, it

St. Francis Xavier lands at Kagoshima, Satsuma Province on the island of Kyushu, in 1549.

was decided on 7 June that over 4,000 Japanese Christians be rounded up and exiled to thirty-four different domains, so that they could be "re-educated" far from the meddling influence and moral support of the resident foreign missionaries, learning to become loyal Shinto subjects. Arrests and relocations continued – a process that lasted from the July 1868 until the eventual return of the surviving exiled Christians in 1873.

These events did not go unnoticed abroad. In an article published on 18 October, 1868, the *New York Times* stated: "A few days ago our correspondent at Nagasaki gave an account of the banishment of two shiploads of Christians from that place under peculiarly painful circumstances." It goes on to mention the issuance of a new decree of persecution that "directs that Christians be arrested and banished – that is, handed over in small detachments to the different Daimios or Princes throughout the empire".

The article concludes with a call for action led by the US. "We think, however, that a joint protest from the Christian governments of the world – a protest headed by the Mighty and Awful Republic of America, whose power is known and dreaded throughout the planet – might penetrate the ears even of the Mikado [Emperor] and impel him to better behavior toward the Christians of his empire [...] Men should not be persecuted for being Christian in the Nineteenth Century". Similarly, one of France's principal broadsheets, *Le Figaro*, reported on 12 October, 1868 – just six days before the *New York Times* article – that "a decree of the Emperor of Japan prohibiting Christianity had been posted publicly [*affiché aux portes*] in Yokohama".

Foreign governments did indeed protest, including those of the US, Britain, Germany, and France; but in response, Japanese officials repeated that Christianity was incompatible with the Japanese polity and that foreign governments had no right to interfere in such internal matters. As these debates continued, in 1871 Japan resolved to send an international mission to the West to renegotiate the unequal treaties. The group of Meiji luminaries included Ōkubo Toshimichi 大久保利通 (1830-78) and Itō Hirobumi 伊藤博文 (1841–1909), later Japan's first prime minister, and was headed by Iwakura Tomomi 岩倉具視 (1825-83), minister of foreign affairs and ambassador extraordinary. While in the US, the question of religious freedom of the Japanese came up in discussions with the secretary of state, Hamilton Fish, who tried to persuade the delegation to compromise on this issue. This question would come up repeatedly wherever the embassy went in Europe, where equal pressure was brought to bear on the Japanese to desist from any further persecution of Christians.

Instrumental as a go-between in this uncomfortable conversation was Mori Arinori 森有礼 (1847-89), originally from the domain of Satsuma, who found secret passage out of Japan in 1865, just three years before the collapse of the Tokugawa regime. He studied first at University College London, and then in the United States, where he briefly joined the Brotherhood of the New Life, a communal religious group inspired by the mystical and visionary theology of Emanuel Swedenborg (1688–1772).

After his return to Japan, Mori was called to government service and appointed the first Japanese ambassador to Washington, DC. In November 1872 he drafted an extraordinary document in English and addressed it to Prime Minister Sanjō Sanetomi 三条実美 (1837-91), entitled, "Religious Freedom in Japan, A Memorial and Draft of Charter" – a copy of which he promptly sent as a gift to his friend, Theodore Dwight Woolsey, the former president of Yale College and a leading intellectual of his day. His principle argument in favour of religious freedom can be summed up by its opening remark: "Among many important human concerns, the one respecting our religious faith appears to be the most vital. In all the enlightened nations of the earth, the liberty of conscience, especially in matters of religious faith, is sacredly regarded as not only an inherent right of man, but also as a most fundamental element to advance all human interests".[5]

He then acknowledges the various objections being voiced in Japan regarding allowing Christianity back into the country, after the "troubles" it had allegedly caused in the past – a reference to the "closed country" policy enacted by the Edo *bakufu* in 1639. He also addresses the idea that the Japanese people are not yet prepared to take such a bold step into a future of religious freedom, lest social cohesion and the rule of law suffer as a result. Such objections, in fact, formed the core of the Meiji government's response to foreign powers advocating the end of the Christian persecution.

In a bold statement, he responds that every country that had hitherto embraced Christianity had benefited and found it a blessing. This, Mori contends, was "because the society which receives the addition of a new knowledge, and a power of the character of the Christian morality and faith, will necessarily better its condition by becoming both wiser and

Mori Arinori (1847–1889).

Monument commemorating the rediscovery of the Hidden Christians, ōura Tenshudō, Nagasaki.

stronger". He links this assertion directly to the notion of civilisational progress among the community of nations.

But Arinori's purpose in drafting such a charter was not simply pragmatic and transactional. In his remarks he returns to the philosophical principle of individual rights and responsibilities. "Since religion is entirely a matter of individual belief, no one or government can be presumed to possess the authority of repudiating whatever faith any man may cherish within himself". Inspired by many of the founding principles of the American constitution and influenced by men deeply committed to religious ideals, including the utopian mystic Thomas Lake Harris (1823–1906), he concludes his argument by reiterating the need for a new set of laws that would guarantee fundamental rights for all Japanese people and a reformed system of education that would build up and sustain these new ideals among the populace.[6]

Arinori went on to become the first minister of education as well as the founder of the Meirokusha 明六社 [Meiji 6 Society], whose purpose was to promote civilisation and enlightenment, with its own journal. Among its original members was none other than Fukuzawa Yukichi (1835–1901), one of the Meiji periods' greatest reformers, who founded Keiō University in 1858, first as a school of Western learning and then as a university. Fukuzawa was also among the first Japanese to set foot in the United States, when the *Kanrin-Maru* sailed into San Francisco Bay in 1860, following the Harris or Ansei Treaty that opened Japan to international trade against its will. Another member of the Meiji 6 Society was the Confucian scholar and educator, Nakamura Masanao (1832-91), an early convert to, and vigorous promoter of, Christianity. He would introduce the writings of John Stuart Mill to Japan and translate *On Liberty* into Japanese in 1872, the same year that Mori published his essay on religious freedom, and a year before he founded the Meirokusha.

Curiously, the man who served as interpreter for the Iwakura embassy when the question of religious freedom was being discussed was Niijima Jō 新島襄 or Joseph Hardy Neesima (1843-90), who secretly arranged passage to the United States in 1864, was baptised two years later, and studied at Amherst College and Andover Theological Seminary. Once he returned to Japan he would found a Christian school in Kyoto, which subsequently became Dōshisha University.

As these great debates were taking place in the United States, Europe, and within Japan itself among young and dynamic intellectuals, many

Japanese Christians continued to suffer great hardship. One of the very worst persecutions took place in Tsuwano, in Shimane Prefecture under the watchful gaze of the zealous local domain lord, Kamei Koremi 亀井 茲監 (1825-85), who was also vice-minister of rites. Initially, at the advice of his fellow domain samurai and *kokugaku* scholar, Fukuba Bisei 福羽美 静 (1831–1907), they tried to persuade the Christians with arguments and debated with them. When this failed to yield any results, they decided to resort to compulsion.

In the woods above the city, where a small chapel and memorial stand today, a young samurai by the name of Morioka Yukio 森岡幸夫 (d. 1878) attempted to force the Christians to apostatise through starvation, exposure in freezing waters, burning with fire, and flagellation with whips. Detailed ledgers were kept of the interrogations; families and their members were all listed, including small children and even infants. The ledgers distinguish between two categories of prisoners: those who 'did not change heart', or *fukaishin* 不改心', and those who did [*kaishin* 改心]. Records indicate that in some cases the whole family agreed to abandon their faith – at least in public. In others, the entire family refused to do so. And in yet other cases, some members of the family held fast to their faith, while others abandoned it.

Altogether 253 Christians from Nagasaki were exiled to Tsuwano, 128 in 1868 and another 125 in 1869. Of those, fifty-four apostatised and sixty-eight did not. A further forty-one died as a result of the torture and mistreatment. In this group there were ten infants. Many years later, a number of photographs were taken of survivors who returned home. In one of them, taken in 1930 of the Tsuwano group, we see Moriyama Jinzaburō 守山甚三郎, the leader of the group and himself a samurai, whose fourteen-year-old brother, Yujirō 祐次郎, had died as a result of torture and abuse but had not given up his faith.

In the case of Tsuwano, the apostates were given separate lodging from those who were still under interrogation, and sufficient food. Their public apostasy notwithstanding, they were not allowed to return home or otherwise leave the area. Survivors would later recount how many regretted their apostasy and made every effort to provide food in secret to those still imprisoned and tortured. Thanks to their compassion, many survived who otherwise would have died of starvation or on account of the harsh conditions they were forced to endure, particularly in the winter.

Finally, convinced that Japan could not take its place among the civilised nations of the world as long as religious freedom was not guaranteed, the Meiji government relented; and on 24 February, 1873, the previous decree boards banning the "evil religion" – which had been reinstated on 7 April, 1868 – were removed once and for all. Notifications were also issued abolishing the religious investigation ledgers that had been kept since the 17th century. Finally, after five years of exile and persecution, in mid-March of 1873, exiles were granted the freedom to return to their homes in Nagasaki.[7]

In his memoirs written years later, Morioka, who had led the persecution in Tsuwano and tortured the fourteen-year-old Yujirō with exposure to the cold and whips, noted how at one point he asked himself: "What am I doing? Torturing a child! Am I a samurai? Am I a man?"

In an extraordinary moment of reconciliation, eyewitnesses claim that when the order from Tokyo to cease the persecution reached Tsuwano, the three principal samurai in charge of the interrogations, including the aforementioned Morioka Yukio, summoned their fellow samurai and the Christian leaders, Moriyama Jinzaburō, Takagi Sen'emon, and two others, and apologised for what had happened. They then invited them to partake in a festive dinner. They tried to explain their motivations for the persecution and praised the Christians highly for being loyal to their heavenly lord. Rarely has history recorded such moments when former enemies, persecutor and persecuted, sat down at the same table to reflect together upon the recent past.[8] The story of Tsuwano is thus a very significant – if not isolated – episode in the history of the last persecution of Christianity in 19th-century Japan.

Finally, on 11 February, 1889, sixteen years after the release of the Urakami Christians from their respective places of exile all across Japan, the Meiji Constitution was officially promulgated by the emperor. Article 28 specifically addressed the question of religion and its practice. It stated: "Japanese subjects shall, within limits not prejudicial to peace and order, and not antagonistic to their duties as subjects, enjoy freedom of religious belief". This statement reflected a carefully crafted compromise. It upheld the principle of religious freedom, which the government found it could no longer deny, but defined it within the confines of what would not cause disturbance to the harmony of society as a whole. What might be "prejudicial to peace and order" remained open to interpretation by the authorities.

In fact, half a century later, the militarist government in Japan would use that loophole to exert enormous pressure on Japanese Christians during the Second World War to conform to Shinto norms in the name of loyalty to the emperor and to the nation. One of the most famous cases was the Yasukuni Shrine incident, which involved the Jesuit-founded Sophia University in Tokyo. The military training officer stationed at the university, Kitahara Hitomi, took sixty students to the nearby Yasukuni Shrine and ordered them to bow in front of the enshrined deities. Three Catholic students refused – sparking a political crisis that lasted for many months. The university was soon labelled unpatriotic by the press, which subsequently carried out a public campaign denouncing Sophia graduates and implying that they would not be employable after their studies on account of their un-Japanese stance. This ploy temporarily saw student numbers decline, until the non-religious character of the Yasukuni ritual was publicly clarified and affirmed. This eventually allowed a solution to be worked out among all parties, including the Archbishop of Tokyo, Jean-Baptiste Alexis Chambon MEP (1875–1948), who intervened with the all-powerful Ministry of Education. Nevertheless, a Christian university had risked losing its accreditation and its reputation as a bona fide institution on account of a handful of students who declared their intention to abide by their constitutional right to religious freedom of conscience. The limits of article 28 of the Meiji Constitution had undergone a severe test.

Ironically, the man who had advocated so eloquently for religious freedom for all citizens would not live to enjoy the rights he had so fervently fought for. On 11 February, 1889 a Shintoist radical approached and fatally stabbed Mori Arinori as he was leaving his home to attend the historic ceremony that would mark Japan's adoption of a modern system of laws. He died the following day, the first victim of a human right that, thanks to him, had found a place, even if somewhat tenuously, in the new Meiji Constitution and in Japanese society. The French press, not knowing what to make of this new constitution – which was drafted on a Prussian model – did not hold back in their Eurocentric mockery in a report "from abroad" posted in *Le Figaro* on 13 February, two days after it came into effect. Their publicly expressed bias and disdain aside, no one could deny that a new and turbulent era in Japan had begun; and having embarked on this new path, there was no going back to the tranquility of the days before Perry's black ships had first appeared on the horizon.

1. For an overview of the Meiji Restoration, see Hane, Mikiso and Perez, Louis G. *Modern Japan. A Historical Survey* (Boulder, Co: Westview Press, 2013), pp. 83–200.
2. For an overview of Shinto in the Meiji Period, see Hardacre, Helen *Shinto. A History* (New York: Oxford University Press, 2017), pp. 323-402.
3. See Ketelaar, James Edward *Of Heretics and Martyrs in Meiji Japan. Buddhism and its Persecution* (Princeton, NJ: Princeton University Press, 1993).
4. See Hur, Nam-lin *Death and Social Order in Tokugawa Japan. Buddhism, Anti-Christianity, and the Danka System* (Cambridge, MA: Harvard University Press, 2007), pp. 1–106.
5. Arinori, Mori *Religious Freedom in Japan. A Memorial and Draft of Charter* (privately printed, 1872), p.3.
6. For an introduction to the life and times of Mori, see *Mori Arinori's Life and Resources in America,* ed. annotated, and introduced by John E. Van Sant (Lanham/Oxford: Lexington Books, 2004).
7. For a summary of this diplomatic history, See Abe, Yoshiya 'From Prohibition to Toleration: Japanese Government Views regarding Christianity, 1854–73', in *Japanese Journal of Religious Studies*, vol. 5 2/3 (1978), 107–38.
8. For a detailed account of the persecutions of the Nagasaki Christians between 1867–73, known as the 'Fourth Destruction of Urakami' [*Urakami yonban-kuzure*], see Urakawa Wasaburō, *Tabi no hanashi* (Nagasaki: Nagasaki Kōkyō Shingakkō-ban, 1938; revised and reprinted in 2003).

Admiral Matthew Perry arrives in Edo Bay, 1854.

THE DRAMATIC CHANGES OF THE TWENTIETH CENTURY

Lars Vargö

On the 8th of July 1853, an American naval vessel under the command of Admiral Matthew C. Perry arrived in Edo Bay, to demand access to Japanese ports and the opportunity to establish trade links with Japan. Perry threatened to use force should Japan refuse. The Japanese ruling elite was acutely aware of what had happened to China during the Opium Wars of 1840–42, so Perry's threat was effective. The following year, the so-called Kanagawa Agreement was signed, initiating a process that would see Japan open up to the outside world after a long spell of self-imposed isolation. Other nations followed America's lead, and the period leading up to the Meiji Restoration in 1868 was characterised by a series of bilateral agreements that shook Japan to the core. This was not merely the opening of ports and the signing of treaties – the very cornerstones of Japanese society were beginning to be remodelled. It was obvious to Japan's rulers that the self-imposed isolation that had begun in the first half of the 17th century had damaged the country and caused it to fall behind. If Japan was to avoid the same tragic fate that had befallen China, reform would be necessary in almost every sphere.

The visit of that American vessel was the starting point for the Meiji Restoration, culminating fifteen years later, in 1868. Military rule under a shōgun was abolished and, for the first time since 1185, the emperor was once again able to assume the position of head of government. The capital city was moved from Kyoto to Edo, which was renamed Tokyo. A number of delegations were sent overseas and foreign experts were invited to Japan to share their knowledge. Japan hoped to learn what the West had to offer from the very best. Different models of society were sought, meaning the Chinese civilisation, so often a source of inspiration in the past, began to be seen as hopelessly conservative and underdeveloped. China, after all, had not succeeded in repelling Western demands, so if Japan was to survive in this tough new climate it would be necessary to build completely new foundations.

The construction of a new Japanese nation was not entirely dissimilar to the colonisation of a foreign land. The religion was to be changed, the national dress given a new style, new holidays and the Gregorian calendar were to be introduced, all with the purpose of creating a new and more effective centralised state. Compulsory schooling and military service was introduced in 1873 and reform after reform demanded changes in legislation. Ideologue Fukuzawa Yukichi described Japanese society as comprising "many millions of people separated by many million walls". The shōgunate had ruled the country with an iron fist, yet it had been divided into over 200 provinces, each with laws, routines and military forces of their own. Bringing Japan together as one nation under a united modern legislature presented a formidable challenge.

The new Japanese state emerged as authoritarian, but the desperate search for an appropriate societal model also meant that proposals advocating an open society could be tabled. In 1874, an association known as Meirokusha was founded, with the aim of stimulating free and open debate. The group published *Meiroku zasshi* [The Meiroku Periodical], which would come to play an important role in an increasingly lively social debate. Meirokusha remained active until 1900, but its influence was short-lived. By 1875, reactionary forces within the government began to initiate legislation restricting media freedom. Excessively liberal ideas could undermine the political project that aimed to make Japan at least as powerful as other colonial powers, and increasing numbers of people had begun to question the wisdom of abandoning all Japanese customs and traditions.

So, as Japan adapted to the values of Western civilisation, it did so with a considerable measure of necessary compromise. Adaptations were made to allow the old ways to survive. Limited change was accepted, to avoid the need for wholesale reform. At the same time, many quickly became accustomed to the Western-inspired new social order, and began questioning much of what was traditionally Japanese. The 20th century evolved into a sometimes confused struggle between those who wished to maintain the traditional – exploiting the inherent strength of their culture to become an expanding colonial power – and those who desired as much change as possible in a Western direction. Proposals for a complete return to the old ways were mixed with unrealistic suggestions for abolishing Japanese language and the Japanese religions. Establishing which proposals were plausible, and which were ludicrous, was done as each one confronted reality.

The Battle of Shanghai, 1932.

In the early 1900s, Japan moved from being a society full of hope and aspiration to being a nation burdened by frustration. Radical forces demanded extensive reforms while conservative ones were terrified that the new modern society was expunging all that was truly Japanese. "Electricity has been discovered, and the darkness has reached us," was a phrase often heard at the time.

The political ideologies of Europe found champions in Japan, and the span between left and right was broad, at least to begin with. In February 1906, socialists were given permission to organise themselves as the "Japan Socialist Party" and to hold political meetings. The party survived only for a short time – what alarmed authorities was the successful campaign against an increase in the price of tram travel, led by the party in the summer of 1906. In February 1907, criticisms were raised that the military had been deployed to crush a rebellion at a copper mine in the Tochigi Prefecture, where 3600 miners and sympathisers had destroyed the complex. The party newspaper *Heimin Shimbun* [The Peoples' Press] was blamed for having incited the workers and the party was forced to dissolve.

The socialist movement faced a new setback in 1911, when socialist leader Kōtuku Shūsui and eleven other activists were hanged for plotting to murder the emperor. The event became known as *taigyaku jiken,* "The High Treason Incident", and the years following the hangings were known as the socialist movement's "winter period", [*fuyu no jidai*]. Authorities were now so averse to anything connected to socialism they even banned the publication of a book called *Insect Society*, since the Japanese word for society, *shakai,* was the same one used in the expression "socialism" – *shakai-shugi*.

When Emperor Meiji died in 1912 and Japan entered the Taishō period (1912–1925), the country faced increasing calls for democracy from the broad mass of the people, "Taishō-democracy". However, the high esteem in which many held the Japanese state meant there was no threat to the Imperial family's strong position or the state itself. The word "democracy" was initially translated as *minponshugi*, "people based principle", a term later replaced by *minshushugi*, "people rule principle".

Ideologue Yoshino Sakuzō (1878–1933), argued for the defence of the rights of the individual, the division of power between the executive and the legislature, and a truly representative parliamentary assembly. He was careful to point out that none of this would in any way harm the notion of national unity, *kokutai* – "national essence/character". Yoshino encountered strong resistance from conservative quarters, but had broad support in many political camps for his demands: a government that was accountable to a parliamentary assembly; a second chamber subordinate to the lower house; and suffrage extended to all men with a higher-level education.

There were more radical thinkers, those who found inspiration in Marxism who considered Yoshino's more social democratic or liberal ideas insufficient. The Russian Revolution of 1917 and the communist movement made it increasingly difficult for Japanese authorities to turn a blind eye even to those ideas that could be considered social democratic. In 1920, however, radical trade unionists went as far as to distance themselves from representative democracy and parliamentary debate, agitating instead for "direct action". Furthermore, the trade union movement was infiltrated by relatively powerful anarcho-syndicalist forces, who rejected almost anything that could be considered support for the state and the Imperial family.

In 1922, the Communist Party of Japan was founded in secret, and its influence on Japanese trade unionism was substantial. The varying sources of ideological inspiration, combined with the increasing oppression by authorities, was, however, an unbeatable recipe for unleashing sectarian struggles within the leftist movements. Additionally, Moscow's great influence upon the underground Communist Party meant that the effects of political putsches and campaigns in Russia were felt in Japan. As the death of Emperor Taishō in 1925 ushered in the Shōwa period, not only did Japan's aspirations to conquer territories in Korea and China become clearer, the government also grew increasingly intolerant of political opposition.

In August 1931, the Japanese prime minister, Hamaguchi Osachi, was murdered by a nationalist extremist outside Tokyo's main railway station. Hamaguchi had been a very active prime minister, who had, amongst other things, followed austere economic policies and signed a series of agreements with foreign powers regarding naval forces in the Pacific. This made him unpopular among expansionists. In February and March of 1932, the far-right *Ketsumeidan* [League of Blood] group staged a drawn-out attempted coup. The group were intent on punishing those responsible for the poverty and suffering affecting rural areas. Around two-dozen politicians and businessmen were singled out as being particularly

Daily Herald

No. 4997 — SATURDAY, FEBRUARY 20, 1932 — ONE PENNY

BATTLE FOR SHANGHAI BEGINS

Cabinet Appoints Council of Action

ARTILLERY DUEL STARTS JAPAN'S GREAT DRIVE

All Day March of Armies to the Front Lines

THE great battle for Shanghai has begun. Machine-gun and light artillery fire has broken out, heralding the start of a great Japanese offensive and the Chinese 19th Army is preparing to defend the North Station.

Meanwhile, speedy Government action has been taken in this country. Yesterday, an emergency conference of the Cabinet was called and a Council of Action appointed, ready to take action if need arose. Day and night the Cabinet will be kept in touch with events. The League Council took action at Geneva yesterday, and, on China's appeal, the Assembly is to be convoked on March 3.

In New York yesterday the Japanese yen opened at 33.50, the lowest level reached recently. There was a slight rally later.

[A special diagrammatical map is on the Back Page.]

THE 19th ARMY PREPARES FOR BIG OFFENSIVE

From Our Special Correspondent
EDGAR SNOW

SHANGHAI, Saturday.

AS I write the rapid exchange of machine-gun fire and light artillery at the North Station are an indication that the great battle for Shanghai has begun.

It has been quiet all day, but now, as zero hour approaches, there is every sign of the most sanguinary warfare since the guns blazed on the Western Front of Europe.

It is learned from a reliable Japanese source that Japan's ultimatum to China to withdraw 19 miles from Shanghai Settlement has been rejected.

Letters of acknowledgment to the ultimatum have been delivered to Major-General Uyeda, the Japanese commander, from the Chinese Consul, Yu Tsi-Ko.

Beyond the general crossed a piece of reply it is believed that the Japanese will wait for the expiration of the time limit, which is 7 a.m. to-day (12 p.m. Friday, British time).

Any moment now they may launch a great offensive against the Chinese 19th Army, which is broadly drawn up, fully prepared for war.

Geneva Time's letter to Japan, when she can declare points in the ultimatum was as follows:—

I have noted the contents of your letter. The troops in my command are an integral part of the National Government of the Republic of China which directs all their activities.

I have therefore submitted your letter to the Chinese Minister of Foreign Affairs.

And so we anxiously await the battle.

League Calls Assembly After Dramatic Scene

From Our Special Correspondent
GENEVA, Friday.

I HOPE that it will be possible to secure the postponement of the ultimatum," said M. Paul Boncour, in low, earnest tones.

The answer came clearly across the Council Hall of the League. The clock on the wall spoke.

One, two, three, four, five, six, seven, eight, nine. In a few hours the Japanese attack begins. It happens now to talk of appealing for postponement.

The Chinese Delegate, Dr. Yen, rose, the League Council has been done this evening, and he has done this evening, might even to be like it. As quickly as he had been given the attention, the quickest line in the Council was surely not to the mind of his audience. The Japanese representative counted to Dr. Yen's appeal.

That has no other meaning meaning than that Japan is to use now.

In view of the urgency of the matter it was decided to appoint a Council of Action, which is to be an call Government on the week-end, ready to take swift action should the situation become serious.

Members of this Council are:—
Mr. Baldwin.

SEVEN WHO WILL WATCH

PREMIER APPROVES OF EMERGENCY COUNCIL

From Our Political Correspondent

Alarming news from Shanghai led to speedy Government action yesterday when a conference of Cabinet Ministers was hurriedly called in the House of Commons.

The grave fears of the Cabinet Ministers, so they came into the Lobby after the meeting was a clear indication of the disturbing news which had been received from the Far East.

Confidential apprehensions exist as to the future of the British and American subjects in the Shanghai Settlement.

In view of the urgency of the matter it was decided to appoint a Council of Action, which is to be on call throughout the week-end, ready to take swift action should the situation become serious.

Members of this Council are:—
Mr. Baldwin.

Lord Hailsham, Secretary for War;
Sir Bolton Eyres-Monsell, First Lord of the Admiralty;
Mr. J. H. Thomas;
Mr. Neville Chamberlain;
Sir John Simon; and
Sir Samuel Hoare.

Instructions were given that the Admiralty and the War Office should make the preparations for the week-end and that responsible officers should be on duty day and night so that the Cabinet can be kept in constant touch with events.

Arrangements for the evacuation of British and American citizens in the Shanghai Settlement should it become no longer possible to guarantee their safety are now complete.

Instructions for the evacuation of British and American citizens in the Shanghai Settlement should it become no longer possible to guarantee their safety are now complete.

In Government circles the view is held that nothing is to be gained by sending Naval re-enforcements to the Far East. It is felt that the ships of the British Fleet on the China station are powerful enough already to cope with any situation that might arise.

The Prime Minister, who is at Chequers, has been apprised of these emergency measures, and will be in constant telephonic communication with the Foreign Office and the Service departments.

DE VALERA LIKELY TO LEAD FREE STATE

ELECTIONS GIVE HIM BIGGEST PARTY

From Our Own Correspondent
DUBLIN, Friday.

MR. DE VALERA will head the biggest Party in the next Free State Parliament.

This fact is certain from the results of the General Election, now to hand, as follows:—

	To Date	Last Elections
Cosgrave Party	—	62
Independents and Farmers	—	15
Independent Labour	—	6
Other results will be announced to-morrow.		
Fianna Fail	—	44
Independents	—	14
Republicans	—	5
Labour	—	13

Already De Valera's total supporters have increased to 73,000, and when the final returns are announced, it is probable he will be found that the Fianna Fail supporters will be able to say stronger than those of Mr. Cosgrave.

Whether Mr. De Valera will replace Mr. Cosgrave as President of the Executive Council of the Free State may be in doubt until the new Dáil meets. Everything will depend on the decision of the Labour Party, who will hold the balance of power.

Proportional representation is in force, and the total first preference votes so far cast for the various parties compared with last election are:—

	1932	1927
Cosgrave Party	—	—
Independents	—	—
Independent Labour	—	—
Fianna Fail	—	—
Labour	—	—

So far, all of the ministers in the last Government, save one have retained their seats. Mr. Heffernan, Parliamentary Secretary for Posts and Telegraphs, being the sole defeated.

All of the members of Mr. De Valera's shadow Cabinet have been elected.

Ernest Blythe, the Minister for Finance and the former International Rugby footballer, who was the Government Party candidate for Dublin North.

The Labour Party, though small in numbers, will probably hold the balance of power.

But there will be no rushing as far as Labour is concerned. It will remain independent of both Mr. De Valera, the Speaker, who is re-elected automatically were contested.

The remaining seven at Sligo-Leitrim will not be filled until March 1, the date originally fixed for the meeting of the Dáil.

In the new Dáil Parliament four of these seats were held by Cosgravites and three by De Valera's supporters.

The new Dáil will be the official registrar until March 9, when the Republicans assume office.

Whatever happens, Mr. De Valera will be unable to put into operation his programme for the reform of the Treaty.

MAINLY FAIR

(See Page Three)

Lucid an Louis Heyn-Renders..... Leisure; Saville's County 6
Radio Programmes 4
Crossword and Home Picture Winnows 8
Serial: Hiking, Cycling and Gardening 9
4,000 Hospitals Contest 10

5,000 MILES TO SETTLE SWEEP DISPUTE

Novice Airman's Dash for Ceylon

A YOUNG Irish amateur airman starts from Heston, Middlesex, this morning on a 5,000-mile intrepid flight.

This is the "record mission," of Mr. M. C. A. Self, the novice pilot, who is flying to Colombo in the first stage of a week's "rest" flight.

When he arrived Ceylon he is to attempt to present the ownership of one of the smaller suites ticket in the recent Irish sweep. Four people claim that the prize money is their due.

After landing the Ceylon dispute it would be expected of him to go away with complete authority.—Air details will appear in Back Page.

FIGHT TO CONTROL MUSIC-HALL MILLIONS

VARIETY INTERESTS AGAINST FILM GROUP

By HANNEN SWAFFER

AN epic fight for the control of Moss Empires is going on. It is the greatest drama in the history of the modern theatre.

Millions of pounds are involved. It is the future of a score of theatres and, more than that, the livelihood of thousands of British artists of every kind; yes, and the living of hundreds of electricians, stage hands and musicians.

The meeting of Moss Empire shareholders has been called at the Holborn Restaurant next Friday. By the first time in 50 years, the annual meeting is to take place away from Edinburgh, the headquarters of the company, which was founded there by the late Edward Moss, who started as a phrase in the Waterloo Market.

SMALL SHAREHOLDERS

The move to London is inspired by the fact that, now, most of the capital is owned by London shareholders.

On the other hand, much of the capital is held in amounts of £3 or £10, by small savers, whose fathers, or wives, themselves, backed either Edward Moss, whom they had always known.

Mr. Thomas Ormiston, M.P., a well-known Scottish film exhibitor, who has been behind the scene opposition, and is hoping to be representative powers of these small Scottish shareholders.

These people, ignoring as they are organized, are a move hitherto behind the scenes.

BEAVERBROOK v. OSTRER

Massed in array would seem to be Lord Beaverbrook's interests on one side, and those of Gaumont-British, whom the Ostrer Brothers control, on the other.

If Lord Beaverbrook and his interests take it—it is a head count of an even greater kind in the control of the Gaumont Company.

Indeed the following everything, based from the Moss Empire affair, only after a six months' struggle, lies in the fact of general recoveries—a battle at how a mere revelling of the action or figure of the opposition may turn out.

Those are a possibility that the holders of a very large number of shares may vote against the direction of the company, in certain cases, and that may not meet in opposition to the present state of the proprietors of the amusement, and may consequently lose one of the directors.

"SATISFACTORY"

The committee is satisfied, however, that, with certain emergencies, private schools are conducted in a reasonably satisfactory manner, if not splendid in many cases.

Compulsory inspection of all private schools was made in a report, but not of the Education Committee of the L.C.C. as long ago as last May.

SIR THOMAS LIPTON'S BIG GIFTS IN WILL

£1,000 EACH FOR SECRETARY, COOK AND DOCTOR

SUBSTANTIAL gifts to former servants and friends are contained in the will of Sir Thomas Lipton, details of which the "Daily Herald" is able to print to-day.

These gifts include:—
£2,000 to Margaret Story, whose mother and brother were in his employment.
£1,000 to his cook, Mrs. Chambers.
£1,000 to his personal secretary, Mr. William Morrison Duncan.
£1,000 to Miss Edward Story;
£1,000 to his chauffeur, Ronnie Dawson; and of the New York heirs, Sir Thomas leaves £500.

£1,000 FOR DOCTOR

Dr. Fairweather, his medical attendant, receives £1,000, and trustees who receive special bequests are:—

Col. Duncan Neill ... £1,000
Mr. J. A. Spens (the writer) £1,000

Each of the six trustees and executors also gets £200 for acting as well.

Mention is made in the will of selected bequests and suits. These are to be opened by Col. Duncan Neill and the other trustees, and Gilroy Glenn, Sir Thomas's friend, the architect.

Directions are left concerning the disposal of his memories, College, at Southgate.

BEQUEST FOR HOSPITALS

This is to be sold within one year, and after payment of his funeral expenses the proceeds are to be applied in accepting T.E.A. property is to be "to indicate information and hospital, or institutions for the relief of the poor and destitute, as in the city of Glasgow and Edinburgh in sums as directed at a fund suggested for the trustees." Other bequests to the will are:—

£1,000 to Mr. Henry McAuley Bulling.
£1,000 to Charles Keith.
£1,000 to Henry Cruickshank of Killearn.
£1,000 to Charles Wright of Belfast.
£1,000 to Mrs. Walker, of Regent's Park.
£1,000 to Mr. McLaren.
£1,000 to J. B. Cassman.

Licensing Order for Private Schools

INSPECTION and licensing of all private schools by the Board of Education is likely, the "Daily Herald" learns, to be a recommendation of the Departmental Committee appointed by Sir Charles Trevelyan when Education Minister in the late Labour Government.

The report of the committee will not be published until May.

It has been revealed that some private schools are conducted on premises which are thoroughly unsafe, and in a manner which is detrimental to the children taught in them. There are nearly 500 private schools unrecognised by either the Board or Local Authorities.

Indeed the following everything, kissed from the Moss Empire affair, only.

CHICAGO with the LID OFF!

In "The People" to-morrow Shaw Desmond lifts the lid off Chicago and its rackets. "The Hub of America" is rotten to the core with graft—graft that clogs the wheels of justice—and the gangster reigns supreme. You must read this startling revelation to understand something of the crimes of crimes that astonish and shock all civilised nations.

A WARDER'S KEY TO THE HEART OF A RED HAIRED GIRL

An ex-warder lays bare the heated truth that has taken the naked soul and innermost feelings of hard-bitten criminals. Beginning in "The People" to-morrow are Warden Wagner, for 13 years governor of San Quentin prison, tells the naked truth. "The" New Rolls of the London Metropolitan, started with a very hearty conclusion for care machinery, which proves appeased. Much of it was ever exciting in their course, but Japan had forwarded and promised that civil war with money and now and encouragement.

The People TO-MORROW

£4,000 Cash Prizes Must-be-Won

(Continued on Page Nine.)

The front page of Daily Herald.

responsible for Japan's supposed weakness, and attempts were made to eliminate them through systematic political assassination. Two were successfully murdered: the boss of the Mitsui Company, Baron Takuma Dan, and the finance minister, Inoue Junnosuke, before most of the insurgents were rounded up. Some were given prison sentences of up to fifteen years, but were released long before they served their time. In May 1932, another attempted coup took place, in which Prime Minister Inukai Tsyoshi was murdered at his official residence by a group of young cadets. Inukai had advocated friendly relations with China. Those responsible were imprisoned, but like their predecessors they were released long before their sentences had expired.

One of the leading philosophers and representatives for the new thinking was Kita Ikki (1883–1937). In his 1906 book *The Theory of Japan's National Polity and Pure Socialism*, Ikki argued for a form of national socialism in which the fundamental principles of traditional society were combined with socialist ideas. He often invoked *kokutai,* a vision in which the emperor and the people would be considered a single entity, where the emperor became a people's monarch in an ideological structure interwoven with Shintoism, Japan's traditional animist religion. According to Kita, the transformation of Japanese society was doomed to failure because of capitalism and the bureaucracy's exploitation of the people. In 1919, he published his *Outline Plan for the Reorganization of Japan,* a book in which he expanded upon his ideas.

On the 26th of February 1936, another coup attempt took place in Tokyo. This time, the instigators came very close to succeeding. A group within the army, "The Imperial Way Faction," mutinied and attempted to seize power by exterminating the ruling political elite. Several members of the government were murdered, including finance minister Takahashi Korekiyo, and the general inspector of military training, General Watanabe Jōtarō. Once the murders were carried out, the mutineers occupied Nagata-chō, the Tokyo neighbourhood that then, as now, was home to most government buildings. After three days they finally gave up, on the direct orders of the emperor. Thirteen officers and four civilians, including Kita Ikki, were executed, while several leading officers were stripped of their positions. The coup attempt failed, but it was to inspire further drastic interventions from the fanatics, and ultimately lead to an increasingly totalitarian society. The violence left its mark and the military began to steer its own course.

Much to the surprise of the watching world, Japan had defeated China in the first Sino-Japanese War of 1894–1895, as well as Russia in the Russo-Japanese War of 1904–1905. These conflicts were waged largely around the Korean Peninsula. As a consequence, Japan had assumed effective control of Korea, which was annexed in 1910. Japan began a brutal regime intended to expunge Korean culture and assimilate it completely.

The expansionist rush continued. In 1931 Japan invaded Manchuria and successfully established the puppet Manchukuo regime. January 1932 saw the "Shanghai Incident" take place. A number of Japanese Buddhist monks were attacked on the street in broad daylight by locals; several later died from their injuries. Japanese marines landed with the intention of punishing those responsible, but were held off by Chinese resistance, which led to the dispatch of more Japanese forces. Fierce battles ensued between the Chinese 19th Route Army and Japanese troops, who were soon bolstered by reinforcements. The 19th Army were forced to retreat, but further Japanese attacks were averted thanks to a British-American initiative that lead to a peace agreement in May 1932. Japan's conduct was criticised at The League of Nations, who demanded that Japan withdraw from China, particularly Manchuria. In February 1933, that criticism turned sharper still. Japan's response was to leave the organisation altogether, in March of that year. Japan's expansionist policies became increasingly unambiguous. From an economic perspective, the most important prize was the natural resources of northern China.

As Japanese troops consolidated their conquests in Northern Manchuria, they came into direct conflict with the Soviet Union. A war was avoided thanks to China's Eastern Railway – controlled by the Soviet Union – being sold to Japan in 1935. The nationalist Chinese regime began to turn its attention towards Chinese communists, leaving Japan to rule its puppet state unimpeded.

In 1937, Japanese troops were sent into China. Battles broke out across the country, but the Japanese military leadership split into two camps – the expansionists and those favouring a more restrictive policy. The latter group advocated for Japan to concentrate its resources on establishing Manchukuo as a viable economy, something that could serve Japanese interests. If further forces were to be deployed into China, it would necessitate a full-scale mobilisation, in turn requiring an expanded and onerous war budget to be passed, they claimed. They also feared Japan was over-stretching and the battles would serve only to bolster Chinese resistance – a concern that would eventually be proved right. The expansionists maintained there was no cause for hesitation: the subjugation of China was essential. Japanese troops crushed all military resistance in Beijing and Tianjin. In central China, Japanese troops marched from Shanghai to Nanjing, which fell under brutal occupation in December 1937. During the so-called 'Nanjing Massacre', thousands of people, mostly civilians were murdered indiscriminately in a six-week period that stretched into January 1938.

In the period after 1936, up until the end of the Second World War in 1945, the ideological differences between adoration of the emperor and the militarists' theories were erased. Whether or not he supported the move, the emperor became the symbol of Japanese expansionist desires, and most Japanese were probably convinced that the emperor would be executed by the Allies. According to traditional Japanese thinking, emperor and foot-soldier alike must take responsibility for their actions. The occupying Allied forces, however, had other ideas. They believed that Japan's transformation to a democratic state would be best achieved if the emperor, with his historical ties and powerful symbolism, was allowed to remain. Japan was transformed into a democracy after the war, with the emperor becoming ceremonial head of state with no power.

The question of how Japan might have progressed if the emperor and Imperial household had not been allowed to remain will never be answered. As it was, the post-war development of the country turned out to be a formidable success. Under the new 1947 constitution, the emperor was simply a symbol of the nation. Political power was to emanate from the people. Japanese society became pluralist and its economy began to follow market principles. The progress made was such that as far back as the 1960s, the world began to speak of "The Japanese Miracle". Japanese productivity went through the roof, and they proved themselves world-beaters in one industrial sector after another. Some economists used Japan's success story to call into question certain economic orthodoxies. The Japanese way of leading and organising companies was held up as a shining example. It was said that Japan had something special, something worth studying and emulating. The idea of Japan's dominance as unassailable was at its most established at around the same time as the Berlin wall fell, and Emperor Shōwa died. It was that time that American author and polemicist, Francis Fukuyama himself of

Japanese descent, declared "the end of history" – with liberalism seen as the undisputed victor.

At the same time, however, many began to argue that Japan had gone too far, and that the country's success had been facilitated by finding itself in a privileged position. Japan was accused of hampering access to its own market whilst simultaneously avoiding taking any responsibility for security by – for example – spending its resources on defence. A few American congressmen, claiming that Japan was competing on an uneven playing field, appeared before the media to symbolically take a sledge hammer to a Japanese radio on the Capitol steps. Another representative went as far as to say that the US should not have dropped two atom bombs on Japan, but four.

As the surrounding world's frustrations grew, so too did Japan's self-esteem. Several politicians succumbed to delusions of grandeur, explaining that Japan's exports were so successful because Japan was simply better. America was said to need Japan's ethnic homogeny. The pronouncements began to smack of racism.

This new Japanese hubris took a serious dent when the economic bubble burst at the end of the 1980s. It was becoming increasingly evident that the economy was built on false hopes rather than a solid base, or at least that it had much less substance than had been thought. The value of stocks on the Tokyo exchange began to plummet dramatically. The long-standing munificence of financial institutions was revealed, bad credits could no longer be hidden from view, the national debt had mushroomed, bankruptcies were increasing and unemployment was rising alarmingly. At the same time, the American economy entered a boom of its own. Talk of Japan being the solution to everything made way for the country being cited as an example of how badly wrong things can go if actors in the market are not given a free reign, or if bureaucrats and politicians are afforded too much power. Criticism was specifically levelled at what was described as the Japanese variety of capitalism – "Japan Inc". The fate of the exceptional Japanese went from admired miracle to cautionary tale.

In the years that followed, Japan was struck by a series of further catastrophes. Religious doomsday sect Aum Shinrikyō, who, it turned out, had plans to kill everyone except their own members, had been allowed to develop undisturbed, with Japanese police in the dark about their plans. In 1995, sect members carried out a Sarin gas attack on the

Kobe earthquake, 1995.

Tokyo metro. In Kōbe, an earthquake not only claimed more than 6,000 lives, it also ruthlessly revealed the incompetence of the rescue effort services. Ten years earlier, in 1985, five-hundred-and-twenty people had died in an air crash on a Japanese mountainside, leading to accusations being thrown at Boeing, the aircraft operators, and the American work ethic. It transpired that the aircraft had been compromised by corner-cutting during maintenance in the USA.

After the earthquake in Kōbe it emerged that Japanese workers had been just as likely to take shortcuts and that these probably caused the collapse of a large elevated motorway. In the rubble of the concrete pillars, tin cans and scrap iron was found in place of solid reinforcement rods. The motorway had been hurriedly constructed to be completed in time for the 1970 World Expo.

In the 1990s, Japan was regarded as a nation with almost insurmountable problems. It was not just the economy that was struggling. Government members resigned one after another after persistent and embarrassing corruption scandals, while decision-makers in the public and private sectors alike seemed to be struck by complete paralysis. To make matters worse, occasionally controversies with neighbouring countries flared up over their insistence that apologies were still owed for previous actions, or over some ill-informed Japanese politician speculating whether Japan really had conducted itself badly during the Second World War and the years leading up to it.

In 2011 Japan experienced one of its worst-ever disasters. A submarine earthquake northeast of the main Japanese island of Honshu gave rise to a devastating tsunami, which as well as killing more than 20,000 people, also sent several nuclear reactors in Fukushima into meltdown. If the rain and wind had travelled southwards, the 36 million residents of the world's largest city – Tokyo – would have been forced to evacuate.

When Prime Minister Abe Shinzō assumed power in December 2012, the government tried a new approach. The economy was to be restored via a series of deregulations, structural reforms and stimulus packages. The ageing population was acknowledged as a major problem, and without significant growth and a guarantee that sufficient labour would be available, Japan's prospects looked bleak. Abe's economic policy came to be known as Abenomics and despite it not leading to any immediate or widespread change, the Japanese ship began gradually to change course.

Even if growth was less than dramatic, Abenomics was still felt to have had an impact. Corporations started to recover, unemployment all but disappeared, and the gloom of the 1990s began to dissipate.

The ageing population and the declining number of citizens remains a great challenge. The national debt is larger than ever, but pessimism now faces competition in the form of a new optimism. The government has begun to actively advocate increased migrant labour, and also wishes to see more women becoming active in the workforce. Once again, Japan is searching for new solutions. The transformation will not be as dramatic as during the latter half of the 19th century, and the country does not need to seek out a radical new form of society or face the temptation to invade its neighbours. Instead, Japan today can address its problems in partnership with the global community, by astutely applying the wide-ranging lessons learnt during the tumultuous 20th century.

CONTRIBUTORS

ELISABET YANAGISAWA AVÉN, Doctoral Student, University of Gothenburg.

OLEG BENESCH, Senior Lecturer (Assistant Professor), East Asian History, University of York.

NATASHA BENNETT, Curator of Oriental Collections, Royal Armouries, Leeds.

JAQUELINE BERNDT, Professor in Japanese Language and Culture, Stockholm University.

JOHN BREEN, Professor, International Research Center for Japanese Studies, Kyoto.

BLAINE BROWNELL AIA, NCARB, LEED AP, Professor and Interim Department Head, University of Minnesota School of Architecture.

THOMAS D. CONLAN, Professor of East Asian Studies and History, Princeton University.

KARL FRIDAY, Professor, Graduate School of Humanities and Social Sciences, Saitama University.

KRISTINA FRIDH, PhD, Researcher, University of Gothenburg.

ROGER GOODMAN, Nissan Professor of Modern Japanese Studies and Warden of St Antony's College, University of Oxford.

JAMES L. HUFFMAN, H. Orth Hirt Professor of History, Emeritus, Wittenberg University, Ohio.

ANNE E IMAMURA, Professor, Department of Sociology, Georgetown University.

JAMES E. KETELAAR, Professor of Japanese History, University of Chicago.

JOHN LIE, Professor of Sociology, University of California, Berkeley.

MARGARET MEHL, Associate Professor, University of Copenhagen.

PIA MOBERG, PhD, CEO Japaco.

PETER NOSCO, Professor, Japanese History and Culture, University of British Columbia.

INKEN PROHL, Professor, Institute of Religious Studies, Heidelberg University.

NAOKI SAKAI, Goldwin Smith Professor of Asian Studies, Cornell University.

DICK STEGEWERNS, Associate Professor Japan Studies, University of Oslo.

DR STEPHEN TURNBULL, Research Associate, SOAS Japan Research Centre, University of London.

M. ANTONI J. UCERLER, S.J., Director, Ricci Institute of Chinese-Western Cultural History; Associate Professor of East Asian Studies, University of San Francisco.

CONSTANTINE N. VAPORIS, Director, Asian Studies Programme, Professor of History, University of Maryland, Baltimore County.

LARS VARGÖ, PhD in Japanese studies, former Swedish Ambassador to Japan.

ANNE WALTHALL, Professor Emerita of Japanese History, University of California, Irvine.

MICHAEL WERT, Associate Professor, Marquette University.

DR CHRISTAL WHELAN, Writer/Anthropologist, Boston University.

PROFESSOR MARK WILLIAMS, Professor of Psychology, Director of the Oxford Mindfulness Centre, University of Oxford.

KOSAKU YOSHINO (1953–2018), Professor, Department of Sociology, Sophia University.

Image Rights©

Cover, front: ©Gallica Digital Library/Public domain
Cover, back: ©National Diet Library Digital Collections
14: ©Topfoto/TT Nyhetsbyrån
p. 17: ©Kitazawa Rakuten/Wikimedia Commons
p. 18–19: ©Stephane Bidouze/Shutterstock
p. 24–25: ©Rene Burri/TT Nyhetsbyrån
p. 27: ©Kosaku Yoshino
p. 30: ©Topfoto/TT Nyhetsbyrån
p. 36: ©Seth Wenig/TT Nyhetsbyrån
p. 38–39: ©Toru Hanai/TT Nyhetsbyrån
p. 42: ©Itsuo Inouye/TT Nyhetsbyrån
p. 45: ©Creative Commons
p. 56: ©Album/TT
p. 58–59: ©Honolulu Museum of Art
pp. 61, 64, 66, 68: ©Dick Stegewern
p. 73: ©Ng Han Guan/TT Nyhetsbyrån
p. 76: ©AusGS2/Alamy
p. 79: ©Kirk Treakle/Alamy
p. 84: ©Japanexperterna.se/Creative Commons
p. 92: ©Kohei Hara/Getty Images
p. 95: ©Coward Lion/Alamy
p. 98: ©Pascal Mannaerts/Alamy
p. 102: ©Emelie Asplund/TT Nyhetsbyrån
p. 108: ©Rawpixel Ltd/Alamy
p. 111: ©The Lewis model/Richard Lewis/CrossCulture/©Pia Moberg
p. 117: ©The Chadberg scale/©Pia Moberg
p. 122: ©Shigeru Tamura/Creative Commons
p. 124–125: ©Sean Pavone/Alamy
p. 130: ©Sean Pavone/Alamy
p. 134: ©Tuul and Bruno Morandi/Alamy
p. 138: ©Åsa Ekström/Kadokawa
p. 143: ©Ton Koene/Alamy
p. 144: ©Åsa Ekström/Kadokawa
p. 152: ©Elstner Hilton/Creative Commons
pp. 154–155, 158, 161©Hasegawa Tōhaku/Emuseum/Creative Commons
pp. 172, 177, 179–181, 184–186, 188–190: ©Photo: Kristina Fridh
p. 192: ©Photo: Blaine Brownell
p. 196: ©Photo: Blaine Brownell
p. 199: ©John S Lander/Getty Images

p. 201: ©Photo: Blaine Brownell
p. 203: Creative Commons
pp. 204: ©Photo: Blaine Brownell
p. 207: ©Photo: Blaine Brownell
p. 214: ©Chiesa del Gesù, Rome
p. 217: ©Kobe City Museum/Creative Commons
p. 222: ©Shikabane Taro/Creative Commons
p. 227: ©26 Martyrs' Museum, Nagasaki
p. 232: ©Creative Commons
p. 235: ©Jim McIntosh/Choir of La Recoleta/Creative Commons
p. 238: ©Granger Historical Picture Archive/Alamy
p. 243: ©Osaka City Museum of Fine Arts/Creative Commons
p. 246: ©Album/TT Nyhetsbyrån
p. 248: ©Sapphire123/Creative Commons
p. 251: ©Domestic and Foreign Missionary Society/Creative Commons
p. 254: ©Creative Commons
p. 257: ©Creative Commons
p. 262: ©Olle Wester/TT Nyhetsbyrån
p. 267: ©Shikabane Taro/Creative Commons
p. 270: ©Creative Commons
p. 275: ©Atlaspix/Alamy
p. 280: ©Historic Images/Alamy
p. 285: ©Creative Commons
p. 288: ©Jules Brunet/Creative Commons
p. 293: ©Creative Commons
p. 296: ©Utagawa Kuniyoshi/Creative Commons
p. 299: ©National Museum of Denmark/Creative Commons
p. 300: ©Library of Congress/Creative Commons
p. 303: ©Courtesy of the author, Anne Walthall
p. 304: ©Album/Alamy
p. 307: ©Courtesy of the author, Anne Walthall
p. 308: ©The Tokugawa Art Museum/Creative Commons
p. 313: ©Emuseum.jp
p. 316: ©Fujiwara no Takanobu/Kyoto/Creative Commons
p. 321: ©The Picture Art Collection/Alamy
p. 324: ©Yamaguchi Museum/Creative commons
p. 327: ©Public Domain/Wikimedia commons
p. 332: ©Keystone France/Creative commons
p. 336: ©Kanō Masanobu/Jizō-in Temple/Creative Commons
p. 341: ©Musee Guimet/Creative Commons
p. 345: ©Gallica Digital Library/Public domain
p. 350: ©Royal Armouries

p. 353: ©Royal Armouries
p. 354: ©Royal Armouries
p. 356: ©Courtesy of The Metropolitan Museum of Art
p. 359: ©Royal Armouries
p. 362: ©Royal Armouries
p. 365: ©Royal Armouries
p. 368: ©Library of Congress/Creative Commons
p. 370: ©LACMA/Creative Commons
p. 373: ©Hiroshige/Smithsonian Design Museum/Creative Commons
p. 374: ©Kôchi kenritsu toshokan, ed. and pub., Kaizanshû, vol 4: rekishi hen 3 (1976)
p. 379: ©Zanitycomau/Creative Commons
p. 384: ©Katsushika Hokusai/Creative Commons
p. 388: © Princeton University
p. 394–395: © The Trustees of the British Museum
p. 397: ©Photo: Michael Wert
p. 401: © The Trustees of the British Museum
p. 404: ©LACMA
p. 407: ©Florilegius/Alamy
p. 408: ©Bain News Service/Creative Commons
p. 413: ©National Library of Congress/Public domain
p. 422: ©YAY Media AS/Alamy
p. 425: ©Geographicus Rare Antique Maps/Creative Commons
p. 428: ©Creative Commons
p. 431: ©New York public library digital collections
p. 434: ©Creative Commons
p. 440: ©Geographicus Rare Antique Maps/Creative Commons
p. 443: ©The Asahi Shimbun/Getty Images
p. 446–447: ©Wikimedia Commons
p. 450: ©Creative Commons
p. 456: ©ART Collection/Alamy
p. 460: ©Philipp Franz von Siebold & Joseph Gerhard Zuccarini/Creative Commons
p. 463: ©Creative Commons
p. 466: ©Hendrik Hollander/Creative Commons
p. 472: ©Historical Institute at the University of Tokyo
p. 475: ©Historical Institute at the University of Tokyo
p. 481: ©The Metropolitan Museum of Art
p. 488: ©Reprinted here with the permission of Iida Yoshiki
p. 491: ©National Diet Library Digital Collections
p. 494: ©Wikimedia Commons/National Diet Library Digital Collections
p. 496–497: ©National Diet Library Digital Collections
p. 499: Seitoku Memorial Picture Gallery
p. 502: ©The Library of the International Research Center for Japanese Studies, Kyoto

p. 508: ©Creative Commons
p. 509–510: ©Daderot
p. 513: ©Felix Choo/Alamy
p. 516: ©Historical image collection by Bildagentur-online/Alamy
p. 521: ©The Protected Art Archive/Alamy
p. 528: ©M. Antoni J. Ucerler, S.J.
p. 533: ©Giovanni Battista Gaulli/Cabral Moncada Leiloes/Creative Commons
p. 536: ©Classic Image/Alamy
p. 539: ©Courtesy of the National Archives of Japan, Tokyo.
p. 540: ©M. Antoni J. Ucerler, S.J.
p. 546: ©Wilhelm Heine/Creative Commons
p. 549: ©akg-images/TT Nyhetsbyrån
p. 552: ©John Frost Newspaper/Alamy
p. 557: ©Pacific Press Service/Alamy

JAPAN'S PAST AND PRESENT

© Bokförlaget Stolpe 2020

In association with Axel and Margaret Ax:son Johnson Foundation for Public Benefit
The essays are based on the following five seminars:
Japanese Self-Images – The Idea of Uniqueness (2016); Japanese Architecture –
Tradition and Modernity (2016); Japan's Christian Century and the Kakure Kirishitan (2017);
The making of Samurai in Tokugawa Japan (2017);
Japan Past and Present: Society, Thought and Religion in Meiji Japan (2018)
Edited by: Kurt Almqvist, President, Axel and Margaret Ax:son Johnson Foundation,
and Yukiko Duke Bergman
Image editor: Tove Falk Olsson
Text editor: Fay Schopen
Proofreading: Philippa Ingram and Fay Schopen
Design: Patric Leo
Layout: Petra Ahston Inkapööl, Patric Leo
Repro: Italgraf Media, 2020
Print: Printon, Estland via Italgraf Media, 2020

ISBN 978-91-6397-205-8

Stolpe

AXEL AND MARGARET AX:SON JOHNSONS FOUNDATION
FOR PUBLIC BENEFIT